DATE			

HUMANIZING ORGANIZATIONAL BEHAVIOR

HUMANIZING
ORGANIZATIONAL BEHAVIOR

Edited by

H. MELTZER, Ph.D.

Professor of Organizational Psychology
Washington University
Director, Psychological Service Center
Saint Louis, Missouri

and

Frederic R. Wickert, Ph.D.

Professor of Psychology and
Graduate Business Administration
Michigan State University
East Lansing, Michigan

CHARLES C THOMAS · PUBLISHER
Springfield · Illinois · U.S.A.

Published and Distributed Throughout the World by
CHARLES C THOMAS • PUBLISHER
Bannerstone House
301-327 East Lawrence Avenue, Springfield, Illinois, U.S.A.

© 1976, by CHARLES C THOMAS • PUBLISHER
ISBN 0-398-03500-8
Library of Congress Catalog Card Number: 75-23293

With THOMAS BOOKS *careful attention is given to all details of*
manufacturing and design. It is the Publisher's desire to present books
that are satisfactory as to their physical qualities and artistic possibilities
and appropriate for their particular use. THOMAS BOOKS *will be true*
to those laws of quality that assure a good name and good will.

Printed in the United States of America
W-2

Library of Congress Cataloging in Publication Data

Main entry under title:

Humanizing organizational behavior
    Based on symposia at the 1973 and 1974 annual meetings
of the American Psychological Association.
    Bibliography: p.
    Includes index.
    1. Psychology, Industrial—Congresses. 2. Industrial
organization—Congresses. I. Meltzer, Hyman, 1899-
II. Wickert, Frederic Robinson, 1912-
III. American Psychological Association.
HF5548.8.H93   658.3   75-23293
ISBN 0-398-03500-8

CONTRIBUTORS

CLAYTON P. ALDERFER, Ph.D.
*Associate Professor of Organization
and Management
Yale University
New Haven, Connecticut*

CHRIS ARGYRIS, Ph.D.
*James Bryant Conant Professor of
Education and Organizational Behavior
Harvard University
Cambridge, Massachusetts*

KENNETH L. BALL, Ph.D.
*Vice-President, Orchard Corporation of America
St. Louis, Missouri*

BERNARD M. BASS, Ph.D.
*Professor of Management and Psychology
University of Rochester
Rochester, New York*

MICHAEL BEER, Ph.D.
*Director of Organizational Development
Corning Glass Works
Corning, New York*

GERALD F. CAVANAGH, D.B.A.
*Associate Professor of Management
and Organization Sciences
Wayne State University
Detroit, Michigan*

MARVIN D. DUNNETTE, Ph.D.
*Professor of Psychology
University of Minnesota
Minneapolis, Minnesota*

ELI GINZBERG, Ph.D.
*A. Barton Hepburn
Professor of Economics
Columbia University
New York, New York*

v

DOUGLAS T. HALL, Ph.D.
Professor of Organizational Management
Northwestern University
Evanston, Illinois

EDGAR F. HUSE, Ph.D.
Chairman, Organizational Studies
Boston College
Chestnut Hill, Massachusetts

EDWARD E. LAWLER III, Ph.D.
Program Director and Professor of Psychology
University of Michigan
Ann Arbor, Michigan

FRED MASSARIK, Ph.D.
Professor of Behavioral Sciences
University of California, Los Angeles
Los Angeles, California

H. MELTZER, Ph.D.
Professor of Organizational Psychology
Washington University
St. Louis, Missouri

WALTER R. NORD, Ph.D.
Professor of Organizational Behavior
Washington University
St. Louis, Missouri

HJALMAR ROSEN, Ph.D.
Professor of Psychology
Wayne State University
Detroit, Michigan

BORJE O. SAXBERG, Ph.D.
Professor of Management and Organization
University of Washington
Seattle, Washington

FRED I. STEELE, Ph.D.
Consultant, Development Research Associates
Boston, Massachusetts

ROBERT A. SUTERMEISTER, M.A.
Professor of Personnel and Industrial Relations
University of Washington
Seattle, Washington

THE AMERICAN ASSEMBLY
Clifford C. Nelson, President
Columbia University
New York, New York

FREDERIC R. WICKERT, Ph.D.
Professor of Psychology and
Graduate Business Administration
Michigan State University
East Lansing, Michigan

PREFACE

ORIGINALLY THE PRESENT volume was called *Humanizing Organizational Psychology* because it was the outcome of symposia by that title chaired by H. Meltzer at the 1973 and 1974 American Psychological Association annual meetings. Both symposia were sponsored by the Consulting Division (Division 13) and co-sponsored by the Industrial-Organizational Division (Division 14). The response of Mr. Payne Thomas after hearing the presentation at the 1973 APA meeting is what led to the preparation of this book. "There is a book in it, will you edit it?" is in essence what Mr. Thomas wrote the senior editor. The participants in the symposia whose contributions are included in this book are Edward Lawler III, Fred Massarik, Douglas Hall, Marvin Dunnette, Bernard Bass and Walter Nord.

The concern underlying the symposia and this book was occasioned by a survey of convention programs, training programs and current literature in both organizational psychology and what is called organizational behavior in departments of management. This survey indicated that organizational psychology and organizational behavior were centered on developing technology that lost sight of its reason for existence—the humanizing process. In this connection it is interesting to note that the two symposia on Humanizing Organizational Psychology were preceded by two also chaired by H. Meltzer under the same auspices which led to the Humanizing Organizational Behavior theme, namely, Social Psychology in Industry: A Needed Revolution, in 1972, and Clinical Psychology in Industry: A Needed Revolution, in 1971, which represented efforts to unfreeze the field for change toward the humanizing theme. The need, therefore, seemed to be to prepare a book that would have humanizing as the main theme in the light of which knowledge and techniques would be included as contributions that would help facilitate or make possible the reinforcement of the humanizing process.

Considered from this point of view the topics seemed to fall naturally into four categories, and the book, therefore, was divided into four parts. First, the nature, extent and social significance of humanizing organizational behavior are considered as a general theme. Belonging with the theme is a consideration of major contemporary problems in organizations today, such as union leadership and workers, and minority groups, including women. These and related frontier problems confronting the organizational psychologist are presented in Part I under the title "Human Realities in Contemporary Organizations." Once the nature and extent of the reality problems we are concerned with are clearly enough understood, then the next consideration is an action theme.

The first step in an action theme is diagnosis for understanding. As a consequence, Part II is concerned with the problem of diagnosing for understanding and managing under the title of "Diagnosing Organizations for Purposes of Humanizing." In Part II are considered organizational diagnosis, the purposes of humanizing and the means of humanizing the organization. Also considered is a very important factor to remember—the development of requisite knowledge and skills is not enough for humanizing. Necessary also is the feeding of the new knowledge past organizational barriers and into the structure of society's institutions.

Continuing with the action theme is the need for considering the problem that used to be expressed in terms of matching men and jobs and is now more realistically conceived as a way in which to help actualize the needs of individuals and also attain organizational objectives in a collaborative manner. Needed is knowledge about individualizing the organization. That is what is considered in Part III under the title "Individualizing the Organization: The Individual and the Organization."

The last action theme is on organizational development considered from the point of view of humanizing rather than primarily as strategies and techniques for satisfying managerial purposes. Accordingly, Part IV, called "Facilitating the Development of the Humanizing Organization" contains contributions on improving individual and organizational effectiveness within one large organization in a humanizing manner; humanizing relations of key people in an organization; moving an organization from an authoritarian style of management to a relatively democratic and humanizing one; and a description of a planned humanizing organization in action, initially designed to be humanizing. In addition to strategies in the form of cases, Part IV also includes studies relevant for a fuller consideration of the humanizing process in organization development. These are humanizing the physical setting at work which deals with what nowadays is often referred to as the environment crisis in human dignity, the search for the effective and humanizing work organization, and on organizations of the future.

The plan was to prepare a book that presents a reasonably representative sample of the possibilities for humanizing an organization in the world we live in. No pretense was made of having an all-exhaustive study. The design was to have it representative and comprehensive enough for use by the people for whom the book is intended—doctoral students, organizational consultants, M.B.A. students interested and specializing in organizational behavior as well as administrators, managers and staff specialists, a good many of whom have knowledge of techniques or technology for the purpose of facilitating organizational effectiveness and do not give due consideration to the humanizing process involved that can be a part of the strategy.

Consultants to organizations can help in processing the humanizing of organizational effectiveness. In settings which permit and encourage human values the consultant is in position to contribute significantly toward the development of expressive behavior which can expand the self-esteem of each participant and help contribute toward the development of patterns of values in relationships which promise well for democratic life in America. In the field of organizational behavior the challenge to psychologists as well as to the managerial group in industry and other organizations is, in the words of Glenn Frank, to be "not merchants of dead yesterdays but guides unto unborn tomorrows." In the meantime it would be well for us to keep in mind Gardner's idea of providing for self-renewal, "In the ever-renewing society what matters is the system or framework within which continuous innovation, renewal and rebirth can occur." In bringing about change it is well to remember that the social responsibility of words flows much more freely than social responsibility of deeds, and it is deeds that yield results.

Because the outlook for organizational behavior from 1975 onward will be conditioned by approach and speed of action, the words used by Lincoln in his opening of his House Divided Speech in 1858 can serve as a framework for the development of a move toward humanized organizational behavior. Lincoln said, "If we could first know where we are and whither we are tending, we could better judge what to do, and how to do it."

The four parts of this book parallel the four themes given by Lincoln. *Where we are* is considered in Part I, *whither we are tending* in Part II, *what to do* in Part III, and *how to do it* in Part IV.

ACKNOWLEDGMENTS

THE EDITORS WISH to express their indebtedness and gratitude to the many people who have contributed to the preparation of this book:

To Mr. Payne Thomas for the invitation to edit the book.

To the six participants of APA symposia on Humanizing Organizational Psychology chaired by H. Meltzer who prepared their presentations for publication—Bernard Bass, Marvin Dunnette, Douglas Hall, Edward Lawler, Fred Massarik and Walter Nord.

To the contributors who prepared studies in their specialties and who went to the trouble of preparing special presentations for this volume—Clayton Alderfer, Kenneth Ball, Michael Beer, Edgar Huse, Gerald Cavanagh, Eli Ginzberg, Walter Nord, Hjalmar Rosen and Fritz Steele.

We are also grateful to the following and their publishers for permission to reproduce copyrighted material—Chris Argyris; Clifford Nelson, President of The American Assembly; Borje Saxberg, and Robert Sutermeister.

Deserving of special appreciation is Mrs. Marcy Bennington who participated in the preparation of the book from the initial stages of correspondence with people invited and follow-up correspondence and who, in addition, did some editing. For help in page proofing we express our thanks to Mr. David Diedrich and Ms. Barbara Malin.

For a professionally competent job of proofreading done in a very accommodating manner, the editors are particularly grateful to Mrs. Willie Bjorkman.

Also deserving of special appreciation is Walter Nord who helped in evaluating and editing at certain stages about select studies.

CONTENTS

HUMANIZING ORGANIZATIONAL BEHAVIOR

Part I

HUMAN REALITIES IN CONTEMPORARY ORGANIZATIONS

INTRODUCING PART I . . .
WHERE WE ARE

FOR A REALISTIC consideration of humanizing organizational behavior the first need is for a frame of reference based on knowledge of existing realities in contemporary organizations—where we are. To bring about a change in the direction of humanizing organizational behavior it is necessary that the liberation of capacities is no longer seen as a menace to organizations and established institutions so that the unfolding of human capacity can operate as a socially creative force. Many businessmen, union leaders and government officials express the feeling that many of our institutions are out of whack with the times and that they are not likely to synchronize with reality very soon unless very definite changes are brought about at the earliest possible time. The first paper, by Saxberg and Sutermeister, starts the consideration of realities with the thesis indicated in the title, namely, "Humanizing the Organization: Today's Imperative."

In their presentation they consider present realities about organizations and changes needed to bring about humanizing of them. Emphasized is the need for a concept of the human being as a total man, man as an end rather than a means. Saxberg and Sutermeister then hook this up with the need for making work more meaningful and satisfying. Ethical and value problems are considered by them including a consideration of existentialism seen by many as "every person doing his own thing." The general conception they consider is in line with Bennis' well-known consideration of what we do on the way to the future in humanizing organizations. This chapter serves as a background for the consideration of the more specific problems presented by other contributors in Part I. The general presentation in this paper along with the more specific considerations of

5

special problems which follow are all purposed to give an idea of where we are as the best reference point for knowing where to go and how to get there.

The first relatively specific problem considered is "The Changing World of Work." The inclusion of this contribution was made possible by the accommodating attitude of the President of The American Assembly, Mr. Clifford Nelson. The challenge is to indicate the need for a new and larger view of the world as well as a look at the quality of worklife it reflects. The idea is that the improving of the place, the organization and the nature of work can lead to a better work performance and a better quality of life in our society. Nobody can argue against the desirability of that happening. Is it happening, to what extent is it happening, and what knowledge is available to make it more likely to happen are the purposes of including "The Changing World of Work" in the present book. A consideration of the world of work makes one think immediately in terms of responses and attitudes of workers who do the work. To what extent do they express job satisfaction or job dissatisfaction? What is the meaning of the results for social action by the organization?

Organizational psychology now has available new knowledge for use. Emphasized in The American Assembly contribution is the need for redesign of work with attention to human factors rather than to plant factors only on the assumption that to a large extent the work place has remained authoritarian in an open society. Innovation and dissemination of new ideas available for action are needed because what is emphasized is the time factor, that the time is now for putting proposals in action. The doing of it calls for flexibility, mobility and innovative procedures all considered in this excellent summary of The American Assembly in 1974.

In "The Changing World of Work," the presentation is of the American scene, but we now have knowledge about what is taking place in the direction of humanizing in Europe. Perhaps the most informed man about the problem of humanizing the European assemby line is Eli Ginzberg. His contribution, specially prepared for this book, gives a clear, relatively full picture of what he discovered in his experience with managers, labor leaders, government officials and research personnel as he visited The Netherlands, Sweden, France, Italy and Israel. He reports his observations on the use of job redesign, job enrichment, job rotation, job enlargement and decentralized decision-making. One important problem that he observed in the various countries is the impact of union management relations and how they differ from country to country. Management in many instances, he found, was becoming somewhat more professional. Political reform and economic realities play a role in the changes he observed in organizations in the various countries. What needs realizing is, as Ginzberg expresses it, that each country is caught up in a historical time schedule all its own. Why Flexi-Time and humanizing are more readily acceptable for change in some European countries than in the United States, one can learn from the study of Dr. Ginzberg's chapter, "The Humanizing of Europe's Assembly Line."

Are union organizations, as they are now composed and work, a help or a hindrance to the humanizing organizational process? There are unions and unions, and one could say almost anything about their role and be right in some measure, in some places. There are many contradictory opinions and some indifference on the part of consultants concerning the role of union problems. Because of this fact we searched for and found a contributor who could present a consideration of the role of unions in humanizing organizational behavior in an informed and objective manner. We found such a person in Hjalmar Rosen, who not only has scholarly familiarity with the literature, but also has had actual experience with unions, union leadership and union organizations as well as managerial organizations. This is presented in his chapter, "Union Organizations: A Challenge to the Utility of Organizational Humanizing Attempts."

In his paper, Rosen raises the problem of whether a union leader leads as an agent of the led or as an agent of union organization. The role and significance of union organization for the humanizing process are considered in the light of a broad perspective by Rosen. Included in his consideration are unionism, its nature, origin and development; leadership and membership involvement; the dynamics of the human side of union enterprise; and the role of leadership style in organizational behavior.

An extremely interesting contemporary problem is, of course, minorities and women. To consider this problem we were very fortunate to have Gerald Cavanagh prepare a special chapter for us about problems of minorities and women which is called "Humanizing Influences of Blacks and Women in the Organization." Cavanagh, along with Purcell, has written a comprehensive book, *Blacks in the Industrial World: Issues for the Manager*, about black workers; they have the knowledge, insight and attitude for an objective consideration of the problem in an open society. The stories of both blacks and women in organizations are surveyed by Cavanagh from the historical point of view and from the humanitarian point of view. Taken into account are the root sources for the problems as they developed and what is needed at the present time in the light of a newly perceived humanizing attitude. He also reviews the facts about blacks and women in the role of supervisors and what kind of supervisors they turn out to be and what their strengths and weaknesses are in this connection. Some case illustrations of actual role-taking by a supervisor and changes in his perception of reactions to black workers are included. Factors which impede effective concern for interpersonal relations on the part of men as compared to women are considered. All of the facts that he presents about the current state of affairs are interpreted by Cavanagh as ways of making it all move in the direction of having a creative organization where innovation and creativity are vital elements.

In the next contribution, Marvin Dunnette presents his ideas and attitudes about organizational psychology under the caption "Mishmash, Mush and Milestones in Organizational Psychology: 1974." He defines *mishmash* as a hodgepodge, *mush* as drivel and presents the negative side of the fence in terms of his disappointments in psychological research and studies. Such disappointments include the use of untested instruments, the use of sophisticated predictive methodologies which have not yielded much of consequence, the insignificant yield from theory and research about motivation, and also lack of research in training. In his milestones he includes such things as Cronbach's emphasis on utility and personal decision-making, research programs on taxonomies of human performance, critical incident methodology, humanized behavior modification methods, job enrichment, domain referenced testing, management by objectives and action research. The flavor of the contribution one can get by reading it as Dunnette expressed it.

The contribution ends with a very hopeful picture that the road is broad and clear for the science of organizational psychology to become more human and to transmit this humanness to practice and to the organizational and societal entities of the future. This contribution will, of course, be most relevant to professional and organizational psychologists, but can be of use also to managers and executives who wish to be informed about the foundations of knowledge that can be of use to them.

The foregoing presentations represent an attempt at giving a picture of human realities in contemporary organizations to serve as a frame of reference for further consideration of the humanizing of organizational behavioral problems with which the four parts of this book are concerned.

─── Chapter 1 ───

HUMANIZING THE ORGANIZATION: TODAY'S IMPERATIVE*

BORJE O. SAXBERG AND ROBERT A. SUTERMEISTER

IN A RAPIDLY CHANGING society, the needs and responsibilities of organizations are changing. Unfortunately they are changing at a rate which is not as fast as the changing expectations and needs of the individual workers. Too many workers in too many organizations are dissatisfied with the dehumanizing effects of their work. Too many organizations too often for too many workers are providing jobs which, as the workers perceive them, rob them of self-esteem and challenge. As a result, too many workers manifest symptoms of alienation and disenchantment which result in turnover, absenteeism and indifference which are costly to the organization, the chief objective of which was to profit from productivity. It is becoming increasingly apparent that what is urgently needed is a change in the management of organizations so that they not only provide jobs but provide a quality of work life which can be satisfying enough to the workers for them to be motivated to cooperate in attaining organizational objectives. In short, the imperative for the seventies is for organizations to become more humanizing.

Early settlers obtained for themselves respect, dignity, a

* Revised from an original version, from Borje O. Saxberg and Robert A. Sutermeister, "Today's Imperative: Humanizing the Organization," *The Personnel Administrator*, January-February:53-58, 1974. Reprinted by permission of the authors and publisher. © The Personnel Administrator, 1974.

challenging life and rewards for achievement through their individual efforts. Important words included honesty, punctuality, uprightness, integrity, sobriety, frugality, diligence and hard work. Work under the Puritan Ethic, as pointed out by Max Weber, achieved a spiritual meaning as a calling or vocation. It was work for survival, and thus its importance was beyond doubt, but the very words of the work ethic have a quaint sound in today's ears just as many other values are being questioned today.

EXISTENTIALIST ETHIC

Existentialism has emerged as a new philosophy justifying a person's *doing his own thing*. The individual is viewed as wholly responsible for himself, for his actions and for his decisions. He cannot hide behind the excuse that the organization forces him to do something, that the rules require it of him, and that he is a victim of circumstances. Each person is expected to explore and understand what he wants to make of himself. What counts is the *here and now*, the *becoming*. History is of no significance as it belongs to the past.

Consequently, the existentialist ethic views work as only one alternative among many paths which an individual may choose to follow in searching for a meaning to his life. It imputes equal importance to other paths—leisure activities in the setting of today's affluent urban society.

There is increasing evidence of the emergence of a third ethic of behavior—the rip-off ethic—partly reflecting the work success ethic running aground on existentialist shores. Our success-oriented society appears to hold out the promise of equality as measured by the possession of material goods. Life's experiences appear to suggest otherwise. The rip-off ethic involves a widespread disregard for private property rights. Possessions are obtained by liberating them or *ripping-off* from other individuals or organizations. The increase in white-collar crime, the looting in ghetto areas during natural catastrophes or in accidents, the petty stealing and shakedowns in the halls of elementary and high schools, the incidents of office and locker room thefts on university campuses, and the general disregard for rights of ownership are manifest in increased emphasis on security—locks, alarms, neighborhood guard duty, community crime watch service and others. The rip-off ethic stands as a commentary on the frustration experienced by many individuals with a societal order which presently lacks a shared set of value attitudes, or a code of behavior.

INDIVIDUALS ARE CHANGING

Warren Bennis has suggested that the changes in the prevailing values of society have had a very pronounced effect on the organization and its members' values.

The emergence of the leisure ethic and its focus on each person doing his own thing was referred to earlier. The alternative commitments available to employees can be viewed as

CULTURAL VALUES

From:	To:
Achievement	Self-actualization
Self-control	Self-expression
Independence	Interdependence
Endurance of Stress	Capacity of Joy
Full Employment	Full Life

ORGANIZATIONAL VALUES

From:	To:
Mechanistic Forms	Organic Forms
Competitive Relations	Collaborative Relations
Separate Objectives	Linked Objectives
Own Resources Regarded as Owned Absolutely	Own Resources Regarded also as Society's Resources

divided between work in one organization, professional knowledge and values regardless of the particular work place, and an emerging view of a balance between demands by the organization, by the work itself and concerns with individual, community and societal objectives.

Traditionally we have expected the great majority of individuals to have a lifetime commitment to one organization. In the past decades this has been a common pattern; all employees were conditioned to look upward, to strive for achievement within their organizations. Perhaps they could also be accused of having lost some of their ability to face risks and create an exciting and imaginative organization in the process.

A number of individuals today are characterized by a professional loyalty—a lifetime commitment to their profession and work, and less concern with the fate of the particular organization they happen to be working for at the moment. They are committed at different times to different organizations. Until recently they have tended to rest secure in their confidence in a marketable skill across organizational boundaries, across industry boundaries and even across international boundaries. This professionalism may also partially account for the trend toward increased organizational mobility in middle and top management. Young executives frequently leave their organizations and do not serve out their periods of apprenticeship as their superiors have done. Such mobility may be a deliberate search for new opportunities with increased responsibilities and rewards, but it may also be a declaration of independence from the organization's objectives and goals as too all-absorbing and powerful.

TOTAL MAN

An increasing number of individuals, managers as well as employees, are giving greater allegiance to the concept of the total man. They assume obligations not just to their organizations, but also to their professions, to their families, to the larger community in which they live, and to other interests they have developed. Thus, an employee may no longer be willing to regard himself as owned, body and soul, by the one world of the organization or by the profession to which he belongs. The co-worldly individual may refuse to transfer to a different geographical area or to assume unwanted responsibilities even though he thereby loses a promotion or even his job. The organization is only one part of his life, his profession is another, and his

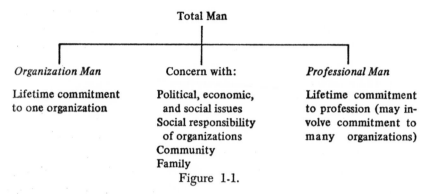

Figure 1-1.

concern for society, community and family loom large in his decisions.

An individual's commitment to a particular organization is influenced more strongly than ever before by wife and family. A wife's increased sensitivity to equality through her own career goals or to a concern for a preferred living and educational environment in which to raise the family is today a critical input in a decision whether or not to remain with one organization or in a particular location.

In light of these changes in society's work values and changes in individuals' expectations and aspirations, management must assume today less predictability and control of employee behavior, and thus show greater attention to the human factor.

HUMANIZING

There are some traditional personnel and industrial relations activities which are vital to an organization—recruitment, selection, placement, training, compensation and fringe benefits, collective bargaining, grievance processing, etc. The technical knowledge and expertise in this area remains important as line management must be able to rely on technical advice and competent counsel in their decisions affecting people, but the humanizing process goes beyond the traditional personnel and industrial relations function.

Organizations must find and retain a motivated work force

to assure their own survival. In a world of new and changed values and attitudes, work in any organization must yield, in addition to a living income, a satisfactory and fulfilling life experience for the employees. This requires humanizing the organization and a view of man as an end rather than a means.

So far management generally has failed to provide a sufficient outlet for man's creative and productive interests. This is reflected in the increasing pressure for a reduction in the work week or for early retirement as answers to unpalatable working conditions. Yet, what assurance do we have that man will be better able to fulfill himself through a reduced work week, earlier retirement or other escapes from work? There emerges the real problem of avoiding boredom. We feel that less attention should be paid to escape from work and more to making work a satisfying experience.

DIFFERENT PATHS

An analysis of the individual's work life suggests that an employee has certain needs he or she attempts to fulfill. One can choose among several different paths in fulfilling them and in reaching for a satisfactory life experience—(1) seek life satisfaction through job activities in business and industry or in other organizations such as government, military, education, church, medical or voluntary; (2) seek life satisfaction through off-job activities; or (3) both on-job and off-job activities can make contributions to one's life satisfaction as was already suggested under the concept of total man.

Looking at the job activities path, one may desire a job full time, part time, temporarily or intermittently. For the time an employee spends on the job, one may seek satisfaction of physiological needs only, paying a penalty of time in return for a paycheck, expecting other needs to be fulfilled in off-job activities. Instead of merely satisfying physiological needs, the employee also may seek to satisfy social needs. Some can satisfy such needs even though the work they perform appears to be routine and unchallenging. Much has been written about the monotony of work. However, monotony is a state of mind of the worker rather

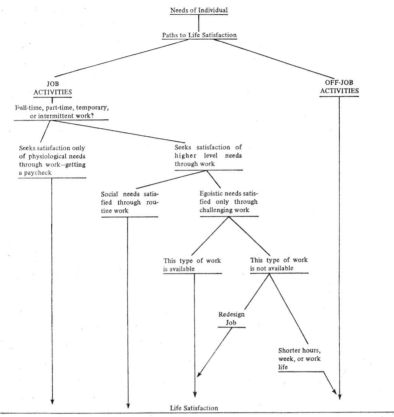

Figure 1-2.

than a built-in component of the job. What is monotonous to one may not be to another.

For other individuals egoistic needs will be activated in addition to physiological and social needs. They can be fulfilled only by work which itself is meaningful, challenging and stimulating. Management has the choice of matching the individual to the job or redesigning the job to meet the needs of the individual. In the future, management must demonstrate true creativity in redesigning jobs to make them meaningful and challenging to assure itself of a work force, to say nothing of one that is motivated and committed to the organization.

Organizations and management have only scratched the surface so far in changing methods to respond more adequately to the needs of employees. Massive additional efforts will be required. New opportunities and new approaches must be devised which will make it possible for an individual to achieve life satisfaction through work experiences. When all efforts to redesign the job have been exhausted, only then should the solution be sought in minimizing the work through fewer hours per day; fewer days per week; more holidays, vacations and sabbaticals; or early retirement. These measures may also provide an opportunity of retooling, and thus a shift in the organization's general employment pattern.

WHAT TO DO

What specifically have organizations already done, or what can they do to give more attention to employees' goals and objectives, and thus support the individual in his search for life satisfaction?

1. Employees can be considered as *job customers* just as organizations consider the public as *product consumers.*

2. With the changing values in society, organizations will be called upon to recruit and hire persons potentially trainable and qualifiable instead of selecting only those already trained and qualified. This emphasizes *including in* rather than *screening out* the potential employee. Anyone who presents himself for an available job opening may have to be accepted for probationary employment until proven untrainable.

3. Selection will become a two-way street. Why should it remain a one-way street in which the employer alone decides whether an applicant is suitable for job openings? Why not let the applicant view the various jobs which are open, even try out several to determine which is most suitable for him? If the applicant tries out the job in advance and then takes it, the chances of the reality of matching his expectations are much improved.

4. Organizations need to ascertain the desires and goals of employees and maintain up-to-date inventories of this information.

5. Use of flexible hours and schedules will increase. Employees who can work less than eight hours a day because of home commitments will be accommodated. Some firms already provide *split schedules* where two workers agree to keep one job filled and arrange between themselves which one of them will work at any particular time or day.

6. Perhaps the concept of life-time employment will gain greater acceptance as one point of stability in an individual's life. Long a norm in Japan and frequently in Germany, a core work force at least is assured of permanent jobs. If a recession occurs, the total payroll is reduced as payments are cut back. Surplus employees go into training status to acquire new skills and new knowledge, giving them a versatility of later value to the organization.

7. Employees in the future must have alternative choices related to their lives and careers. For some there may exist a need to intersperse other activities, such as service work or community work, with work.

8. The creative, innovative talents of management must be directed toward making jobs more meaningful for those employees who are satisfied with nothing less than that. One way is to redesign jobs to allow and encourage greater participation by employees in decision-making. Instead of having responsibility only for the doing of the job, employees will have responsibility for the planning and inspection or control aspects as well.

9. Employees in the future will demand more control over their own fortunes and destiny. Jerry Wurf, President of the American Federation of State, County and Municipal Employees has stated, ". . . white collar workers will not turn down higher salaries, but this is not their main reason for unionizing. The main reason is so that they can be a part of the process that determines their destiny." This statement is equally relevant to other groups in our society, e.g., women, blacks, students and others.

Most union agreements today call for grievance procedures culminating in arbitration. This is another step in the *humanizing process* since arbitrators tend to be especially sensitive to actions of management which are arbitrary, capricious or discriminatory.

10. Organizations will increasingly work toward humanizing their operations. Some recent illustrations point to the effects of the difference between a traditional mechanistic approach and a humanizing approach in treating employees.

When General Motors established its super assembly line to build the new Vega® in Lordstown, Ohio, it designed the most advanced automatic car assembly line plant in the world, the fastest ever built. However, the new employees of an age group in the low twenties—members of the new generation—protested against this integration of human effort into the mechanical colossus. The number of grievances reached some 5,000 with little apparent effort by management to come to grips with them during the *breaking-in period.* The dissatisfied employees went on strike and closed the plant.

11. Organizations will reduce or be forced to reduce time spent on the job for routine jobs which cannot be redesigned. Perhaps not every job can be made satisfying, interesting and meaningful. We face some situations where there are more employees seeking meaningful work than there are meaningful jobs. In these cases the impact of work on the individual and his life must be minimized.

OVERVIEW

Work values in society are changing rapidly. Our society is presently searching for acceptable standards of behavior. Individuals' values, expectations and aspirations are also undergoing rapid change as societal values change. People want more freedom to *do their own things* and to strive for total life satisfaction through one or more paths that they, not the employer, choose. Management has a responsibility to create organizations which are sensitive, aware and knowledgeable about the needs of employees. Only by developing such sensitivity and knowledge can the organization contribute to the life satisfaction of employees at the same time it is furthering its own goals.

In short, management must increasingly humanize the

organization, providing part-time, temporary or intermittent employment; routine or meaningful jobs; or sometimes even escape from jobs in response to the varied needs of the employees and changing values of society.

Chapter 2

THE CHANGING WORLD
OF WORK*

THE AMERICAN ASSEMBLY

T HE WORLD OF WORK is caught up in the cross currents of rapid change. Problems of the work place including job satisfaction demand immediate attention and action.

Three distinct forces are involved—the institutions and the jobs they provide, the society at large and the individual worker. Each is changing at different rates of speed and with different degrees of responsiveness. The individual worker and the society are changing much faster than the institutions and the quality of the jobs they provide.

Disaffection and discontent are a reflection of increasing education and rising aspirations rather than of alienation. Worker disaffection also mirrors the problems of society generally. It is a symptom of a dynamic society that is questioning itself in order to achieve a better society.

The society must take a larger view of work and examine how it relates to increased or decreased satisfaction with life both on and off the job. The issue is made clear by focusing on the expectations workers bring to the job and on the distinction between economic and psychological work satisfaction. While

* The Final Report of the Forty-Third American Assembly held at the Arden House, Harriman, New York, November 1-4, 1973. Reprinted with the permission of Clifford Nelson, President, The American Assembly.

the employer is primarily motivated to create and maintain a productive work place, this is not incompatible with a high quality of working life provided there is a balanced relationship among human, technical and economic factors.

Worker reactions also reflect a conflict between changing employee attitudes and organization inertia. Employees want challenge and personal growth, but work tends to be simplified and overspecialized. Employees want to be involved in patterns of mutual influence, but organizations are characterized by decision-making concentrated at the top. Employees want careers and self-development, but organizations design rigid career paths that sometimes impede fulfillment of these goals. Employees want more opportunity to achieve self-esteem, but many organizations emphasize impersonality.

Some have argued that the press and the professors have created a straw man on the issue of worker discontent. The Assembly does not agree. The problem exists at many levels of both private and public employment. It affects white-collar, blue-collar, professional and service employees.

Our lives are organized around our jobs. The work ethic is deeply embedded in our cultural values. For Americans it means a commitment to productive labor involving security, independence, self-esteem and dignity.

Yet the work ethic is often thwarted. The inefficiencies and impersonality at many work places, decision-making which excludes participation by individual workers, and insufficient recognition or reward to workers for high-quality output all contribute to increasing consumer complaints about the quality of goods and services. Increasingly, workers question both employer decision and the concept of work for work's sake alone, but the desire to accomplish something and to do so effectively remains.

New cultural trends are transforming the work ethic. These include the changing definition of success, reduced fears of economic security, a new sharing of labor between the sexes, and a spreading disillusionment with a narrow definition of efficiency.

As the economic needs of workers are met there will be increasing demands for improvement in the quality of working life. These demands will not substitute for the need for basic economic reward and security. Neither can we ignore the fact that millions of workers are still struggling to achieve a modicum of economic security and an opportunity to earn an adequate income. They are often obliged to sacrifice considerations of improvements in the quality of working life in their struggle to survive.

Big organizations often provide greater financial reward for workers than small organizations but are sometimes a breeding place for worker discontent. The individual can be diminished in these giant organizations where special attention needs to be given to the quality of working life.

Unions have contributed significantly to the improvement in wages, hours, working conditions, the quality of work life, and the advancement of the interests of all workers. Union leaders, for their part, are concerned about the talk of *job enrichment.* Many suspect it is a code word for speedup or a device to undermine unionism. The challenge now is for labor and management to work at resolving issues of the work place in a nonadversary atmosphere with a goal of improving the quality of working life.

Finally, it is recognized that needed changes must be sought within the context of rising international economic competition and other economic pressures.

REDESIGN OF WORK

Employers should place the same emphasis toward the design of human work that they have long placed upon the design of the physical plant. In the long-range interests of the enterprise they should be as innovative and concerned about the needs and feelings of the workers as they are with their profits. A broad spectrum of experiments should include basic changes in the production process, improving health and safety conditions, more attractive surroundings, reduction of special privileges and greater equity in amenities, consideration of more flexible work schedules, use of work teams and more decentralized decision-making. New designs in the work place can more nearly satisfy the needs of workers while they enhance overall vitality of the organization.

Many workers want and should have more of a voice in the world of work. Work is so critical and vital to their lives that to continue to exclude them from participation in decision-making is to remain out of step with the rest of society. At the same time, it is recognized that not every worker wants to be consulted regarding his or her job. While authority is an integral factor in the operation of our society, the bases of authority should be competence and contribution, not just arbitrary rank.

The work place cannot remain authoritarian within an open society. Increasing organizational democracy will contribute to an increasingly free society.

EMPLOYERS

Management has the capacity for initiating changes in the work place, and some have successfully done so. The record of successful experiments, while small, is encouraging. This Assembly believes that significant social and economic gains can be made if more experiments are introduced to improve the quality of the working life. A restructuring of work and work organizations holds promise of more effective development of employees while adding to their work satisfaction without adverse effect on the companies' costs and with potential gains in productivity.

To advance such experiments top management must recognize and seek to allay the insecurities of their middle managers, foremen and workers. Middle managers and employees often resist any reduction of their power and authority since this may be viewed as a threat not only to their authority but to their jobs.

Too often managers underestimate the capabilities of their employees. If authority were reasonably decentralized or released, management could gain substantially. Therefore, improvements in the quality of working life and increased participation in development of human talent will benefit the organization just as it serves individual aspirations.

UNIONS

Unions have, since their inception, been seeking to *humanize* work. The current ideas of improving the quality of working life are basically an extension of this long-range goal. Unions have primarily sought and have achieved significant economic gains and substantially increased job security. This should not obscure their long-term struggle for improvement in the quality of working life. Unions properly resent the view that they are not concerned over this issue.

Unions rightly fear that some management people will attempt to use *job enrichment* as a guise for speedup. Yet, this fear should not be a bar to the possibilities of genuine improvement in jobs. Improved quality in work life may increase productivity and often will, but this should not be the only factor considered. Unions will probably be reluctant to participate in experiments to change work unless there are rewards to the worker. This is legitimate.

Unions should continue to move ahead, cooperating and in some cases spurring management to induce change. Unions should participate in experiments and play a larger role. There are new and encouraging precedent-setting breakthroughs in recent union-management initiatives in the case of the steel and auto workers. Relations between management and labor unions have improved perceptibly over the past two decades, thus new opportunities exist in their mutual interest to improve the quality of working life.

GOVERNMENT

The issue of human dignity at work is an important national goal. It must be high on the national agenda. Government at all levels has long recognized a commitment to enhance the work place environment. But to these commitments it should establish a new national policy that improvement in the quality of working life for all workers is desirable to raise standards of living, protect mental and physical health and welfare, and advance individual fulfillment.

Government should conduct surveys aimed at establishing and tracking levels of job dissatisfaction and factors associated with job dissatisfaction. It should identify the extent of the problem for a wide variety of organizations and provide information for different segments of the working population. Government should encourage research and development in work design, fund experiments, convene national conferences, support worker exchange programs, distribute literature and stimulate and perhaps subsidize these efforts.

It should not be overlooked that governments at all levels employ 18 percent of the nation's labor force. Many of the recommendations for improving the quality of work life in other sections of this report apply to federal, state and local governments.

Advantage should be taken of the well-documented military manpower program (which exceeds 40 billion dollars annually), and use should be made of these continuing studies to establish models on social issues pertaining to youth, minorities and women.

INNOVATION AND DISSEMINATION

Improvements in the quality of working life will benefit from the discovery and application of effective methods of redesigning jobs and other changes. The present level of information and know-how is inadequate. We need new institutional arrangements to accelerate change. We need talent and organizations on the shop floor and in the office to deal with and advance the quality of working life. These concepts can be applied to both union and nonunion situations.

Agencies for Change

There is a need to establish nonprofit institutes to further the improvement of the quality of working life. These should be funded jointly from private and public sources. Funds should be contributed by government, foundations, management and unions so that all are involved and all have a stake in the outcome. These institutes would stimulate and assist management and labor in developing experiments and programs and in the measurement of the full range of their effects. They should serve not only as a stimulus for experimentation but should reflect changes around the world. They should develop professional talent equipped to facilitate change.

In addition, universities and other established educational institutions should continue to conduct research into and evaluate experiments on improving the quality of working life and distribute their findings. Moreover, schools of business, engineering, law, labor relations and other disciplines training people directly involved in designing and managing work must include in their curricula greater consideration of factors affecting the quality of working life.

Work issues should also become the concern of civic, religious, educational, neighborhood and other organizations to increase the linkage between the work place and the community and to achieve new approaches to workers' needs in the broadest possible framework.

ADAPTING TO CHANGE

While the nature of work is central to discussion of the quality of work life, other aspects of work frequently cause strong and specific worker discontent. Improving only job tasks may not be sufficient to improve worker satisfaction unless these other factors are also improved.

The following recommendations presuppose the development and maintenance of a high level of employment without which they cannot be fully implemented.

Flexibility and Mobility

Rigid rules and restrictive customs regarding work should be reexamined. Acceptable programs are needed to enhance mobility, develop the use of human resources, fulfill human potential and advance economic welfare. Many employees want job mobility and more options in their fringe benefits, pensions and other deferred payments.

The barriers to job change presented by economics, geography, invalid credential requirements and other factors should be reduced or eliminated.

Part-Time Employment

More and better part-time jobs would greatly increase the opportunities and choices for all workers, particularly women, youth, handicapped and older workers who seek such opportunities. Such jobs are more easily harmonized with new lifestyles combining work, education, home and family. Current wage and benefit practices which discriminate against part-time workers must be changed so as to increase opportunity and ease labor shortages in particular occupations or industries.

Transitions Involving the Home, the School and the Work Place

Many young people are poorly prepared for the world of work. Schools, in cooperation with government, business, unions and parents, should improve methods for career development. Career education and cooperative education programs should become an integral part of the school system. Provisions must be made for the financial commitment and job redesign which such programs require. Moreover, all people must have access to education throughout their lives with minimal financial and occupational disruption. Continuing education upgrades existing careers, advances second careers and generally enriches lives.

Discrimination

Despite progress, ethnic and racial minorites, women, youth and older workers still suffer severe discrimination in public and private employment. Our progress is significant only in contrast to where we were a decade ago. We must develop a more effective national effort to achieve opportunity for full participation in the work force at all levels of employment. The Equal Employment Opportunity Commission (EEOC) must be sustained and strengthened. The handicapped also need more opportunity to enter the world of work and establish their full place in society.

This effort would help give these groups access to employment and begin to meet their most basic aspirations for decent jobs, income security and a sense of self-worth. The continuing discrimination against ethnic and racial minorities resists change and must be eliminated. A full employment economy will accelerate the achievement of these objectives.

Women

Women represent the single largest sector of the population that has been blocked from access to meaningful jobs and careers. To improve the opportunities of those who seek work out of the home requires that they have access to financial aid for educational opportunities, preferably prior to or at the time they are ready to enter or reenter the work force.

It also requires employers and trade unions to remove all barriers to equal employment, compensation, training and promotion. Women must receive equal pay for equal work. Greater flexibility in hours should be provided by employers so that both husbands and wives can arrange their schedules with greater ease. A substantial expansion in educational day care and after school care centers will further improve opportunities for meaningful working careers for women and should be undertaken by employers, unions and government, and where applicable, fee schedules should be geared to family income.

Middle-Aged and Older Workers

Options for older workers are often severely limited. Not only is their age an artificial handicap to other employment, but deferred benefits are tied to their jobs and lost if they leave. Moreover, there are few opportunities for them to find additional education or training. The labor market itself is a frightening place.

Increased mobility and second career chances are needed. They also strengthen the institutions where work is performed since organizations often carry employees who are marginal performers, blocked, frustrated and relatively unable to make a worthwhile contribution. Continuing education with income support would broaden the options available to workers. More funds are required from both public and private sectors.

Pension Plan Reform

It has been assumed and accepted that both employers' and employees' interests are served by establishing pension plans which put a high premium on staying with one firm. This philosophy is not compatible with the need for flexibility, mobility and individual freedom in our society, nor does it serve the best interests of the firm. In too many enterprises, executives, middle managers and rank and file workers have left the firm mentally but will not leave physically until they retire.

Pensions represent the single most important deferred benefit of American workers. Private retirement plans now cover nearly 50 percent of the private work force, more than double the proportion for 1950. However, it has been estimated that more than half of all the workers covered by these plans will draw few, if any, benefits under present law. In addition, half of the American labor force is without *any* private pension plan coverage.

We must therefore expand pension coverage and endorse comprehensive federal pension reform legislation, especially provisions for early vesting and adequate funding.

CONCLUSION

Something, clearly, is stirring. In part, we are witnessing changes in personal values that are seen and felt not only in the United States but around the world. In part, we are experiencing the latest chapter in the continuing story of the quest for fulfilling American goals and aspirations—a fair and equitable society, an opportunity for each citizen to participate in the forces that affect his life, and a confirmation that the democratic process does, indeed, work for all. Now that challenge is emerging at the most basic level of work itself, the questions have come down to society's responsibility to provide a higher quality of working life and increasing opportunities for those millions on the fringe who for so long have endured the reality of a life in which all our fine talk about job enrichment and job humanization is meaningless. We believe that the changes we advocate can help us work toward a more democratic and more productive society. They will not solve all the problems; they are a beginning.

Our view is pragmatic—improving the place, the organization and the nature of work can lead to better work performance and a better quality of life in the society. A crisis, though it may not presently exist, could confront us if business, labor, educational institutions, community leadership and government fail to respond. If we are lulled by our successes of the past, and if we presume they inevitably will carry over into our future, we are mistaken. They will not. While we differ on specific points and proposals, we are united in one belief—these questions are vital. The time has now come to put our words and proposals into action.

Chapter 3

THE HUMANIZING OF EUROPE'S ASSEMBLY LINE

Eli Ginzberg

T HOSE OF US WHO have studied the problems of jobs, work and manpower lately have been required to turn our attention from the issue of employment itself to that of work satisfaction, or more properly, work dissatisfaction. Note, for example, the enormous amount of attention paid to the wildcat strike at the Vega assembly line at Lordstown, Ohio, and to the rising rejection of collective-bargaining agreements by union locals whose members believe that their national leadership is disregarding unsatisfactory working conditions. Note, too, the growing interest among leading corporations—A.T.&T., General Foods, Polaroid, Procter and Gamble, Chrysler—in experimenting with job redesign, enrichment, rotation, enlargement and decentralized decision-making, all of which are aimed at removing some of the major sources of employee discontent with work conditions. Even the enthusiastic public response to the revival of Charlie Chaplin's *Modern Times* suggests popular empathy with the plight of the industrial worker.

THE PLIGHT OF THE INDUSTRIAL WORKER

In Europe, as the writer learned during a trip through The Netherlands, Sweden, Norway, France and Italy, and in Israel, the subject of work satisfaction is attracting even more attention than in the United States. He talked with managers, labor leaders, government officials and research personnel about some of their new experiments in work structuring. In addition, many hours were spent in plants observing a number of these experiments which ranged from autonomous work groups in a television assembly unit to efforts at job enlargement and enrichment in automotive assembly plants.

One of the things that strikes an American studying industrial and economic conditions in other countries is the way in which each particular society is caught up in its own historical time schedule. Thus, over and over again, European managers waxed enthusiastic over their discovery of the new doctrines of decentralization and consultative management, doctrines that have flourished in the United States at least since the end of World War II. On the other hand, almost without exception, European managers are far more sensitive than their American counterparts to the play of ideological and political forces that place severe limits on their ability to remedy workers' broad discontent through restructuring the work they perform.

The role of social science in this regard has been significant. In the early 1950's the Tavistock Institute in London developed a new synthesis composed of the technology of Frederick W. Taylor and Elton Mayo's perception of the factory as a network of social relations, which has come to be called the *sociotechnical approach*. In the early 1960's, Tavistock became associated with E. Thorsrud of Norway, who was about to launch a cooperative effort among management, labor, government and social scientists to modify the work environment in order to make a tangible improvement in the quality of life. Ten years of active experimentation followed; Thorsrud is now the acknowledged leader among European practitioners of sociotechnical methods.

The workers and representatives of management who take part in such experiments are, of course, pursuing, or believe they are pursuing, their own interests. The interests of management, while diverse, are easy to discern. On the other hand, they stem from the fact that many companies have come to face great difficulty in recruiting industrial workers, particularly from the native labor force. For most of the last decade, the majority of the countries of Western Europe (and Israel also) have been confronted with a labor market that has ranged from tight to very tight. All of the European countries visited, Italy excepted, have had to import foreign workers. In Italy the automobile plants in Turin were being staffed increasingly with labor recruited from the southern part of the country. Industrial employers had also sought to expand the number and proportion of female employees, but this group turned out to be a rather shallow labor pool. Relatively few women can be enticed into blue-collar jobs, especially if heavy, noisy and dirty work is involved.

LABOR MARKET CONSIDERATIONS

Recently, each of the labor-importing countries has become aware of the social and political disabilities of having a large foreign labor force in its midst. There are very real drawbacks if the foreign workers remain for only a year or two; and if they seek to settle more or less permanently, all sorts of difficulties arise with respect to such elements as the provision of housing and schooling, and the social and political relations between the immigrants and the host society. When tight labor markets begin to loosen and unemployment increases, great pressure develops to restrict the importation of foreign labor. Employers who have come to depend on such labor see themselves caught in a bind; they are unable to recruit local labor, and they run the risk of having their foreign supplies cut off. If, through changes in work-structuring, industrial employment can be made more attractive to the native population, employers might be able to surmount their recruitment problems.

Another inducement for management to restructure work has been provided by such factors as increases in absenteeism and turnover, and other evidence, imagined or real, of low motivation and low morale. There is as yet little hard data to back what is a general impression. In fact, alternative explanations having little or nothing to do with actual job dissatisfaction seem to offer just as reasonable an accounting for counterproductive worker behavior. In Italy, for example, a recent change in the social security system no longer requires that a worker who takes a day off because of illness be examined by a physician, and many workers now view the liberalized sick benefits as paid time off.

In addition, management has looked for ways to increase plant productivity in order to compensate for higher wage costs. Trade unions in France and Italy have been successful in achieving major reforms such as transferring blue-collar workers to the monthly payroll and upgrading a significant proportion of unskilled and semiskilled workers. Work structuring offers a prospect of offsetting the cost of these innovations.

MANAGEMENT BECOMING PROFESSIONAL

As European companies have grown in size and complexity, their managements have become more professional. One consequence of this trend is increased attention to established organizational relationships and supervision. Many companies have found themselves burdened with excessive layers of supervision which slow decision-making, retard productivity and prove burdensome to those at the bottom of the hierarchy. Experimentation with work structuring by enlarging the responsibility of the worker on the line often provides an excuse for making fairly radical organizational changes, including collapsing several layers of supervisors. Moreover, in Sweden, where hourly wages are the exception in industrial establishments, each change in the production system in the past usually provided the occasion for intensive negotiations between management and labor about norms, piece rates and bonuses. One tangential benefit of work-structuring has been to reduce, if not eliminate, such complex negotiations.

In Western Europe and Israel, then, there is a minority of managements who, faced with a range of problems centered around recruitment and utilization of manpower, have decided that they have little to lose and perhaps much to gain from experimenting with changes in work structuring. If successful, they believe their companies will benefit in terms of increased productivity and profits as well as in terms of improved worker satisfaction.

As for the workers, why have they been willing to participate in experiments that could not be launched and surely could not be successfully implemented without their cooperation? What have they seen as their own possible gain? To begin with, most factory work in Europe—as in the United States—leaves much to be desired. It is characterized by excessive noise, poor ventilation, frequent breakdowns in machinery, poor supervision, infrequent rest periods and a host of other conditions workers find irksome. As a result, any effort on the part of management to address itself to these problems will be seen as a boon provided the workers are convinced that the new approach is not aimed at getting them to produce more without commensurate adjustment in wages. Since most experiments require the cooperation of only small numbers of worker volunteers, it is usually easy to counter this fear.

The volunteers frequently respond to improved communications and expanded decision-making power which are integral parts of many work-structuring experiments. They like the idea of having more to say about the specifics of the production process, and they enjoy the regularly-scheduled conferences at which they learn about how their work fits into the larger picture. They also like the fact that the experiments relieve them of one or more layers of supervision and that they are given more opportunity to use initiative. In the case of autonomous work groups—a leading form of experiment—the members frequently relish the camaraderie that develops, and most of them find themselves under less pressure than when the pace of work was set by the machine.

There are additional reasons why workers support the experiments. Most important is their conviction, in many cases justified, that if the experiment proves itself, they will be able to earn more through upgrading, higher wage rates, larger bonuses or all three. Sometimes they see in them the promise of reaching other long-deferred goals such as getting rid of piecework or being placed on the monthly payroll, thereby enjoying the same perquisites as white-collar workers.

REALITIES OF LABOR-MANAGEMENT CONFLICT

The experiments also expand the scope and responsibility of the local labor representative. In most European countries and in Israel either the national unions or the national trade union organization (L.O. in Sweden and Histadrut in Israel) have long dominated the collective-bargaining process. The worker in the plant and his local trade-union representative are both pawns in a strategy of national negotiations, but no significant changes can be made without local trade-union participation. While the national trade-union leadership has seldom been enthusiastic about these experiments, they generally cooperate because they recognize the mounting evidence of local restiveness and see the experiments as a relatively safe outlet for the drive for greater local autonomy. And it is, after all, risky for the leadership to drag its feet, for it must play a key role in any serious program aimed at improving the work environment.

A word about the research community and governmental officials. Thorsrud explained his initial interest in work-structuring in terms of his disenchantment with radical political solutions—that is, with the Soviet and Yugoslav versions of Communism—and of his equal distaste for the banality and materialism of industrial capitalism in its American version. He was impressed with the desirability of infusing fresh life into the social democracy of the Scandinavian countries which were finding it increasingly difficult in the post-World War II years to advance into new terrain. The more pragmatic members of the Western European research community, while less concerned with the larger problems of values and politics, share Thorsrud's desire to find an alternative to the confrontation and conflict that have for so long characterized labor-management relations.

It was only one small step, therefore, for some political leaders such as Jacques Chaban-Delmas, the former French premier, to join the ranks of the new converts. In outlining his platform for reelection late in May, 1972, Chaban-Delmas made reform of the working environment one of his key planks, specifically stressing a superior profit-sharing plan, worker participation at board level, and improvements in the work place.

In Sweden the establishment coalition consisting of representatives of management, labor, government and the research community prepared a working paper, "The Quality of Working Life," for the Stockholm Conference on the environment, the only presentation directed specifically to this subject. But these are exceptional examples. The subject is still too esoteric to have caught the imagination of most politicians or governments.

In any case, with about a decade of experimentation in Norway and the Netherlands (Philips), and with briefer but more intensive efforts in the other countries, it is beginning to be possible to draw up some kind of balance sheet.

The first thing one notices is how slowly the experiments have proceeded in both Norway and the Netherlands. The senior staff of Philips is aware of this and finds its experience with small-scale experiments at job enlargement and autonomous work groups in radio and television production to have been exaggerated out of all proportion. A visitor to Eindhoven-Philips headquarters concludes that the firm has pursued some interesting experimentation for its own sake since the management hesitates to make any real jump from experimentation to policy. There have been no radical changes in the basic production system, and it is questionable whether there will be. A manager pointed out that the successful autonomous group that was assembling twenty-six television sets a day could produce thirty but refused to do so. When asked whether he had discussed a reduction in hours or a higher bonus with the members of the group, he looked aghast!

In Norway, on the other hand, the slow pace reflects Thorsrud's determination to advance only in unison with the principals—management, labor, government. He is committed to the idea that the planning, the success and the errors of work structuring must be left to those who have to live with the changes. The Norwegian experimenters believe that other entrepreneurs regard them as deviants, enamored of a method that makes no sense to sound businessmen. Nor have the national trade-union leaders shown much enthusiasm for the new approach, although one or another has been willing to participate. The modesty of the Norwegian record, therefore, reflects a conjunction of Thorsrud's determination to progress only with the active participation of all the principals and the difficulty of eliciting the cooperation of any large number of them.

The efforts in the other countries are too recent to justify any clear-cut conclusion, but certain notes come through loud and clear. First is the critically important fact that, with the possible exception of a large office machine and electronics concern in Italy, nowhere has management been sufficiently convinced by the experimental results to have altered basic production processes. Until managements move to alter their basic operations, the entire approach remains in the realm of the abstruse.

This is not to say that there have been no significant spin-off effects from the experiments. Many firms have come to appreciate the considerable gains to be made in moving toward decentralization, flattening their organizations and removing one or more layers of supervision. More importantly, they have come to recognize that there are also gains to be made from improved communications with their work force and from involving employees in decisions that bear on their own working conditions.

In addition, there are spin-offs as far as workers and their trade union organizations are concerned. Many workers have actually secured important improvements in their working conditions. At Volvo in Göteborg, Sweden, the men who operate the big body presses, where noise level is excessively high, now can take a break in a special noise-proof retreat in their immediate area, and Olivetti, south of Turin, Italy, has linked work structuring to upgrading a thousand or more workers with corresponding increases in their wages.

Moreover, one finds in these several countries links between work structuring experiments and reductions in hours, shifts from piece work to hourly or monthly pay, improved bonuses and other priority objectives of trade unions. Such objectives might well have been achieved by the trade unions without these experiments, but the gains would have come more slowly.

While no *national* trade union leader talked glowingly about the experiments per se (Ben Aharon, the former leader of Histadrut, was convinced of the need for fundamental changes in the work but in terms of protecting the dignity and intelligence of man), much favorable comment came from *local* labor leaders who were directly involved in introducing changes at the work place. It seems likely then that the experiments are doing little to reduce the basic tensions between national unions and their locals that exist in the United States, Western Europe and Israel. However, by providing new scope for local leaders, they may be easing their relations somewhat. Workers appreciate whatever limited attention is paid to local issues.

Thus, all has been neither gain nor loss. Indeed, before one can choose to be either an optimist or a skeptic, one must attempt to place work structuring in the larger context of those political, social and economic forces that will be the major factors in determining any transformation of industrial societies in the decades ahead.

CHANGES IN THE WORLD OF WORK

The proponents of work-structuring stress that, once earnings are above a subsistence level, workers become less interested in income than in other forms of satisfaction. The question remains, however, whether labor leaders and workers do, in fact, act in accordance with this idea or whether they are simply and constantly interested in fighting for more money. There is little hard evidence from the collective bargaining table to support the work structure theory. This means that, although workers are definitely concerned about improving the conditions of the work place, they are even more interested in higher wages, shorter hours, more paid vacations and higher retirement benefits. Workers question, and probably rightly, the degree to which conditions on the factory floor can be improved. They do *not* question that they will be better off if they earn more and work less. Only the self-assured manager and the moralistic social scientist are certain that, if workers work fewer hours, they will not know what to do with their leisure. Workers themselves are not in the least beset by such worries. Hence, if workers want more pay for less work and if managers want more work from them for the same pay but with altered work conditions, the confrontation that the sociotechnical theorists look forward to dissolving is likely to be with us for a long time. Work-structuring is not likely to usher in the demise of the union.

There is talk in Western Europe, just as in the United States, that the day may not be far off when certain types of manufacturing will no longer be profitable. If this generation of young workers and the next really balk at accepting less desirable types of factory employment, if the countries involved run out of second-class citizens such as workers from the south of Italy or blacks in the United States, and if these countries refuse to permit large numbers of foreigners to settle among them, then the outcome is clear. Certain manufacturing operations will move to other countries where workers have fewer options and lower expectations. To illustrate, in the United States, after the seasonal migration of Mexican farm laborers was prohibited in the mid-1960's, certain stoop crops could no longer be raised. In France, one of the oldest and most profitable radio manufacturing plants is seeking new production ideas in the Far East as well as new markets!

Certain industrialists question whether they will still be able to manufacture at home a decade hence, or whether they will be forced to relocate to less developed countries where, regardless of working conditions, the opportunity to earn one dollar and fifty cents an hour to two dollars an hour is welcomed. The rapid growth of low-wage manufacturing operations in developing countries is threatening the competitive advantages long held by more advanced European firms. Unless the latter can increase productivity, they may lose out in the competition with labor-intensive manufacturers of goods ranging from clothing to radios.

In this perspective, experiments with work structuring are

forced responses of management. The fact that only a small number of such experiments were initiated in countries with tight labor markets underscores management's preference for the conventional solution—tapping new sources of labor supply—rather than for major structural innovation.

However, the assumption that, in a struggle between management and labor over productivity, profits, wages and working conditions, international competition will discipline labor to accept terms it would otherwise reject is wrong for two reasons—labor bargains in the short run; international competition, to the extent it operates, has an impact in the long run. Morever, one of the interesting consequences of the greater degree of European economic hegemony is the increasing cooperation among national unions. All trade unions with agreements in Ford plants in Western Europe are coordinating their demands and aiming for a multinational settlement. Labor can play the multinational game about as easily as management.

Wide as the gap is in the United States between most blue and white-collar workers, and between workers and managers, the gap is that much wider in Europe. While the present gap is being narrowed in varying degrees in Scandinavia, France and Italy by transferring blue-collar workers to the monthly payroll and equalizing their fringe benefits, it is difficult to see how work-structuring efforts can effectively cancel out the differences between the man who uses his muscles eight hours a day and one who sits at a desk manipulating words, figures or people. Someone once remarked that when he first became an office worker, he could not believe that what he was doing was work, for it bore no resemblance to his earlier life in the factory. Some of the more reflective managers recognize this difference and see no way of eliminating it other than by rotating workers between the office and the factory—an experiment, needless to say, that has yet to be structured. They view problems with the labor supply as going beyond improvements in the immediate work environment, and even beyond adjustments in wages and benefits, because resistance to blue-collar work will continue as long as the dominant value systems assign it to the lowest rung of the social totem pole.

It is no accident that almost all the experiments in work-structuring involve blue-collar workers. Only in Sweden are white-collar workers included in the experimental design, but these efforts smack more of work simplification than of work-structuring, and nowhere is attention being paid to lower and middle management. Presumably they are deemed to be highly productive and to be enjoying their work, a presumption without a shred of supporting evidence. Every time the question was raised about work dissatisfaction among middle management, employers were speechless.

POLITICAL REFORM AND THE LABOR MOVEMENT

This brings us to the relation between work-structuring and the broader problem of political reform. Here we must distinguish between the countries where the social democrats have long been in control (Sweden, Norway and Israel) and the situation in France and Italy.

The long-term political ascendancy of the labor movement in both Scandinavia and Israel is under attack from within and without on a whole series of fronts—ideology, organizational structure and leadership. The dissidents include many members of the younger generation, the professional classes, disadvantaged minorities and, in fact, increasing numbers of the general public who have begun to question whether the labor establishment can solve urgent national problems. Evidence of growing restiveness and disillusion can be read in wildcat strikes, alienation of youth, the growing hostility of unemployed intellectuals, the strident criticism from opinion leaders on the right and left, all of which indicates a loss of confidence in the institutions that labor built with so much loving care to hasten the new society. No one other than the idealistic Thorsrud sees work-structuring as being responsive, or having the potentiality of becoming responsive, to the political malaise threatening social democracy.

The situation in France and Italy is different. The more progressive sectors of French management have not yet recovered from their nightmarish experience of 1968 when they were saved by the Communists who refused to join the ranks of the revolutionaries, but the wiser managers know that the discontents that fed the uprising are still present, and that the next time the rank and file may join the students. Hence, a great many adjustments must be made as quickly as possible on many fronts—including improving the work place, increasing the worker's share and enlarging his role in the decision-making process. It is far from clear that the conservative political and business leadership in France will be able to make the long-delayed accommodations that are required to assure broad support for a system whose legitimacy is under serious attack. France needs not another de Gaulle, but a Franklin Roosevelt. No one expects work-structuring to provide more than an assist in the task of social reform.

The Italian scene is even more unstable. The economy is being radically transformed while the political structure and class relations are changing very slowly. Work-structuring has little to contribute to solving the urgent problems that demand attention—the swelling ranks of the educated unemployed, the abysmal poverty of the south, the gap between workers' expectations and the ability of the economy to meet them.

Despite the substantial improvement in the lives of the working population of Western European countries and of Israel during the past quarter century—gains reflected in increased real income, higher educational attainment, improved social benefits, more leisure—a pervasive unease exists. European workers are increasingly bereft of the ideology, political organization and leadership necessary to channel their discontents and formulate new goals.

Workers always welcome an opportunity to improve their conditions of work just as they press for more wages and shorter hours, but when workers begin to question whether the good life consists only of more consumer goods, and when they are unclear about what they really want and have even less idea about how to realize whatever vision they have of a better future, adjustments at the work place are a limited response at best. If workers direct a major effort to this new frontier, the issue that remains open is what may lie beyond. If recent

European experience tells us anything, it is that management will explore a great many alternative ways of meeting its manpower needs before embarking upon large scale experimentation. Management continues to prefer seeking solutions in the market.

Chapter 4

UNION ORGANIZATIONS: A CHALLENGE TO THE UTILITY OF ORGANIZATIONAL HUMANIZING ATTEMPTS

HJALMAR ROSEN

IF, INDEED, THE GOAL of organizational humanization is individual satisfaction in the broadest sense, what must be the nature of an individual's interaction with an organization that will bring that state of affairs into being and maintain it? Perhaps it would be well to initiate our analysis by discussing the significance of formal organizational membership for the individual.

Human beings, having a prolonged period of maturation before they are able to fend for themselves, develop a strong dependency upon others for their survival. Only through the utilization of means controlled by others can the individual grow into maturity—and, for that matter, maintain his existence once he is mature. This dependency, however, immediately imposes constraints upon the individual. The individual must learn to abide by, if not accept, the demands made upon him by others in return for their support.*

Infant and childhood dependency upon others provides the basis for socialization, i.e., acceptance of the fact that one must operate within the framework of others' constraining demands in order to have others accept the demands the individual makes upon them that are necessary for the individual's survival. It

---

* Freudians would refer to this process as development of a superego that acts as a control for the highly individualistic and asocial needs of the person (id).

is the socialized individual who has learned the social exchange relationship that becomes involved with formal organizations. The socialized individual has learned to expect that organizational membership has both assets and liabilities. To the extent that an individual is able to choose his organizational affiliations he will make his choice in terms of those organizational affiliations that have the promise of the greatest relative gain/loss ratio.

Turning now to the union organization, to the extent that the individual has freedom to join or not and freedom to maintain or terminate his affiliation, to that extent will the organizational membership be a factor in his satisfaction. Although organizational constraints (costs) are inevitable, such costs would be accepted as long as they were counterbalanced by gain to an extent that would compare favorably with other options perceived to be available to him. However, the situation outlined does not jibe with current reality of union membership for a number of very good reasons.

UNIONISM—ITS NATURE, ORIGIN AND DEVELOPMENT

Unionism in its inception was a protest movement; its purpose was to provide the powerless individual worker with a social vehicle by which to achieve a greater power equalization with the employer, thereby increasing the probability of achieving a more equitable, qua satisfying work relationship with the employer in the pursuit of his economic livelihood. The logic of union effectiveness in the realm of power equalization is based upon the assumption that power is additive. A traditional organizational tactic provides a dramatic illustration of this point. In an organizing campaign the union organizer takes a single thread and calls a puny member of the audience to the stand and asks him to break it. The task is completed easily. The organizer states, "Even the weak employer can break the individual worker." Then the organizer counts out as many threads as there are potential members and twists them together. Calling a burly member of the audience, the organizer asks the person to break the cord. No amount of straining will achieve the task. "Together *sic* in a union, we are invincible."

However, if a union is to be successful in the sense of being a vehicle for need gratification, it must be able to marshal the unionized employees into a cohesive body to stand behind the demands made upon the employer. Obviously (and there are rare exceptions in terms of *bottleneck* positions and units), the greater the number of union members among the employees, the higher is the probability of successful goal achievement. This *fact of life* led to the need for the union to develop some mechanisms to insure that employees would join the union and would maintain their affiliation. Over the history of unionism in the United States this has led to the development of closed shop, union shop or agency shop clauses in the contract as well as maintenance of membership agreements.* In reality, such organizational constraints, necessary for successful bargaining for employee demands, inevitably limit the freedom of the individual to choose in terms of his perceived best interests. Consequently, they contribute to dissatisfaction and to an apparent need for humanization of the person-organizational relationship.

A second critical set of factors that create potential dissatisfaction and a need for humanizing the organization relates to the governance and control philosophy and mechanisms characterizing union organizations. The philosophical-political framework of the union organization is that of representative democracy, although some would claim that this is an ideal rather than a real representation. To the extent that unions operate within a framework of representative democracy, however, one would be prone to see this as a critical condition to insure humanization rather than as a deterrent. For, after all, one of the most

---

* Closed shop called for all current employees within the bargaining unit to join the union as a condition of employment. This has been declared illegal. The union shop clause called for all new employees to join the union. The agency shop clause requires that even nonmembers must contribute *via* reduced dues to the support of the union, and all new employees must join as a requirement of employment. Maintenance of membership refers to the fact that one must remain a member in good standing to remain employed.

vaunted humanizing strategies is participative decision-making.*
We must remember, however, that effective humanizing must
be assessed in terms of individual satisfaction in the sense of
individual need gratification. Representative democracy in a
union organization or elsewhere has two characteristics that bear
on humanization. The first relates to the *will of the majority;*
the second to policy determination and organizational direction
being delegated to elected officials or leaders who hold positions
within the organization of the union rather than having positions
comparable to their constituency.

Considering the first issue, with a majority rule with regard
to goals, demands, procedures, etc., there inevitably will be a
minority of members who will not see their best interests being
served by the majority decision, and consequently, resulting in a
reduction of their satisfaction with the union as an agent of need
fulfillment. *If* they were able to withdraw or terminate their
membership and/or join or develop a more compatible organization, the problem would not be critical. But, in terms of bargaining effectiveness, such options are rarely available within the
union movement.* Consequently, given such constraints, there
is a need to cope with resultant potential feelings of nonfulfillment.

With regard to the second problem, union leadership does
not function within a role comparable to that of its constituency,
and as a consequence may be viewed by the constituency as
not being committed to service the goals of the membership.
Perlman (1928) refers to the problem in terms of differences
in time perspective between union leadership and membership.
Selznik (1957) refers to the problem in terms of differential

---

* Participative decision making is a key concept of such humanistic
theorists as McGregor (1960), Argyris (1957), Likert (1961, 1967) and Herzberg (1959, 1966).

* The two-party system of the Printing Trade Unions does permit an option
for disgruntled membership (Lipset, Coleman and Trow, 1956). Leadership
is maintained in power only as long as it fulfills the demands of the majority.
Opposition party leadership (provided for within the political structure) constantly forces existing leadership to be sensitive to membership needs. Even so,
this mechanism does not cope with the minority member who is forced to accept
the will of the majority.

information available to leaders and members resulting in decisions being based upon different information as a function of role. Rosen and Rosen (1957) discuss the issue in terms of the broader and longer range perspective necessary in the union leadership role. Moreover, in translation of and bargaining for demands emanating from the membership majority via participative decision-making, leadership functioning within the context of their role will inevitably introduce modifications, and although the long-range intent and impact may be equivalent, there often appears to be glaring disparity from the membership demands. Even for the majority member, then, there is the possibility that feelings of nonfulfillment will occur.

LEADERSHIP AND MEMBERSHIP INVOLVEMENT

Unions via their readership are not unaware of the potential for membership disgruntlement built into their system of representative democracy nor of the potential impact such disgruntlement could have upon the viability of the union as an organization and the maintenance of leadership within it. As any political strategist would operate faced with a condition of political democracy, they attempt to develop means by which the union and their positions within it are protected and maintained.

To the extent that the union under current leadership direction has been successful in acting as a need gratification vehicle for the majority of the membership, members will be prone to follow leadership recommendation. They will support leadership recommendations by vote even on issues that do not appear to have any critical need fulfilling function per se. Let us explore this aspect more fully.

Let us first consider the means developed for increasing membership and insuring membership stability. Preparing the groundwork for greater membership inclusion within the bargaining unit, emotionally-toned arguments concerning the *free loaders* are developed, e.g., Is it fair and just for us (extant membership) to sacrifice in terms of dues, time and effort to achieve gains for those who, at best, contribute nothing toward their achievement? Psychologically, the problem is cast within an equity framework. To the extent that by comparison others (nonmembers) achieve equivalent outcomes with lesser or no inputs, inequity exists. Once this point is established, it becomes relatively predictable that members will vote for some type of inclusion clause to be a key bargaining issue. Once achieved in contract negotiations, it literally forces nonmembers, as a condition of employment, to either join the union or contribute toward its support by dues assessment. Following the achievement of such a clause, the union leadership is provided with an opportunity to convince nonmembers who are contributing to the support of the union financially to see such a condition as inequitable for them because they are provided with no voice in developing demands consistent with their needs—a situation that the union leaders can point out *easily can be rectified by becoming a member in good standing.*

Within the current state of affairs, membership per se is not mandatory for those within the bargaining unit who choose not to join the union, but, over time, almost total inclusion of the bargaining unit is guaranteed by requiring all newly-hired to join as a condition of employment. Eventually, through attrition, nonmembership status will disappear, *but,* as time passes, an ever greater proportion of union members are persons who had no choice in joining and who at best may be apathetic regarding their membership role in the union organization. Moreover, as this type of membership becomes predominant, it has an impact upon union leadership.

There becomes less active involvement on the part of the rank and file in terms of active participation in policy determination, not due to organizational constraint but by choice. The abysmally low involvement of members in union meetings is a widely-noted phenomenon. Greater and greater responsibility for both intra and interorganizational affairs falls upon the shoulders of the leadership. The *Let George do it* attitude or *slot machine unionism* dominates. (One should note, in passing, that similar phenomena occur within the context of nations characterized by political systems of representative democracy.) The impact upon leadership is a strengthening of a we-they differentiation initially stimulated by lack of role comparability. A consequent result is the development of a belief among union leadership that they represent the essence of the union organization and that the maintenance of their positions within the organizations is critical for the survival and welfare of the system. "The Leader as Agent of the Led" position becomes transformed into the "Leader as Agent of the Union Organization" (Rosen and Rosen, 1955). In this role the union leadership takes the responsibility to direct the constituency in ways that they consider are best for them.

The leader enlarges his role to include characteristics of counselor, teacher and even perhaps father figure. It is inevitable, to the extent that such role reformulation occurs among union leadership, that membership will be viewed to an ever increasing extent as children who must be guided in courses of action determined by leadership to be in the best interest of the membership and of the organization.

To insure that the *father knows best* determination is maintained in the face of possible objection on the part of the membership, a number of intraorganizational mechanisms may be employed. We shall not attempt at this point to be inclusive, but rather illustrative, because the dehumanizing product of the various strategies is much the same.

One common strategem is to develop an election by slate, i.e. election of all officials by the unit at large rather than by the particular membership serviced by the particular leader. At best, a full-time, paid union official only services a few thousand members. If that official's maintenance of office were dependent upon election by immediate constituents, the likelihood of position maintenance often might be in doubt. To the extent that leadership role is primarily defined (and sanctioned) by a leadership body who is forced to assume a broader and longer-range perspective to ensure the maintenance and survival of the union organization, the specific leader may upon occasion be put in the unenviable position of being at odds with his constituency. To insure the continued contribution (of such an official) of the accumulated experience and expertise to the organization as a whole, the slate system provides that the leader will be elected by a membership among whom only a few have direct knowledge and reaction to his leadership activities. As the power base broadens, there is less direct accountability to immediate constituency and the potential for growing disillusionment among that constituency that they indeed have a meaningful input.

An alternate political strategy with much the same impact is the organization wide election of a leadership elite who in turn appoint subofficialdom to service membership. Particularly, in this case, the loyalty of lower echelon union leadership (accountability) is to the organization power elite rather than to the constituency. Again, this provides the very real potential for rank and file disgruntlement.

A final illustration of a strategem quite different from those previously outlined relates to informational control. This strategem involves careful preparation of *solutions* to upcoming issues by the union leadership in advance of known crises, e.g., bargaining demands, etc., that require immediate resolvement. Not only are solutions formulated, but there is sufficient time to develop overwhelming support of the recommendations in terms of search for and integration of relevant data. The leader, when faced with the crisis, a situation demanding immediate action, presents a well-prepared and documented position. Because those who have the right to evaluate and act upon the recommendations or to participatively determine alternative solutions are caught in the press of expediency, there is little else to do but accept leadership recommendations. Upon occasion there are a few members who are sufficiently motivated and farsighted to have considered the issues prior to the crisis, but without the benefit of the organization's mechanisms for information retrieval and expert opinion, their solutions are often less well-founded, although in many cases their verbal challenges are hard for leadership to answer. The bane of any union leader is the "Contract Lawyer," the foresightedly involved but informationally and experientially-deficient protestant member. Although participation under these conditions is formally possible, realistically participation is restricted to a *rubber stamping* of predetermined solutions with little or no opportunity for meaningful input in terms of optimizing personal need fulfillment.

DYNAMICS OF THE HUMAN SIDE OF UNION ENTERPRISE

Let us now examine a number of humanizing theories and strategems in terms of their applicability and relevance to union organizations and union leadership.

Theory X and Theory Y

Although McGregor's contributions are more conceptual than action-oriented, it is worthwhile to assess union organizations within such a framework. It should be recalled that Theory X and Y as postulated by McGregor (1960) refer to assumptions regarding human nature upon which two opposing managerial styles are formulated. Theory X posits (1) man has an inherent dislike of work and will avoid it if he can; and (2) because of this dislike, people must be coerced, directed, controlled and threatened with punishment to get them to exhibit organizational desirable behavior; and (3) the average human being prefers to be directed, wishes to avoid responsibility, has little ambition and wants security above all. In contrast, Theory Y, based largely upon Maslow's Need Hierarchy Theory (1954) posits (1) man does not inherently dislike work; (2) man will exercise both self-control and self-determination in pursuit of goals to which he is committed; (3) such commitment is a function of egoistic and self-fulfillment needs that *can* be associated with organizational goal achievement; (4) given the proper conditions, man will not only accept, but seek, responsibility; (5) talent, regarding creativity, ingenuity, etc., is broadly distributed among organizational members; and (6) under current organizational conditions, man's potential is, at best, only partially utilized within the organizational setting. The principal theme of Theory Y is that man can best achieve personal need gratification by expending his efforts toward organizational goals reflective of his needs.

Superficially, to the extent that one can translate X and Y to fit union organizations, unionism in its inception and certainly in its ideology is wedded to the assumption inherent in Theory Y. Union governance formally provides for participation and contribution of its constituents; in fact, membership is the essential resource of the union organization. Self-direction and self-control via representative democracy *can be* exercised. There is the opportunity for satisfaction of higher order needs and the possibility to be creative and imaginative in organizational problem-solving. There also is the opportunity to move upward in the organizational hierarchy even though existing leadership often tenaciously attempts to prolong its tenure. However, in spite of the attempts to maintain status, it should be pointed out that line leadership in unions almost uniformly has come from the rank and file. In summary, the structure and function of unionism provides the potential—an opportunity for Theory Y both to characterize the organization and to function.

Is that potential utilized? Is modern unionism characterized by a Y philosophy and implementation in terms of Y premises? Probably not, although there may be isolated cases that are consistent with Theory Y. If not, is Theory X a more accurate model of reality? The lack of membership involvement certainly seems to parallel the *inherent dislike of work and responsibility* premise of Theory X. Certain unions at certain times, e.g., Teamsters and Longshoremen, also seem to have operated in a fashion compatible with the coercion premise of Theory X, although in general this is not a characteristic strategy of union leadership. The general apathy of union membership puts few constraints upon union leadership. Avoidance of responsibility and drive toward security do seem to be characteristic of membership as it is epitomized in the concept of slot machine unionism.

Without indulging in any speculation at this time as to the dynamics underlying this apparent paradox one could state with reasonable generalizability that the built-in potential for a Theory Y organization in unionism seems to have been transmuted, in many cases, into an actuality that appears to be more consistent with Theory X. The critical question, and one where there is a very real dearth of empirical evidence to be brought to bear, relates to the dynamics of changes that have occurred. One can engage in many speculations, but for the sake of brevity let us only consider two.

The first would posit that *power-hungry, Machiavellian union leadership* has distorted the intent for their own ends. The second would posit that the assumptions of Theory Y may not be viable within the framework of an interactive, formal organization with inherent goals of maintenance, growth and survival. Obviously, as presented, the interpretive choices are both too simplistic and too unilateral. An attempt to integrate the dynamics suggested by the two alternatives may be both more fruitful and more realistic.

The union as an organization provides the framework (potential) for Theory Y to function, but does not demand compliance regarding involvement from union constituents in terms of their organizational behavior. There are actually more formal constraints upon union leadership to operate within the framework of Theory Y than upon union membership. It is true, as Selznik (1957) has pointed out, that there are many necessary, but nondramatic, housekeeping chores that must be fulfilled for the purpose of organizational maintenance that do not directly or immediately relate to either tangible and/or salient gains. Membership tends to be nonparticipative in such critical, but routine, organizational functions. The lack of involvement could reflect a foreshortened time perspective concentrating on immediacy (Lewin, 1951). Certainly Perlman (1928) suggested such a dynamic.

The question arises as to whether or not McGregor's Theory Y assumptions may only be valid under certain restricted conditions, i.e., when the issues at hand are perceived by the constituents to be both critical and salient. Participation for the sake of participation would seem to have little positive reinforcement value as anyone who has sat through committee meetings well knows.

Turning to the possible explanation involving union leadership motivation from the union leadership's perspective, the non-utilization of Theory Y potential of the union organization by membership may lead them to see more validity in the assumptions of Theory X. Assuming for the moment that they adopt such a point of view, in the vast majority of cases, acceptance of this philosophy by union leadership would only have critical impact *if* union leadership attempted to undermine the potential for membership involvement through subtle and manipulative strategies in areas where the membership had high stakes. Again, the critical question, and one unanswerable in the context of the business organization where Theory Y would be a dramatic intervention, is whether or not the assumptions of Theory Y can be valid over time and across issues in a formal organizational structure. A corollary question, and one with considerable theoretical implications, is whether or not the *potential* rather than *actuality* regarding participation and involvement is sufficient for a humanistic organizational atmosphere. It would seem that one must have the need to exercise the potentials of Theory Y and to behave in terms of them before the full benefits to the individual would be derived. Obviously, in terms of limited research data, this remains a moot point.

Likert's System Four and Linking Pin Theory

Flowing directly from Theory Y is Likert's System Four (participative group) and linking pin theory and implementation. In brief, System Four (Likert, 1961) is based upon the sub-principles of (1) organizationally supportive relationships (with supervisors) that develop the member's belief in his contribution to the successful achievement of organizational goals; (2) high performance expectations, i.e., commitment to high performance in the pursuit of organizational goals; and (3) group decision-making within intact organizational subunits that are coordinated in the achievement of organizational goals via a linking pin structure, i.e., an organizational condition where the spokesman, official or leader of a subunit is a member of a higher level organizational decision-making body—literally a mechanism by which the official represents his constituency but is responsible for the possible broader ramifications of the subunit decision that he presents for discussion and evaluation at the higher organizational level. The union structure inherently incorporates the linking pin concept in both grievance (shop) and local organizational structure. Each official position-holder who receives recommendations (or demands) from his immediate constituency brings that information to the next higher level for evaluation (and action if necessary). Technically, the issue could be brought to the top governing body for review. Actually, however, the input rarely reaches the topmost officialdom with issues terminating in their upward movement largely in terms of their scope of relevancy to the organization.

As linking pin structure suggests, as each additional level becomes involved, a broader scope of decision variables are introduced, with the tendency for the initial demands of the involved constituency to be modified. When the demand has been evaluated—accepted, rejected or modified at the highest appropriate level—that information flows downward, accompanied by reasons for the decision, back to the affected, initiating constituency. When the system works (limited by communications transmission error inherent in all communication) there is no guarantee that the end product will be an acceptable resolution for the initiating party or parties, and certainly low probability that it will be perceived as an optimal resolution. This becomes a classic case where that which is optimal for the individual (or small body of individuals) may not be optimal for the organization, the net result being that the organization and its leadership may be perceived as ineffectual or even detrimental by the affected member(s).

Although linking pin strategy in conjunction with System Four may optimally provide for both participative decision-making and feedback, *if* the constituency, for whatever reason and no matter how adequate the feedback, has needs rejected in terms of fulfilling them not being in the best interest of the organization, that constituency is not apt to perceive the resolution as coming from a humanistic organization. There seems to be an inherent fallacy in assuming that any system, however elegant conceptually and philosophically, that does not provide for optimization as the involved parties define it will be perceived as humanizing or humanistic. In short, it suggests that the very nature of organizations negates the possibility that such a system will be viewed as being humanistic by constituency over time and across conditions.

There is no question that frustration of members' needs by an organization that is considered to be arbitrary and non-responsive by the member is potentially more dehumanizing than an organizationally-imposed frustration that has resulted from systematic evaluation of the member's demand by appropriate (elected) representatives, accompanied by feedback justifying such a resolution. Yet, no system will insure the acceptance of frustration per se. Abstractly, one may accept the premise that the greatest good is for the many rather than the few, but when that results in frustration the agency of that decision may be perceived as being restrictive, depersonal and nonrepresentative. Only when the need for participation is more dominant than the specific needs involved in the demand could or would the *ideal* response occur. In fact, if the various human relationists had more carefully considered Maslow, they would have realized that the lower order needs, so characteristic of both bargaining and grievance issues, take precedence over the higher, i.e., participation in their formulation and in attempts at their achievement, when they are both unmet.

In the case of unionism, at least in the United States, the union organization is largely a vehicle for economic and security need fulfillment. That has been and remains its salient function.* No matter how well a union provides for higher order need gratification incorporated in participative decision-making via its decision and governance mechanisms, if it does not maximize, in the assessment of the membership, its primary function, i.e., economic and security fulfillment, and if the member has little or no choice for terminating the relationship, the union organiza-

---

* Walter Reuther, among others, discovered that union members rather narrowly define the scope of the union's functions. Political action, for example, in spite of Samuel Gompers' "reward your friends and punish your enemies" has only had *desired* and predictable influence during times of economic depression. With affluence the trade union member often opts for other than union political guidance.

tion is apt to be perceived by many as a source of frustration, not as a responsive, humanistic agency.

THE ROLE OF LEADERSHIP STYLE IN ORGANIZATIONAL BEHAVIOR

Thus far we have concentrated our analyses on the opportunity for participative decision-making—a key concept in the human relations movement. Let us now turn to strategems relating to organizational leadership, particularly with regard to those that are professed to improve leader-follower relationships. Again, we do not intend to be all inclusive, but rather concentrate upon representative theories and approaches.

Whether elected or appointed, the styles and behavior of those in organizational leadership positions have a significant impact upon the reactions of members to the organization. Aside from several highly charismatic union officials, e.g., Walter Reuther, John Lewis, Sidney Hillman and perhaps James Hoffa, who symbolized their unions and their unions' successes in improving the lot of the working man to the membership, very little is known about the *day in, day out* leaders who play such a vital but less dramatic role in union functioning (Sayles and Strauss, 1955; Hudson, 1951, etc.). Whether or not such officials create, destroy or have little impact upon a humanistic environment within a union organization is at this stage of knowledge yet another moot point.

Superficially, one might posit a close positive relationship between (1) a consideration style of leadership, i.e., person-centered, and (2) organizational membership morale, i.e., identification with and involvement in the organization. Certainly, there is evidence to support a prediction of a positive relationship between such a leadership style and subordinate positive affect (Fleishman, 1962). However, it should be pointed out that such supportive data have been found in employee organizations with the focal leadership being appointed rather than elected. A question arises as to whether or not such a leadership style would have equivalent impact within a union structure having largely elected leadership. Small group research, for example, suggests that elected leaders can and do act in a more task-oriented style (initiating structure) and utilize less consideration than do appointed leaders. Moreover, they seem to be able to do so without severe repercussions in terms of affective indicators.

Perhaps under elected leadership conditions, the member qua follower feels more secure of the leader's commitment to the memberships' best interests, and, consequently, is less demanding of overt style regarding consideration and more accepting of control exercised by the leader to achieve their common objectives. In a union organization, then, with line officials for the most part being elected, person-centered style of leadership may be a less effective humanizing strategy than in the work organization where leadership is largely appointed.

Again, we must come back to the function of the organization as perceived by its members. In the case of the business organization the employee must bargain off his acceptance of control and direction of his activities by the organization and its agents for various compensations that the organization provides in return. The business organization has a critical constituency that includes not only employees, but the investor-stockholder as well. Both labor and capital resources are necessary to the organization; and the leader-manager must attempt to strike a balance that will satisfy both. The business leader can no more unilaterally support the employees in their quest for maximization than he can support the investor.* To the extent that the business leader is responsive to the needs of his labor force subordinates, i.e., considerate, employee-centered, etc., positive affective outcomes seem to be forthcoming.

But, take the case of the union organization and its leadership. By and large, leadership is *elected to serve the interests of the membership.* The union organization itself developed to fulfill a service function for its constituency. The union leader

---

* Strauss (1963) has written a perceptive analysis of the inherent conflict between organizational need and the need of the individual. Although historically "Organizational need *Uber Alles*" has dominated, there has at least been a voiced concern with employee needs and interventions to accomplish such ends.

has had as his primary function *delivering the service,* whether that be in the form of contract negotiations and/or grievance settlement. What is being suggested is that the demands made upon a union and its leadership by union members are *ends* rather than *means*-oriented. Given such conditions, *getting the last apple out of the barrel* becomes the dominant credo. A considerate, person-oriented union leader may be reacted to favorably, but only if that leader, through his activities in behalf of the membership, maximizes *pay off* for them. To the extent he accomplishes this end he will gain support. If he fails to *deliver,* no matter how personal-oriented he may be, he will be rejected as an ineffective, albeit perhaps well-meaning, instrument.

At this point, we are suggesting that membership reaction to a union organization and its leadership is far more dependent upon the extent to which desired ends are achieved than upon the particular leadership style employed in their achievement. This is in sharp contrast to employee assessment of a company organization and its leadership. The goals of a company, at best, are only tangentially related to serving its employees' best interests. Whether or not such goals are achieved has little direct import to the employee.* As a consequence, there is apt to be greater concern with and reaction to leadership style. For example, task-oriented leadership in pursuit of maximizing organizational goals nonsalient to the employees can generate resistance and antagonism. On the other hand, supervisory warmth and concern with the employees as human beings is likely to generate positive affective responses both to the leadership and the organizations they represent.

It is not the intent to suggest that leadership style is irrelevant in the union context. Rather, it is suggested that the impact upon the assessment of the union and its leadership by union membership is less dependent upon leadership style than it would be in a company organization.

---

* Obviously, whether or not a company organization remains viable affects the welfare of the employee in terms of both job stability and capacity to bargain successfully for added benefits; yet, except in times of crisis, employees do not tend to perceive the relationship.

Far more important than style per se for the union leader is the capacity to (1) assess the critical needs of the majority of the membership and (2) determine what can be done organizationally to retain their support or, perhaps more accurately, to not alienate them to a point of generating active rebellion. In short, the union leader has to be able to size up his membership.

It is questionable whether or not any given leadership training strategem or combination of them (often prescribed for organizational management development) can facilitate this process within the context of unions. On the face of it, sensitivity training, with its goals of self-insight concerning the impact of one's behavior upon others, empathy (i.e. ability to deduce the reactions of others) and awareness of those interactional processes that facilitate group functioning, might appear to be an appropriate intervention, but, in terms of questionable validity of such approaches (Campbell and Dunnette, 1968), it would be hazardous to recommend sensitivity training as a valuable intervention, let alone a panacea.

Group decision-making (among leadership) would provide another possible alternative. One descriptive study in the context of a union organization (Rosen and Rosen, 1955) suggests that there may be significant benefits to be derived from pooling the experience and expertise of a number of union leaders in developing optimal strategies. A broadening of the number of alternatives considered as well as the possible consequences associated with their utilization (often in terms of membership reaction) occurred. However, in the field context there is not sufficient evidence nor controlled studies to justify opting for such a strategy.

In short, particularly within the union organizational framework, a critical need exists for leadership to be able to predict majority membership needs and reactions to union practices and policies in pursuit of union maintenance and growth via servicing the membership. Unfortunately, there do not appear to be any well-validated approaches that one can recommend that will guarantee to achieve such ends.

SUMMARY

Four interrelated themes become apparent when one attempts to analyze the potential utility of attempting to introduce humanizing approaches into the union organization. The first relates to the fact that unions, in theory at least, are structured upon the principle of representative democracy; and, in so being, at least provide the bases for participative decision-making, Y organizational philosophy and the linking pin concept so critical to System Four theory.

Essentially, union organizations have the key conditional variables required by the human relations movement and provide the groundwork for most, if not all, humanizing attempts within organizations. Corollary to this theme is the evidence that such opportunities are utilized by the union members to a minimal degree, a situation that may lead union leadership to function, in many cases in a manner that would appear to run counter to the basic principles of organizational humanization.

In part, this apparent paradox of under or unutilized humanistic potential may be accounted for by the inherent limitations imposed by representative democracy in providing for maximization of member need gratification for those members who take positions dissonant from those of the majority. This creates a situation which in turn threatens organizational cohesion and stability, and, in turn, leads to leadership recommended strategies that make union membership a condition of employment in the guise of union and agency shop and maintenance of membership clauses. The net effect of such attempts to guarantee organizational maintenance limits the members' opportunity to withdraw from the organization they perceive not operating within the framework of their best interests.

A second major theme relates to whether or not the opportunity to participate can and does compensate for potential frustration of more basic and salient members' needs regarding the purposes of the union organizations. A disgruntled minority are apt to be disenchanted with the organization and its leadership even though the structure has given them an opportunity to voice their case. In other words, participation and other humanistic strategies may not be sufficient within the framework of a union organization to provide gratification, particularly when there is little or no opportunity to leave or break ties with the frustrating organization.

The third theme suggests that in the context of the union organization with its inherent service orientation, leadership ability to assess the active membership majority, both in terms of their demands and what solutions they will settle for, is far more critical than leadership style per se in determining how members will evaluate the union and its leadership. Unfortunately, at the current state of knowledge there is little basis for recommending specific management development techniques to better meet this leadership need.

A final and implicit theme that was developed suggests that efforts to humanize organizations, if fully implemented, may not achieve the intended purposes. Analysis of union organizations in terms of humanizing strategies and mechanisms suggests that, even if one were able to implement organizational democracy, there would be little guarantee that such potential would be actively utilized by the organizational member. Moreover, to the extent it were, there always would be a significant minority who would not see the practices and policies determined by the majority of participating members as best serving their interests.

Organizational membership imposes constraints and limitations upon individual need fulfillment. Within the context of some organizations, i.e., those that historically have ignored membership needs, efforts at humanization can lead to improvement.

REFERENCES

Argyris, C.: *Personality and Organization.* New York, Harper and Brothers, 1957.

Campbell, J. P., and Dunnette, M.D.: Effectiveness of T-group experiences in managerial training and development. *Psychol Bull, 70:*53-104, 1968.

Fleishman, E. A., and Harris, E. F.: Patterns of leadership behavior related to grievances and turnover. *Personnel Psychology, 15:*43-56, 1962.

Herzberg, F.: *Work and the Nature of Man.* Cleveland, World Pr, 1966.

Herzberg, F.; Mausner, B., and Snyderman, B. B.: *The Motivation to Work.* New York, Wiley, 1959.

Hudson, R. A.: The social role of the shop steward. Unpublished Ph.D. dissertation. New Haven, Yale U Pr, 1951.

Lewin, K., and Cartwright, D. (Ed.): *Field Theory in Social Science.* New York, Harpers, 1951.

Likert, R.: *New Patterns of Management.* New York, McGraw, 1961.

Likert, R.: *The Human Organization.* New York, McGraw, 1967.

Lipset, S. M.; Coleman, J. S., and Trow, M.: *Union Democracy: Inside Politics of the International Typographical Union.* Glencoe, Free Press, 1956.

Maslow, A. H.: *Motivation and Personality.* New York, Har-Row, 1954.

McGregor, D.: *The Human Side of Enterprise.* New York, McGraw, 1960.

Perlman, S.: *A Theory of the Labor Movement.* New York, MacMillan, 1928.

Rosen, H., and Rosen, R. A. H.: Decision making in a business agent group. In Tripp, R. (Ed.): *IRRA Annual Proceedings, 1:*287-297, December, 1955.

Rosen, H., and Rosen, R. A. H.: The union business agent's perspective of his job. *J Administration and Industrial Relations, 3:*49-58, 1957.

Rosen, H., and Rosen, R. A. H.: Personality variables and role in a union business agent group. *J Appl Psychol, 41:*131-136, 1957.

Sayles, L., and Strauss, G.: *The Local Union.* New York, Harper and Brothers, Part III, 1953.

Selznik, P.: *Leadership in Administration.* Evanston, Row, Peterson, 1957.

Strauss, G.: Some notes on power equalization. In Leavitt, H. J. (Ed.): *The Social Science of Organization.* Englewood Cliffs, P-H, 1963, pp. 41-84.

Chapter 5

HUMANIZING INFLUENCES OF BLACKS AND WOMEN IN THE ORGANIZATION

GERALD CAVANAGH

THE CLASSIC STEREOTYPES of both blacks and women are in many ways similar. Blacks and women are said to be less capable of abstract thinking, innately submissive, emotionally unstable and physically suited to more menial tasks. These stereotypes are only now beginning to dissolve. Because of community pressure and government legislation, blacks and women are now moving into managerial positions in organizations. In the process these organizations and their members are losing their biases and acknowledging the important contributions that these minorities make to the organization.

This paper will seek to demonstrate that not only are blacks and women not accurately described by the negative performance stereotypes above, but, on the contrary, they perform well and contribute much to humanizing the organization. Their presence has a beneficial effect on interpersonal relations, communications and organizational atmosphere and structure. The major proposition of this paper is that blacks and women have made important contributions to the organization beyond those of their white male counterparts.

BLACKS IN THE ORGANIZATION

Many contributions of blacks toward humanizing the organization are obvious to even the casual observer. Separate washrooms, water fountains and locker rooms which were required by law in most southern states were demeaning and dehumanizing to both blacks and whites (Purcell and Cavanagh, 1972). Black protests initiated a process in which the separate facilities were eventually removed, thus freeing whites from the results of their own dehumanizing actions and also of many of their parallel biases and prejudiced myths.

Selection and promotion criteria rather systematically excluded blacks from good jobs and especially from supervision. Personnel tests and other devices for screening job candidates were often invalid. Firms received orders from the Equal Employment Opportunity Commission that they demonstrate that these tests were valid predictors or drop them; and the record will show that most of these tests are no longer used. Organizations could not show that these devices were good predictors of who would be the better performers on the job.

The elimination of these invalid tests was a benefit to both the organization and its employees. From the standpoint of the firm, they were able to hire and promote qualified and capable people who would have been excluded by the previous criteria. Moreover, individuals themselves were thus able to obtain work more commensurate with their aspirations and abilities.

Biases Dissolve

The most obvious humanizing influence of blacks in the organization was simply a result of blacks working side by side with whites. Most of the whites also came from segregated neighborhoods. Their entire life had been spent in a white ghetto and their attitudes toward nonwhites had largely been based on stereotypes.

The industrial plant often provided an environment for racial mixing that could not be achieved in other institutions—schools, clubs, churches and neighborhoods. Bias and racial prejudice were broken down by the person to person contact of whites and blacks in the plant. The blacks who were pioneers in a previously all-white plant were often harassed and hasseled, but most kept their cool. Many of the breakthroughs occurred in the 1950's and early 1960's, but in some cases are occurring even today.* These pioneers were strong and talented men and women; generally they were markedly superior in intelligence, poise and ability to their white peers. In their willingness to put up with the early abuse and prejudice they were able to change the attitudes of most of their white co-workers. As one white woman in a General Electric plant put it, "I was happy to find out how wrong I was about Negroes."† The harassment was more obvious and lasted longer in plants in the South, but it also occurred in the North, although a bit more subtly. Thus, these brave, overqualified and sensitive black pioneers helped to make the white world more humane.

New Values at Work

There are additional, still more subtle and yet more pervasive and long-lasting humanizing benefits that blacks bring to the organization. The advent of large numbers of young unskilled blacks into the firm in the late 1960's brought new values to the work place (Cavanagh and Stewart, 1974). Many of these blacks were coming to their first industrial job and were fearful; they expressed their fears and anxieties less in words than in body language and actions. The industrial plants appeared to them to be a huge, noisy, unknown labyrinth. If their supervisor and fellow workers did not seem to them to be at least somewhat friendly and helpful, their distrust and fear would be heightened. That fear would express itself especially in tardiness, absenteeism and turnover. Because, among other reasons, the workplace was so threatening, they expressed their dissatisfaction by not coming on time, by missing work (especially on Mondays and Fridays) and by quitting.

Management facing this new work force often initially countered the new tardiness, absenteeism and turnover problems with increased discipline along with such activities as attendance

---

* See Purcell and Cavanagh, 1972, pp. 58-60, 97-99, 125-128, 176, 181-185, 195-199.

† Previously unpublished interview segment from Ford-funded research project from which resulted Purcell and Cavanagh, 1972.

contests and plant open houses, but it generally did not take them long to realize that any substantial moves that were made to correct the difficulties had to direct themselves to humanizing the work environment. Researchers and managers themselves found that any attempt to retain these young and sometimes disadvantaged workers must include a thorough orientation to the job and a good supervisor for the new worker.*

More specifically, it was found that any concerted effort to lessen tardiness, absenteeism and turnover must include the following elements:

1. A thorough orientation to the life and work of the plant. The new worker must not only be shown such basics as where the washroom and cafeteria are, but also he must understand the importance of his job—where it fits in and what he contributes to the final product.
2. The new worker must be assigned to a sensitive, knowledgeable and flexible foreman who demonstrates (a) a personal interest in the worker, (b) effective two-way communication with the worker, and (c) honest and fair discipline.

These insights into the importance of job orientation and a sensitive foreman are not new. They have been suggested in varying forms for some time (McGregor, 1960; Likert, 1967; Maslow, 1964). The new element is that these organizational qualities are now not merely suggestions of researchers and academics; they have become recognized as essential by firms that employ significant numbers of the new work force. In effect, blacks provided management with an early warning system of new interpersonal demands and expectations.

Supervisors from foremen to plant managers acknowledged how their hard-nosed, exclusively production-oriented stance was no longer as effective. The new work force demanded that they be more sensitive to the individual person and to the general

---

* Purcell and Cavanagh, 1972, esp. pp. 65, 69-71, 81-86, and pp. 242-272 passim. The conclusions on the importance of supervisors' support were updated by Beatty, 1974.

organizational climate that they created. Many supervisors found the challenge threatening, but most were able to shift their managerial style to meet the needs and demands of these new minority workers. Supervisors were challenged in the concrete to a new management style that organizational development seminars could only theoretically point to as desirable.

The above disruptions, abrasions and challenges led to two major benefits for the organization, each a humanizing influence— (1) a better treatment of and more intelligent use of the human beings who made up the organization and (2) a more open and flexible organizational structure.

Militant blacks who were able to obtain more considerate treatment for themselves ironically initiated a climate that embraced black and white alike. The new work force, and especially black, disadvantaged youth demanded this more considerate personal treatment, and in so doing, they encouraged supervisors to develop a management style that is today generally more effective. A supervisor in a Virginia General Electric plant was typical when he expressed the demands made on him and his own changes in attitude after a young disadvantaged worker was hired into his section.* This Southern-born foreman was asked what he thought of programs to bring disadvantaged into the plant, "If you'd ask me a year ago, I'd told you probably somepin' different . . . If a bum don' want to work, leave him outside. Yah know?"

The foreman then described the twenty-five-year-old black man now in his unit as a fellow who "was on the streets for three years, gamblin', yah know, hustlin' for a livin'." This foreman found out that he could talk to this young black, he could communicate, ". . . but you have to do it in his language. You can't do it in your language. OK?" The supervisor was drawn out of his own frame of reference into that of this worker who had very different values.

This foreman described how the young black reacted to authority and how he handled it when he missed a day of work,

---

* Interviewed as part of the foreman sample in the study cited above. The supervisor is quoted in Purcell and Cavanagh, but this portion of the interview is previously unpublished.

> . . . I know you couldn't drive that guy for anythin' in the world.
> Mo' you drove him—I know this—mo' he'd go in the other direction.
> So I went back couple days later and talked to him again, spent
> about 15 minutes with him talkin' to him, and he's a good worker.
> . . . I said "Don' you know you let me down? I had you in heah
> to do a job, and you let me down. Why didn't you call me up at
> home and tell me you weren't able to come to work?

After their heart-to-heart talk at the plant, the young black
man expressed his appreciation, in the foreman's words, "He just
stuck out his han' and said, 'I never had nobody do that fo'
me before.'" I said, "You work for me; I'll work for you!"

This same foreman then went on to describe how his own
attitudes have changed.

> I enjoy workin' with 'em. That's why I've changed mah min'.
> I enjoy workin' with that guy . . . I jest get a kick out of it, and I
> can't say that there's anything I enjoy mo' than workin' with him
> and seein' 'im work. It's jest kinda gratifyin' in a way I guess.

This foreman's attitude change was quite common. If a foreman was to successfully manage young black workers, he soon
found that he had to become more flexible and sensitive to them
as persons. Management came to know this quickly, and so
assigned young blacks to supervisors who were sensitive and more
concerned with relating to the individual person.

Moreover, in the last few years most large national firms have
initiated the policy that one of the criteria for the standard
rewards of pay increases and promotion for supervisors is that
supervisor's ability to relate to minority workers and to identify
their special talents (Purcell and Toner, 1974). This major policy
change has put all industrial supervisors on notice that their job
description has now widened; in addition to their standard production duties they will be required to be more sensitive to their
individual employees. Sensitivity to the individual, which previously had not been seen as such a valued quality for a supervisor, is now judged as far more important.

The young black worker came into the plant with different
values. He presented these values strongly and sometimes even
harshly. That young worker demanded that he/she be treated
as a person. Because of equal employment opportunity law, plus

pressure from the larger society, supervisors are now expected to be more sensitive to the needs and person of the workers thanks largely to black workers.

Improved Communications

The value system of young black workers and of plant management are thus seen to be quite different. The initial reaction of both groups is most often defensive, and conflict results. That conflict is manifested in the turnover, absenteeism and tardiness discussed above, and also is shown in a lack of communication and resulting disagreements on the plant floor. The organization will evidence a low tolerance for this conflict if the organization is inflexible and highly bureaucratized (Lawrence and Lorsch, 1967). When roles and relations are stable in a large organization, communications can become stylized, minimal and thus less accurate.

Demands for the organization to perform under changed circumstances tend to open that organization up. Supervisors realized that they had neither the information nor the expertise to work with the large number of young blacks who were coming into the organization. They thus became more open to new values, new methods of managing and upward communication from their own people.

Increased and more accurate information flow was encouraged by various worker and foreman training programs. These ranged all the way from in-plant programs specifically focused on working with young black workers (sensitivity training, role-playing, the Bell and Howell foreman training programs) to university-sponsored management training programs.

Foreman training programs generally have a significant component that is geared to aid the supervisor in becoming more sensitive to different values, interests and life-styles of the young and the black worker. This trained supervisor is better able to supervise the younger black worker.

The industrial organization has also found that it is more successful in dealing with black workers if it does so straightforwardly without trying to sell them. In presenting an orientation to the workplace, turnover was found to be far less when all of the difficulties of the work were honestly discussed (Wanous, 1972). So, because of the increasing number of blacks in the firm and the varying values that they brought with them, communications have generally been improved both among workers and especially between worker and supervisor.

Blacks as Supervisors

The appointment of black supervisors does not automatically create good relations with black employees. It depends more on whether that new supervisor is capable, open and earns the respect of the work group. On the other hand, in rating workers, black foremen tend to judge their black employees more favorably than do white foremen and to make more perceptive distinctions, although they also could be very critical (Purcell and Cavanagh, 1972). Black supervisors tend to rate white subordinates less favorably, and some of this seems to depend on personality rather than job skills (Flaugher *et al.*, 1969).

Ironically, when a black supervisor was appointed, whites and Spanish-speaking accepted that person as their supervisor more readily than did many of the blacks. Former fellow black employees gave the new black foreman a disproportionate number of problems (Purcell and Cavanagh, 1972).

In sum, black supervisors, as long as they are selected on merit, perform their responsibilities more than adequately. Although they have better perceptions of their black employees, they find that those same black employees are, in the beginning, often more difficult to deal with.

WOMEN IN THE ORGANIZATION

Women in organizations have been victims of role stereotoypes in much the same fashion as blacks. These stereotypes and biases have in the past severely limited the contributions of both groups to the organization. Women and blacks have been restricted to generally menial work of lesser responsibility. This section of the paper will attempt to show that this restriction has deprived the organization of talents and contributions that would have been immensely beneficial and also that, where allowed to operate according to their ability, women have much to contribute to humanizing the organization. We will examine the contributions that the woman makes to the organization (1) as a worker and (2) as a supervisor.

Women as Workers

Until rather recently women have been restricted to clerical, nursing, teaching and semiskilled operative-type of jobs. This artificial discrimination has placed an upper limit on the jobs that women could aspire to. As a result, industrial plants have typically had women workers of greater ability and education than their men co-workers.

In two southern electrical plants where women constituted the majority of the work force these women had an average of one year more schooling than did the men in the plant. This was true in spite of the fact that the men had better jobs with far more responsibility and were receiving better pay.*

From the standpoint of the organization, it was getting more talent and ability than it was paying for. Women brought their unique talents and abilities to the work place at a fraction of what they would otherwise cost. This is the classic picture of the results of job discrimination. Although it is now illegal in this single way, discrimination was and is of benefit to the organization.

Women as Supervisors

Until rather recently discrimination against women deprived the organization of the unique contributions of women as supervisors. Although empirical evidence does indicate some varying characteristics, values and interests, these have often been both

---

* Purcell and Cavanagh, 1972, pp. 105, 185. These figures indicate that blacks had more education than did whites. Within both groups, women had more years of schooling. For example, at Memphis Fairbanks, women were on much lower level jobs, yet they averaged 12.1 years of schooling, while men averaged 11.2 years. Fully one-third of the women operatives had some college education.

overemphasized and interpreted to the disadvantage of women. Full participation of women in the organization demands putting behind the sexual biases that restrict the ability of women to contribute to the organization (Rosen and Jerdee, 1974, 1973; Pheterson, Kiesler and Goldberg, 1971), while at the same time recognizing the unique and valuable qualities of the woman supervisor.

Better Interpersonal Relations

Society expects women to be more concerned with interpersonal relations, and studies have shown that they generally respond in that fashion. Women tend to be more compassionate, sympathetic and affectively integrated (Tyler, 1965). In organizations, men perceive more conflict in their group than women do, and men feel a more normative pressure on values. Women value more highly a friendly environment (Bartol, 1974) and tend to talk over personal problems with their fellow workers. The woman's relationship to the organization emphasizes interpersonal relations more so than does a man's (Wilson, 1973).

Several factors impede effective concern for interpersonal relations on the part of men. As the male sex hormone, testosterone, is increased in animals, they tend to display increased aggression (Scarf, 1972). Findings for men do show that they demonstrate more competitiveness and aggression than do women, but the extent to which this is due to their male physical characteristics is disputed.

Secondly, society, as noted above, expects men to be more concerned with achievement, power and the external task. This sort of concern has often made men less patient with concern for interpersonal relations.

Finally, for a variety of reasons, men are not as sensitive to the needs and motives of others, especially those of women. Specifically, women are able to be sensitive to, and to predict what motivates men while men do not accurately ascertain preferences and motives of women (Burke, 1966). The failure of men is largely because of their stereotype of feminine inferiority. This lack of perception and greater influence of stereotypes on the part of men supervisors inhibits their ability as supervisors. On the other hand, a woman's more accurate perception of others enables her to better understand each person who is her subordinate, and thus build on individual work motives.

Women are as effective as producers, and as supervisors; they possess substantially the same job orientation as do men (Saleh and Lalljee, 1969). In addition, women are more likely than men to value good co-workers (Centers and Bugental, 1966; Mannhardt, 1972). When given the opportunity to manage, women do an effective job. Moreover, their concern about interpersonal relations can lead to an interpersonal, consensus-oriented management style.

Given the opportunity, women not only prove to be effective managers, but also are able to integrate their unique concerns for the individual into their leadership style. Fakenham Enterprises is a common ownership English firm in which women hold all of the positions of responsibility beginning with the managing director (Kasindorf, 1973). With no business experience these women have developed their own management style. Although English newspaper and magazine articles have portrayed this small group of women as engaged in a love-in, financial advisors and outside consultants have commented on how mature and realistic is their operation. "Almost all decisions are reached by consensus; only infrequently must a vote be taken."

The white male in leadership roles tends to be concerned with tasks, career and promotion, while the woman tends to place greater value on interpersonal relationships. Graphically summarizing what seems to be a narrower male perspective on work was a young Negro woman contract specialist at the General Electric plant in Lynchburg, Virginia, ". . . I think a white man is so concerned with saving money and putting it in the bank, he doesn't take time to enjoy it. And he's just turning to an old old man with nothing."* This woman is not naive; she has a graduate degree in business and has management responsibility,

---

* Previously unpublished interview segment from research project, from which resulted Purcell and Cavanagh, 1972.

yet she still feels that white males are not very sensitive to human needs, either their own or those of others.

Whether latently or overtly, many are concerned that these greater interpersonal concerns of women will work to the disadvantage rather than to the advantage of the firm. The case is made that women may become too emotional, involved with people and disturbed when they are under pressure or criticized. A woman management consultant replies,

> . . . a woman could not have achieved her professional stature and education if she were unduly temperamental. Women are not too emotional to be entrusted with the life and death situations in a hospital or in the home, but somehow there is a fear that a profit and loss crisis will shatter them (Buchanan, 1969).

The contributions of a woman's greater affective integration and her sensitivity to the situation can be an aid in a wide variety of organizational settings. Those in the occupation have pointed out how a policewoman in a tense situation is better able to detect others' feelings and so frequently diffuses potential violence. Women lawyers are often better able to keep their cool than are men. A woman hearing examiner for a federal regulatory agency explains her success. She describes herself as, "more sensitive to other people's feelings. I never try to embarrass attorneys" (Bird, 1973).

Although both the experimental literature and field study accounts of women as managers do indicate differences in management style between men and women, it is probably also true that many contributions of women will not be manifested for some time to come. Women who have moved up the management hierarchy have had to emulate the predominant masculine-oriented management style in order to do so (as with Uncle Toms among blacks). Nevertheless, the evidence that we do have indicates that women will tend to adopt a more interpersonal management style and will undoubtedly exhibit less aggressive and competitive behavior with their male co-workers. Competitive and aggressive behavior between individuals and departments in the same organization can be seriously dysfunctional, thus this contribution of women in leadership roles will probably aid the organization to overcome an element that brings not only a blockage of communication, cooperation and hence efficiency in performing the task, but also creates a strained and distrustful working environment.

Communications

Encouraging better communications within the organization is often a priority concern of management. Firms such as General Electric have developed elaborate and expensive staffs that are entrusted with the communications function. Admittedly, communication within the organization often is limited to the plant newspaper and top down communications; nevertheless any experienced manager knows the importance of two-way communications.

It is precisely in the realm of two-way communications that a woman can be most successful. If she has the latitude to work in a favorable environment, her sensitivity to co-workers will enable her to be aware of ignorance and misinformation. As supervisor she can then see the need to provide the necessary information so as to aid cooperation and even consensus. These communication talents aid the woman in supervising,

> . . . much of the real decision-making in organizations takes place behind the scenes, where you negotiate, or persuade, or influence, and women have lots of early training and cultural indoctrination in being sensitive to the hidden cues that represent the real resistance of the persons whom they are persuading (Bird, 1973).

There is evidence that men will not express their feelings as readily to another man as they will to a woman. A friendly-dependent management style is considered more appropriate for supervisors of either sex when used with subordinates of the opposite sex (Rosen and Jerdee, 1973). While this may be somewhat due to sex stereotypes, it remains a reality. Moreover, these expectations can be used to the considerable advantage of both the organization and the individual woman supervisors. An example of its benefits,

. . . Anna R. Hoffman has built an impressive career on this fact. She has served as the eyes and ears of two Presidents of the United States, improved the morale of the armed forces by relaying the gripes of soldiers to the high command as the only woman Assistant Secretary of Defense, settled bitter labor disputes, and furthered the careers of a half-dozen political and business leaders, including the Rockefeller brothers (Bird, 1968).

A woman's greater concern for interpersonal relations and her sensitivity to the attitudes, feelings and motives of others enables her to be more aware of especially nonverbal communications. She is thus in a position to pursue her newly gained insight, to clarify it verbally with the people involved, and finally to replay that information to where it is needed.

THE CREATIVE ORGANIZATION

Innovation and creativity are vital elements for any organization that expects to operate effectively in a changing society. Paradoxically, success in the past often brings rigidity; what has worked in the past will surely work in the future. Success often breeds a fear of change, and this may well be the malaise that many United States firms have fallen into in the post-World War II era. Much of the current loss of confidence in the industrial firm and other American institutions undoubtedly stems from their complacency, rigidity and their preoccupation with their own survival and growth over serving the needs of the people who are customers and citizens.

The purpose of this last section of the paper is to demonstrate that the introduction and promotion of blacks and women in an organization help to bring about and to sustain an organizational climate that encourages innovation and creativity.* New attitudes and values that are introduced by blacks and women demand that management consider these new values and goals. The organization thus becomes more of an open system, and hence more flexible and creative (Maurer, 1971).

---

* Gary Steiner, 1965, says that among the elements of an organization that encourage creativity are heterogeneous personnel, even marginal and unusual types (pp. 16-18).

Organizational incumbents can be blind to new information, strategies and opportunities. Generally individuals tend to interpret events around them consonant with their own previous experiences and attitudes, filtering out what is in disagreement with them and their needs and accepting only what is in agreement with them (Festinger, 1957). When individuals and an organization are subjected to conflict from within and/or criticism from without, they are alerted to new information and new attitudes (Coser, 1956). They are thus put in a position where they can adapt and innovate.

As has been pointed out above, blacks and women come into the organization with backgrounds and attitudes that vary from the dominant white males who currently determine organizational climate and policies. Blacks ask for greater personal sensitivity on the part of their supervisors and co-workers, and they also ask that they themselves have some understanding of the long-term value of the work they are doing. Women tend to be more affectively integrated; hence, they too tend to place a greater value on interpersonal relationships on the job. Sensitivity to interpersonal relations and a need to understand the value of the job are two of the most important problems facing organizations today, and the fact that they were raised early and unmistakably by blacks and women is to the long-run advantage of the organization. Blacks are more sensitive to injustice whereas the older white male has lived with lower expectations for years.

It is of considerable advantage to the organization to have present people of varying values. Small group research has demonstrated that, while a deviant may not always be popular and may indeed cause considerable conflict, nevertheless her/his presence considerably increases the chances that the group concerned produces better and more creative solutions to problems (Boulding, 1964). In sum, in spite of feelings often to the contrary, it is not to the best interests of the organizations to hire and promote the same sort of people. Blacks and women bring varying backgrounds and attitudes and, thus, a broader perspective to the organization. The organization is therefore urged to face this new information and new attitudes, and thus is given the opportunity to become more flexible and creative.

SUMMARY AND CONCLUSIONS

This paper has attempted to demonstrate that blacks and women contribute much to humanizing the organization. Both blacks and women have higher expectations for interpersonal relations with their supervisors and co-workers. Blacks, women and youth, because of their higher expectations, have been largely responsible for bringing into being a wide variety of sensitizing programs for organizational behavior.

Women are more affectively integrated and, hence, they also more highly value good personal relationships on the job. Women are not as competitive as men. They seek a more open and collaborative organizational climate, and their presence often tends to encourage such a climate.

The varying values of both blacks and women introduce new information and new attitudes into the firm. Any organization operating in a changing environment needs some new challenges in order to keep itself flexible and creative. Blacks and women, when they are heard and given responsibility, provide some of the more important new information and attitudes for the organization.

BIBLIOGRAPHY

Bartol, K. M.: Sex differences in job orientation: A reexamination. *Proceedings of Annual Meeting of Academy of Management, 43,* 1974.

Beatty, R. W.: Supervisory behavior related to job success of hard-core unemployed over a two-year period. *J Appl Psychol,* 59:38-42, 1974.

Bird, C.: *Born Female: The High Cost of Keeping Women Down.* New York, McKay, 1968.

Bird, C.: *Everything a Woman Needs to Know to Get What She's Worth.* New York, McKay, 1973.

Boulding, E.: *Conflict Management in Organizations.* Ann Arbor, Foundation for Research on Human Behavior, 1964.

Buchanan, E.: Women in management. *Personnel Administration,* 32(5): 21-26, 1969.

Burke, R. J.: Differences in perception of desired job characteristics of the opposite sex. *J Genet Psychol, 109*:27-46, 1966.

Cavanagh, G. F., and Stewart, J.: Short versus long-run effects of the introduction of black workers into the firm. In Sethi, S. P. (Ed.): *The Unstable Ground: Corporate Social Policy in a Dynamic Society.* Los Angeles, Melville, 1974, pp. 404-420.

Centers, R., and Bugental, D. E.: Intrinsic and extrinsic job motivators among different segments of the working population. *J Appl Psychol, 50*:193-197, 1966.

Coser, L.: *The Functions of Social Conflict.* New York, Free Press, 1956.

Festinger, L.: *A Theory of Cognitive Dissonance.* Evanston, Row, Patterson, 1957.

Flaugher, R. L.; Campbell, J. T., and Pike, L. W.: *Ethnic Group Membership as a Moderator of Supervisor's Ratings.* Princeton, Educational Testing Service, Bulletin PR-69-5, 1969.

Kasindorf, J.: England: Revolt in a shoe factory. *MS Magazine, 2*:16-18, 1973.

Lawrence, P. R., and Lorsch, J. W.: *Organization and Environment.* Boston, Graduate School of Business Administration, Harvard University, 1967.

Likert, R.: *The Human Organization.* New York, McGraw, 1967.

Manhardt, P. J.: Job orientation of male and female college graduates in business. *Personnel Psychol, 25*:361-368, 1972.

Maslow, A. H.: *Motivation and Personality.* New York, Har-Row, 1964.

Maurer, J. G.: *Readings in Organization Theory: Open System Approaches.* New York, Random, 1971.

McGregor, D. M.: *The Human Side of Enterprise.* New York, McGraw, 1960.

Pheterson, G.; Kiesler, S., and Goldberg, P.: Evaluation of the performance of women as a function of their sex, achievement, and personal history. *J Pers Soc Psychol, 19*:114-118, 1971.

Purcell, T. V., and Cavanagh, G. F.: *Blacks in the Industrial World: Issues for the Manager.* New York, The Free Press, 1972.

Purcell, T. V., and Cavanagh, G. F.: Alternate routes to employing the disadvantaged within the enterprise. Twenty-Second Annual Meeting of the Industrial Relations Research Association, New York, 1969.

Purcell, T. V., and Toner, F. J.: Two major corporate strategies toward full minority participation in business. In Sethi, S. P. (Ed.): *The Unstable Ground.* Los Angeles, Melville, 1974.

Rosen, B., and Jerdee, T. H.: Influence of sex role stereotypes on personnel decisions. *J Appl Psychol, 59*:9-14, 1974 .

Rosen, B., and Jerdee, T. H.: The influence of sex-role steretoypes on evaluations of male and female supervisory behavior. *J Appl Psychol, 57*:44-54, 1973.

Saleh, S. D., and Lalljee, M.: Sex and job orientation. *Personnel Psychol,* 22:465-471, 1969.

Scarf, M.: He and she: Sex hormones and behavior. *New York Times Magazine,* May 7, 1972, p. 30.

Steiner, G.: *The Creative Organization.* Chicago, U of Chicago Pr, 1965.

Tyler, L. E.: *The Psychology of Human Differences,* 3rd ed. New York, Appleton, 1965.

Wanous, J. P.: Matching individual and organization: The effect of job previews. Proceedings of the Academy of Management, 1972.

Wilson, G. A. G.: *Sex Differences in Organizational Dynamics.* Unpublished doctoral dissertation. Ann Arbor, University of Michigan, 1973.

Chapter 6

MISHMASH, MUSH AND MILESTONES IN ORGANIZATIONAL PSYCHOLOGY: 1974*

MARVIN D. DUNNETTE

INTRODUCTION

SOME READERS MAY have been lured by the strange title. Titles come easy to the writer; content and substance usually seem more difficult. A more sedate title and one more in keeping with the subject is "Disappointments, Accomplishments, and Goals for Organizational Psychology: 1974." Nonetheless, here are the dictionary definitions of mishmash, mush and milestone so that the reader may, as he sees fit, classify various parts of what is said into each.

Mishmash is defined as a mixture thrown together without coherence, a *hodgepodge*, a *jumble*.

As the writer reviewed various parts of the field while preparing this paper, its mishmash, hodgepodge, jumbling nature became increasingly obvious, and it requires no further elaboration. Each of us must certainly have experienced his own sense of mishmash in the field of psychology, and no attempt will be made to identify or label the elements further.

Mush, in addition to being defined as a kind of boiled corn meal that may be eaten either hot or cold, is said to be something that is soft and spongy or shapeless, a formless mass, weak sentimentality, *drivel.*

* Address presented by Marvin D. Dunnette at the symposium on Humanizing Organizational Psychology in 1974 at the convention of the American Psychological Association in New Orleans, 1974, and updated into 1975 for this book.

Here, too, it's possible for anyone to find his own drivel without any help. For the writer, the current major focus of *mush* in organizational psychology is to be found in the organization development movement, particularly in relation to its stated intentions and objectives. The idea of optimizing human and social improvement or to optimize task accomplishment or to accomplish some blend between the two, fine sounding as it is, seems very *mushy* and inexplicit. Moreover, such objectives as open problem-solving climates, building trust and collaboration, developing reward systems that recognize both organizational missions and the so-called growth of people, and increasing self-control and self-direction are difficult to get hold of. They seem to become spongy, shapeless and formless as one seeks to grasp them, and one gains an impression that those who play with such substances may not yet have been toilet-trained. But, the writer recognizes that this is but his own view of what seems mushy in organizational psychology. Labeling things as mushy or not mushy could be an interesting exercise, but it's of little consequence really, and doesn't do much for us in understanding where we stand today in the field of organizational psychology.

Milestone, for the writer's purposes, is best defined as a significant point in any progress or development.

This definition seems to imply that milestones are to be regarded only as markers indicating significant points of advancement. The writer prefers to view milestones in a broader way—as marking not only the points of advance, but also as marking any significant point of change, the wrong turns as well as the right ones, the low roads as well as the higher, failure as well as success.

Thus, we come to the real subject matter—and the changed title, "Disappointments, Accomplishments, and Goals for Organizational Psychology: 1974."

DISAPPOINTMENTS

1. In 1962, the writer commented in the *Annual Review* chapter as follows:

Major shortcomings in most personnel functions stem from a

too ready acceptance of untested instruments, packaged procedures, and yesterday's solutions to today's problems. Personnel management as a profession and industrial psychology as a science need people who are not content simply to "please" businessmen and managers—particularly if such acceptance is achieved with less than a full commitment of available knowledge and resources. Thus, the merit of what personnel men and psychologists do in industry must come to be judged on the basis of their own emerging standards of professional and scientific conduct rather than on the broadly variable standards of differing business enterprises (Dunnette, 1962).

A major disappointment in organizational psychology today is that evidence is far too meager that we have yet managed to bridge the gap between merely responding to the needs and demands expressed by our clients and the more legitimate scientific enterprise of leading and educating those clients to undertake solid behavioral science research. Our sins of omission throughout the past decades cut across many arenas, but they are most clearly discernible in our historical reluctance to see to it that our science was a science for *all* persons and not merely one for white, middle class males. In 1961, Taylor and Nevis stated that,

too many untested tests are too readily available to too many unqualified testers. Little real research is being conducted with respect to personnel selection in industry, and almost none on devices other than aptitude and personality tests (Taylor and Nevis, 1961).

And, in 1965, Biesheuvel laid the groundwork for a broadened perspective in personnel selection when he urged that,

it will be necessary to see selection in the wider context of more fully developed methods of recruitment and counselling, the definition of job requirements, the characteristics of various types of work organizations, and the factors determining motivation within them. Personnel selection is only one element in a complex system of manpower utilization, and neither its requirements nor its success can be properly apprised without taking the other elements that determine the functioning of the system into account (Biesheuvel, 1965).

Current and apparently never-ending hassles about test usage recommendations, interpretations of government guidelines, and how to carry out a proper validation study seem to indicate that we have done a very poor job indeed of seeking to educate and to lead clients as opposed to merely being responsive to their every whim.

2. Related to the above disappointment is the continued use of marginal practices, instruments and technologies by a not inconsiderable number of psychological brethren. These practices range all the way from suggesting that nearly anything can be accomplished by using a short ten-minute test to filling the popular literature with prescriptive statements about all the good things that will follow if managers will merely change certain things in their organization or undertake the use of various nostrums according to prescription. In a somewhat different but relevant context, Guion (1967) has referred to such approaches as "nothing more than arrogance put forward as the facade of ignorance."

3. Another disappointment over the last several years is that statistically more sophisticated prediction methodologies, in particular those using moderator, subgrouping or control variable approaches, have not yielded much of consequence. Certainly the ghostly barrier of validities around .50 suggested by Hull (1928) is still with us, and many, Phil Ash (1975) in particular, argue that the barrier is at a much lower level in reality than the .50 suggested by Hull.

4. The great surge of theorizing and research about motivation has failed to yield much. Equity theory spawned much research, but it has seen its heyday, primarily probably because of grave difficulties in operationalizing the equity concepts as they might apply to task or work-related outcomes other than pay. It seems apparent also that the several versions of expectancy-type theories have produced little of consequence. The writer (Dunnette, 1973) summarized a series of studies done under his direction and concluded that no more than 2 or 3 percent of task performance variance could be attributed to measurable differences in motivational parameters. In his upcoming *Annual Review* chapter, Locke (1975) argues at length that many of the crucial assumptions, human cognitive require-

ments and measurement approaches inherent in expectancy formulations are faulty and unrealistic. He notes further that only a very few studies have shown treatment effects of any consequence when ability variables have been controlled.

5. Perhaps most distressing over the last decade (and this could just as well be extended to cover the last century, the writer suspects) has been the embarrassing lack of solid evaluation research in industrial training programs, ranging all the way from cognitive or knowledge courses to such programs as computer simulations of team functioning and encounter groups, team development or other group process-oriented efforts. John Campbell, never the optimist, was especially pessimistic in his 1971 *Annual Review* chapter. He found the "bulk of (training) literature to be voluminous, nonempirical, nontheoretical, poorly written, and dull" (Campbell, 1971). In 1974, Back counted 149 evaluation studies of group intervention techniques. He found that few used behavioral measures of any type; fewer still obtained information from anyone other than the training group participants, and almost none of the evaluation studies used control groups. Back (1974) concludes, "the best way to understand the group intervention movement is to look at it simultaneously as a psychological technique and a social problem."

6. Leavitt and Bass (1964) wrote the first *Annual Review* chapter with the title "Organizational Psychology" just a decade ago in 1964. They held out much hope for this new field because they saw it as a merging of the energies of industrial, social and experimental psychologists to do research on large organizations. They wrote that "Systems-oriented, dynamic approaches to psychological problems in industry dealing with the interaction of organizational and human behavior are replacing static correlational surveys" (Leavitt and Bass, 1964). Yet, in 1966 Porter still found it necessary to comment on the need for a marriage in industrial psychology between fields of "personnel-differential" and "social-organizational." In 1967, Quinn and Kahn found that "Organizational psychology shows a great deal of redundancy without attaining the benefits of replication" and in referring to systems-oriented research, they wondered whether or not the

"approach will become a dominant guide to empirical work or whether 'system' will become merely the latest *in* word among organizational psychologists."

That the marriage has still not been consummated should be obvious to all of us as we note the continuing tendencies for various camps to emphasize certain pet theories, methodologies and subject matter areas in the research undertaken by their advocates. This constitutes the final and perhaps, substantively and theoretically, the most damaging disappointment the writer noted in his review of the last decade's activities.

The upshot of these six disappointments, the writer believes, is that we as psychologists must say that we still don't know the *real* meaning of job satisfaction; that we don't have a solid grounding on how to change people through counselling, training or development; that we don't yet know how to talk about, much less how to measure total systems, organization, unit or even group effectiveness; that we have no new and better statistical or psychometric methods for predicting behavior; that we do not *really* know what the consequences may be when a person says he works hard or what would cause him to feel that he is doing so; that we do not in other words yet have a useful theory of effort; and that we have not yet learned how to integrate the contributions of the so-called camps and sub-disciplines of organizational psychology into a cohesive whole.

What we have here is a field that seems fragmented and disconnected. No cohesive thrust seems immediately apparent beyond the soft and essentially unproven value systems that undergird current practices in organization development. However, the appearance of disarray is probably due mostly to an overemphasis on techniques and weak theories with an accompanying underemphasis on some of the concepts which *do* seem to be standing the test of time. Another look at developments over the last ten to fifteen years in industrial and organizational psychology *does* reveal certain milestones that can give us some greater cohesion in the thrust of both research and practice in organizational psychology.

ACCOMPLISHMENTS

Criteria

In considering organizational psychology's milestones or accomplishments, the writer found himself adopting certain implicit criteria. These criteria became explicit only *after* he had already listed areas of accomplishment and was then seeking to rationalize them by exploring what, if anything, they seemed to have in common. Here are the criteria the writer appeared to be using.

Social Usefulness

The areas of significant accomplishment seem mostly to have either immediate or potential social utility as opposed to merely being of academic interest (and he does mean *academic.* Many developments, theories especially, seem to have been devised as much for their usefulness in establishing scholarly or so-called academic credentials as for any other purpose).

Behavior Relevance

Most of the areas about to be mentioned seem to have already shown their usefulness for predicting or governing *behavior* in organizations or to have good potential for doing so.

Simplicity

The writer has always been surprised with the degree of complexity that many psychologists seem to be willing to introduce into their theories and ideas; he prefers simplicity. The story is told that, during World War II, the most predictive indicator of successful adjustment to service in Alaska was a YES response to the question, "Do you like cold weather?" The writer believes the science of psychology is still so imprecise that very simple concepts, methods and techniques are likely to be more fruitful than those that are unduly complicated.

Verifiability

Critical to the advancement of science is the ability of others to confirm and extend what has been reported by an investigator. Thus, developments that are heavily dependent upon insight or intuition instead of publicly communicable and verifiable facts were not chosen as significant accomplishments for the purpose of this listing. To a large degree, this criterion tended to rule out many imprecisely-stated theories and techniques supported only by evangelical testimony.

Milestones

Here, in the writer's opinion, are the major current accomplishments of organizational psychology up to and including part of the year 1974. Most of these will be seen as old friends or, perhaps, "old hat." Even so, they merit continued and increased attention.

1. *Cronbach's* (Cronbach and Gleser, 1965) emphasis on utility in personnel decision-making is one such milestone. The notion of utility is not at all new, but it seems to be widely ignored, perhaps because it is so easy to be lulled into a sense of contentment by the act of computing a correlation coefficient. The imperative of providing equal opportunities for employment for all persons should long ago have made more apparent to organizational psychologists the importance of interpreting personnel decision procedures according to cost concepts—costs related not only to errors of selection but also costs related to erroneous rejection of potentially successful applicants. Obviously, utility is not readily expressed as a single index; instead, it reflects a way of thinking, an emphasis *not* on trying to reduce everything to some common scale, but instead a directive to identify and list all possible personnel decision outcomes accompanied by a judgmental weighing of the costs and values (individually, organizationally *and* societally) associated with each.

2. A second milestone is to be found in the work of such persons as Fleishman (1972), McCormick (1972) and Owens (1975) in their programs of research on taxonomies of human performance. The writer suspects that many readers will feel a sense of surprise and perhaps revulsion at the suggestion of such *old* ideas as being among the best we have in organizational psychology. The writer hopes that no one would argue too long with his contention that the understanding and measurement of

task requirements and human performance capabilities are fundamental to the effective and accurate linking of humans and jobs
in complex organizations. The most pervasive source of dissatisfaction expressed by today's work force is that their abilities
are not being utilized. In his opinion, appropriate utilization of
human abilities at work will come much more quickly from
the disciplined thinking and research of taxonomists such as
Fleishman and McCormick than from an emphasis on such mushy
concepts as *growth, trust* and *self-direction*.

3. Thus, the writer suggests that a third milestone for
organizational psychology was the development by Flanagan
(1954) of critical incidents methodology and its recent rebirth
in the form of methods for tying down very explicitly the
behavioral requirements of different jobs. Articulating exactly
what behaviors have led to success or failure in different job
settings is too rarely done. As a result, employees often have
limited and distorted knowledge of what is expected of them.
Their only recourse usually is to learn the ways in which they
can screw up in jobs through methods of trial and error rather
than through carefully-formulated training and development
efforts.

4. The fourth milestone, deserving greatly increased attention
from organizational psychologists, involves the behavior modification methods flowing directly from, but going beyond, the
principles of Skinnerian and Pavlovian conditioning. John Campbell, in his 1971 *Annual Review* chapter, reserved his greatest
optimism for these methods. He saw them as the most likely
way of assuring significant advances in training technology in
the years ahead. As is now known, the method has been used
with great success in a number of industrial settings under various
labels such as contingency management and social modeling.
The latter has been carried forward by Goldstein and Sorcher
(1974), Johnson (1974) and Johnson and Sorcher (1974) in
their use of video tape to show learners a model who behaves
in a desired way and is reinforced. Learners are then asked to
model or mimic the same behavior, and they, too, are reinforced
for doing so. Many behaviors not previously in the learner's

repertoire are generated and reinforced. Recently Porter (1973) has summarized and discussed the wide range of strategies utilizing basic reinforcement principles which are applicable to organizations. Those who cringe at the thought of *controlling* people via behavior modification should find Porter's paper helpful along with an interesting one by Nord (1969) wherein he argues that the operant conditioning model has a great deal of similiarity, conceptually, to the poorly specified so-called humanistic theories of such persons as McGregor (1960), Maslow (1969) and Herzberg (1966).

5. Speaking of Herzberg, the writer believes a fifth milestone in organizational psychology is the technology of job enrichment which was popularized by Professor Herzberg through his emphasis on the importance of work itself (Ford, 1969). The idea that a liking or disliking for the activities involved in one's job may have important implications for sticking with the job and finding satisfaction in it is, of course, nothing new. It extends back at least as far as the beginning of vocational interest measurement. The special contribution of the practitioners of job enrichment has been to emphasize that jobs should be changed to fit the likes and dislikes of job incumbents rather than depending exclusively on hiring persons who already have appropriate interests. Though widely seen as a means of motivating employees, job enrichment can also be viewed as a kind of individualized means of changing jobs so that they match more fully the patterns of abilities possessed by employees. In other words, much of the power of job enrichment programs probably resides not merely in *What Employees Want To Do* but also and perhaps more importantly within the area of providing jobs that better utilize employee abilities—that is, "What Employees *Can* Do."

6. A sixth milestone for organizational psychology has been developed primarily by our colleagues in education and probably is still relatively foreign to organizational psychologists. The writer refers to the emerging field of *domain referenced testing* (Hively *et al.*, 1974), which is also known by the more widely used but semantically more confusing label, *criterion referenced*

testing. Domain referenced testing is of great importance to organizational psychologists because it, too, demands a disciplined specification of the domain of behaviors required for doing a job properly. After the domain has been specified, items are developed to test the entire domain of job performance; as such, the approach comes considerably closer to psychometricians' traditional definitions of content validation and to industrial psychologists' methods of developing job-sample tests. However, in contrast with individual differences-rooted *norm referenced testing* which has as its traditional purpose the selection and behavior prediction of examinees, domain referenced testing has its roots in learning theory and provides incremental measures that are useful for evaluating *growth,* or, more precisely, learning progress. The progress of learning is measured by forming tests with sample pools of items from the total test item domain and auditing each learner's progress at various stages in the teaching sequence. In the writer's opinion, domain referenced testing will become of great importance to organizational psychology because it is vastly more diagnostic and therefore far more responsive than norm referenced testing to the training and development needs of applicants and job incumbents. Though norm referenced testing will still be used for many prediction and selection situations, domain referenced testing affords greatly increased opportunity for assuring equal employment opportunities to all persons. It supplements traditional selection standards with solid diagnostic indicators pointing the way for required training and development of selectees.

7. A seventh milestone has several different labels—namely *goal setting, intentionality* and *management by objectives.* The appeal of these concepts lies mostly in their simplicity. The author believes a person will indeed work best toward goals which he has accepted and which he states he intends to accomplish. Again, an important strength in this contribution stems from the behavioral specificity required for goals to be established. In the process of setting a goal, an individual learns what he is supposed to do whereas previously the task may have been unclear. Carried into the day-to-day world of work, management

by objectives may be viewed simply as a form of performance appraisal involving the mutual setting of goals between an employee and his or her boss, thereby bringing more order and mutual understanding to what may have been an ambiguous situation. Another appealing feature of goal-setting, of course, is that it too allows ability parameters to enter into the performance contracts between superior and subordinate rather than depending upon motivational parameters alone. In his upcoming *Annual Review* chapter, Locke (1975) cites and discusses a number of field studies of MBO and goal-setting programs. Results of these studies are helpful in defining the important practical parameters of the MBO approach and in suggesting areas where more research should be done.

8. The writer is somewhat hesitant to mention the eighth and final milestone because it differs quite substantially from the others suggested in that it is much softer—even somewhat mushy— and certainly less clearly specified. Nonetheless, the writer agrees with Friedlander's and Brown's (1974) suggestion in this year's *Annual Review* chapter that action research is one important avenue for advancing knowledge in organizational psychology. Action research is best carried out by a clinician who possesses the unusual experimental acuity of a Freud or a Piaget. For the writer, action research implies naturalistic observation, and this in turn demands detailed and complete observation of naturalistic events, a willingness to introduce single parametric changes in order to observe clinically their effects on other parameters and on outcomes, and an ability to document fully the processes of clinical experimentation that have been tried and what their outcomes have been so that hypotheses may be either disconfirmed or confirmed. The writer hopes it is clear that he does not define action research as merely involving some OD practitioner wallowing around in an organization doing his thing. Friedlander and Brown (1974) define the need and the nature of action research, or, as the writer prefers to call it, naturalistic observation, when they contrast the form of *what is needed* with what has gone before. They state,

Thus far (research) has chosen to play a relatively uninvolved and distant role in the change-practice situation. Thus far it has focused on producing data for research needs rather than practice needs. As a result, we have theory from an external research perspective only. We have generally failed to produce a theory of change which emerges from the change process itself. We need a way . . . to become a science in which knowledge-getting and knowledge-giving are an integrated process, and one that is valuable to all parties involved. We believe that a theory of planned change must be a theory of practice, which emerges from practice data and is of the practice situation, not merely about it (Friedlander and Brown, 1974).

SUMMARY

Now to summarize what has been said by suggesting two common themes among the six disappointments and also the general thread of communality among the eight areas labeled as milestone-accomplishments.

The disappointments are readily seen to stem from two major causes, one stylistic and the other, probably cognitive. The writer believes it is the style of many organizational psychologists to be content with pulling the wool over their clients' eyes. Not only do we tend to be overly deferent to client needs and slow to lead them by pushing for more and better behavioral science research, we also take advantage of our acceptance by offering and monitoring the use of untested and underevaluated instruments and techniques.

Cognitively, the disappointments stem from too great a readiness to utilize overly complicated models, whether they be models of motivated behavior, models of statistical prediction strategies or models involving broad-scale, so-called systemic research strategies. These efforts to deal with great complexity just have not worked out, and we should take the hint and become more simple-minded and less mush-headed.

In contrast, the milestones are all characterized by solid efforts to specify required, desired or intended *behaviors* and to observe and record, either retrospectively or *in vivo*, task and organizationally-relevant behavior as it unfolds in the work setting. These behavior-relevant and behavior-based methods and conceptions seem to provide the only solid base we have for deriving organizational psychology theory and practice in the years ahead.

At the risk of redundancy, let me be quite specific about what our goals should be as we move into the second half of the seventies.

First, it is our hope that we will see a more disciplined emphasis on behavior-recording and observation through on site naturalistic observation and systematic clinical-experimental hypothesis-testing, task studies and analyses, gathering and conceptual clustering of critical job behaviors and further development of taxonomies of human performance.

Second, it is the author's hope that testing technology will revolve about efforts to specify the desired behavioral end products of individual-job-organizational interaction within the context of domain referenced testing in addition to the traditionally psychometric orientation of norm referenced testing.

Third, it is the author's hope that future approaches to organizational and individual change may give increased emphasis to methods which take account of *both* ability and so-called need or motivational parameters. Three such methods have been suggested that currently are being espoused and practiced under the labels of (a) *behavior modification* (social modeling and contingency management technology), (b) *work itself* (job design and job enrichment technology), and (c) *intentionality* (goal-setting and management-by-objectives technology).

Fourth, and finally, we hope that a primary basis for evaluating and auditing our practices in the years ahead will flow more fully from the *utility* conceptualization suggested so long ago by Cronbach and Gleser (1965), and that this may at least come to supplement and eventually to replace our current fixation with correlational methodology as the primary means of determining the validity and social usefulness of our practices.

The writer believes the indirect consequences of the above emphases will be toward humanizing organizational structures and processes in the years ahead. The emphasis on behavior study and behavior measurement will lead inevitably to more fundamental knowledge about individual motives, their development, modifiability and behavioral correlates. An empirically-based technology of training processes will lead inevitably to better organizational planning and make possible individual and organizational changes which are planned and focused instead of haphazard.

We can hope, then, ultimately that our science of organizational psychology will lead the way toward organizational practices which may lean less on the development of institutional nationalisms, supplanting such loyalties with broader and more socially-relevant loyalties to all humanity while still retaining the great strengths of individualism.

The road, it seems, is broad and clear for the *science* of organizational psychology to become more human and to transmit this humanness through *practice* to the organizational and societal entities of the future.

REFERENCES

Ash, P., and Kroeker, L. P.: Personnel selection, classification and placement. In Rosenzweig, M. R., and Porter, L. W. (Eds.): *Annual Review of Psychology*, vol. 26. Palo Alto, Annual Reviews, Inc., 1975.

Back, K. W.: Intervention techniques: Small groups. In Rosenzweig, M. R., and Porter, L. W. (Eds.): *Annual Review of Psychology*, vol. 25. Palo Alto, Annual Reviews, Inc., 1974.

Biesheuvel, S.: Personnel selection. In Farnsworth, P. R.; McNemar, O., and McNemar, Q. (Eds.): *Annual Review of Psychology*, vol. 16. Palo Alto, Annual Reviews, Inc., 1965.

Campbell, J. P.: Personnel training and development. In Mussen, P. H., and Rosenzweig, M. R. (Eds.): *Annual Review of Psychology*, vol. 22. Palo Alto, Annual Reviews, Inc., 1971.

Cronbach, L. J., and Gleser, G. C.: *Psychological Tests and Personnel Decisions*. Urbana, U of Ill Pr, 1965, Second Edition.

Dunnette, M. D.: *Performance Equals Ability and What?* Technical Report Number 4009, ONR Contract Number N00014-68-A-0141-0003, NR 151-323, Minneapolis, University of Minnesota, 1973.

Dunnette, M. D.: Personnel management. In Farnsworth, P. R.; McNemar, O., and McNemar, Q. (Eds.): *Annual Review of Psychology*, vol. 13. Palo Alto, Annual Reviews, Inc., 1962.

Flanagan, J. C.: The critical incident technique. *Psychol Bull, 51*:327-358, 1954.

Fleishman, E. A.: On the relation between abilities, learning, and human performance. *Am Psychol,* 27:1017-1032, 1972.

Ford, R. N.: *Motivation Through the Work Itself.* New York, American Management Association, 1969.

Goldstein, A., and Sorcher, M.: *Changing Managerial Behavior.* Elmsford, Pergamon, 1964.

Guion, R. M.: Personnel selection. In Farnsworth, P. R.; McNemar, O., and McNemar, Q. (Eds.): *Annual Review of Psychology,* vol. 18, p. 286. Palo Alto, Annual Reviews, Inc., 1967.

Herzberg, F.: *Work and the Nature of Man.* Cleveland, World, 1966.

Hively, W. *et al.:* Domain referenced testing. *Educational Technology,* June, 1974.

Hull, C. L.: *Aptitude Testing.* New York, Harcourt, Brace and World, 1928.

Johnson, P. D.: Use of social modeling methodology for supervisory training. Unpublished technical report, Minneapolis, Personnel Decisions, Inc., 1974.

Johnson, P. D., and Sorcher, M.: Behavior modeling training: Why, how, and what results. Paper delivered to the National Convention of Plant Engineers, Kansas City, Missouri, November 7, 1974.

Leavitt, H. J., and Bass, B. M.: Organizational psychology. In Mussen, P. H., and Rosenzweig, M. R. (Eds.): *Annual Review of Psychology.* vol. 15. Palo Alto, Annual Reviews, Inc., 1964.

Locke, E. A.: Personnel attitudes and motivation. In Rosenzweig, M. R., and Porter, L. W.: *Annual Review of Psychology,* vol. 26. Palo Alto, Annual Reviews, Inc., 1975.

Maslow, A. H.: *Motivation and Personality.* New York, Har-Row, 1969.

McCormick, E. J.; Jeanneret, P. R., and Mecham, R. C.: A study of job characteristics and job dimensions as based on the Position Analysis Questionnaire (PAQ). *J Appl Psychol,* 56:347-368, 1972.

McGregor, D.: *The Human Side of Enterprise.* New York, McGraw, 1960.

Nord, W.: Beyond the teaching machine: The neglected area of operant conditioning in the theory and practice of management. *Organizational Behavior and Human Performance,* 4:375-401, 1969.

Owens, W. A.: Background data. In Dunnette, M. D. (Ed.): *Handbook of Industrial and Organizational Psychology.* Chicago, Rand McNally, 1975.

Porter, L. W.: Personnel selection. In Farnsworth, P. R.; McNemar, O., and McNemar, Q. (Eds.): *Annual Review of Psychology,* vol. 17. Palo Alto, Annual Reviews, Inc., 1966.

Porter, L. W.: The rewarding environment. In Dunnette, M. D. (Ed.): *Work and Non-Work in the Year 2001.* Monterey, Brooks-Cole, 1973.

Quinn, R. P., and Kahn, R. L.: Organizational psychology. In Farnsworth, P. R.; McNemar, O., and McNemar, Q. (Eds.): *Annual Review of Psychology,* vol. 18. Palo Alto, Annual Reviews, Inc., 1967.

Taylor, E. K., and Nevis, E. C.: Personnel selection. In Farnsworth, P. R.; McNemar, O., and McNemar, Q. (Eds.): *Annual Review of Psychology.* vol. 12. Palo Alto, Annual Reviews, Inc., 1961.

Part II

DIAGNOSING ORGANIZATIONS FOR
PURPOSES OF HUMANIZING

INTRODUCING PART II . . .
WHITHER WE ARE TENDING

For humanizing organizational behavior, the realities confronting us are many and complex and frontiers beckoning us are urgent. This is what we can learn from the contributions in Part I. In Part II we will be concerned with the first essential move for intelligent action—diagnosis, organizational diagnosis. What we wanted was a consideration of the problem of organizational diagnosis in a manner that was explicitly related to the theme of humanizing organizations. This is precisely what Dr. Alderfer does in his contribution which he specially prepared for this book under the title of "Boundary Relations and Organizational Diagnosis."

The point of view that he expresses is one which has evolved from research, theory and practice in applied behavioral science. As a result his contribution is a systematic presentation "devoted to organizational diagnosis as a specialty worthy of attention in its own right." The paper proceeds in three steps—(1) defining of organizational diagnosis, (2) specifying a number of major variables and related empirical findings to provide a basis for focusing on certain aspects of an organization during diagnosis with an analysis of organizational variables to propose a set of contingencies which specify which techniques are most appropriate at each phase of diagnostic process. Organizational boundaries, we are advised, can be identified concretely and subjectively. Included are case studies about differences in the permeability of organizational boundaries (overbounded or underbounded systems) and the effects they have on human relations as well as performance. The relationship of both types of systems to the problem of authority is well considered. Also presented is the nature of communication problems and how it differs in relationship to boundary conditions. The relationship of the systems to economic conditions is explored. Dr. Alderfer reports findings about the nature of system boundaries which exert a powerful effect on the kinds of human problems to be uncovered by diagnosis. In general, Dr. Alderfer's impression is that, particularly in overbounded systems, theory, technology and data exist to make significant changes in the direction of humanizing.

The second chapter in Part II is "Self-Managing Systems, Z.E.G., and Other Unthinkables." This was a presentation at the 1974 APA symposium by Bernard Bass. Of the papers presented at that symposium, this was by far the most comprehensive and interdisciplinary in nature. It starts with the contention that it is impossible to talk about humanizing organizations without looking at what has been happening to the industrial society world-wide and what is likely to happen during the years to come. Bass' consideration in realistic terms of the possible consequences of zero economic growth is consonant with considerations of limits of growth and related kinds of research problems which have been reported and usually lead to a pessimistic outlook. Bass does not agree and what he attempts to do in this chapter is to relate self-planning, self-direction and self-control which pay off in outputs of productivity and satisfaction. He presents documented evidence and illustrations for each concept. The general conclusion is that self-managed person-systems approach is an optimal solution. To use his words, "It can please the devils' materialistic interests in efficiency and the saints' humanistic interests in satisfying work."

"Humanizing Organizations: The Potential Impact of New People and Emerging Values Upon Organizations," the third chapter which appears in Part II, is based on Hall's presentation at the 1973 APA symposium. Hall considers the population not considered by others to any significant extent—new people, meaning young people—and particularly some of the concepts that emerged from a consideration of this kind of population. The generation gap he redefines as being more accurately called the value-perception gap. He enumerates and considers some of the value areas in which young people expect more and perceive less. Included are basic concern about goals and values; action as being more important, the cry being to do it; and the importance of personal integrity, honesty, openness and realism.

The emphasis in humanistic terms is on personal growth and development. He generally contends that ironically the values of the counterculture are quite congruent with the principles which have guided humanistic organizational development efforts. The youth movement and the direction in which it seems to be moving are considered in some detail in this contribution. The social significance of the youth movement and its implications are considered at the end of the paper.

The last chapter in Part II is "Economic and Socio-Cultural Barriers to Humanizing Organizations." It is based on a symposium presentation at the 1974 APA meeting. Emphasized in this contribution by Nord are background assumptions which overlook constraints such as the individualistic focus with a disregard of the group. Each individual is treated as an end, but seldom is the focus explicitly on the human potential of all the people taken together as a whole. Another constraint factor considered is the emphasis on the lower level needs. An economic problem presented by Nord is organizational profits and growth as goals. It is contended that too many previous studies emphasized micro rather than the macro level focus. There are differences in economic class attitudes-economic class competition and a market system which seem to generate forces which conflict with humanistic goals. An interesting generalization made is that reasons are sought for the existence of conflict rather than reasons for the absence of conflict. Another interesting problem well-considered in this paper is the distribution of power and its consequences. The bureaucratic structure is described as being characterized by an implicit power struggle orientation which increases in-fighting, empire building, rivalry and a sense of futility.* In general, what Nord argues for in this paper is

---

* Bennis, who is often quoted for what he says about the dehumanizing effects of bureaucracy, has, since he became president of the University of Cincinnati, changed his mind somewhat about that and justified bureaucracy in some instances as a need.

that organizational psychology may become a stronger force for humanization by increasing the degree to which the sociocultural system is taken as a unit of analysis and lower-level participants as client. Nord therefore advocates more macroanalysis and an awareness of the influence of our own personal worlds and background assumptions as leading to a more meaningful outlook.

Chapter 7

BOUNDARY RELATIONS AND ORGANIZATIONAL DIAGNOSIS*

CLAYTON P. ALDERFER

INTRODUCTION

THIS PAPER PRESENTS a point of view about organizational diagnosis which has evolved from research, theory and practice in applied behavioral science. During the last ten years there has been a rapid increase in the amount of professional literature in this area (Friedlander and Brown, 1974). Most attempts to treat organizational development in detail give some attention to diagnosis (e.g., Argyris, 1962; Beckhard, 1969; Schein, 1969; Lawrence and Lorsch, 1969; Margulies and Raia, 1972), but there are only a few systematic presentations devoted to organizational diagnosis as a specialty worthy of attention in its own right (Argyris, 1970; Levinson, 1972; and Mahler, 1974).

Argyris (1970) proposes a behavioral science intervention theory featuring three primary tasks—generation of valid information, provision of informed choice and development of internal commitment. He conceptualizes diagnosis as primarily a *process* in which the three tasks are essential regardless of the substantive issues involved. While he discusses many levels of organiza-

* Invited paper presented at the District of Columbia Psychological Association, November 15, 1974. The ideas and experiences on which this paper is based have been developed in collaboration with L. Dave Brown, Robert E. Kaplan and Ken K. Smith. Al Glickman, Richard Hackman, Carol Schreiber and Fred Wickert provided helpful comments on an earlier version of the paper.

tional variables, his primary focus is on interpersonal relations, particularly among top executives and between the top group and the consultant. Levinson's (1972) approach to organizational diagnosis is to provide a data-gathering guide modeled after a psychiatric examination outline. He conceptualizes an organization as an open system maintaining equilibrium among internal subsystems, between itself and other systems, and within larger subsystems of which it is a part. As something of a complementary contrast to Argyris (1970), Levinson (1972) devotes most of his work to the *content* of the diagnostic study, although he also demonstrates a rich understanding of the emotions associated with the diagnostic process and the importance of coping effectively with these feelings. Argyris (1970) analyzes the advantages and disadvantages of organic versus mechanistic research methods, and Levinson (1972) proposes the use of various types of instruments for data collection, but neither of these writers provides extensive detail on instrumentation for diagnosis. Walter Mahler (1974), on the other hand, gives about 90 percent of his book to the presentation of instruments for collecting diagnostic data about organizations.

This chapter proceeds in three steps. First, it begins with a definition of organizational diagnosis, a set of activities that has several phases and generally involves major tension between understanding and change. Second, it specifies a number of major variables and related empirical findings to provide the bases for focusing on certain aspects of an organization during diagnosis. Finally, it brings together the nature of organizational diagnosis with an analysis of organizational variables to propose a set of contingencies which specify which techniques are most appropriate at each phase of the diagnostic process.

I. A DEFINITION OF ORGANIZATIONAL DIAGNOSIS

Organizational diagnosis is the process of publicly entering a human system, collecting valid data about human experiences with that system, and feeding that information back to the system to promote increased understanding of the system by its members. Among a growing array of social technologies, organizational diagnosis is not a change strategy per se, but a precursor to change. The purpose of an organizational diagnosis is to determine whether change is desirable based on a widely-shared understanding of the system.

The role of organizational diagnosis in affecting the life of a human system is loosely analogous to the part played by medical diagnosis in maintaining the physical health of an individual, but the distinction between organizational diagnosis and action cannot be as clearly marked as that between medical diagnosis and prescription. When an organizational diagnosis is conducted the system is altered by the entrance of outsiders, the solicitation of information and attention to issues identified by these processes. Since these events are not normally a part of organizational activities, diagnosis itself is a change. In fact, each phase of the diagnostic process has some tendency to provoke change.

Sometimes the mere fact of entering a system may lead members to change their standard ways of operating. At the outset of a study of a private boarding school, for example, the faculty decided that they needed an independent forum to discuss issues of concern to them. With the consent and support of the school administration, the faculty established such a forum (Alderfer and Brown, 1974). Although this development came about as the faculty were deciding whether to approve an organizational diagnosis, it was not prescribed by the consultants. There are instances, however, where, in order to decide whether to conduct a diagnosis, consultants do alter the normal ways people relate to each other. Beginning the study of a group of interrelated municipal social service agencies, the diagnosticians felt that it was important for the heads of all relevant bodies to meet in order to agree about the scope of the diagnostic activity. They later learned that conflict among this set of leaders was so great that they normally did not meet face-to-face except at ceremonial occasions. Unknowingly, at the time, the diagnosticians were changing the normal pattern of interpersonal relationships among people simply to determine whether diagnosis was feasible.

Systematic collection of valid information about the experiences of organization members is not an every day event in most systems. Nondirective interviewing, an activity that occurs in many diagnoses, is a powerful process for releasing feelings in people (Rogers, 1961). Sometimes individuals leave interviews with their morale temporarily enhanced because of the cathartic experience. Others may decide to act differently because of insights obtained in the process of responding to an interviewer's questions. Group methods in the conduct of diagnoses bring individuals together to talk about common concerns they have or to complete a questionnaire about their reactions to organizational life. In either case, consciousness about a common fate in the organization may increase as a result of interaction that is necessary for data collection. This greater awareness may lead to a temporary reduction in alienation among employees, to stimulation for change or to a decision that change is hopeless.

Finally, organizational diagnosis commits a system to paying attention to the results of the study. A diagnosis conducted according to these concepts arranges for data to be shared publicly within limits of confidentiality. Feedback methods promote interaction among the people who participated in the diagnosis to confirm or disconfirm the findings, provide a check on whatever analyses or inferences are made by the diagnostician, and reduce the likelihood that major findings of the study will be ignored. Feedback processes are designed to promote interaction among those parts of the system which data indicate would benefit from greater exchange around common problems. This approach to designing feedback sessions increases the likelihood that change will follow from the diagnosis if it is called for by the data.

Thus, while the intent of an organizational diagnosis is to test the feasibility of change, not promote it, the process is likely to influence the system in which it takes place. As a result, the role of the organizational diagnostician is fraught with ambiguity and conflict at each step in the diagnostic process. The professional goal is to produce a valid and widely-shared analysis of the system which is the target of the study. Once this objective has been agreed upon by all relevant parties the diagnostician cannot proceed in a passive manner, avoiding all influence attempts in order not to change the system he is attempting to understand. In the period preceding an explicit decision to plan for change, however, the diagnostician's interventions should be confined only to those activities which are necessary for achieving a valid diagnosis.

This approach to organizational diagnosis arises from the interaction of two traditions in social science. First, there are the long-standing methods of participant observation and survey research which have led to much of the basic knowledge we have about organizations. Users of these methods, even when they disagree with each other, usually accept a comparatively passive role toward the organizations they study (Sieber, 1973). Second, there are the newly-emerging social technologies of experiential learning and social intervention (Bennis, 1966; Hornstein, *et al.*, 1971). Professionals from this orientation have developed methods which permit them to intervene in social systems to effect change. Thoughtful, reflective analyses of the phenomena being changed, however, are often missing (Alderfer, 1974).

Drawing on both of these traditions, the present view of organizational diagnosis rests on the following guidelines:

1. The diagnostician should attempt to influence a client when intervention is necessary to complete the diagnostic process defined above.

2. However, the diagnostician should *not* attempt to influence a client system when that influence is not necessary for effective diagnosis, no matter how great a perceived opportunity for constructive change exists.

These two guidelines provide no hard and fast criteria for resolving questions of when to intervene during diagnosis. The decision still rests on the judgment of the diagnostician, but they do provide a way to confront the dilemma. As a result the diagnostician should be clearer to himself and to the client about his mission despite its ambiguity.

II. CONCEPTUAL AND EMPIRICAL BASES FOR ORGANIZATIONAL DIAGNOSIS

Human organizations are open systems regularly engaged in interaction with their external environments. They import material, energy and information from outside the system, transform these resources, then export their products back to the environment (Rice, 1963). Organizations and subsystems within them are distinguished from their environments by the boundaries which regulate transactions between the system and environment and thereby determine what is part of the system and what is outside of it. Organizational boundaries may be identified both concretely and subjectively. Publicly-observable, concrete boundaries include walls, fences, maps to mark spatial boundaries; clocks to indicate time boundaries; and membership lists and organizational charts to specify human boundaries. Subjective boundaries refer to the human feelings that often are associated with concrete boundaries. They pertain to how much the individuals and groups develop a sense of territoriality, feel that events have begun or ended, and participate in a spirit of cohesion and community with their fellows. Open systems theory recognizes the interdependence among subsystems within systems as well as the relations between a system and its environment. Rather than seeking explanations in one-way causality, this framework generally assumes two-way causality among variables (Berrien, 1968). We therefore assume that concrete and subjective boundaries influence each other. Subjective boundaries may lead to the formation of concrete boundaries as when neighbors who wish to reduce their interaction with each other build fences. Concrete boundaries may lead to the development of subjective boundaries as when maximum security prisoners become increasingly alienated from society as a result of their confinement. Under long-term stable conditions, concrete and subjective boundaries tend to parallel each other.

The permeability of organizational boundaries refers to the ease with which resources are passed back and forth between a system and its environment and among the subsystems within an organization. Relatively impermeable boundaries mean that exchanges are difficult, and the organization is in danger of becoming closed off from needed interaction. Excessively permeable boundaries mean that the distinction between organization and environment is nearly obliterated, and the system faces the possibility of being indistinguishable from its environment. Either highly permeable or impermeable boundaries represent a problematic condition for an organization. Figure 7-1 shows the hypothetical relationship between boundary permeability and organizational vitality (Alderfer, 1975). A system characterized by highly impermeable boundaries tends to be rigid and over-controlled, while a system with extremely permeable boundaries is chaotic and disorganized. While these two boundary conditions represent opposite ends of a continuum there is a tendency for some systems in marked disequilibrium to vacillate between the

System Vitality as a Function of Boundary Permeability

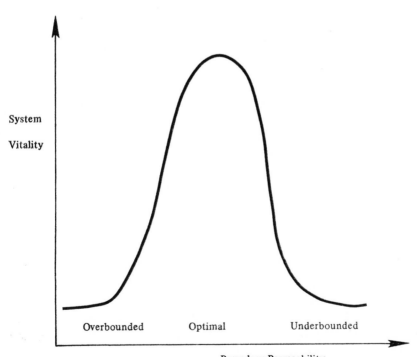

Boundary Permeability

Figure 7-1.

extremes. The chaos and disorganization of a prison riot is often a reaction to excessive control and deprivation experienced by inmates. Conversely, student protest led to the stationing of national guardsmen on college campuses and the decrease of boundary permeability when university leadership thought that chaos was sharply increasing.

The hypothesized relationship between system vitality and boundary permeability is also based on systematic empirical evidence. Several investigations show results consistent with the proposition from different kinds of organizations. A review of selected parts of this literature indicates that both overbounded and underbounded systems lose vitality, though in different ways.

Two Overbounded Systems

Data from two overbounded systems have been reported from an elite upper class independent boarding school (Alderfer and Brown, 1974), and one of the established corporations in the United States (Bray, Campbell, and Grant, 1974).

The independent boarding school showed many characteristics of being overbounded. It was a total institution for the boarding students who made up more than 80 percent of the student body. These students found their daily lives took place completely within the confines of the school. They ate at the school, attended classes in its buildings, participated in athletics on its grounds, played in the corridors of its buildings, and slept in the dormitory rooms. Students were permitted to leave school for holidays and selected weekends, but otherwise their whole lives were confined to school property and activity. Located in New England, the school's already impermeable boundaries became even more restrictive with the onslaught of winter. Hazardous weather limited the degree to which students could roam on school grounds, and activities tended to be further confined to school buildings.

Even before systematic data were collected, informal reports suggested that morale declined as the school year progressed. Time series data collected during a year-long diagnosis confirmed this effect both for successive months during the school year and across the four classes of students. Student satisfaction declined throughout the year until near the end when it rose slightly for first, third and fourth-year groups. A similar pattern was also observed for student reports of their sense of growth from academic activities. As the boundaries of the school became more confining, indications of student vitality declined. When the temporal and spatial boundaries became more permeable either by the ending of the school year or the ending of a school career, the direction of these curves changed to an upward direction.

Students and faculty at the boarding school had their own way of understanding these phenomena. When the time series curve was shown to the students, they christened it the BFD curve. BFD was not an example of social science jargon being inflicted on unsuspecting subjects, but rather a case of clients labeling their own problems. BFD was shorthand for *big fucking deal*, terms that both symbolized and expressed the overall sense of apathy and alienation that gripped the school community. Students actually conceptualized it as a social disease. They talked about catching it, avoiding it and recovering from it (Alderfer and Brown, 1974).

Two remarkably similar trends were reported for a group of management recruits whose experience with the Bell System was followed for a period of eight years (Bray, Campbell, and Grant, 1974). Although specific data on the boundary characteristics of the Bell System were not provided in the study, there is enough common knowledge about the system for one to reasonably assume that if the organization departs from optimal boundary permeability in any way, it does so in the direction of being overbounded. Thus, the longer one stays in the system, the more impermeable he would experience the organization to be. Bray *et al.* found that general management attitude, a scale with items very similar to overall satisfaction as measured in the boarding school study, progressively declined throughout the eight-year period they observed. They also found that values on a scale measuring fulfilled expectations about the use of abilities and career progress, items that were quite similar to the sense of academic growth in the boarding school study, declined markedly over the same eight-year period.

Time series data of the sort in the boarding school and A.T. & T. studies are not yet frequently found in the social science literature. Their common trends document a phenomenon of systems with quite different objectives de-energizing people in very similar ways.* They illustrate how overbounded systems progressively drain vitality from their members.

Another similar finding between the boarding school and Bell System studies pertains to interpersonal behavior. In the Gaight study (Alderfer and Brown, 1975) it was found that the prevalence of sarcastic behavior among students increased from the first to the second to the third year, then decreased somewhat in the fourth year. In individual interviews and in group meetings, we learned how painful and confusing sarcasm could be. The typical sarcastic exchange contained two quite conflicting messages; usually one was positive and the other was negative. A student who excelled in academic, extracurricular and athletic activities was labeled "Perf" by his peers. Behind the admiration for his achievements was only thinly veiled derision. Students, describing their personal experiences with sarcastic interaction, noted that after they realized what the social norms were, they would begin conversations sarcastically because they believed that the best defense was a good offense. For the school as a social system the prevalence of sarcasm posed a two-fold problem. First, it tended to produce psychological distance between people rather than enhance a sense of community. Second, it resulted in frequently distorted communications; people were generally confused about which of the mixed messages they should accept as real.

The Bell System study also documented changes in interpersonal behavior as managers remained in the Bell System. At the time of initial assessment, the management recruits were measured on a wide range of variables. The variable that showed the highest correlation with *expected* success in the corporation

---

* Glickman (1961) found a similar trend in another overbounded system, the United States Navy. Over a three-year period an overall attitude index declined more than twenty points.

at the time of recruitment was human relations skills with a coefficient of .66. At the time of reassessment, after the recruits had worked in the company for eight years, their human relations skills were measured again using the same methodology. The correlation of this variable with *achieved* success in the business was then the second highest among the twenty-five indicators measured by the assessment process, but the size of the correlation had dropped to .32. It was not only the magnitude of the relationship between human relations skills and corporate success that changed over the eight year-period; the actual level of human relations skills of the managers decreased during this time. Reassessment showed that behavioral flexibility, likeableness and interpersonal skills decreased significantly. Bray *et al.* comment,

> Such results are surprising, to say the least. The recruits certainly had much more opportunity for group interaction during their years in the business. It would be reasonable to expect such practice to improve interpersonal skills. Furthermore, it is difficult to conceive of people losing interpersonal ability (except for cases of mental illness). It seems more likely that ability has not been lost but that manifest behavior has for some reason changed in the direction of being less effective.

The boarding school and Bell System studies revealed similar effects of prolonged membership in overbounded organizations. Morale dropped, perceived utilization of human abilities declined, and the effectiveness of interpersonal communications decreased. One important difference between the studies was that the boarding school research covered a shorter period of time and included evidence of what happened as termination from the system approached. In the school setting there was evidence that anticipation of crossing this time boundary was associated with changes in otherwise downward trends. A similar effect was not observed for the Bell System data, but eight years into a career in that organization is still relatively near the beginning.

Two Underbounded Systems

Data from underbounded systems have been reported from a classic study of technological change in British coal mines (Trist,

Higgin, Murray, and Pollock, 1963) and an investigation of students at an American Indian boarding school (Alderfer, Hammerschlag, Berg and Fisher, 1972).

Trist *et al.* examined the consequences of different methods of social organization for the mining of coal. For generations prior to the advent of a new technology, coalmen had organized themselves as six-person groups who shared the same physical location in a mine and whose pay was jointly determined. Members of these so-called marrow groups selected their own members and held autonomous responsibility for all shifts in their territory. The marrow groups therefore controlled their spatial, temporal and human boundaries, but the introduction of the conventional longwall method of coal-mining radically altered traditional work group boundaries by completely disrupting marrow groups. Individual miners no longer belonged to self-selected work teams who shared full responsibility for a common territory on all shifts. Instead they tended to function as individuals with narrowly-defined roles specifying the work to be done on each shift. There was a high degree of destructive competition between men in different roles on the same shift and among the different shifts. Overall, the new mining technology fell far short of realizing the economic gains which had been expected for it.

As the investigators spent time observing and interviewing in the mines, they discovered that a new form of social organization had emerged in some settings. The researchers called the new system a composite method of coal-mining because it combined characteristics of the old marrow group organization with the new mining technology. A complete composite method consisted of four features. First, rather than separating functions by shifts, the members on each shift were prepared to pick up the mining cycle wherever their predecessors left off, thereby assuring task continuity. Second, individual miners were expected to perform multiple tasks rather than single functions in mining coal although not every team member had to perform all tasks. A team as a whole, however, had to have within it members who collectively could perform all tasks. Third, members of a team were self-selected, insuring that they accepted differences among themselves from the outset. Finally, all members of a work team shared a common paynote from which all took equal amounts of money since it was assumed that they made equivalent contributions. Typically, the new groups were much larger than the traditional marrow groups, containing approximately forty members rather than six, but most importantly, their group boundaries were once again congruent and solidified.

On all measures reported by the research team, the composite method functioned more effectively than the conventional long-wall system for both the individual miner and the organization. Individual miners reported more satisfaction with their work and a greater sense of relationship with other miners. The men appeared less fatigued and felt less strain. Older miners said they expected to have a longer work life under the new system than under the old. Absence rates were more than cut in half under the new system as compared to the old. Demands for coordination and settlement of jurisdictional disputes by management were reduced under the composite system. The composite system operated at 95 percent of technical efficiency while the conventional method ran at only 78 percent of potential, and the conventional system lagged on its work 69 percent of the time compared to only 5 percent lag for the composite method. The Trist *et al.* study showed that the breakdown of group boundaries and their subsequent replacement are tremendously significant events for individuals and organizations.

A study comparing the intra and intertribal relations among several groups of adolescents at a Bureau of Indian Affairs boarding school showed similar phenomena (Alderfer, Hammerschlag, Berg and Fisher, 1972). The pattern of group relations differed markedly among four different tribes at the school. Especially noteworthy was the pattern of one tribe who showed many indications of complete breakdown of their group boundaries. This group reported the most aggression against other tribes at the school, the least support from members of their own tribe, and the most fighting among members of their own tribe. Their behavior and attitudes contradicted the commonly-held proposition that external aggression by a group is associated with internal cohesion because this tribe was highest on both internal and external aggression (Levine and Campbell, 1972). Moreover, they reported the greatest decrease in respect for Indian heritage and traditions and in respect for themselves as a result of being at the school. School records indicated that members of this tribe had the highest drop-out rate of any tribe at the institution. Overall, as a group they seemed to be a system in a high degree of disorganization and chaos.

In both the coal mines and the Indian school there were some similar consequences of group boundaries breaking down. Overt conflict was heightened. Among the miners, noteworthy strains were observed among men with different roles and between adjacent shifts of workers. Members of the culturally-depressed Indian tribe fought more with members of their own tribe and with other tribes at the school than did other groups. Member attitudes in underbounded systems tend to be pessimistic, especially with regard to themselves. Miners found their work less satisfying after the breakup of the marrow groups. Only after the formation of new groups did some of the older members say they expected to have a longer work career as a result of the change. Members of the hostile Indian tribe reported the greatest drop in self and heritage esteem of any tribe in the school. Neither miners nor Indians were effective in using special technologies introduced to further individual and system benefits. The conventional longwall method of obtaining coal turned out to be much less effective than originally expected, and the boarding school could not educate or in other ways help Indian students who were dropping out. The breakdown of group boundaries spelled dismal consequences for individual members and for the larger social system in which they were embedded.

Comparison of Over and Underbounded Systems

In terms of boundary conditions, over and underbounded systems are nearly mirror opposites, but deeper examination of the two system conditions indicates that the two kinds of pathologies are not so simply specified. The foregoing quantitative studies plus clinical data from a number of organizational diagnoses identify a number of specific parameters which more precisely differentiate the two conditions. They are authority, role definition, communication, human energy, affect, economic condition and time span of concern.

Both kinds of systems evidence problems with authority. In overbounded systems the nature of authority is well-defined, often profusely detailed. There is relatively little doubt about who can make which decisions or who reports to whom. The result is that overbounded sysems frequently constrain initiatives from below, and needed information is held only by those authorized to do so. In contrast, the nature of authority in underbounded systems is typically unclear. Sometimes it appears as though several individuals and groups hold responsibility for the same thing. Other times needed work does not get done because no one has been assigned to do it.

Closely related to problems of authority are those of *role definition*. In overbounded systems member roles are too finely specified, taking away many opportunities for enlarging the use of one's abilities from naturally occurring events. Underbounded systems suffer from members being uncertain about any limits or priorities in their work. As a result, they tend not to plan effectively and often respond to events on a crisis basis.

Difficulties with the management of human *energy* also vary as a function of system boundaries. Underbounded systems typically have difficulties harnessing energy to do work. People are often geographically dispersed and pulled in so many ways by conflicting pressures that they find difficulty in moving decisively in any single direction. Overbounded systems have problems releasing the energy that is contained within them. While they frequently do not lack resources, the members of overbounded systems find themselves blocked from moving by system boundaries which become barriers.

Communication problems also differ as a function of boundary conditions. Members of overbounded systems have comparatively few problems meeting with one another or engaging in face-to-face interaction. Their difficulties arise because of what and how they communicate. They distort and withhold information from each other, often engaging in elaborate games that may give the appearance of valid exchange, but beneath the surface they serve mainly to enhance self-interest of the communicator. Members of underbounded systems are more likely not to meet to discuss common problems. Diffusion of authority, role definition and energy keep people apart in underbounded systems.

The nature of the *affect* experienced and expressed also varies under different boundary conditions. In overbounded systems member affect tends to be experienced as ego and ethnocentrism; individuals and groups are inclined to attribute positive qualities to themselves and ingroups and negative qualities to others and outgroups. Emotional expression also tends to be generally more suppressed (or repressed) in overbounded systems. Emotional expression in underbounded systems is less constrained than in overbounded systems and is of a different quality. The affective experiences of people who belong to underbounded systems tend to be more dominantly negative than those in overbounded systems. Targets for the hostile and anxious feelings experienced by individuals and groups in underbounded systems tend to be both themselves and others. They tend to be both intra and extrapunitive. In this sense, the members of underbounded systems tend to be less ego and ethnocentric than members of overbounded systems, but the tendency for extremely under and overbounded systems to transform themselves rapidly into their *opposite* condition may mean that an underbounded system of today with little ego or ethnocentrism may become an overbounded system of tomorrow with a great deal of ego and ethnocentrism.

Over and underbounded systems also tend to differ with respect to *economic* condition. Overbounded systems tend to have more certain and wealthier economic positions than underbounded systems (Aldrich, 1971). Underbounded systems are typically shorter of funds and live with greater uncertainty about sources of income than overbounded systems. This property is tied to the relationship between physical and psychological boundaries. Ultimately, the loss of economic support threatens the physical boundaries of a system.

Finally, over and underbounded systems differ in the *time span* of their hazards. Underbounded systems continually face issues of survival. They live with a crisis-oriented mentality. Overbounded systems typically do not face short-run disaster. Their danger comes from a slowly increasing loss of capacity to cope with forces impinging upon them. As time passes, overbounded systems become less able to recognize and respond to problems that confront them.

III. IMPLICATIONS FOR THE CONDUCT OF ORGANIZATIONAL DIAGNOSIS

The preceding sections offered a definition of organizational diagnosis and a set of concepts for understanding organizational behavior. This last section explores the implications of the definition and analysis for the conduct of organizational diagnoses. It relates a point of view about organizations to the series of strategic choices that must be made in the diagnostic process. Under and overbounded systems are sufficiently different that methods which facilitate effective diagnosis in one kind of setting often inhibit it in another, and vice versa.

Entry in Under and Overbounded Systems

Entry into a system usually begins by contacts with the leadership. In overbounded systems, formal leaders usually have the authority to commit their units to a diagnostic project, but in underbounded systems it may even be difficult to find out who all the relevant leaders are. A diagnostician entering an overbounded system may be tempted to accept the invitation of those in formal command rather than negotiating a separate agreement with each sector of the system. He usually has the option, however, of finding out who all the relevant groups and individuals are simply by asking for an organization chart. If the leadership decides they want to proceed with a diagnosis, he can make his agreement contingent on acceptance of the project by others in the system (Kahn and Mann, 1952).

On entering an underbounded system, the diagnostician often

may *not* find an organization chart to guide his thinking about how to proceed with entry. Significant people may not be present at his introductory meeting, and he may find himself facing pressures to become aligned with one or more conflicting individuals or groups. If the diagnostician does not recognize these signs or fails to act quickly to make contact with the relevant conflicting parties, he may find that his capacity to establish trustworthy contacts with certain parts of the system is severely impaired (Lewicki and Alderfer, 1973).

One way a diagnostician has to bridge the gap between his own standing outside the system and the interacting groups inside is to form a liaison group consisting of representatives from all relevant groups. This group then becomes something like a microcosm of the system being studied, but the ease with which such a group can be formed varies with whether the total system tends toward being over or underbounded. For underbounded systems such a group will be harder to form because people will be less accustomed to regular interaction with each other, and the liaison group will be more like an intervention. Thus, in underbounded systems the diagnostician may have to establish a series of relationships with individuals to maintain liaison rather than being able to work with a group representing a cross section of the system.

The greater diffusion of energy characteristic of underbounded systems implies that the diagnostician may have to invest more time and energy to determine whether diagnosis is feasible than he would in an overbounded system. Pragmatically this means that it will take more exploratory meetings to reach a decision about proceeding. The poorer economic picture of underbounded systems also suggests that the financial costs of a diagnosis will be more problematic in underbounded systems than in overbounded systems.

Because diagnosis begins with entry, the diagnostician's initial inference about the kind of system he is facing is quite important in determining his mode of proceeding.

Data Collection in Underbounded and Overbounded Systems

The major purpose of data collection activities is to obtain valid information about member experiences with a system. In pursuit of this goal, the diagnostician potentially has in his tool kit all the traditional methods of social science—archival records, observational systems, various types of interviews and questionnaires—but these technologies produce useful information only if they are employed in ways that recognize that research itself is a social process which requires active cooperation among investigators and respondents.

Superficially, the collection of information from organization members may be an easier task in overbounded than in underbounded systems. The more structured authority relations of overbounded systems make it possible for high-ranking leaders to order all members to attend a meeting to answer questionnaires. A great deal of the data on which the field of organizational psychology rests comes from just such events, but while one may order an employee to a room, there is little that management can do to require a person to answer questions that honestly reflect real experiences with the system (Argyris, 1970). There are some other generalizations about data collection that apply to both under and overbounded systems.

The last several years have witnessed not only a great recognition of the reactive effects of much of social research, but also the development of methods that permit and encourage greater real participation of respondents in the design and utilization of research instruments (Maslow, 1966; Argyris, 1970; Kelman, 1968, 1972; Alderfer, 1968; Alderfer and Brown, 1972). Results from these studies suggest that investigators can obtain more valid data if they employ certain types of methods sequentially. Data about the more threatening aspects of organizational behavior become more accessible by more structured methods if these techniques are used *after* a period of data collection by less structured methods.

Unstructured, open-ended data collection methods by participant observation and nondirective interviewing serve several functions in the early phases of a diagnostic study. Their use can decrease the likelihood that investigators impose preconceived ideas on respondents and thereby overdetermine the content of information. Their use also helps to make researchers better listener-observers of how members experience and behave in their systems. Inevitably, when the diagnosticians behave as effective listeners, respondents become more motivated to provide accurate information. In part, this happens because rapport between investigator and respondent decreases threat, but it also happens because, as the diagnostician becomes more knowledgeable about the system, respondents sense that it will be more difficult to mislead him. If more fixed response, statistically-oriented instruments are used later rather than earlier in the study, researchers can examine the convergent validity obtained by different instruments which purport to measure the same trait (Campbell and Fiske, 1959) after having reduced one major source of method variance that arises from problematic features in the client-researcher relationship.

The ease with which more structured instruments can be used in underbounded settings is probably less than in overbounded systems despite whatever gains can be achieved in relationship improvement by using unstructured methods first. The disorganization present in many underbounded systems makes it difficult to establish standard conditions for administering research instruments. Morever, underbounded systems are likely to include participants whose educational differences are very great, thereby raising the issue of whether identical questions would be understood in the same way by different respondents.

While sequencing methods promotes greater empathy between the investigators and clients, many studies have more than role differences present. The group identifications of investigators also influence their ease of creating mutual understanding with clients. Race, for example, has repeatedly been demonstrated to affect the nature of data obtained in social surveys (Hyman, 1954; Schuman and Hatchett, 1974). Underbounded systems are often likely to contain members whose group identifications differ from university-trained diagnosticians. One way to bridge such group identification differences is to form diagnostic teams whose members share many of the same group identification differences as system members. Another way is to find liaison people from the client systems with individuals who are able to help the researchers understand the views of people quite different from themselves.

Feedback in Underbounded and Overbounded Systems

Data feedback serves several functions. It is the time when investigators report their findings back to the client system where it was obtained, usually by a series of meetings designed to facilitate full exploration and joint understanding of data. These sessions provide members with another opportunity to see and question the analyses of their system which the outsiders have developed. Feedback sessions provide at least two ways to confirm or disconfirm the validity of diagnostic results. On the one hand, clients may agree or disagree with the results. On the other hand, their behavior in the meetings may reproduce or refute hypothesized system dynamics. Feedback also serves as a link between diagnosis and action. It may be the terminal event between client and consultant or it may mark the beginning of a new phase in the relationship in which action is taken based on the findings (Alderfer and Brown, 1974).

As a general rule, feedback sessions are likely to provoke some defensiveness and resistance from clients (Alderfer and Ferriss, 1972). Resistance may mean that clients are reluctant to accept *the truth* as reported by diagnosticians, or it may mean that the diagnosis is limited or wrong. The tendency for human beings to resist painful insights is no less true among diagnosticians than it is among clients. Because the nature of feedback may promote an adversary relationship between client and consultant, it is desirable if clients and consultants can develop an atmopshere of mutual exploration of data and analyses. Two means that facilitate these ends are: (1) the information presented is minimally inferential and (2) to offer explanations for the data presented tentatively as hypotheses or

themes for discussion rather than as final conclusions. The feedback meetings then may become settings where clients are
encouraged to produce additional data to confirm or disconfirm
the findings for *each other* rather than for the consultants.

The design of feedback meetings depends on both the nature
of the findings and the social system where the information was
collected. Probably the most common group method for feedback
is bringing people together in *family groups* of superior and subordinates. Issues most effectively discussed in this kind of setting
pertain to the internal dynamics of the work team, *provided*
that enough trust already exists in the group to permit exploration of such subjects (Mann, 1957; Schmuck and Miles, 1971).
To feedback data pertaining to the wider social system, a series
of meetings with people who share common problems but do
not necessarily report to the same superior may also be arranged.
The peer group-intergroup method of feedback consists of a
series of meetings which are initially focussed on concerns common to peers in the organization and subsequently directed to
interface problems between different groups in the system
(Alderfer and Holbrook, 1973). The peer group-intergroup
method may be employed when broader systems issues are of
primary concern and when family group meetings are inhibited
by lack of confidence between superiors and subordinates.

Differences between feedback in over and underbounded
systems may arise in two ways—the need for intervention prior
to feedback and the role of cognition in feedback meetings.
Because of the more ambiguous authority relations and the
generally higher level of conflict in underbounded systems, it
may be necessary to intervene in some human relationships prior
to feedback simply to insure that relevant parties appear at
meetings. In one case diagnosticians employed third party peacemaking (Walton, 1969) to work through tensions between a
supervisor-subordinate pair in a public agency prior to their
meeting with a larger group to discuss issues of interagency
relations. Both parties had acknowledged that problems existed
between them before the feedback meeting, and it seemed that

feedback about more systemic issues would be facilitated by the intervention.

The higher level of emotionality in underbounded systems somewhat changes the more common relationship between experiential and cognitive learning that is followed in group relations education. Usually diagnosticians attempt to generate data before presenting concepts and theories to aid people in understanding their experiences. The function of new data or experience is often implicitly to raise questions with individuals about existing ways of making sense of their experience. In overbounded systems this sequence also serves to release suppressed emotionality, but in underbounded systems the problem is often less that of releasing pent-up feelings and more that of containing disruptive conflict. Consequently the design of feedback sessions for underbounded systems may begin with intellectual work. This approach may reassure people that some understanding of their system can be had and thereby permit them to explore additional issues with greater security.

CONCLUSIONS

Organizational diagnosis proceeds in three phases from entry to data collection to feedback. At each stage in the diagnostic process the professional has choices about the degree of intervention appropriate to the system being studied. The diagnostician should intervene only as much as is necessary to complete the diagnostic study effectively no matter how promising an opportunity to effect constructive change is perceived.

The diagnostician also confronts choices about which techniques to employ at each stage of the diagnostic process. The nature of system boundaries exerts a powerful effect on the kinds of human problems to be uncovered by diagnosis. Specifically, underbounded systems present a different syndrome of difficulties than overbounded systems, and the nature of system boundaries influences which approaches to entry, data collection and feedback may be used most fruitfully. Under some conditions it is appropriate to use methods that mirror system characteristics in order to obtain a valid picture of the organization. Under other conditions, it is more effective to use methods that counteract systemic tendencies in order to prevent organizational patterns from undermining the diagnostic mission.

REFERENCES

Alderfer, C. P.: Change processes in organizations. In Dunnette, M. D. (Ed.): *Handbook of Industrial and Organizational Psychology.* Chicago, Rand, 1975.

Alderfer, C. P.: The relevance of human intellect and organizational power for organizational development. In Adams, J. D. (Ed.): *Theory and Method in OD.* Fairfax, Learning Resources Pr, 1974.

Alderfer, C. P.: Comparison of questionnaire responses with and without preceding interviews. *J Appl Psychol, 52:335-340,* 1968.

Alderfer, C. P., and Brown, L. D.: *Learning from Changing: Organizational Diagnosis and Change.* Beverly Hills, California, Sage, 1975.

Alderfer, C. P., and Brown, L. D.: Designing an empathetic questionnaire for organizational research. *J Appl Psychol, 56:456-460,* 1972.

Alderfer, C. P., and Ferriss, R.: Understanding the impact of survey feedback. In Hornstein, H., and Burke, W. (Eds.): *The Social Technology of Organizational Development.* Fairfax, Learning Resources Pr, 1972, pp. 234-243.

Alderfer, C. P.; Hammerschlag, C.; Berg, D., and Fisher, S.: Group relations and the expression of aggression among American Indians. Unpublished manuscript, 1972.

Alderfer, C. P., and Holbrook, J.: A new design for survey feedback. *Education and Urban Society, 5:437-464,* 1973.

Aldrich, H.: Organizational boundaries and interorganizational conflict. *Human Relations, 24:279-293,* 1971.

Argyris, C.: *Intervention Theory and Method.* Reading, A-W, 1970.

Argyris, C.: *Interpersonal Competence and Organizational Effectiveness.* Homewood, Irwin-Dorsey, 1962.

Beckhard, R.: *Strategies of Organizational Development.* Reading, A-W, 1969.

Bennis, W. G.: *Changing Organizations.* New York, McGraw, 1966.

Berrien, F. K.: *General and Social Systems.* New Brunswick, Rutgers U Pr, 1968.

Bray, D. W.; Campbell, R. J., and Grant, D. L.: *Formative Years in Business.* New York, Wiley, 1974.

Campbell, D. T., and Fiske, D. W.: Convergent and discriminant validity by the multitrait-multimethod matrix. *Psychol Bull, 56:81-105,* 1959.

Friedlander, F., and Brown, L. D.: Organization development. In Mussen,

P. H., and Rosenzweig, M. R. (Eds.): *Ann Rev Psychol,* 25:313-341, 1974.

Glickman, A. S.: *The Career Motivation Survey: Overall Attitude and Re-enlistment Trends.* Washington, United States Navy Personnel Research Field Activity (Research Report 61-2), June, 1961.

Hornstein, H. A.; Bunker, B. A.; Burke, W.; Hornstein, M., and Lewicki, R. J.: *Strategies of Social Intervention.* New York, The Free Press, 1971.

Hyman, H. H.: *Interviewing in Social Research.* Chicago, U of Chicago Pr, 1954.

Kahn, R., and Mann, F.: Developing research partnerships. *J Soc Iss,* 8:4-10, 1952.

Kelman, H. C.: The rights of the subject in social research. *Am Psychol,* 27:989-1016, 1972.

Kelman, H. C.: *A Time to Speak.* San Francisco, Jossey-Bass, 1968.

Lawrence, P. R., and Lorsch, J.: *Developing Organizations: Diagnosis and Action.* Reading, A-W, 1969.

Levine, R. A., and Campbell, D. T.: *Ethnocentrism: Theories of Conflict, Ethnic Attitudes, and Group Behavior.* New York, Wiley, 1972.

Levinson, H.: *Organizational Diagnosis.* Cambridge, Harvard U Pr, 1972.

Lewicki, R., and Alderfer, C. P.: The tensions between research and intervention in intergroup conflict. *J Appl Behav Sci,* 9:424-449, 463-468, 1973.

Mahler, W. R.: *Diagnostic Studies.* Reading, A-W, 1974.

Mann, F. C.: Studying and creating change: A means to understanding social organization. In Arensberg, C., *et al.*: *Research in Industrial Human Relations.* New York, Harper and Brothers, 1957.

Margulies, N., and Raia, A. P.: *Organizational Development: Values, Process and Technology.* New York, McGraw, 1972.

Maslow, A. H.: *The Psychology of Science.* New York, Har-Row, 1966.

Rice, A. K.: *The Enterprise and Its Environment.* London, Tavistock, 1963.

Rogers, C. R.: *On Becoming a Person.* Boston, HM, 1961.

Schein, E. H.: *Process Consultation: Its Role in Organization Development.* Reading, A-W, 1969.

Schmuck, R. A., and Miles, M. B.: *OD in Schools.* Palo Alto, Nat Pr, 1971.

Schuman, H., and Hatchett, S.: *Black Racial Attitudes, Trends and Complexities.* Ann Arbor, U of Mich, 1974.

Sieber, S. D.: The integration of fieldwork and survey methods. *Am J Sociol,* 78:1335-1359, 1973.

Trist, E. L.; Higgin, G. W.; Murray, H., and Pollock, A. B.: *Organizational Choice: Capabilities of Groups at the Coal Face Under Changing Technologies.* London, Tavistock, 1963.

Walton, R.: *Interpersonal Peacemaking: Confrontations and Third-Party Consultation.* Reading, A-W, 1969.

Chapter 8

SELF-MANAGING SYSTEMS, Z.E.G. AND OTHER UNTHINKABLES*

Bernard M. Bass

It is impossible to talk about humanizing the organization without looking at what has been happening to industrialized society worldwide and what is likely to happen during the years to come. Since the last APA the energy problem has become the energy crisis, and the pollution crisis has become the pollution problem. As have New Zealanders, Norwegians and Oregonians on occasion, we may vote for slower rates of economic growth in the interests of maintaining a better environment. To conserve increasingly expensive nonrenewable resources and to reduce pollution we may be forced to slow down United States economic growth from the average long-term 3 percent rise per year to say 2 percent or less with possibly extended periods of zero growth, and this long-term economic change is likely to have humanizing or dehumanizing effects on industrial organizations depending on what we can do about it.

POSSIBLE CONSEQUENCES OF ZERO ECONOMIC GROWTH

If this thinking is unthinkable, Day (1973), Chief, Demographic and Social Statistics for the United Nations, has examined

* Address presented by Bernard M. Bass at the symposium on Humanizing Organizational Psychology at the convention of the American Psychological Association in New Orleans, 1974.

in detail the social consequences of *zero economic growth* (Z.E.G.) if such should become naturally or as a matter of policy the future state of industrialized society.

Toynbee (1974) sees such a slowing down of GNP in the developed countries as inevitable. The barbarians knocking at the gates of the Newest Rome are the developing nations who have the resources to develop. Industrialized Rome will be pushed into decline by the rising developing nations. Inside the Newest Rome, as Toynbee sees ahead, conflict will increase to partake of the increasingly scarce goods and services that remain. In a siege economy, dictated by severe regimentation, salvation will come beyond freedom and dignity by turning to new spiritual concerns. Presumably we shall move into a new medievalism with feudal multinational organizations. We shall be loyal to our firm, not to our country.

At the other extreme from Toynbee are those who still believe that a technological utopia lies ahead. The current pollution and energy problems will long since have disappeared by the turn of the century as a consequence of man's scientific genius (Geiger, 1973).

Although we may see neither the fall of the Newest Rome nor technoutopia, we are likely to experience a near future in which

1. Real incomes grow more slowly than heretofore for the current work force.
2. Taxation to provide public services increases to the point that it is confiscatory at higher levels. (The United Kingdom currently and Scandanavia to some degree have already achieved these levels, and it wouldn't take much more for those in New York to feel close to this.) At the same time, health, education and welfare become available for the asking.
3. The cost of nonrenewable resources, pollution and taxes continues to rise in the absence of increased purchasing power; goods become increasingly expensive.
4. Progress and growth norms are replaced by survival and maintenance norms.

5. While psychologists increasingly experiment with ways to connect compensation received with performance accomplished (sophisticated piece rates) social forces push in the opposite direction to increasingly divorce compensation from work done. Financial inducements and benefits become more difficult for organizations to provide and are weaker in their effects.

A slowing down of growth of the GNP does not imply reducing all of us to beggary. Rather, it may mean that more of us are forced to live in apartments, to give up the second automobile, and to use returnable bottles. This can come about as a consequence of free market forces as well as through legislated national economic policy.

The slowing down in the rate of increase in income and standard of living can yield an unfavorable present in contrast with the past. A sense of relative deprivation may cast a pall. The outlook of the 13 million unemployed during the Great Depression or the masses of underemployed in India today may give some insight into the potential for a psychological mass depression. Fewer jobs and overqualified job occupants with the threat of discharge hanging over one's head are real dehumanizing possibilities, but there is an alternative.

ECONOMIC AND SOCIAL DETERMINANTS OF ORGANIZATIONAL OBJECTIVES

In 1952 the writer suggested that the ultimate criterion of a firm's success should be measured by the extent the firm provides satisfactions for its various constituent members and clients, owners, managers, employees, customers and the community-at-large (Bass, 1952).

Henry Manne (1973) is a most outspoken critic of this position, mirroring the thinking of Friedman (1962), Hayek (1960), Kelso and Adler (1958) and Powlison (1950). Any business expenditure for social responsibility (apart from the good will it may earn) is a nonprofit maximizing expenditure, and in a free market for products, corporate managements who pursue such social responsibility in a substantial way against the self-interests of their stockholders may risk losing out in the competitive market of stockholders.

> . . . the corporate system requries that, by and large, companies be operated exclusively in the interest of the shareholders. . . . As shareholder dissatisfaction grows, market forces, working invisibly and automatically, provide the correct solutions. . . . This market for corporate control functions in various ways, most prominently through tender offers, proxy fights, and mergers. In its less overt form it constantly pressures corporate executives to operate the company in the shareholders' interest. . . . (Manne, 1973).

Many scholars beginning with the Berle and Means (1968) seminal attack on big business and including Phillips (1963), Reder (1947), Gordon (1961), Simon (1957) and Dent (1959) share my position as do a majority of a sample of 3,453 subscribers to the *Harvard Business Review.*

> Only a small minority feel that a corporation's duty is only to its owners, as described in nearly all classical business doctrine. More than 60% believe that the interests of owners must be served in competition with interests of three other groups—i.e., employees, customers, and the public (Ewing, 1971).

Nevertheless, I have a strong feeling that the incentives to manage firms to satisfy the interests of the different groups depend on the respondent's beliefs about their mutual interdependence. Supposedly it is good for business to have satisfied customers and employees; supposedly employee morale is good for employee productivity, but we know that the correlation between morale and productivity can range from low negative to high positive. At the same time, when profits are threatened, concerns for employee welfare are likely to diminish. Concern for good human relations may increase with the profitability rather than vice versa. The pursuit of work nonmaterial satisfactions seems to thrive and is tolerated by materialists mainly in prosperous times. Come a recession with company belt-tightening, and everyone knows what can happen to programs to improve job satisfaction (Bass, Binder and Breed, 1967).

HUMANIZING ORGANIZATIONS AND
NATIONAL POLICIES

However, we could have long-term economic recession without long-term psychological depression. Although the earth materially may need to be maintained as a system in homeostasis rather than as a growing system, nevertheless, limits do not need to be maintained on the growth of psychic inputs of new information and psychic ouputs of added nonmaterial satisfactions. We need to start getting more psychic *bang for the buck*—more psychic rewards from the same expenditures of energy and nonrenewable resources.

What is also needed is more selective material growth. There can be a continued rise in per capita income and real welfare by shifting from goods production to services and leisure, from status-display goods (i.e., auto fender fins) to intrinsically satisfying goods (i.e., sturdier fenders), from polluting and resource-wasting goods to pollution-combatting and resources-conserving goods, and from population growth to Z.P.G.

What is also needed in a capitalist society is a strong survivalist orientation with a government active particularly on behalf of future generations since individuals pursuing their own short-term interests cannot deal with long-term environmental adversities (Benoit, 1974).

John Stuart Mill said the same thing and said it better in his *Principles of Political Economy* first published in 1848. Mill (1896) examined the "stationary state of wealth and population." It was a state "dreaded and deprecated" by most economists of his day. Nevertheless, he did not find it undesirable. On the contrary, he noted that the increase of wealth is not boundless; the stationary state ultimately is unavoidable. Nevertheless, most economists of his day looked at such a termination of growth as ending in shallows and miseries. However, he declared,

> I am not charmed with the ideal of life held out by those who think that the normal state of human beings is that of struggling to get on; that the trampling, crushing, elbowing, and treading on each other's heels . . . are the most desirable lot of human kind. (They are) the disagreeable symptoms of one of the phases of industrial progress (Mill, 1896).

Coupled with a policy promoting zero population growth and protection of the environment Mill advocated for his stationary society a progressive redistribution of wealth to generate an affluent working class so they could also "cultivate the graces of life."

Further, he argues that,

> If the earth must lose that great portion of its pleasantness which it owes to things that the unlimited increase of wealth and population would extirpate from it, for the mere purpose of enabling it to support a larger, but not a better or happier population, I sincerely hope, for the sake of posterity, that they will be content to be stationary long before necessity compels them to it (Mill, 1896).

There would be in a stationary world as much scope as ever for all kinds of "mental culture, and moral and social progress; as much room for improving the Art of Living, as much more likelihood of its being improved, when minds ceased to be engrossed by the art of getting on" (Mill, 1896).

Currently, when we look at living standards, the measurement of consequence is Gross National Product per capita. The more goods and services produced by a country for each of its inhabitants, the higher the index and, therefore, the higher the standard of living. The pursuit of happiness is measured by a materialistic criterion. The social and human costs of producing the goods and services are not accounted for. Humanistic values per se are irrelevant to GNP except to the extent that a high GNP per capita signifies a relatively rich country with surpluses of goods and services beyond what are required for meeting the needs for survival and security. And in wealthier countries more concerns for social values occur according to a survey we completed among AISEC students in five Western European countries of varying national GNP's per capita (Bass and Franke, 1972).

Suppose that in addition to constraining GNP, through changes in national policy, economic legislation forced up the price of goods based on nonrenewable resources and, at the same time, services in health, education and welfare were promoted by policy (i.e., subsidized) since their consumption does not pollute or use up resources. As part of this promotion, firms would receive tax credits for their contributions to health, education and welfare. For example, health tax credits could be given for the medical services, safety and occupational health records maintained by firms. Education subsidies or tax credits could be given for adult education programs organized by the firms (as is done in France). Firms would receive welfare tax advantages for transferring employees to training cadres (as Japanese firms do) instead of laying them off because of seasonal slowdowns in demand. The goods of those countries that did not subscribe to such policies would have to be dealt with by tariff policies in those countries that did.

If the pursuit of happiness is to be promoted by national policy, then again firms could be rewarded for the extent to which they provide satisfying rather than dissatisfying jobs in the same type of occupation. Tax credits could be tied to absenteeism and avoidable quit rates. Just as research support, assistance and tax benefits can be applied in increasing dosages to reduce costs associated with oil exploration and production so similar inducements could be provided for increasing job satisfaction and better interpersonal relations. As firms were finding it increasingly difficult to offer financial benefits for work done and had to turn to offering interpersonal and personal inducements as well as rewards intrinsic to the work itself, they would find support at the national level in fiscal and monetary policies that rewarded the firms for their humanistic contributions.

Increased humanization may be one of the significant consequences of a national policy that slows up material growth rates. Curiously, contrary to McClelland (1961), Franke (1974) makes a much stronger case for showing that lack of need affiliation themes in children's readers of 1925 forecasts growth of Gross National Product in the ten big rich countries ($r = -.82$) rather than themes of need achievement which are also negatively related ($-.45$) to growth. Dehumanization (as seen in low need affiliation themes in children's readers in 1925) gave rise to rapid economic growth from 1950 to 1968.

Heretofore, we have always been asking what it takes to push for more GNP. McClelland thought it might be through promoting high need achievement. Franke more accurately shows it might better be from promoting low need affiliation. If Franke is right and there are cause-effect linkages between the themes, ideologies and norms that emerge that motivate productivity per capita, we may need to start promoting more need affiliation in today's children for the next generation. They will be better suited for a world of slow or zero economic growth rates. Such high concern for affiliation presumably will be consistent with humanizing the organization.

As for long-term economic trends and political possibilities outside the firm that could enhance humanization trends inside the firm, it has been stated that in the world to come we will need to pay more attention to nonmaterialistic rewards within the firm. This effort can be enhanced by national policies that reinforce the social responsibilities of private enterprise and reward maintaining a broadened outlook towards the ultimate criteria of organizational success.

REFORMATION AND COUNTERREFORMATION

Now, to look at the current scene where Hegelian dialectics may be at work. The humanistic reformation of the 1960's may be threatened by a materialistic counterreformation in the 1970's. Needed may be a new synthesis—self-managing systems.

Between the first edition in 1965 of *Organizational Psychology* (Bass, 1965) and the forthcoming second edition in 1976 (Bass and Ryterband, 1976) the Division of Industrial Psychology has become the Division of Industrial and Organizational Psychology. More sophisticated theories of organization and of leadership have been formulated and tested. The systems approach to organizations has become a common point of view.

Motivation to work is seen as a complex function of what the employee expects to get from working, how much he values what he thinks he can get, his experience in succeeding as a consequence of his performance, and whether he has alternative ways of obtaining what he wants. Different segments of the work force seek different satisfactions from work (Porter, Lawler, and Hackman, 1975).

The decade has also been marked by societal changes of consequence. Organizing for health, education and welfare has become much more salient. Concern for more efficient delivery of services to the consumers and also the workers has increased greatly. At the same time (articulated by Lawler, Levinson and Hall last year at the symposium: Humanizing Organizational Psychology, 1973), increasing consideration is being given to the potential alienation of the manual worker and the career concerns of the manager. Automation of routine work has become the rule rather than the exception. Affirmative action programs for upgrading the disadvantaged minorities, particularly women and black employees, have increased greatly the focus on understanding what elements in a job environment can be modified to accommodate the needs and abilities of a wider range of job applicants. A variety of flexible alternatives to the eight-hour day, five-day work week are being introduced. Internationalization has proceeded as rapidly as forecast. We are now likely to discover as many or more innovations in organization in Sweden, Japan and Yugoslavia as in the United States.

Organizational development, the process involved in organizational improvement, has grown from the practice of a few pioneering consultants to a network of 1300 external and internal organizational change agents.

Indeed, we have humanized industrial psychology to a considerable degree in the past decade. Nevertheless, we are faced with a counterreformation against a humanistic approach to work and organizational life. Thus, *Newsweek* (April 29, 1974) brands concern about worker alienation as "sociological chic of the 1970's." Three Rutgers' psychiatrists claim that 95 percent of assembly line workers at a General Motors plant in Baltimore are satisfied with their jobs and 71 percent find no part of their job to be tiring or upsetting. The job is not a source of meaning but a means toward enjoying other pursuits and security. This is corroborated in a four-country survey of automobile assembly line workers. Particularly in the less affluent countries of Argentina and Italy, work on the assembly line is seen as a way to spend the day which is less boring than staying away from work (*Human Behavior*, April, 1974).

Commenting on the Rutgers findings, the *Wall Street Journal* has this to say,

> . . . They seem to be closer to the truth than previous explanations that often bordered on pop sociology.
> A re-reading of some of the more popular literature on the subject makes it pretty clear that a good many interpreters took workers' natural gripes and complaints far too seriously.
> After all, what job isn't without its less pleasant aspects? What occupation isn't less than stimulating eight hours a day?
> What worker, or for that matter, what chairman of the board, doesn't sometimes feel that his efforts are insufficiently rewarded or appreciated?
> Some people will probably always try to get by on as little effort as possible. But many people still take pride in the work they do for a living and most people would seem to be reasonably satisfied.
> Assembly line workers, as the Rutgers medical team discovered, are not that much different.
> Actually, what is probably more prevalent than "blue collar blues" is the alienation from middle class values of certain social critics, especially those who project their own dissatisfaction onto reasonably contented workers (*Wall Street Journal*, May, 1974).

United Auto Workers' president, Leonard Woodcock, is quoted as saying that concern for blue-collar blues is nothing more than "elitist nonsense" by some scholars and journalists. Labor on the left and economists on the right join hands in the cry that job satisfaction is determined by whatever is put into the paycheck (Sheppard, 1971).

Everybody and everything has a price. If you want an all-volunteer army, all you need to do is to buy it. If 35 percent of Ford workers at its small and intermediate automobile assembly plants exercise their option to refuse to work overtime beyond fifty hours a week (*Democrat and Chronicle*, Rochester, New York, April 27, 1974), it's because the increment in their pay for such overtime is too low. Raise the increment if you want them to work the extra time. If Winston Churchill's lady friend won't sleep with him for £5, she will for £10,000. This really defines the problem for the counterreformation.

What's the price? The fact that such prices are meaningless impossibilities is irrelevant since the problem as posed by the counterreformation has been solved, but in the real world, when

Volvo was faced with high rates of absenteeism, wage increases which might reduce such absenteeism would have bankrupted the company. Willingness to keep working on the assembly line was seen to be much more readily affected by making the job itself more attractive through enlargement and team organization.

The counterreformation would treat organizing in the same way. The secretary-boss relationship is inefficient. The secretary has to stop typing to answer the telephone or to run errands. Put her in a large typing pool with the best available equipment so that she and the other former secretaries are members of a formal administrative service with allegiance to that service unit, not to her former boss. She now can spend full time on her formal duties. Ignored are all the negative effects of dehumanizing the secretary's role as well as all the extra informal functions she performed, releasing her boss from being tied down with many of the details of his office. Ignored are the human values contributed by a close secretary-boss relationship of mutual benefit to both (Bass and Baker, 1962).

The counterreformation sees planning as the prerogative of financial and marketing specialists fully equipped with a variety of forecasting models. What need for interpersonal chitchat when you can spell out what objectives need to be met and the mathematically optimal way to meet those objectives? Ignore as messy trivialities the many payoffs from bottoms-up planning such as higher productivity, greater creativity, more commitment, more confirmatory behavior and better understanding of what needs to be done (Bass, 1970).

The counterreformation deals with problems of production as simple mechanical problems. Once the problem has been defined in simple terms (give or take a few assumptions about the nature of human motivation, incentives and communications) with a single objective function to maximize the present value of the firm, then a mathematical model can be applied to provide the answer to the problem. But, as Ackoff (1972) notes, managers who solve such neatly-defined problems still have a mess on their hands because the "problem" so often is embedded in a larger system of markets, finances, personnel and personal preferences, an organic whole with interrelated parts.

The counterreformation was underway within many departments of psychology during the 1960's. As industrial psychology became stronger in its applications and increasing numbers of psychologists were employed full-time in industry, leading departments of psychology abandoned industrial psychology programs. Although behavioral science has become increasingly visible in management education both at undergraduate levels and in management development programs, it has been taking a beating recently at graduate management schools (the University of Rochester is an extreme example) where the behavioral science focus on limited rationality, subjectivity, relativity of values, small samples and large ambitions make it a target of attack as too soft intellectually for the ivory towers. Last year I spoke at length about the scientism in social science which may be at the core of the counterreformation in academia (Bass, 1974).

An attack from a different quarter by Tausky (1973) suggests that dehumanizing work is in the eye of the beholder, which in turn is conditioned by societal norms. "A shared meaning system can bestow honor and purpose on any activity." Humanizing the organization may not require job enlargement as much as valuing what one is doing in the organization even if it is the most menial of tasks. It is true the Incas could make hoeing potato fields a religious ritual and, therefore, endow the activity with great value, but just how can we endow the many jobholders of jobs in the United States which lack variety, skill demands, discretionary opportunities, prestige and so on with a sense that what they do for a living has purpose, meaning, honor and dignity when our culture in all its forms says just the opposite? The humanistic reformers say let's automate all such jobs out of existence or, if this is not possible, modify the jobs to make them more attractive, or give the job holders the opportunity to move on as soon as possible to more attractive work. The counter-reformers say pay such job holders a competitive wage, a wage higher than they can obtain on any other job open to them.

HUMANISTIC VERSUS MATERIALISTIC
POSITIONS IN MANAGEMENT

There is merit in both the humanistic and materialistic positions. One cannot foresee eliminating all menial work. Both costs and physical constraints bar such a development. Somebody will be needed to collect bed pans for a long time to come. However, we may need to provide higher wages for such unattractive work because fewer applicants will be available to accept such jobs. At the same time, attractive jobs with more applicants can be filled at lower salaries. Bellamy's (1967) solution in 1889 to the problem in *Looking Backward* when far more manual labor was the rule was to create a national service. All able-bodied youth would be expected for a few years to cover these kinds of jobs. We may have to come to Bellamy's solution eventually.

Let's give the materialistic devils their due. Humanistic saints wince when notified that they are not getting an expected salary increase; they agonize over the likely resale of their three-year-old automobile; they are comforted when there is a good surplus in their bank account and worry about just how big a mortgage they can handle on the new house.

Materialists can also point with alarm to the excesses of humanism for the humanistic reformation has spawned the radical Anabaptists of our times whose extremism generates counter-reformatory reactions. Autonomy is translated into anarchy, freedom into license, cooperation into confrontation, influence based on merit into coercion based on power. Intellectual discourse and research are rejected as irrelevant head trips. Professional responsibility is replaced by loyalty to causes.

For the writer the problem is that both the humanist reformers and the counterreformationists are often so dogmatic and single-minded in their beliefs that they fail to see the equipotentiality of outcomes of systems, multiple causation and partial effects. Man for the humanists is the self-actualizing idealist who lives for more than bread alone. For the counterreformation, man is basically a selfish animal best understood in terms of simple pleasure-pain principles which translate into calculi of income and expenses, costs and benefits, and profits and losses. Those of us in organizational psychology are particularly sensitive to how inadequate to account for worker motivation are the materialistic partisans of Adam Smith and Frederick W. Taylor and how inadequate as well are the humanistic partisans of Henry Thoreau and Abe Maslow. For we see that the biggest source of variance often lies in individual differences. In fact, here is the most powerful generalization of all—*People differ in what they expect from their work.* It is for this reason that any movement toward humanization, whenever feasible, needs to try to provide *elective* opportunities, flexible policies, self-planning and optional arrangements. For example, in a survey completed in three companies, a student of the writer found almost two completely polarized camps when he queried professional employees about their desire for collective bargaining. The scientists and engineers were almost all for it; the accountants and the economists were almost all against it.

Curiously such elective opportunities are just what the counterreformationists keep pushing for in the marketplace *outside* the enterprise. Each consumer should be completely free to sink or swim in the free economy. Each worker should be free to negotiate his own wages and terms of employment. Each parent should have vouchers to use in deciding on his children's schooling. The entrepreneur should be free of regulation, but he also should be free to impose his demands on whoever *freely* chooses to work for him or not to work for him. The writer argues here for more freedom *within* the enterprise although not as a free competitive market but rather as a cooperative collectivity of systems, teams or small groups.

The word *elective* is important. Not everyone wants to be master of his own fate. There are many dependent people in this world who are comfortable only when they are satisfied they are doing what they have been told to do. How situational contingencies affect one's desire for autonomy is illustrated by Leon Festinger's comment in Moscow in 1966 that security is knowing that in a room with six lines of waiting people, one is standing in the correct line.

Nevertheless, the freedom to plan for oneself pays off, although not for everyone. For instance, a simulation which made possible comparing the behavior of European managers under planning by self and by others showed generally that self-planning was more efficient, but the differential was much greater in Latin countries than in the United Kingdom, the Low Countries and Scandinavia, and disappeared for Germans for whom both conditions were equally efficient (Bass, 1972).

In a humanistic utopia, powerful moral and aesthetic values guide decision-making so people live in harmony without coercive authority or repression. Each individual can realize his unique potential for self-development. It is plain living and high thinking (Geiger, 1973) and contrasts with a technological utopia where impersonal application of efficiency criteria in decision-making coupled with scientific and technological advances lead to successful coping with all difficulties; rising living standards; and healthy, happy, rational people in a peaceful and well-ordered society. It is plain thinking and high living (Geiger, 1973). In the technological utopia, economies of scale dictate the big organization, but big organization is antithetical to humanistic ideology which stresses small-scale production and worker skill and cooperation rather than hierarchical, impersonal relationships. An organization which is big can't be humanistic; a humanistic organization can't be big.

Nevertheless, the O.D. movement has focuses on how to change a big organization to make it more in accord with humanistic values by reconciling the organization's activities and goals to the needs of the organization's members (Argyris, 1962). It seems more attention could be given to what may be needed to help the organization's members learn to live with organizational imperatives. Simon (1957) is probably right. A hierarchy of some sort is a natural optimal form for large productive organizations. Nevertheless, our culture and counterculture join forces in creating masses of counterdependent future members of the work force. We should be teaching people to understand more about the uses and abuses of authority and how to live with the proper uses and how to cope with the abuses.

The writer ran a two-hour workshop for about forty members of a humanist group. He explained that the purpose was to provide everyone with the experience and the opportunity to share feelings about directing others and following orders. This would then be contrasted with the experience of carrying out a self-planned activity. The first step was for each participant in a twosome to tell his partner what to do for three to five minutes as well as how to do it; then each participant was to monitor and correct the action if the order was not followed to his satisfaction. One young man jumped up and said that what was proposed was unethical; a second took the writer aside and said he just couldn't bring himself around to give someone else an order; a third asked if he could leave. Fortunately, everyone completed both experiences of giving and receiving orders. A number commented on how surprised they were to find that in this situation they were more comfortable following orders rather than taking the responsibility for their own direction. One woman noted that she could and did give herself a much more difficult assignment than she could ask her partner to carry out.

In the same vein, contingent studies of managerial style strongly support the contention that almost every manager is directive at times. No manager is just consultative or just delegative or just participative or just negotiative (Bass and Valenzi, 1974). Directiveness is more likely to be seen among introspective subordinates doing routine tasks in a highly-ordered, tightly-constrained organization. It is more effective with subordinates who seem to be secure in their own sense of fair-mindedness (Bass, 1976).

It seems that before we can humanize the organization we need to do the obvious for both the saints and the devils. We must catalog the boundary conditions when and where humanistic considerations cannot be ignored. Conversely, we need to indicate the limits of materialism and rationalism. Just as we looked earlier at possible economic trends so we also must consider the powerful social trends at work today which may move these boundaries considerably. While the counterreformation tries to return organizations to classic doctrines of the nineteenth century, the humanistic counterculture spreads from college youth to noncollege youth. A sample of 3,522 persons between sixteen and twenty-five, only one third of whom were in college, were interviewed in 1973. Only 56 percent would agree that hard work always pays off, but 79 percent had agreed in a 1969 survey. Conversely, 74 percent would welcome less emphasis on money in 1973 compared to 54 percent in 1969. Yankelovich (1974) sees these expressed values boding major changes at the work place in the coming years. The 1960's generation gap was between college youth and their parents. Today's gap is more likely to be between youth, in general, and their parents. "The new values off campus pose a new and different kind of challenge in the workplace . . . (the young employees') incentives and what they want as payoffs have begun to change."

Chiefly wanted are jobs that provide self-expression and self-fulfillment. Wanted also are opportunities for special education to seek new aspirations. Only three out of ten are optimistic about finding such jobs.

The young employees are less fearful of economic insecurity, but they assume that their employers cannot or will not provide security. They are inclined to take less crap than older workers, are less responsive to hierarchical discipline and fear of being fired, and are not as automatically loyal to their organizations. They are much more cognizant of their own needs and rights (Yankelovich, 1974).

In the original manuscript of a chapter Ed Ryterband and the writer prepared for Dunnette's "Work and Nonwork in the Year 2001" (Bass and Ryterband, 1973), he envisaged the world of the twenty-first century divided politically into the haves and the have-nots. Hopefully it was lack of space that forced Dunnette to omit the final paragraph. This excised soothsaying forecast that

> . . . some of us will be working harder than ever in more complex and challenging jobs than we face today. But gratifications from creative success experiences at work will be comparably greater. The boundaries between work and play for the creative elite will be less distinct than they are today. At the same time, for those who cannot find work satisfying, greater opportunities will exist for leisure and play with minimally secure guaranteed incomes.

Greater polarization is likely between those who become more committed and dedicated to work, science, art and business and those who opt to "drop out." Many of the young "drop outs" of today will be the old "drop outs" of 2000 A.D. Post-industrial society may come to have grudgingly accepted the legitimacy of their position by 2000 A.D. but the political lines of the 21st century may indeed be drawn between those whose life goals center around inner experiences, play, leisure and social relations.

Geiger (1973) has gone way beyond me suggesting a three-class society for the twenty-first century—the elites, the leisured nonelites and the dissenting groups. The elites would be the self-actualizing achievers with a redemptive mission to further social progress and individual improvement. Achievement and rationality would be the binding motifs of this class.

The leisured nonelites would resemble our retirement communities but would be much younger in average age with little interest in perpetuating themselves. Social approval and hedonism would be the binding motifs of this class. The dissenters would be the dropouts from both the elite and the leisure groups, alienated from the achieving or affiliating groups of elite and leisured nonelites; in short, the self-oriented types the writer described in the late 1950's (Bass, 1960) as opposed to the task-oriented elite and the interaction-oriented leisured nonelite. (Little did the writer realize then how rapidly such self-orientation would grow in the United States in the 1960's.)

THE PROMISE OF SELF-MANAGED SYSTEMS

What does this mean for humanizing the organization now, for we still have a quarter-century before the millenium arrives? By developing self-management systems the writer believes we can increase the pursuit of humanistic aims in organizations today without conflicting with the materialistic goals of enterprise.

The principle to follow is that *The minimum size system with the resources to complete a subtask of the organization should be self-managed.*

Typically, a primary group consisting of a supervisor and those reporting directly to him contain the minimum essential information and resources to carry on a subtask, to import needed information and energy, and to export products to other systems inside or outside the larger organization.

It is this system to which the writer addresses himself and which he and Enzo Valenzi have built as the unit of analysis for survey feedback (Bass, 1976) to study contingencies of management style. This system can be described by thirty-one factored variables. Inputs include organizational, group, task and personal variables. Transformation processes involve leadership, power, structure and information variables. Outputs include variables of satisfaction and effectiveness.

The writer shares with Brewster Smith (1973) the concept that self-actualization is egocentric and ethnocentric in character although Yankelovich's survey, previously mentioned, suggests that increasingly it is becoming a norm in the new youth of America. Nevertheless, as a life goal, self-actualization, for instance, may be more important for accelerated rather than decelerated managers according to our data on managers from eight countries. Wide individual differences emerge in concern about self-actualization even at this level (Bass, 1976). Moreover, the writer believes self-actualization as a concept fails to give sufficient weight to the individual as a person embedded in a particular environment—that is, it says more about what the person ought to be and how the environment might provide experiences to promote the interests of such a person. It does not look at what a person-environment system ought to be. The writer borrows freely from open systems theory, seeing the person-environment as a system of inputs, transformation and outputs of energy and information. Development and growth in response to feedback of discrepancies between objectives and attainment are characteristic. Another characteristic of such a system is its equifinality. It can reach a heightened level of activity, for instance, through many different ways of development.

The management of such a system involves planning, directing and controlling its development. The writer proposes that a system is mature the more such development can be achieved and the higher the level of such development relative to the system's potential through self-planning, self-direction and self-control, and the less it must depend on others planning for it, others directing it or others controlling it.

Note that who shall plan, direct and control is a matter which transcends the person. It may depend as much or more on the others in the system as well as policies, the nature of the task, etc.

Organizations that provide environments and develop people to foster self-management are likely to achieve a heightened level of effectiveness where effectiveness is measured in terms of long-term satisfaction of its sponsors, its clientele or customers and its members.

Self-managed systems put both motivational and informational processes to work within the individual members of the system to increase the consistency between supporting actions and carrying them out. Kelman (1974) has summed up what we know about attitudes, commitment and freedom to decide,

> A high degree of choice about . . . induced action is particularly conducive to attitude change. . . . If the person is undecided as to whether to carry out the action, then the higher his degree of choice, the more likely he is—in the process of arriving at the necessary decision and firming it up—to reexamine his attitudes and to marshal forces in support of the action that he finally selects. . . . The fact that he is given the choice may force him to engage in a process of active self-persuasion to find attitudinal support for the action he has already decided to take.
>
> Once the decision to act has been made, the person's motivation to meet the demands of the task in which he has agreed to participate may bring a further process of reexamination of attitudes into play. . . .
>
> The motivational processes generated in the action situation are accompanied by informational processes that are similarly conducive to attitude change. . . . He may thus acquire data about the characteristics of the object, about the value implications of various policies, about the distribution of opinions on the issue, and about the expectations held by relevant reference groups (Kelman, 1974).

The motivational and informational processes generated in self-management improve all three aspects of management—planning, direction and control.

Self-managed systems can look like Likert's (1967) over-lapping groups, but they don't have to. Self-managed systems can make every employee a manager following Myers' (1968) strategy, but they don't have to. Self-managed systems can become autonomous groups (Herbst, 1954), but they don't have to.

What is minimally sufficient for a self-managed system is for its members to know its boundaries, inputs, transforms and outputs. What processes and structure emerge should be consistent with what is known about the system's boundaries, inputs, transforms and outputs. How much is known, prescribed in advance, determined by forces outside the system's control will obviously vary. One system may have as a given an appointed superior who represents it with higher authority. Another system might consist of just one person in isolation running a weather station, but the principle remains that if it has the resources, as much as possible, its planning, direction and control should be self-managed.

In the sociotechnical approaches of Fred Emery (1959), Eric Trist (Trist and Bamforth, 1951), Einar Thorsrud (1972; Emery and Thorsrud, 1969) and Lou Davis (1971; Davis and Taylor, 1972) one can see numerous examples of how jobs as well as industrial processes can be redesigned to permit such self-planning, self-direction and self-control.

Self-planning, self-direction and self-control pay off in outputs of productivity and satisfaction. Thus,

1. SELF-PLANNING. Data on several thousand managers from twelve to fifteen countries suggest that self-planning leads to greater objective output at lower costs. It is also more satisfying. Eight reasons can be cited—greater sense of accomplishment, more effort to confirm own decisions, more commitment, more flexibility, greater understanding of plans, better use of manpower, fewer communication errors and less competitive feelings between planners and doers (Bass, 1970).

2. SELF-DIRECTION. The manager and his subordinates are a system. Self-direction is least for all when the manager commands and the subordinates obey or when the manager delegates

and the subordinates execute. Self-direction is greatest in the manager-subordinate system when consultation or participation is practiced. Satisfaction is also greatest for all concerned when consultation or participation is practiced (Bass and Valenzi, 1974).

3. SELF-CONTROL. When behavior can be self-regulating, again efficiency is maximized and satisfaction is greatest. The manager-subordinate system which builds in self-regulating feedback loops optimizes the system's efficiency.

To conclude, the writer believes that a self-managed person-systems approach is an optimal solution. It can please the devil's materialistic interests in efficiency and the saints' humanistic interests in satisfying work.

REFERENCES

Ackoff, R.: The second industrial revolution. Unpublished manuscript, 1972, pp. 8, 35.

Argyris, C.: The integration of the individual and the organization. In Argyris, C., *et al.* (Eds.): *Social Science Approaches to Business Behavior.* Homewood, Irwin-Dorsey, 1962.

Bass, B. M.: The substance and the shadow. *Am Psychol, 29*:870-886, 1974.

Bass, B. M.: The Bass-Valenzi management styles profile: In Burke, W. (Ed.): *Current Issues and Strategies in Organization Development.* New York, Behavioral Publications, 1976.

Bass, B. M.: Greater productivity and satisfaction through self-planning. Proceedings of the First International Sociological Conference on Participation and Self-Management. Dubrovnik, Yugoslavia, December, 1972.

Bass, B. M.: When planning for others. *J Appl Beh Sci, 6*:151-171, 1970.

Bass, B. M.: *Organizational Psychology.* Boston, Allyn, 1965.

Bass, B. M.: *Leadership, Psychology and Organizational Behavior.* New York, Harper, 1960.

Bass, B. M.: Ultimate criteria of organizational worth. *Personnel Psychol, 5*:157-173, 1952.

Bass, B. M., and Baker, P.: A secretary's lot is a happy one: Or is it? *The Secretary, 22*:2, 4, 6, 8, April, 1962.

Bass, B. M.; Binder, J. M., and Breed, W.: *Profitability and Good Relations: Which Is Cause and Which Is Effect?* Management Research Center Brief 4, Pittsburgh, University of Pittsburgh, 1967.

Bass, B. M., and Franke, R. H.: Societal influences on student perceptions of how to succeed in organization: A cross-national analysis. *J Appl Psychol*, 56:312-318, 1972.

Bass, B. M., and Ryterband, E. C.: Organizational Psychology, 2nd ed. Boston, Allyn, 1976.

Bass, B. M., and Ryterband, E. C.: Work and non-work: Perspectives in the context of change. In Dunnette, M. D. (Ed.): *Work and Non-Work in the Year 2001*. Monterey, Brooks-Cole, 1973.

Bass, B. M., and Valenzi, E. R.: *Contingent Aspects of Effective Management Styles*. In Hunt, J. G., and Larson, L. L. (Eds.): *Contingency Approaches to Leadership*. Carbondale, Southern Illinois University Press, 1974, pp. 130-157.

Bellamy, E.: *Looking Backward, 2000-1887*. Cambridge, Harvard U Pr, 1967 (first published in 1889).

Benoit, E.: A survivalist manifesto. *Society*, March/April:14-25, 1974.

Berle, A. A., and Means, G. C.: *The Modern Corporation and Private Property*. New York, HarBrace, 1968 (first published in 1932).

Davis, L. E.: The coming crisis for production management; technology and organization. *Int J Production Research*, 9:65-82, 1971.

Davis, L. E., and Taylor, J. C.: *Design of Jobs*. London, Penguin, 1972.

Day, L. H.: Social consequences of zero economic growth. '*Em Déwgnois Koywvlxwv 'Eqewwy a' rqiunoy, 1973*, pp. 166-175.

Dent, J. K.: Organizational correlates of the goals of business management. *Personnel Psychol*, 12:365-396, 1959.

Emery, F. E.: Characteristic of sociotechnical systems. *Human Relations Document 527*. London, Tavistock, 1969.

Emery, F. E., and Thorsrud, E.: *Form and Content in Industrial Democracy*. London, Tavistock, 1969.

Ewing, D. W.: Who wants corporate democracy? *Harvard Business Review*, 49(5):12ff., 1971.

Franke, R. H.: An empirical appraisal of the achievement motivation model applied to nations. Unpublished doctoral dissertation. University of Rochester, 1974.

Friedman, M.: *Capitalism and Freedom*. Chicago, U of Chicago Pr, 1962.

Geiger, T.: *The Fortunes of the West: The Future of the Atlantic Nations*. Bloomington, Indiana U Pr, 1973.

Gordon, R. A.: *Business Leadership in the Large Corporation*, Revised ed. Berkeley, U of Cal Pr, 1961.

Hayek, F. A.: The corporation in a democratic society. In Anshen, M., and Bach, G. L. (Eds.): *Management and Corporations, 1985*. New York, McGraw, 1960.

Herbst, P. G.: The analyses of social flow systems. *Human Relations*, 7:327-336, 1954.

Kelman, H. C.: Attitudes are alive and well and gainfully employed in the sphere of action. *Am Psychol*, 29:310-324, 1974.

Kelso, L., and Adler, M.: *The Capitalist Manifesto.* New York, Random, 1958.

Likert, R.: *The Human Organization: Its Management and Value.* New York, McGraw, 1967.

Manne, H. G.: The myth of corporate responsibility—or—Will the real Ralph Nader please stand up. *Rochester Review,* 1973, pp. 8-10.

McClelland, D.: *The Achieving Society.* Princeton, Van Nostrand, 1961.

Mill, J. S.: *Principles of Political Economy.* 6th Ed. London, Longmans, Green, 1896.

Myers, M. S.: Every employee a manager. *California Management Review,* 10(3):9-20, 1968.

Phillips, C. F.: What is wrong with profit maximization? *Business Horizons,* 16:73-80, 1963.

Porter, L. W., Lawler, E. E., and Hackman, J. R.: *Behavior in Organizations.* New York, McGraw, 1975.

Powlison, K.: The profit motive compromised. *Harvard Business Review,* 28:102-108, 1950.

Reder, M. W.: A reconsideration of the marginal productivity theory. *J Political Economy,* 55:450-458, 1947.

Sheppard, H. L.: Discontented blue collar workers—A case study. *Monthly Labor Review,* 18:25-32, 1971.

Simon, H. A.: *Models of Man.* New York, Wiley, 1957.

Smith, M. B.: On self-actualization: A transambivalent examination of a focal theme in Maslow's psychology. *J Humanistic Psychol, 13*:17-33, 1973.

Symposium. Humanizing organizational psychology. American Psychological Association Meeting, Montreal, September, 1973.

Tausky, C.: Meanings of work: Marx, Maslow and steam irons. American Sociological Association Convention, August, 1973.

Thorsrud, E.: Job design in the wider context. In Davis, L. E., and Taylor, J. C. (Eds.): *Design of Jobs.* London, Penguin, 1972, pp. 451-459.

Toynbee, A.: The future will be a severely regimented one. *Rochester Democrat and Chronicle,* April 21, 1974.

Trist, E. L., and Bamforth, K. W.: Some social and psychological consequences of the longwall method of coal-getting. *Human Relations,* 4:3-38, 1951.

Yankelovich, D.: *A Survey of Youth, 1973.* New York, McGraw, 1974.

┌───┐

──────── Chapter 9 ────────

HUMANIZING ORGANIZATIONS: THE POTENTIAL IMPACT OF NEW PEOPLE AND EMERGING VALUES UPON ORGANIZATIONS*

Douglas T. Hall

└───┘

CONTRARY TO WHAT the title of this paper may indicate, unfortunately, the writer does not think young university graduates actually are effective change agents in complex organizations. At least there has been no research yet to show that the differences in values between recent graduates and older employees have led to much restructuring or humanizing of bureaucracies, although there have been predictions that this would occur as today's students and recent graduates move into established organizations (Hall, 1971b; Culbert and Elden, 1970). These value differences *could* have a revitalizing effect, though, and the writer would like to examine why they do not now and how they might in the future.

THE VALUE/PERCEPTION GAP

Much of what is thought to be a generation gap is more accurately called a value/perception gap. Part of the difference between younger and older people is that they tend to value

---

* This article is based upon a contribution to a symposium on "Humanizing Organizational Psychology," H. Meltzer, Chairman, American Psychological Association, Montreal, 1973.

158

things differently, and part of the difference is that they perceive things differently. When a young person thinks about an issue such as career opportunities for women, he probably values equal opportunities more than someone twenty years older. Furthermore, the young person is likely to stress how far we have to go in this area (and thus be dissatisfied with developments to date) whereas the older person is more likely to look with favor on how far we have come. Dissatisfaction involves a gap between what actually exists and what should be. There is some evidence, at least among Roman Catholic priests, that young people tend to expect more and/or perceive less regarding conditions they value than their older colleagues (Hall and Schneider, 1973), feeding into the gap from both sides.

Some of the value areas in which young people expect more and perceive less are as follows:

1. There is now more concern about basic goals and values, not just different values, but values per se.

2. Action is more important. Merely talking about one's values is suspect. The cry is "Do it!"

3. Personal integrity, honesty, openness and realness are more important. After the revolution, hypocrisy may be a capital offense!

4. Many of the "new culture" (Slater, 1970) values are humanistic, oriented toward personal growth and development. This reflects a shift away from concerns for occupational success and security. The ultimate meaning and purpose of living is more important.

5. There is increased concern for the ultimate social value of one's work, the *consequences* of that work and not just its content.

6. Authority based on age or position is less highly regarded and the authority of one's expertise, personal style, convictions or competence carries much more weight with youth. Shared authority is more important than before (Hall, 1971b).

WHAT RECENT GRADUATES WANT
IN ORGANIZATIONS

How do these values translate into specific organizational conditions that recent graduates might desire? They would probably want more openness and less secrecy about issues such as pay, promotion and hiring practices and about how key organizational decisions are made, why and by whom. They would want to be consulted or involved and to have more influence involving decisions affecting their own lives—promotions, transfers, pay raises, performance appraisals and so forth. They would expect to have a colleague relationship with the boss, to be respected and to share in the important decisions affecting their work group. They would also want the boss and the organization to provide opportunities to learn and grow on the job, to try new activities, to have work assignments reflect their needs as well as the organization's. They would want the organization to be aware of its social responsibilities to groups other than shareholders—to customers, to members of the external community, and to members of the internal organizational community (i.e., employees). Implicit in all of the above, perhaps, is a desire for flexibility and openness on the part of the organization, a receptivity to new ideas and possible changes such as those the new employees represent.

GENERATION GAP: SOMETHING OLD,
SOMETHING NEW

In many ways there has always been a generation gap. A favorite gimmick of several recent popular articles on the generation gap has been to ask the reader to identify the author of a short passage lamenting the impatience, impertinence and stubbornness of modern youth; the author, perhaps not surprisingly, is Socrates. Rather than debating whether the generation gap is old or new, it will be considered very sketchily how it is a bit of each.

First of all, there has always been organizational resistance to change, and young employees have always been important carriers of new ideas, energy and idealism into organizations. In this sense youth represents a societal change agent. However, in the past two hundred years most change in organizations has been technological in nature. Now young people are pushing for a new arena of change—social innovation. Almost every profession has its own generation gap—there are *new* doctors, lawyers, psychologists, sociologists, priests, nuns, film makers, arts managers, teachers and businessmen—and the central issue is always, "How can professional knowledge be applied in the form of service, more attuned to the needs of people?" In the past, the issue was more, "How can professional knowledge and competence be extended?"

There has always been a conflict between the needs and aspirations of the individual and the goals and requirements of the organization. In the past, however, the outcome was that the organization would socialize the person into accepting its goals. Now people are likely to innovate or humanize the organization as well. Even though many young people have always seen organizations as threats to their creativity and individuality, now there is a growing sense of youth identity and *youth power* which reduces the odds against them.

IS THERE A GAP AT ALL?

Studies have indicated that in many value areas (DeSalvia and Gemmill, 1971) and in the need for power (Argyris, 1968) the present generation of students may be no different from present managers. In fact, Argyris (1968) shows how the behavior of antibusiness students is just as high as that of executives in precisely those areas in which the students were criticizing the executives—competition and manipulation.

The apparent generational differences in values are just as great within the present generation of young people as we think they are between young and old (Yankelovich, 1972). In fact, the young-old differences may be due largely to one faction of present youth—obviously not all young people are into the counterculture (Roszak, 1968) and Consciousness III (Reich,

1970). However, even if the counterculture does not represent all youth, it may represent the avant garde of the generation. Fred Davis' (1971) *Transaction* article, "Why All of Us May All Be Hippies Some Day," argues that this group may be showing us possible ways to adapt to the leisure-rich future, to break out of present patterns of compulsive consumption, and to enjoy more fully the here and now rather than endlessly delaying present gratification in favor of future achievements. Even though counterculture freaks may avoid large organizations in droves, some of their values may rub off on the more establishment-oriented peers so that Consciousness III values may temper those of Consciousness II presently found in organizations. Some evidence for this widening acceptance of new values is found in surveys indicating that the values of noncollege youth are becoming less conservative and more like their college counterparts (Yankelovich, 1974). Another indicator is that over the last fifteen years the mean dogmatism scores of college students have decreased significantly (Ondrack, 1971), reflecting a general reduction in authoritarianism.

Ironically, the values of the counterculture are quite congruent with the principles which have guided humanistic organizational development efforts over the last ten years. Although Reich and McGregor may differ in the value they would attach to organized effort, they share beliefs in man's basic goodness; innate capacity for growth; need and capacity for autonomy; and the value of trust, caring and authenticity in interpersonal relationships as aids to growth. In organizations where these evolving forms of management philosophy and style are practiced the gap may be narrower than many young people might imagine.

What actual data are available relative to the generation gap in organizations? Not much, although we can piece together some fragments. As mentioned previously, Ondrack's research shows that dogmatism is decreasing among college students. However, DeSalvia and Gemmill (1971) found students to be more pragmatically-oriented (concerned with power, achievement, money, security, prestige, etc.) and *less* people-oriented than managers; their sample of business administration students at one university was certainly not representative of a cross-section of college students, however. A literature survey by Ondrack (1973) reported similar findings—an increasing concern for individual achievement and independence. Ondrack concludes that near-entrepreneurial work would be more satisfying to contemporary graduates than work in a large hierarchical organization.

A study of Catholic priests by Hall and Schneider (1973) examined the personal value they attached to certain church goals (theological, meaning and relevance, church existence and relating church to society) and the extent to which they felt the church was presently working toward them. Young priests attached much greater value than older priests to making the church more socially meaningful and relevant, although the age groups did not disagree in their perceptions of what the church was actually doing in this area; they agreed it was doing little. On the other hand, old and young agreed that maintaining the existence of church structures per se was not an important goal to them personally, yet significantly more young than old priests saw the church as actually working toward existence as an organizational goal. Young priests were also far less likely than older ones to perceive the church as working toward theological goals, although there were not consistent young-old differences on the personal values of theological goals. Therefore, among the priests the age-related differences in their perceptions of organizational realities were at least as great as the differences in the corresponding personal values. By the coding used, young priests also had much more complex, differentiated views of both personal values and perceived church goals, indicating that the issue of goal-related organizational performance was more salient or important to them than to older priests.

INCREASED REALISM?

There is also evidence presented by Rotter (1971a) and Wrightsman and Baker (1969) that interpersonal trust has decreased among college students in recent years. There have also been steady and significant increases recently in students' perceptions of external (as opposed to internal) control (Rotter, 1971b). While Rotter suggests this finding raises questions about the validity of increased concerns about autonomy among present students, the writer would argue that this change reflects a more realistic view of the environment rather than a reduced concern for autonomy. The career literature abounds with references to the reality shock students feel upon entering organizations when they see their idealistic expectations clash with their experiences. Students may be developing more realistic expectations of organizations and may therefore be better able to cope with organizational problems and resistance to change. Future young employees may be more sober, serious change agents than their predecessors. Again, this suggests that the generational gap may lie as much in youth's perception of organizational realities as it does in their personal values.

WHAT CHANGES HAVE RECENT
GRADUATES STIMULATED?

So much for the desires of young people. Unfortunately, there is little evidence so far of the kind of impact young employees have had. Part of the problem here is that there has been little research on the problem, and it's pretty hard to find positive (or negative) data without research. It is possible to identify specific incidents of young employees applying pressure such as at General Motors and Chrysler assembly plants where young workers have staged wildcat strikes and sabotaged production over the last few years. Personnel managers have described the pressures they feel from young graduates for more openness about pay raises, promotions and transfers, and what criteria are used and why, who decides and why can't the employee have more to say about the decisions.

It is not clear, though, that these pressures from young employees will result in significant organizational change. A classic issue in the literature on organizational careers is the reality shock experienced by the new graduate as his or her pre-employment expectations encounter the daily frustrations of the work world. Generally in the past the result has been a lowering of the young person's ideals and aspirations and his acquisition of a more realistic (or cynical) view of the organization. In this sense there has always been a generation gap. The critical question now is, "Is there less of a tendency for the young person to give up his high aspirations and more of a tendency for him to hang in there and fight to sell and win acceptance for his ideas?" If this were happening, then the young person would be attempting to *humanize* the organization while it was trying to *socialize* him.

Virtually unencumbered by any available data, let the writer offer the speculation that the impact of young people upon organizations has not been great. In universities their impact is obviously considerable, but when they have moved beyond the university into business, government and political organizations there is little evidence of change. When managers and executives have been asked whether they see differences in value and outlook between them and young university graduates, the answer is yes. Then, when asked whether and in what specific ways the young graduates have affected their organization, the responses are less positive and slower in coming. When they can give examples of impact, these are usually in the area of dress, hair length, language and life-style. Managers are hard-pressed to identify specific policies and procedures which have been affected by recent graduates. In one talk the writer gave recently to a group of bank managers (a profession with traditionally few university graduates), when he asked for a show of hands, many university graduates were reluctant even to identify themselves as graduates.

What arouses more pessimism regarding the impact of the young and passive? Kingman Brewster spoke of an "eerie tranquility" on campus, an assessment corroborated by Kenneth Keniston (1971). Bowen (1972) and Yadoff (1972) make similar diagnoses of the student climate. If the present students are not willing to rock the boat on campus, will they be any more likely to do so at I.B.M.?

CHANGES IN THE YOUTH MOVEMENT

The writer offers his view of what has happened to the youth movement with the model shown in Figure 9-1. This model shows the five responses to bureaucracy listed by Merton (1957) as modified and augmented by Hall and Schneider (1973). In our view, the person's values can lead him to evaluate the goals of the organization in one of three ways. If he values both the goals and procedures, i.e., means of achieving goals, of the organization, then he *accepts* the system in its present form. If he values the present goals but not the means used to achieve them, he would advocate *reform*. If he does not value either the present procedures or the present goals, he would tend to *reject* the organization in its present state (even though he may value what the goals or procedures *should be* and may show a high-level

Personal Orientations Toward Complex Organizations

(from Merton, 1957; and Hall and Schneider, 1973).

BEHAVIOR (IN RELATION TO OWN VALUES)

		ACTIVE	PASSIVE
ORIENTATION TOWARD ORGANIZATION'S GOALS	Accept	CONFORMITY	RITUALISM
	Reform	INNOVATION	GRUMBLISM
	Reject	REBELLION	RETREATISM

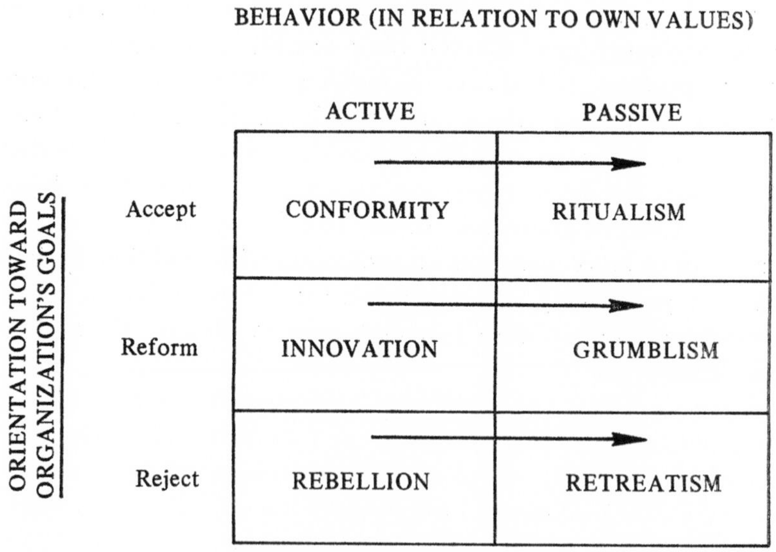

Note: Arrows indicate direction of most likely short-term change.
Figure 9-1.

commitment to the organization by attempting to make changes).

On the horizontal dimension of the model in Figure 9-1 are two behavior-orientations the person may assume. He could be *active* in the sense that he behaves in line with his values, showing that he has actively internalized these values and is attempting to apply them and influence the organization with them, or he could be *passive*, not acting out his values or behaving as though he valued things which in fact he does not; the essence of the passive orientation is that the person's values and behavior are not congruent.

The combination of these two dimensions (values and value-behavior fit) yields a three by two table of personal orientations toward an organization. Five of the cells are filled by the five responses to bureaucracy described by Merton (1957). The *conformer* actively supports the goals and procedures of the organization. The *ritualist* accepts the procedures, but not necessarily the goals, so he looks like an accepter, but he is not behaving out of an internalized value commitment. He goes along, keeps the peace and doesn't make waves. The *innovator* endorses the values but not the procedures of the organization according to Merton and works to reform the procedures. However, Merton has no category for our passive-reform cell, the person who would like to see reform but does not act on that desire. We have called him the *grumbler*. The *rebel* accepts neither the goals nor the procedures. The *retreater* similiarly rejects the present form and purpose of the organization, but does nothing to influence it.

Considering the possible changes in the university population over the last few years, the changes seem to deal more with behavior (the horizontal, active-passive) dimension in Figure 9-1 than with values (the vertical dimension). Rebellion seems to have given way to retreatism while innovation has given way to passive reform. The writer believes that the reformist and radical values have not changed, meaning that rebels have not become innovators, and innovators have not become conformers or ritualists. It is probably more likely that a person would move horizontally on this model than vertically, at least over a one or two-year time period. In time, of course, over several years of a person's career, one's values change as well (Hall, 1971a).

Indeed, this tendency toward retreatism, especially in the face of the power of technology and large impersonal institutions may help explain the resurgence of interest in Charlie Chaplin, his trimphant return to the United States, his special Oscar award, and his current folk-hero status. To Merton, Chaplin's bum is the epitome of the retreatist. Merton quotes Kardiner (1945) as follows:

> (Chaplin's bum) is perplexed by the dilemma either of being crushed in the struggle to achieve the socially approved goals of success and power . . . or of succumbing to hopeless resignation and flight from them. Charlie's bum is a great comfort in that he gloats in his ability to outwit the pernicious forces aligned against him if he chooses to do so and affords every man the satisfaction of feeling that the ultimate flight from social goals is an act of choice and not a symptom of his defeat (Kardiner [1945] quoted in Merton [1957]).

If youth is presently rather quiet, this is not the same quiet as that of the silent generation of the 1950's. The youth of the fifties were passive because of nonconcern; they didn't care greatly about personal values and goals, and were essentially ritualists in terms of the present model. Present youth is greatly concerned about values and process, but they have probably become passive because of the failure of their active attempts to change our social institutions. There is probably considerable energy and anger behind this alienation; it should not be mistaken for apathy.

WHY HAS YOUTH BEEN INEFFECTIVE IN CHANGING ORGANIZATIONS?

What accounts for this apparent lack of success of young innovators and rebels? They have at least three important factors in their favor. First, there is a general awareness of youth by older people in our society; while the attitudes toward youth are probably conflicting, there is a growing respect for the ideas and contributions of young people as witnessed by the lowering of the voting age in the United States and parts of Canada. Also, many of the youth values regarding noneconomic issues, e.g., quality of life, consumerism, community and social responsibility, seem to be gaining greater acceptance among the general public, and the top managements of organizations seem to be getting somewhat unfrozen on these issues.

A third and most important factor is that these desires of young graduates are generally consistent with the humanistic theories of organizational behavior such as McGregor, Likert and Argyris which are gaining increasing acceptance in organizations. These theories all stress man's innate need and capacity for growth and autonomy given the appropriate conditions and the value of shared authority, open communication and good interpersonal relationships as aids to growth. While it is certainly possible to show ways in which young graduates do not always behave in line with these theories, it seems safe to say that these process-oriented models fit youth better than the method-oriented writings of F. W. Taylor, Urwick and Gulick, or Koontz and O'Donnell.

Why, then, have youth's change attempts had little success? Why have young employees been rather ineffective interventionists and change agents? Part of the answer probably lies in a comparison of the change methods of an organization development specialist and those of the young employee.

According to Richard Beckhard (1969), organization development is an effort that is (1) planned, (2) organization-wide (3) and managed from the top to (4) increase organizational effectiveness and health through (5) planned interventions in the organization's processes (6) using behavioral science knowledge.

Many of the change attempts by young employees are not systematically planned, but rather arise spontaneously as in the process of trying to sell an idea to one's boss. A key departure from the OD model is that young employees are generally isolated from one another and engage in individual rather than collective action. Thus, the influence attempts are not coordinated and organizationwide. One person (a voice in the wilderness) has little chance of influencing a complex organization. Because the young employee is at or near the bottom of the organization, it is obviously hard for him to initiate change from the top. However, there is probably much more sentiment favoring change at or near the top than most new employees realize; these "leading parts" (Brown, 1971) at the top, in collaboration with young employees, could greatly strengthen a change effort, but young employees often do not think in terms of such collaboration.

The goals of the young employee might be somewhat different from those of the OD specialist in that the young member might be more concerned about changing the job conditions or goals of the organization than in improving its effectiveness or health. His change attempts might well be aimed at organizational processes (such as communication), but he probably doesn't make much use of behavioral science knowledge. In fact, this is the area where administration programs were criticized most by managers—we don't train students to sell their ideas and to work well with people.

Argyris (1970) has argued that intervention attempts tend to be more effective when three conditions are present in the relationship between the interventionist and client system—free choice of all parties to continue or discontinue the relationship, open flow of valid information between interventionist and the client system, and the internal commitment of all parties to the change effort.

Although young employees often talk about valuing free choice, their methods are often oriented toward power and the imposition of their changes on others in the organization (Argyris, 1968; Hall and Schneider, 1973). Strategic behavior, convert influence, political behavior and competition rather than collaboration are often the methods of young Turks. The young employee is not a neutral third party as is the interventionist. Related to this, young employees are often reluctant to bring conflicts with older employees or managers out into the open for fear of reprisals. This behavior, combined with the covert influence attempts, tends to restrict the free flow of information in the system. Another restriction of information flow regards the new member's information about himself. Because of his strong commitment to his own position, he may be blind to his impact on others, thinking the correctness of his moral position justifies his actions. This may deprive him of useful personal feedback with which he could learn from his mistakes and improve his ability to influence others.

The internal commitment of new graduates may be wavering a bit in recent years as has been indicated with the model in Figure 9-1. Also, if a young employee attempts to coerce others to change (assuming he is still attempting to bring about change), the most he might expect would be compliance-based change, not internal commitment to the change. These considerations would all tend to reduce the effectiveness of the new employee as change agent.

HOW CAN YOUTH STIMULATE CHANGE MORE EFFECTIVELY?

One idea to increase the change-effectiveness of young employees would be for them to consciously think of themselves as organizational change agents. One thing this does immediately is put the organization in the role of client-with-a-problem rather than adversary. In helping this *client* change, young employees could work collectively rather than as separate individuals consciously utilizing behavioral science knowledge and skills (as per the Beckhard dimension number 6). They could diagnose the organization, identifying change and resistance forces (or people), and plan strategies in collaboration with others interested in change for reducing resistance rather than applying coercive pressure for change. They could focus on ways to unfreeze and involve key people at the top of the organization, perhaps by feeding back to them the results of a collaboratively-conducted formal diagnosis. Here the focus for the interventionists would be on involving as many people as possible in discussing the feedback and generating ideas for change collaboratively rather than having the initiators prepare in advance a list of recommendations which the other participants could then only accept or reject.

The behavior of the initiators could serve as a model to others in the organization. The more open, internally-committed and collaborative they were, the more they would encourage this behavior in others and the more likely to succeed any changes would be. This would mean, though, that the young interventionists might not necessarily generate exactly those changes they would most advocate; after all, the risk of participative decision-making is that others might influence the decisions! This approach would mean being committed to a *process* of collaboratively-directed change rather than to specific kinds of change. This, then, is a key dilemma of the young employee-as-interventionist—the more he acts as advocate for particular types of change (through power tactics, coercion, etc.), the lower are his chances of effecting change, but if changes do occur, they will probably be *his* changes. The more he acts as an interventionist, focusing on collaborative processes, the less control he has over the specific changes, but the more likely it is that internalized change will occur.

Regardless of which approach is employed, the first steps are for young employees (1) *to think of themselves as a collective unit,* a true movement, and (2) *to develop systematic plans for change.*

It may be that the youth movement is ready for just this sort of new effort. What Brewster called "eerie tranquility" may be a consolidation and regrouping phase in which young people are examining their methods, facing up to their disillusionment and internal conflicts, learning from their mistakes and developing more effective means of stimulating change. As was mentioned earlier, students in recent years may be developing more realistic expectations of organizations having experienced their "reality shock" in the university after May Day, 1970; after Kent State; Jackson State; assassinations of great leaders; Watergate and so on. They may now be better able to cope with organizational problems and resistance to change with these experiences behind them. Future young employees may be more sober, serious change agents than their predecessors.

Rather than retreat after some initial failures, the present tasks for young employees are to engage in some self-reflection to see how their own behavior may have contributed to these failures and how they can learn from these experiences.* Kenneth Keniston describes these tasks as follows:

It is time for the student movement to become a national movement of affirmation. To transform this movement will require not merely the enthusiasm of Consciousness III, but the professionalism of Consciousness II. It will require not only the celebration of life and the expansion of consciousness, but the respect for hard work, persistence and the dedication that characterized the old culture. It will require an alliance not merely of the young, the privileged and educated, but of those who are not young, privileged, or educated (1971).

What the writer is arguing for is a synthesis of youth's new values and OD's tested methods of effecting social change. If such a synthesis does not occur, we will be faced with a generation of people with reform or radical values and despairing passive stance resulting in a widespread sense of alienation and cynicism. Not only would this mean that organizations feel less pressure to change, but the climate and long-term stability of our society would suffer badly.

REFERENCES

Argyris, C.: *Intervention Theory and Method.* Reading, Addison-Wesley, 1970.

Argyris, C.: Students and businessmen: The bristling dialogue. *Think,* 34:26-31, 1968.

Beckhard, R.: *Organization Development: Strategies and Models.* Reading, Addison-Wesley, 1969.

Bowen, D. D.: American youth: Revolt, con III, or a silent majority. Contribution to symposium, Challenges and Dilemmas of Trends in Youth Culture, Eastern Psychological Association. Boston, April, 1972.

Brown, L. D.: Leading parts and organizational change. In Alderfer, C. P. (chairperson), Multilevel View of Organizational Change, symposium

---

* Drawing an analogy between the personal development of a psychiatric patient and the growth of the student movement, Keniston (1971) describes how patients must confront their own evils and inner conflicts in a process of inner agony and depression. This process may be happening in the student movement with students now in the agony of confronting their own tendencies toward violence and aggression. Out of this agony could come a more realistic, equally-determined movement.

presented at American Psychological Association, Washington, D.C., September, 1971.

Culbert, S. A., and Elden, J. M.: An anatomy of activism for executives. *Harvard Business Review*, November, December: 131-142, 1970.

Davis, F.: Why all of us may be hippies some day. In Friedenberg, E. Z. (Ed.): *The Anti-American Generation*. Chicago, Aldine, 1971, pp. 61-80.

De Salvia, D. N., and Gemmill, G. R.: An exploratory study of the personal value systems of college students and managers. *Academy of Management Journal, 14*:227-238, 1971.

Hall, D. T.: A theoretical model of career subidentity development in organizational settings. *Organizational Behavior and Human Performance, 6*:50-76, 1971a.

Hall, D. T.: Potential for career growth. *Personnel Administration, 34*:18-30, 1971b.

Hall, D. T., and Schneider, B.: *Work Climates and Careers: The Work Lives of Priests*. New York, Seminar Press, 1973.

Kardiner, A.: *The Psychological Frontiers of Society*. New York, Columbia U Pr, 1945.

Keniston, K.: The agony of the counter-culture. *Yale Alumni Magazine*, October:10-13, 1971.

Merton, R. K.: *Social Theory and Social Structure*. Glencoe, Free Press, 1957.

Ondrack, D. A.: Emerging occupational values: A review and some findings. *Academy of Management Journal, 16*:423-432, 1973.

Ondrack, D. A.: Attitudes toward authority. *Personnel Administration, 34*:8-17, 1971.

Reich, C.: *The Greening of America*. New York, Random House, 1970.

Roszak, T.: *The Making of a Counter Culture*. New York, Doubleday, 1968.

Rotter, J. B.: Generalized expectancies for interpersonal trust. *Am Psychol, 26*:443-452, 1971a.

Rotter, J. B.: External control and internal control. *Psychol Today, 5*:37-42, 58-59, 1971b.

Slater, P.: *The Pursuit of Loneliness: American Culture at the Breaking Point*. Boston, Beacon Press, 1970.

Wrightsman, L. S., and Baker, N. J.: Where have all the idealistic imperturbable freshmen gone? *Proceedings of the 77th Annual Convention of the American Psychological Association, 4*:299-300, Summary, 1969.

Yadoff, B.: Decreasing political participation of college students. Contribution to symposium, Challenges and Dilemmas of Trends in Youth Culture. Eastern Psychological Association, Boston, April, 1972.

Yankelovich, D.: The real meaning of the student revolution. *The Conference Board Record*, IX(3), March, 1972.

Yankelovich, D.: *The New Morality*. New York, McGraw-Hill, 1974.

———————— Chapter 10 ————————

ECONOMIC AND SOCIO-CULTURAL BARRIERS TO HUMANIZING ORGANIZATIONS*

WALTER R. NORD

MANY AMERICAN ORGANIZATIONAL psychologists share the general goal of humanizing organizations. While it is comforting to point to our theoretical and empirical contributions, there are indications that the influence of work has been minimal.

A number of writers have commented upon our failure. Miles (1965) reported the strong preference of managers to use the more manipulative "human relations" approach instead of the "human resources" model. Campbell, Dunnette, Lawler and Weick (1970) told us that only a few of what we might expect to be leading organizations in human resource management use anything besides management by objectives; then, Levinson (1970) wrote that many firms which employ MBO do not implement it in a way to achieve humanistic objectives. Moreover, Quinn et al. (1973), after surveying a broad sample of workers, concluded that only a few increases in job satisfaction have occurred in recent years, and those increases which did take place were due primarily to financial gains. Krishnan (1974), based on data from two surveys of executives, concluded

> . . . it appears that the majority of business executives taking part in these studies do not take the view that employees should have the right to participate, through the democratic process, in making

* Presented at the Symposium on Humanizing Organizational Psychology in 1974 at the Convention of the American Psychological Association in New Orleans, 1974, and updated into 1975 for this book.

175

organizational decisions. They do not even favor allowing employees direct input to the decision making process through direct access to the top policy making body or presentation of their viewpoints to the chief executive, except when the nature of the problem is such that the traditional managerial prerogatives will in no way be affected. An absolute majority believe in the traditional managerial prerogatives.

Finally, Walton (1972), Scott (1974) and Nord (1974) pointed to the need for rather radical changes in our values and the scope of our analysis if we are to reach what Walton termed "the frontiers beckoning" us.

While numerous other pessimistic statements are available, the foregoing citations demonstrate the need for asking the question which the writer will attempt to answer in this discussion—Why, by 1974, have we not been more successful in humanizing work organizations?

The writer believes that our failure is partially explained by our narrow focus. We have worked at the microlevel almost exclusively; the firm is the largest unit we analyze. However, we have ignored the impact of the economic and sociocultural context in which these organizations attempt to survive and grow. This milieu induces pressures upon even the best-intentioned manager to treat people, even himself, in nonhumane ways. This chapter will examine how some of these economic and sociocultural forces are in conflict with a number of the proposals organizational psychologists have advanced for humanizing organizations. If we are to humanize organizations we must complement our microfocus with analysis and change of economic and sociocultural forces which constrain humanization.

This chapter examines a selected set of economic and sociocultural forces which, although we have not been aware of them, have had powerful effects on the work of organizational psychologists. In Gouldner's (1970) words, it will deal with some of our background assumptions.

The writer's approach has been to search for themes which seem to underlie much of the work of American organizational psychologists but which they do usually not explicitly acknowledge. No attempt will be made to develop a complete list of barriers to humanization. Moreover, the writer does not maintain that the forces discussed are independent of each other; they are undoubtedly highly intercorrelated since many of them are interwoven with the prevailing ideology of postcapitalistic America.

BACKGROUND ASSUMPTIONS AND OVERLOOKED CONSTRAINTS

Individualistic Focus

One of the most prevalent background assumptions made by members of organizational psychology has been our view of humanization in individual terms. We talk about *each individual* being treated as an end, about *each* person exercising control over his or her own outcomes, and the self-actualization of each individual. Seldom do we focus explicitly on the human potential of all people taken together as a goal.

The problems with this individualistic approach stem from the fact that an individual's personal growth is, in part, a function of one's social environment. For example, consider Maslow's hierarchy of needs; it is difficult to function at the self-actualization level in a social system where crimes of violence are rampant. Similarly, it may be difficult to self-actualize in organizations which are dominated by patterns of competition and a king of the hill mentality. The experience of companies with sensitivity training is a case in point. An article by Calame (1969) described a number of instances where the personal learning from a T-group conflicted with organizational norms. One executive described his post-T-group experiences this way,

> "I came back all charged up and stuck my head in the wringer the first few weeks," recalls the chief of a research lab for a big chemical company, "but I found that the rest of the world I worked in hadn't been exposed to sensitivity and that the people couldn't be expected to react the way I did. It just didn't work out."

Whereas a more social approach would focus on the development of all people taken together, our individualistic orientation induces us to accept social patterns which constrain our ability to achieve humanistic outcomes.

Underemphasis on Lower Level Needs

A second limiting assumption in our work has been our somewhat uncritical translation of Maslow's hierarchy into a proposition that material resources have become less important in our affluent society. In a general way, other things being equal, the writer feels this proposition is correct, but how equal are other things? For instance, suppose that there are forces operating in society which systematically increase material needs or transform the means by which higher level needs are satisfied. Consider the huge outlays of resources and talents devoted to advertising. Have these efforts enhanced the value of material goods in such a way that people have come to perceive these commodities as means to achieve social and ego needs? In short, the needs served by material goods may have changed.

Also, the satisfaction of material needs may be a relative phenomenon. As Festinger (1954), Homans (1961) and others have suggested, one's definition of what he needs is influenced by what people in his comparison group have. As Jencks (1972) noted, the cost of living is more than the cost of buying a fixed set of goods and services, rather "It is the cost of participating in a social system. The cost of participation depends in large part on how much other people habitually spend to participate." As Wool (1973) stated,

> One fallacy in the Maslow-Herzberg model of worker aspirations, as a guide to behavior, lies in its inherently static premises. Even though individual earnings and family incomes have increased steadily over the decades, the great majority of American workers certainly do not consider themselves as "affluent," when they relate their spendable income to their spending needs, for which they now consider an acceptable standard of living.

Large numbers of people, i.e., the 20 million workers holding nonfarm jobs which pay under $2.50/hour (Wool, 1973), do not have their lower level needs satisfied; consequently relatively traditional aspects of work may play a large role in determining what they seek from work. Moreover, Wool added that job security is far from certain for many workers. He wrote, "The most important single set of measures which can contribute to improvements of *quality* of work in America are . . . those designed to increase the *quantity* of work in America." In other words, if workers have more ability to choose among alternative places to work, their work lives would be more satisfying both economically and psychologically. Inflation, recession and unemployment are still vital concerns for many people.

In sum, the existing distribution of resources inhibits the development of large segments of our population. Organizational psychologists have ignored or at least vastly underestimated the magnitude of this constraint. I suggest that substantial blows for humanization can still be struck in traditional ways—increases in the number of jobs available, higher wages and greater job security.

Organizational Profits and Growth as Goals

In spite of our emphasis on the need to treat organizations as open systems, our strategies for humanizing work have focused almost exclusively within individual organizations. This micro-level focus has prevented us from following the system's view to what seem to be its obvious conclusions. For example, general systems theory implies that the internal structure of an organization is a function of its environment. In von Forester's (1968) words ". . . environment and the organism associated with it will be duals to each other in the sense that a particular organism (O) implies its particular environment E(O), and vice-versa. . . ." Later he noted, "An organism that is matched to its environment possesses in some way or another an internal representation of the order and regularities of its environment." Application of this idea to organizations leads to the assumption that organizations map their environments; existing organizations are intimately related to economic, political, technological, legal and value systems characteristic of the larger social systems. If these environmental factors remain unchanged it is questionable whether a variety of changes within organizations can be sustained.

Systems must adapt to environmental contingencies in order to survive. As Terreberry (1968) observed, the process of organizational evolution is analogous to biological evolution. Environments are continually in flux; systems existing in these environments must change in order to survive. If this view of organizational evolution is correct, it follows that we must consider what goals managers must pursue to help their organizations survive in their environments. Clearly, profits and growth are given priority over humanization.

In a number of ways the economic competition and the market system (past and present) seem to generate forces which conflict with humanistic goals. Clearly, the competitive system encourages the use of other people as means rather than ends. Moreover, individuals define their own worth in terms of their economic and social standing relative to other people. Individuals and groups develop vested interests in preserving parts of the status quo which give them advantages over their fellow man. Human welfare is sacrificed for individual advantage.

Heilbroner *et al.* (1973) provided a number of detailed studies where corporate profits and the personal interests were associated with blatant disregard for human welfare. The case of MER/29®, a drug produced by the William S. Merrell Company for the treatment of heart disease, is one of the more shocking examples. Despite evidence that side-effects of the drug included damage to and loss of hair, the drug was promoted vigorously; the data which threatened the marketability of the drug were withheld and/or distorted. A somewhat lengthy quote from the end of the case description summarizes some of the general tensions between profits and human welfare.

> How many other similar cases there may have been before MER/29 and since, it is impossible to know. But FDA Inspector Rive, now stationed at FDA headquarters in Washington and responsible for the recall of drugs, says that at the time, "I didn't think (the MER/29 case) was typical but I was wrong. . . . They were totally geared to the dollar sign. I'm sure there are many other firms similar to them—even today. I suspect (Merrell) got away with the same thing many times before. This is typical Americana: get away with what you can. I really don't think it hurt their consciences at all."
>
> Every day American pharmaceutical firms send out announcements of new miracle drugs, new promises of paradise through medical research. They spend millions of dollars imploring doctors, institutions and clinics to try new items on their patients and then

report the results. When it is convenient to do so, the drug companies themselves prepare letters and articles praising the drugs, which the doctors only have to sign and submit. Surely, many of the drugs involved are useful. But who is to calculate the cost in suffering from untold side effects, who is to count the victims of the harmful drugs, the substances introduced into human bodies by men for whom profit comes first?

Apparently there are numerous instances when individuals perceive their own best interests and/or the corporate goals of profit and growth as being best served by actions which are clearly detrimental to the well-being of other human beings.

Organizational psychologists have failed to study the social psychological correlates of profit maximization. As Williams (1959) has noted, the profit motive can be seen as a social condition, not merely a psychological motive. This social condition plays a major role in the day-to-day lives of organizational participants. The contingencies of reinforcement operating on many organizational participants stimulate behavior oriented to achieving profits at the expense of humanized outcomes.

Organizational Goals Versus Social Goals

Our focus on the internal processes of organizations and our acceptance of the goals of individual firms have led us to overlook the relationship between the producer and consumer as a factor giving meaning to work. We have assumed that the quality of a product and its role in serving human needs are inconsequential to the worker. However, based on a more social view of man, we might have given more emphasis to the role of producing high quality products which directly serve central needs of one's fellow man as a contributor to a person perceiving his work as meaningful. In addition to the conventional assumption that alienation from work is responsible for low quality products, low quality products may also produce alienated workers.

Of course the study of the nature of the product is only one direction where a more full commitment to humanization might lead. It could induce us to give more attention to the role of work ideology in giving meaning to work. It might also induce us to consider what is being done in countries with radically different political systems. Consider the efforts to humanize work in modern China. Whyte (1973) reported that the Maoists, without changing the design of jobs, have attempted to provide meaningful work through an ideology which gives each worker an awareness of the implications of his or her performance for broad political and social objectives. Every organizational decision and action is perceived as having implications beyond the boundaries of the organization. While, as Tausky (1973) noted, the Maoist strategy may not be effective in an affluent, pluralistic society such as our own, Tausky did stress the need for some type of macroanalysis. He wrote,

> The organization theorists who deal with motivation . . . are skimming only the surface of an exceedingly complex dilemma to which the effective remedy implies changes in the fundamental structure of western societies of plenitude. Nevertheless, claims of discovering a key to unlock workers' motivations continue, on the assumption that work effort is a built-in characteristic of man which clumsy work arrangements have blocked from fully emerging. Techniques at the workplace will not alter the social structure which has generated the problem.

A more social definition of our subject matter might also lead us to question the purpose of growth—growth of what? For what? As Meadows *et al.* (1972) have argued, we may need to make some choices about where we as a human race can afford to have growth occur. Our own personal and career interests seem to limit the scope of the questions that we as organizational psychologists ask. We are not concerned with what goals firms seek, but only with helping managers and their firms do better what *they* have chosen to do. Seldom do we seem to ask if the task itself is worth doing.

We can rationalize this position by saying it is not our job to make such value judgments. However, to the extent that all people do not have equal access to our services (and financially most do not) by failing to take an overt value position, we are taking a covert one. For a fully humanized organizational psychology to exist we may need to make deliberate choices about which ends we serve. Incidentally, such choices do not necessarily mean a loss of scientific rigor. They mainly involve a choice of whose interests we allow to define what are significant problems for study and action and what parameters we take as given.

Integrative Assumptions as Constraints

Many of the assumptions the writer has discussed so far are related to our micro-orientation toward both people and firms. Most of the remaining difficulties to be discussed stem from an equally pervasive set of assumptions about the nature of social organization. Borrowing from Dahrendorf (1959), the writer will argue that our work is dominated by integrative as opposed to coercive theories. Integrative theories tend to assume that every functioning social structure is based on a consensus of values among its members. By contrast, coercion theories assume that every society is based on the coercion of some of its members by others.

One of the consequences of our integrative perspective can be seen in the way we approach conflict. We search out reasons for the existence of conflict rather than reasons *for* the absence of conflict. For example, consider the following situation: A corporation has two plants; the plants are located in different communities having very similar demographic characteristics. Both plants have the same production process and are subject to the same general set of policies. However, Plant A is characterized by industrial strife while Plant B is characterized by harmony. How does the typical organizational psychologist look at the problem? It is the writer's feeling that most of us begin to look at the reasons for the conflict in Plant A and fail to question why there isn't more conflict in Plant B. In this sense a passage from Reich (1970) is directly applicable to modern organizational psychology. Reich wrote,

> . . . what has to be explained is not the fact that the man who is hungry steals or the fact that the man who is exploited strikes, but why the majority of those who are hungry *don't steal* and why those who are exploited *don't strike*.

The way we *select* our problems for study and therapy and our integrative assumptions lead us to overlook opportunities for humanizing organizations. All too often we are *tension reducers*. Rules and structures which promote the stability of existing organizations go unexamined; forces which threaten existing organizations are taken as problematic in order to minimize the tension they produce. Consequently social conditions which do not generate threats to existing structures go unexamined even when they may themselves be barriers to humanistic goals.

Power

Our integrative assumptions also are associated with our commonly recognized neglect of social power. While thanks to the work of Seeman (1971), Kipnis (1972), Mulder (1971) and Mulder and Wilke (1970) we know more about power than we did a few years ago, the implications of this recent work challenge some of our generally-accepted strategies for humanizing organizations. Specifically Seeman found that intrinsically rewarding work was not a major factor in reducing alienation; data from the work of Kipnis and Mulder suggest that strategies of power equalization may result in very little improvement in the social relationships experienced by lower level participants. Power differentials, even if diminished temporarily, seem to be associated with social behavior which results in the reestablishment of larger differentials.

Organizational psychologists seem to have underestimated the difficulty in changing the distribution of power. We seem to forget that individuals who currently have power, whether they are in business, government or the labor movement, have an interest in not changing the distribution of power too much.

Moreover, we have given very little attention to the existing distribution of power and its consequences. Krishnan's (1974) findings on these matters are especially informative. He wrote,

> In 1971, the 500 largest industrial corporations and 50 largest companies in banking, life insurance, diversified financial, retail, transportation and utilities fields combined owned $1.3 trillion in assets and employed 20.3 million persons. Compared to the $1.3 trillion assets of these business organizations the GNP of the U.S. in 1971 was approximately $1.050 trillion. This provides some

indication of the extent of the influence business institutions wield in this society. Paul Samuelson has pointed out that the executives and directors combined in a typical corporation own a very small fraction (3 percent) of the outstanding common stock, but still have the formal authority to control the business. . . .

Based on data from his own study and a related one conducted by the *Harvard Business Review,* Krishnan concluded that most executives are not inclined to share this power.

> From the present study and the HBR one, it appears that the majority of business executives taking part in these studies do not take the view that employees should have the right to participate, through the democratic process, in making organizational decisions. They do not even favor allowing employees direct input to the top policy making body or presentation of their viewpoints to the chief executive, except when the nature of the problem is such that the traditional managerial prerogatives will in no way be affected. An absolute majority believe in the traditional managerial prerogatives. The executives do not think that direct involvement/participation by employees is desirable in business organizational decision making even though business as an institution has an overwhelming effect on the social system and the lives of the people in it.

There is evidence from both the psychological laboratory and real world events that people who are given power over others are apt to treat the less powerful in inhumane ways. The research of Zimbardo (*New York Times,* 1973) provides a prime example of this point. Zimbardo designed a simulated prison; some individuals were appointed guards, and others were made prisoners. Very quickly the guards began to treat the prisoners in inhumane ways. So extreme was the behavior of the guards that the experiment, which had been designed to last two weeks, had to be terminated at the half-way point.

Rosenhan's (1973) study of mental hospitals revealed the operation of a parallel process operating in real situations. The powerful, in this case members of hospital staffs, used a number of technical and social processes to distance themselves from their clients. As a result the relationships between the staff and the patients were more of an I-it type than real human encounter.

It takes little imagination to see these same processes operating in our own organizations. Faculty members, executives and even parents exercise a great deal of control over the lives of others. Members of each group behave in ways and establish procedures which result in less than fully human encounters between themselves and lower level participants. Differences in the distribution of power are mapped into the everyday experiences of organizational participants. Far more resources and attention are given to the needs, wants and dignity of the more powerful than those of the less powerful.

These outcomes which are associated with the unequal distribution of power are social in nature; they stem from the character of the role relationships between people. These relationships are an expression of more macrorelationships; their existence depends, in part, on the social structure in which the organizations function. Marx's point about the ownership of the tools of production is an example of this line of thought. The ability of management to treat workers as means instead of ends is dependent upon social relationships which are spawned by the social structure in which the sources of power are concentrated in the hands of a few. Whether the sources of power lie in the ownership of property as Marx suggested or in control of information as Bennis (1974) suggested, their effects are similar —"the rich get richer."

For the most part we have taken the distribution of authority based on the existing distribution of power, whether it is based on property, control of information or whatever, as an unexamined given and have stressed the fact that authority really flows from the bottom anyway. While the writer agrees that lower level participants have, at least potentially, considerable power, we have given too little attention to the power of the higher level participants. Authority conveyed by property rights influences the pattern of social relationships within the organization. In Gouldner's (1960) terms, ownership may act to promote complementary as opposed to reciprocal social relationships. Organizational relationships are complementary in the sense that the owners have *rights* over others, and these others have *duties* toward the owners. In contrast, they are reciprocal when *both* parties have *mutual rights and duties* toward each other. Almost all processes within organizations are somehow influenced by either the manifest or latent power of the owners and/or their agents. Yet we have almost ignored the role of ownership or other sources of legitimacy which are associated with a grossly unequal distribution of power within organizations which induce patterns of behavior which conflict with the fully human treatment of lower level (and even upper) participants in organizations.

In addition to overlooking the more social psychological and sociological factors relating to power, we have overlooked some individual factors as well. People who have power appear to prefer to keep it. Moreover, as Cummin (1967), Livingston (1971) and Winter (1973) have suggested, those who achieve power in a number of organizations in our society tend to have high needs for being powerful. This state of affairs poses an interesting dilemma for those who seek to humanize organizations through power equalization. Those who have power have strong needs for it; they are unlikely to be enthusiastic about voluntary power equalization.

Even if they were inclined to give power away, important questions about how power can be redistributed successfully to other people remain. For example, are the consequences for human development the same from the gift of power as they are from power acquired through struggle? As Reich (1970) and Gorz (1967) have noted, people must be developed in order to exercise power effectively. People who have merely been given power may not be as well-prepared to exercise it effectively as those who have gone through the process of taking it. Those who are given power may not be able to participate effectively for a number of reasons. As Bennis (1973) noted about organizational development,

> OD may unwittingly encourage a bastardized form of 'participative democracy' in our institutions. That is it encourages a political participation by constituents and others who haven't the interest, the time, or competence in furthering the goals of the particular institution.

More generally it may be argued that power cannot be given

by the powerful because the ability to give it implies the ability to retake it. In other words power always remains latent. Frequently subordinates are well aware that their exercise of delegated decisions is being evaluated and can easily be removed. Superiors can always remove sources of gratification which are important to the subordinates. As Gouldner (1970) wrote, "It is the sheer ability of the powerful to do this . . . that is an independent, ever-present element in the servile attitudes that subordinates often develop toward their superiors." Similarly, Levinson (1970) suggested that frequently MBO does not result in any real gains in humanization; it becomes merely a new technique for the superiors to get their subordinates to do what the superiors want them to. In short, the net contribution to humanizing organizations of power equalization strategies which organizational psychologists have marketed so widely may be very small unless it is accompanied by real changes in the distribution of power and central elements in the structure of modern organizations.

Levinson (1973) expressed this point as well as anyone. He observed that almost all of the various management philosophies of this century have acknowledged ". . . that the more powerful have a natural right to manipulate the less powerful." Levinson suggests that subordinates realize that this assumption means they are in a jackass position vis-a-vis their superiors. Bureaucratic structures based on this premise of hierarchy breed dependency, internal competition for power and position, and resentment and defeat.

> Bureaucratic structure, with its implicit power-struggle orientation, increases infighting, empire building, rivalry, and a sense of futility. It tends to magnify latent feelings that the organization is a hostile environment which people can do little to change. . . .

While Levinson does not attempt to deal with the economic and sociological conditions which may be responsible for the existence of the assumption that hierarchy is a given and is necessary, he does explain in very real terms the conflict of the hierarchical assumption and the distribution of power it induces with humanized organizations.

Bennis (1973, 1974) made a similar point in his reflections, changes in his beliefs about the role of consensus as a basis for organizational decisions which followed his move from behavioral scientist to administrator. He noted a number of constraints which he experienced in his new role which limited his abilities to implement the "democratic" procedures he had advanced in his scholarly writings. These barriers included the need to deal with external forces, time pressures and problems introduced by the size of the organization and various constituencies. Moreover, he noted the inadequacy of OD models due to their failure to deal fully with power processes.

Bennis' discussions demonstrate a central theme of this paper—major barriers to changing organizations are social in nature. "Resistance" to change is not just a function of ignorance or selfishness on the part of the powerful. The structure and dynamics of organizations are functions of the systems with which they interact and are embedded.

The Assumption of Shared Goals

In accordance with our integrative theories we assume that the same behavior which aids in human development will serve the interests of the owners and the powerful. This assumption has been shared by most important writers in our field including both Frederick Taylor and Douglas McGregor.

One of the most articulate challenges to this view can be found in Brimm's (1972) comments. Brimm argued that we have focused almost exclusively on how the organizational entity can be made more successful

> . . . in a system where success is defined in terms of organizational productivity, profitability, and survival, plus individual growth, commitment, and motivation. While the latter criteria seem to attribute value to individual development, their ultimate implications are the greater subordination of the person to the organization.

Later Brimm added

> By sharing the ideological framework of the dominant power group change agents are constrained in their ability to perceive a broad range of alternatives for organizational change.

The writer agrees with Brimm; the assumption of high congruence between the interests of those in control of organizations and humanistic goals weds us to the existing distribution of power. Consequently we fail to study the ways in which such a distribution spawns organizations in which the powerful treat the less powerful as means and where the less powerful who attempt to exercise control over their own outcomes are subjected to a variety of "intimidation rituals" (O'Day, 1974).

There may be more inherent conflict between the goals of lower and upper level participants. The changes which are needed to humanize an organization may appear quite different depending on whether we look up or down the organization. For the most part we have looked from the top down. Our entry point into the system constrains the alternatives we consider. Our opportunities for research, careers and consulting are in important ways controlled by people at the top of organizations. Given this position, our impotency to humanize organizations is not all that surprising.

One final point about our relationship to dominant power groups. Many of us have a large stake in the distribution of power that now exists. While it is somewhat old hat to call social scientists servants of power, Gouldner added a new twist. He charged that social scientists may serve power by providing a set of rationalizations which permit the powerful to see themselves as good without giving up their power. In this sense the writer believes it is significant that McGregor and others after him have maintained that Theory Y and related concepts do not change management's prerogatives in any way. Is it too much of a leap to conclude that what Theory Y does do, while protecting management's prerogatives, is give the manager a way of believing he is exercising his power in a humanistic way? If we provide useful rationalizations, we can serve power well without bringing about any significant changes.

CONCLUSION

Throughout this discussion the writer has attempted to point out that organizational psychology, as currently defined and practiced, is closely interwoven with existing economic and social processes. Consequently, we have been, at best, a mild force for humanizing organizations. Are there any alternatives for us short of becoming political activists and sacrificing our scientific attitudes and approaches?

Given the complexity of this question, most solutions will sound simplistic. However, two starting points come to mind. The first is a fuller discussion of our background assumptions and an assessment of their influence on our work. The second possible direction is the use of the concept of reciprocity as a criterion for evaluating our efforts.

The more our actions promote social relationships which are fully reciprocal, the more we are apt to be building the foundation upon which humanized organizations can be constructed. As Lehmann and Young (1974) argued, under conflict conditions of social organization, the appropriate role for professional sociologists is to ". . . take an active role in creating the social conditions under which reciprocity is maximized." Of course, this statement opens more issues than it answers. Even if we could redistribute power, to merely equalize power and let it go at that would not be enough. Rather, we may need to help create a process of change as discussed by Reich (1970) and Gorz (1967) through which lower level participants become equipped to exercise power.

In short, organizational psychology may become a stronger force for humanization by increasing the degree to which we take the sociocultural system as a our unit of analysis and lower level participants as our clients. More macroanalysis and awareness of the influence of our own personal worlds and background assumptions would certainly lead to better science. More attempts to view the requirements for humanization through the eyes of participants at all organizational levels would undoubtedly yield more effective strategies for humanizing these systems.

REFERENCES

A Pirandellian prison. *New York Times Magazine,* April 8, 1973, pp. 38-40.

Bennis, W. G.: An O.D. expert in the cat bird's seat. *Journal of Higher Education,* 44:389-398, 1973.

Bennis, W. G.: Conversation . . . with Warren Bennis. *Organizational Dynamics, 2:*51-66, 1974.

Brimm, M.: When is a change not a change? *J Appl Beh Sci, 8:*102-107, 1972.

Calame, B. E.: The truth hurts. *Wall Street Journal, XLIX:*1, 23, 1969.

Campbell, J. P.; Dunnette, M. D.; Lawler, E. E., and Weick, K. E.: *Managerial Behavior, Performance and Effectiveness.* New York, McGraw, 1970.

Cummin, P. C.: TAT correlates of executive performance. *J Appl Psychol, 51:*78-81, 1967.

Dahrendorf, R.: *Class and Class Conflict in Industrial Society.* Stanford, Stanford U Pr, 1959.

Festinger, L. A.: A theory of social comparison processes. *Human Relations, 7:*117-140, 1954.

Gorz, A.: *Strategy for Labor: A Radical Proposal.* Boston, Beacon, 1967.

Gouldner, A. W.: The norm of reciprocity: A preliminary statement. *Am Sociol Rev, 25:*161-179, 1960.

Gouldner, A. W.: *The Coming Crisis of Western Sociology.* New York, Basic, 1970.

Heilbroner, R. L.; Mintz, M.; McCarthy, C.; Ungar, S. J.; Vandiver, K.; Friedman, S., and Boyd, J.: *In the Name of Profit.* New York, Warner, 1973.

Homans, G. C.: *Social Behavior: Its Elementary Forms.* New York, Har-Brace, 1961.

Jencks, C.: *Inequality. A Reassessment of the Effects of Family and Schooling in America.* New York, Harper, 1972.

Kipnis, D.: Does power corrupt? *J Pers Soc Psychol, 24:*33-41, 1972.

Krishnan, R.: Democratic participation in decision making by employees in American corporations. *Academy of Management Journal, 17:*339-347, 1974.

Lehmann, T., and Young, T. R.: From conflict theory to conflict methodology: An emerging paradigm for sociology. *Sociological Inquiry, 44:*15-28, 1974.

Levinson, H.: Management by whose objectives? *Harvard Business Review, 48:*125-134, 1970.

Levinson, H.: Asinine attitudes towards motivation. *Harvard Business Review, 51:*70-76, 1973.

Livingston, J. S.: Myth of the well-educated manager. *Harvard Business Review, 49:*79-89, 1971.

Meadows, D. H.; Meadows, D. L.; Randers, J., and Behrens, W. W. III: *The Limits to Growth.* New York, Universe, 1972.

Miles, R. E.: Human relations or human resources? *Harvard Business Review, 43:*148-163, 1965.

Mulder, M.: Power equalization through participation? *Administrative Science Quarterly, 16*:31-39, 1971.

Mulder, M., and Wilke, H.: Participation and power equalization. *Organizational Behavior and Human Performance, 5*:417-429, 1970.

Nord, W. R.: The failure of current applied behavioral science: A Marxian perspective. *J Appl Beh Sci, 10*(4):557-578, 1974.

O'Day, R.: Intimidation rituals: Reactions to reform. *J Appl Beh Sci, 10*(3):373-386, 1974.

Quinn, R. P.; Mangione, T. W., and Baldi de Mandilovitch, M. S.: Evaluating working conditions in America. *Monthly Labor Review, 96*:32-41, 1973.

Reich, W.: *The Mass Psychology of Fascism.* New York, FS & G, 1970.

Rosenhan, D. L.: On being sane in insane places. *Science, 179*:250-258, 1973.

Scott, W. G.: Organization theory: A reassessment. *Academy of Management Journal, 17*:242-254, 1974.

Seeman, M.: The urban alienations: Some dubious theses from Marx to Marcuse. *J Pers Soc Psychol, 19*:135-143, 1971.

Tausky, C.: Meanings of work: Marx, Maslow and steamirons. American Sociological Convention, August, 1973.

Terreberry, S.: The evolution of organizational environments. *Administrative Science Quarterly, 12*:590-613, 1968.

von Forester, H.: From stimulus to symbol: The economy of biological computation. In Buckley, W. (Ed.): *Modern Systems Research for the Behavioral Scientist.* Chicago, Aldine, 1968, pp. 170-181.

Walton, R. E.: Frontiers beckoning the organizational psychologist. *J Appl Beh Sci, 8*:601-629, 1972.

Whyte, M. K.: Bureaucracy and modernization in China: The Maoist critique. *Am Sociol Rev, 38*:149-163, 1973.

Williams, R.: *American Society.* New York, Knopf, 1959.

Winter, D. G.: *The Power Motive.* New York, Free Press, 1973.

Wool, H.: What's wrong with work in America?—A review essay. *Monthly Labor Review, 96*:38-44, 1973.

INDIVIDUALIZING THE ORGANIZATION: THE INDIVIDUAL AND THE ORGANIZATION

INTRODUCING PART III . . .
WHAT TO DO

Wᴵᵀᴴ ᴀ ᴋɴᴏᴡʟᴇᴅɢᴇ of whither we are tending gained from
our study of organizational diagnosis we are now ready to consider *What to do* in a well-defined setting which we plan to
consider in Part III entitled "Individualizing the Organization:
The Individual and the Organization."

This central theme is succinctly considered by Lawler's contribution under the title of "Individualizing Organizations: A
Needed Emphasis in Organizational Psychology." This contribution is based on the address presented by Lawler at the APA
convention in 1973. It is Lawler's contention that a humanized
organization is one that can satisfy the needs of its members.
He emphasizes the marked personality differences in human
beings at work. He argues that to assure everyone would be
satisfied and productive, some individuals must be given enriched
jobs and others must be given classic Theory X-type jobs. The
insistent need in a humanizing organization is to treat employees
in more individualized ways. Lawler advocates that people must
be given the opportunity to make important decisions about their
working conditions for themselves rather than have them made
by the personnel department representing management. He
favors emphasizing consideration of potentials for doing rather
than what one can now do in measuring individual differences.
He also indicates that research shows that training needs to be
individualized and that this can be done, though not without
some difficulty. His belief is that the literature now suggests that
only individuals from rural backgrounds with a protestant ethic
attitude, who have strong higher order needs, can be expected to
respond favorably to job enrichment procedures by being more
satisfied and productive.

The next contribution, "Humanizing or Mental Health Implications of Aging in Industry," by Meltzer, is concerned with aging in industry, a topic which is not featured in many comprehensive gerontological volumes. An article, "Mental Health Implications of Aging in Industry," considers such problems as workers' perceptual age differences and perceptual stereotypes, a description of mental health programs, and significant statistical differences reported on four age groups studied in one well-defined setting. Also considered is a problem not too frequently encountered in the literature, namely the problem of age differences in positive mental health of workers. The factors investigated for assessing mental health were self-regard, maturity, personality organization and relations to environment. The general picture of the total index of mental health reveals the growth and decline with age. This and related findings will be of interest to people who work with the aging problem in industry, in counseling or in guidance of mental health problems in industry. All the facts presented have to be considered in the light of the emotional climate of an organization and its organizational effectiveness as related to attitudes expressed.

The next chapter in Part III is by Massarik. The title is "The Humanistic Organization: From Soft-Soap to Reality." It is based on a presentation at the 1973 symposium on Humanizing Organizational Psychology. Massarik considers the humanistic organization as neither Weberian bureaucracy nor Maslowian eupsychia. For perspective he considers seven criteria—valuing, holistic systematic perspective, intentionality, intuitiveness, openness-privacy, identity, paradox variabilty and creativity and meaning. Massarik conceives of the humanistic organization as paying attention to a multiplicity of relevant publics rather than emphasizing exclusively worker satisfaction. He lists thirteen relevant publics. Also considered is the multiplicity of values and goals. The paper ends with a reprise which represents an attempt at organizational realism. It is recognized that the humanistic organization should avoid both single-minded Pollyanna approaches and persistent gloom or fixed cynicism, and should be capable of responding to the genuine complexity of organizations and people—seeing a perspective with plusses and minuses that present themselves in ongoing organizational life. The humanistic organization seeks its unique identity and deals with the varied realities as these unfold in the light of changing values and goals of a broad set of relevant human groupings.

The last contribution, by Walter Nord, is of a different nature. "Behavior Modification Perspective for Humanizing Organizations" describes a process used for change which is not too often identified with an emphasis on humanizing. What Nord tries to do in this article is show that behavior modification per se is neither humanistic nor nonhumanistic. The perspective he describes is that it can be used for humanizing organizations. The early part of the article presents two general features which most humanists see as central to their position. One is to treat human beings as ends as opposed to means, and the other is to seek to advance the degree to which human beings exercise control over their own outcomes. Nord argues that while operant technology can be used to manipulate people, so can almost any advance in knowledge including participative management. With regard to the second criterion it is argued that behavior modification has the ability to enhance human potential, achieve favorable exchanges with the environment, and behavior modification may even turn out to be superior. The humanizing use of behavior modification is considered in this article in terms of its effect on individuality, choice and freedom.

Chapter 11

INDIVIDUALIZING ORGANIZATIONS: A NEEDED EMPHASIS IN ORGANIZATIONAL PSYCHOLOGY*

EDWARD E. LAWLER III

W HAT IS A humanized organization? Humanization can be equated with the degree to which an organization is designed to function in a way that satisfies the needs of its members and that is appropriate to their skills and abilities. Thus, a humanized organization is one that satisfies the needs of its members and that has jobs which fit the skills and abilities of its members.

How do we humanize organizations? The human resource theorists (Likert, Argyris, McGregor) propose one way of doing this. They talk about such things as autonomous work groups, enriched jobs, the Scanlon plan and participative leadership. According to them these practices will lead to high levels of individual need satisfaction, good utilization of everyone's skills and abilities, and to organizational effectiveness, but the writer wonders if practices such as these can produce an organization which satisfies the needs of all people. They will satisfy the needs of more people than will the practices which are prescribed by traditional organization theory. However, they, like the practices suggested by traditional theorists, fail to adequately take into account the differences that exist among individuals in their needs and abilities. McGregor and Argyris correctly point out that not everyone is Theory X in nature, *but* what

* Address presented by Edward Lawler III at the convention of the American Psychological Association in Montreal, 1973.

they don't emphasize is that not everyone is Theory Y in nature either.

Looking at the psychological research on people, one will see convincing evidence that individuals differ significantly in their needs, skills and abilities. This is not to say that individuals aren't similar in many ways, for they are, but to be human is to be unique. To be humanized an organization must recognize the uniqueness and sovereignty of each human being. In practical terms this means that organizations and jobs must be designed to ways that are responsive to the differences which exist among people. Approaches to organization design and management which recommend standardized jobs, authoritarian management and piece-rate pay incentive plans for all don't do this, and neither do approaches which recommend enriched jobs, democratic management and M.B.O. plans for all; therefore neither of these approaches has produced or is likely to produce a humanized organization.

The writer does not wish to take the time here to go through the literature in the areas of job design, leadership, pay, hours of work, selection and training, but wishes to remind the reader that study after study has shown that no practice in these areas elicits the same response in all or most people. It shows convincingly that standardized organization practices do not produce the same behavior on the part of all employees. It is often argued that organizations should treat everyone the same because only if they do this will everyone behave the same. This evidence suggests that only by treating individuals differently is it possible to get them to behave in the same way.

The research on job design nicely illustrates this point. Originally the advocates of job enrichment stressed that everyone could be expected to respond to enriched jobs by being more satisfied and productive. However, the literature now suggests that only rural background, protestant ethic individuals who have strong higher order needs can be expected to respond this way. Thus, in order to assure that everyone will be satisfied and productive, some individuals must be given enriched jobs and others must be given classic Theory-X-type jobs. In other words, in order to elicit the same response from all employees, the employees have to be given different jobs.

INDIVIDUALIZING ORGANIZATIONS

This conclusion suggests that a new emphasis is needed in our thinking about how organizations should be designed, an emphasis on individualization. If organizations are ever to be humanized they must treat employees in more individualized ways. How can organizations be designed so that they can treat everyone as the unique individuals they are? Unfortunately, at the moment there is no easy, obvious answer to this question. Two things are needed before this can become a reality—first, more basic research on how individual differences can be measured and on how they affect behavior in organizations; second, the development and testing of more operational practices and procedures which provide a practical way of treating employees differently according to their needs and abilities.

Before we discuss in detail the kind of research and practices which are needed in order to create individualized organizations we need to consider the general issue of who can best decide what kind of organizational situation is best for an individual. Most organization theorists have argued that the organization is in the best position to do this. Selection and placement programs, for example, are built on the basis of this assumption. The emphasis is not on providing the individual with valid information in order to help him or her make a good job choice decision, nor is the individual given much chance to personalize the job once he has taken it. The emphasis is on the organization collecting the information it needs in order to make good selection decisions and on developing standardized jobs and personnel practices. The assumption seems to be that the organization knows what is best for the individual, and, as a result, the individual doesn't have the opportunity to make very many meaningful choices about what his or her work life will be like.

A change in our thinking with respect to this issue is needed if we are to humanize organizations. People must be given the opportunity to make the important decisions about their working conditions for themselves. My belief is that most individuals can make good decisions about whether particular jobs and particular job characteristics will satisfy their needs and fit their abilities if they are given valid data. In fact, on the average, the writer is willing to bet that individuals can do a better job of choosing for themselves in many areas than organizations can do for them. He is aware that Argyris (1973) and others have pointed out that individuals who turn down enriched jobs often find them satisfying when they are coerced to try them. However, this type of case is felt to be relatively less frequent than cases where individuals are coerced to take enriched jobs and find them to be unsatisfying and not suited to their abilities. Further, even if an individual who is coerced to try an enriched job finds that he or she likes it, the whole experience may simply reinforce the person's feelings of dependency. In order for persons to gain increasing feelings of independence and experience psychological success, they must feel personally responsible for their behavior. Individuals who are coerced into trying things rarely feel that they are in control. Quite to the contrary they feel that once again someone has successfully showed them what is best, thereby causing them to experience psychological failure.

In the writer's view, there is also an ethical issue involved here—that psychologists must avoid deciding what is best for people. Otherwise we will end up taking a manipulative role. This suggests that individuals should be given valid data about what kind of job situation exists but that, in the end, they must decide without coercion to try the situation. The writer realizes a legitimate difference of opinion is possible here. It is reasonable to argue that only after a person has experienced something like an enriched job can he or she reach a valid conclusion about whether he wants it. The fallacy in this argument centers upon the issue of what happens to the individual who is harmed by trying something he or she doesn't want to try; the writer personally does not want to be responsible for this. Although he is not excited about being responsible for employees missing out on something good because they won't try it, he is more comfortable with taking responsibility for this.

RESEARCH ON INDIVIDUAL DIFFERENCES

The work on measuring individual differences that has been done so far has focused largely on measuring the *can do* aspects of behavior for the purpose of selection. The effective individualization of organizations depends on the development of measures which tap *will do* aspects of behavior, e.g., measures of motivation and reactions to different organizational climates, and measures that can be used for placing people in the part of the organization that best fits their needs and psychological makeups.

This is not to say that selection should be ignored; it certainly shouldn't since anything that can be done to keep to a manageable size the kinds of individual differences that exist in an organization and to keep out people who clearly cannot do the job should be done, but it is important that measures of such things as motivation, reactions to different leadership styles, and preferred organization climate be collected and evaluated in relationship to the climate of the organization, the psychological characteristics of the jobs in the organization, and the leadership style of various managers. The same measures are obviously relevant when consideration is given to placing new employees in different parts of the organization or in different jobs. The difficulty in doing this kind of selection and placement at the moment is that there is a paucity of measures of the relevant individual differences, and the needed measures of the organization climate and of the psychological characteristics of jobs do not exist. In many cases it is not even known what the relevant individual difference variables are when consideration is being given to predicting how people will react to different administrative practices, policies and different organization climates.

Research on selection is also needed which recognizes that individuals can contribute to better selection decisions. We need to learn how the selection situation can be turned into more of a counseling situation so that enlightened self-selection will operate. There is evidence that when job applicants are given valid information about the job they will make better choices. Weitz (1956) showed this long ago with insurance agents, and more recently it has been shown to operate with West Point cadets and telephone operators (Wanous, 1973). In the future the most effective selection programs will have to emphasize providing individuals with valid data about themselves and about the nature of the organization. For example, applicants might be shown the results of attitude surveys conducted in the organization, and they could be shown tables indicating the probability that people like themselves will succeed in the job. After this information is presented to the applicant, he or she will make the decision as to whether to join the organization. Before this kind of selection system can be put into effect, however, a great deal of research is needed on how this process can be handled. We need to know for example what kind of information should be presented to individuals and how it should be presented. However, the problems involved in the approach are solvable.

DESIGNING THE INDIVIDUALIZED ORGANIZATION

The research on job design, training, reward systems, hours of work and leadership provides a number of ideas as to how specific organizational practices and job situations can and should be individualized. The research on job design shows that jobs can be fit to people if organizations are willing to tolerate having a wide range of jobs and tasks. One plant in Florida has done this by having an assembly line operating next to a bench assembly of the same product. Employees are given a choice of which kind of job they want. The fact that some want to work on each kind is impressive evidence of the existence of individual differences. Kahn (1973) has suggested that the fit process can be facilitated by allowing individuals to choose among different groups of tasks or modules. In his system workers would bid for those tasks which they would like to do. For this system to work all individuals would, of course, have to know a considerable amount about the nature of the different modules. To be effective this approach will probably also have to take place in conjunction with some job enlargement activities. Otherwise, the employees might be faced with choosing among modules made up of simple, repetitive tasks, thus giving them no real choice. As Kahn notes, the modules concept is intriguing because it should make it easier for individuals to choose not to work a standard forty-hour week. This is important because of the difference in people's preferences with respect to hours of work.

The leadership research shows that people respond to different types of leadership. This could be handled by fitting the superior's style to the personality of subordinates such that the superior who can only behave in an authoritarian manner will be given subordinates who perform well under that type of supervision. The superior who can only behave participatively could be given only people who respond to that style. The superior who is capable of varying his style could be given either people who respond to different styles in different conditions or a mix of people with which he or she would be encouraged to behave differently. The important thing is to place subordinates according to how they respond to different styles and according to the styles of which the leader is capable.

The research shows that training needs to be individualized so that it will fit the needs and abilities of the person to learn. Implementation of this requires careful assessment of the people in terms of their abilities, motivation and good career counseling. Once it has been accepted that not everyone in the organization can profit from a given kind of training, then training becomes a matter of trying to develop people as much as possible with the kind of training to which they will respond. It involves accepting the fact that people may develop quite different leadership styles or ways of behaving in general and trying to capitalize on these by fitting the job the person holds and the groups he supervises to his style. The pay system could also be designed to fit the person. Fringe benefit packages can be individualized as a first step by using a cafeteria pay plan, and people can be placed on pay plans that fit their needs. Those whose desire for money is strong, for example, could be placed on jobs that lend themselves to pay incentive plans.

Creating truly individualized job situations which are suggested by the research obviously presents many practical problems in organization design. It is difficult for organizations to create conditions such that the person who responds to an enriched job and democratic supervision has them and the person who responds to a routinized job and authoritarian supervision has them. One way of accomplishing this could be by creating relatively autonomous subunits that vary widely in climate, job design, leadership style, etc. For example, within the same organization the same product might be produced by mass production in one unit and by unit production using enriched jobs in another. One subunit might have a warm, supportive climate while another might have a cold, demanding one. The size of the subunit would also vary depending upon the type of climate that is desired in it and the type of production it uses. From the point of view of individualization, this variation is not only all right, it is desirable as long as the placement process is able to help people find the modules that fit them.

An organization would have to have an almost infinite number of subunits if it were to try to have one to represent each of the possible combinations of climate, leadership style, incentive systems, job design, etc. This is not practical; and this is where selection, a study of the labor market, attention to the principles of motivation and satisfaction, and the nature of the product and market come into play. By studying the labor market to see what type of people the organization is likely to attract it should be possible to determine what combinations will be needed to fit the characteristics of most of the workers. In most homogeneous labor markets, this may be only a few of the many combinations that are possible. Traditional selection instruments can help the organization decide who will fit into the subunits, and, if individuals are given information about the nature of the subunits, they can often make valid decisions about whether they will fit.

Motivation theory argues that when important rewards are tied to performance, it is possible to have both high satisfaction and high performance (Vroom, 1964; Lawler, 1973). This suggests that all work modules which are created must meet one crucial condition—the reception of some rewards that are valued by members of that part of the organization must be tied to performance. This rules out many situations. For example, a situation in which no extrinsic rewards such as pay and promotion are tied to performance and which has authoritarian management and repetitive jobs should not exist. Finally, the research on job design and organization structure shows that the type of product and type of market limit the kind of subunit which can be successful. For example, authoritarian management, routine jobs and tall organization structures simply are not effective when the product is technically sophisticated and must be marketed in a rapidly-changing environment.

Creating subunits with distinctly different climates and practices is one way but not the only way to create an individualized organization. In small organizations this probably is not possible; thus, it is important to encourage differences within the same unit. This may mean training supervisors to deal differently with subordinates who have distinctly different personal characteristics. It may also mean designing jobs such that one person may do them one way and another person may do them another. For example, in one group a product might be built by a team and passed from one member to another, while in another everyone might build the entire product without help. Obviously, this approach generally will not allow for as much variation as does the approach of building distinctive subunits, but it permits some degree of individualization to take place, and this should lead to improvements over the more traditional approach which stresses standardization.

At the present time it is not apparent how such divergent organization practices as work modules, cafeteria-style pay plans and job enrichment that is guided by individual difference measures can be integrated in practice. With respect to practical application they are not necessarily in conflict nor are they necessarily synergistic. It is important to note, however, that they do share one attribute; they are all attempts to shape organization to individuals rather than the reverse. It seems logical, therefore, to identify these and other similar efforts as attempts to individualize organizations. Hopefully the identification of them as such and the establishment of the concept of individualization will lead to two very important developments—the generation of more practices that will individual organizations and work on how these different practices can simultaneously be made operational in organizations. Only if these developments take place will organizations ever be humanized.

REFERENCES

Argyris, C.: Personality and organization revisited. *Administrative Science Quarterly, 18*:141-167, 1973.

Kahn, R. L.: The work module—A tonic for lunchpail lassitude. *Psychol Today, 6*(9):35-49, 94-95, 1973.

Lawler, E. E.: *Motivation in Work Organizations.* Monterey, Brooks-Cole, 1973.

Vroom, V. H.: *Work and Motivation.* New York, Wiley, 1964.

Wanous, J. P.: Effects of a realistic job preview on job acceptance, job attitudes and job survival. *J Appl Psychol, 58*(3):327-332, 1973.

Weitz, J.: Job expectancy and survival. *J Appl Psychol, 40*(4):245-247, 1956.

──────── Chapter 12 ────────

HUMANIZING OR MENTAL HEALTH IMPLICATIONS OF AGING IN INDUSTRY*

H. MELTZER

INTRODUCTION

AGING IS AN important social issue. Discrimination against aging means a dehumanizing of the aging process for all too many workers who are either unemployed, unemployable or retired from industry. Aging as such does not have a monopoly on discrimination problems, poverty, illness or even housing problems, but it is a serious problem for many people who are aging. Of significance for our purposes is to review, in the form of a survey of facts known about aging in industry, the implications for the humanizing process or mental health implications of aging.

Aging in industry is not featured, in fact is hardly mentioned, in comprehensive gerontological volumes (e.g., Anderson, 1949, 1956), including those sponsored by the Gerontological Society (Birren, 1960; Burgess, 1960; Tibbits, 1960), but some related

* From H. Meltzer, "Mental Health Implications of Aging in Industry," in the main prepared for presentation at the Seventeenth Annual Meeting of the World Federation for Mental Health, Berne, Switzerland, August 3-7, 1964, with research projects sponsored by the Human Relations Research Foundation. The Journal of Genetic Psychology, 107:193-204, 1965, with selected excerpts from H. Meltzer and David Ludwig, "Age Differences in Positive Mental Health of Workers," The Journal of Genetic Psychology, 119:163-173, 1971. Reprinted by permission of the author and publishers of The Journal of Genetic Psychology. © Journal of Genetic Psychology.

considerations are presented. For example, Dr. Kleemeier's chapter, "Behavior and the Organization of the Bodily and the External Environment" (in Birren, 1960), outlines a broad approach toward aging problems in general. In the same volume is the relevant chapter, "Work and Occupational Skills" (in Birren, 1960), by McFarland and O'Doherty. Also, related areas covered include Brozek's (1956) article on age and functional efficiency; Clay's (1956) study on performance in relation to age; Karsten's (1959) study, "Adjustment to Old Age in Industry"; and Welford's (1958) study, "Ageing and Human Skill."

Ageing in Industry, the most comprehensive book on the subject, has been published in England. Clark and Dunn (1956), its authors, used a completely statistical approach concerned with the survival rates for old age for thirty-two occupations as found from the census studies in England. Clark and Dunn's purpose is to survey modern industry from the viewpoint of its oldest opera-tors—that is, they attempt to determine what workers are able to continue in various occupations beyond the midsixties. There is need for studies about age differences in work and life-adjust-ment attitudes in well-defined settings, and a need for facts concerning the social psychology of aging in industry—this means interpreting individual differences with full consideration of organizational effectiveness and emotional climate as emphasized by Argyris (1957, 1962).

The need for considering emotional climate and setting for understanding any given personality is well expressed by D. H. Lawrence (1930) in an essay called "We Need One Another,"

> You may imagine you are something very grand, since few individuals approximate to this independence without falling into deadly egoism and conceit; and emptiness. The real danger is, reduced to your own single merits and cut off from the most vital human contacts, the danger is that you are left just simply next to nothing. Reduce an individual, man or woman, to his elements, or her elements, and what is he? what is she? Extremely little! Take Napoleon, and stick him alone on a miserable island and what is he?—a peevish puerile little fellow. Put Mary Stuart in a nasty stone castle of a prison and she becomes merely a catty little person. Now Napoleon was not a peevish, puerile little fellow, even if he became such when isolated to St. Helena. And Mary Queen of Scots

was only a catty little person when she was isolated in Fotheringay or some such hole. This grand isolation, this reducing of ourselves to our very elemental selves, is the greatest fraud of all. It is like plucking the peacock naked of all his feathers to try to get at the real bird. When you've plucked the peacock bare, what have you got? Not the peacock, but the naked corpse of a bird.

PURPOSE

The purpose of the present study is to review three series of articles concerning work and life-adjustment attitudes (Meltzer, 1963), stereotypes of age preferences for happiness (Meltzer, 1964), and age differences in the positive mental health of workers (Meltzer, 1958, 1960, 1962, 1965). In the light of these studies mental health needs and possible mental health programs dealing with the problem in industry will be considered.

The setting for the studies reviewed involves a history of security and a pattern of management designed to be firm but democratic. The more generalized conclusions are best conceived as applicable to organizations similarly designed and managed.

REVIEW OF STUDIES ON AGE DIFFERENCES IN WORK ATTITUDES

Work and Life-Adjustment Attitudes

For the studies on work and life-adjustment attitudes, 257 subjects were divided into four groups as follows: Group I, composed of 102 workers from nineteen to twenty-nine; Group II, composed of ninety-eight workers from thirty to forty-four; Group III, forty-three workers from forty-five to fifty-nine; and Group IV, thirteen workers from sixty to seventy-seven. All of the subjects were from the parent plant in Saint Louis (see Meltzer, 1958). The results were based on the findings of morale-survey data containing forty-one items, twenty-eight of which refer to work attitudes and thirteen to life-adjustment attitudes. As a simple expression of the general tendency of an individual toward satisfaction or dissatisfaction, a satisfaction index was used. The procedure for obtaining the index followed that used in determining algedonic differences in the study of individual differences in forgetting pleasant and unpleasant experiences (Meltzer, 1930). The formula used is $(S \div T)$ minus $(U \div T)$. S equals responses indicating above-average satisfaction, U equals responses indicating below-average satisfaction, and T equals the total number of responses. The middle or average choice was not included in the calculations; thus, the index is a measure of predominance of satisfaction or dissatisfaction.

The findings in the author's first study on age differences in work attitudes may be summarized as follows:

1. There are many statistically significant differences among the four age groups (Meltzer, 1958).
2. In considering the company as a place to work and items indicative of identification with management and their policies there is a tendency for increasingly favorable attitudes with age.
3. Attitude toward pay becomes increasingly more favorable with age.
4. In most areas tested, satisfaction increases with age.
5. The differentiating age for attitude toward work conditions is forty-five.

The evidence does not prove Harris' (1949) contention that "An old population is more conservative, less creative, less productive, less mobile, and more dependent than the younger one." What the study does show is that the attitude of the older worker can be perceived as a pattern, and that some of the seemingly paradoxical answers obtained make sense in the setting in which they developed. For example, older workers think well of supervisors in general and think that supervisors are interested in them, but they consider themselves neglected in certain types of attention and feel that supervisors play favorites and do not treat them as favorites. When an older worker says he cannot tell how good a job he is doing, he merely means that the supervisor takes him for granted too much and that he would like more attention. The fact that the oldest group of workers gives the most favorable responses to questions about having had its breaks and share of happiness while it rates low in share of recognition makes unifying sense. It makes sense, however, only if the context of the situation and all that characterizes the human relations practices involved are considered (Meltzer, 1958).

Age Preference for Happiness

For the studies on age preferences for happiness in the various groups, subjects were 270 workers of both sexes working for the same company, though located in three different regions of the United States—Northeast, Midwest and Far West. The age ranges were seventeen to sixty-two for women and seventeen to sixty-four for men.

In a second study of age differences in happiness and life adjustment of workers (Meltzer, 1963) the author reached the following conclusions:

1. The feeling of the worker that he has had his *share of happiness* increases with age. There are large and statistically significant differences between all groups with the exception of the two younger groups.
2. The belief of the worker that he has received his *share of happiness* does not seem to differ from age group to age group in terms of statistical significance, but the trend seems to be negatively associated with age.
3. In general *work* takes on more significance with age! *Spare time* decreases in significance with age.
4. With increased age there is increased interest in *steady work* and decreased interest in advancement. Hope for advancement is low in the youngest group; it decreases with age; and it is practically absent in the oldest group.
5. The correlation of *share of happiness* with two items indicative of *self-concept* is relatively consistent, with a coefficient of contingency of .45 for one and .38 for the other. The correlations with two items classified as perception of others are inconsistent, one being the highest the other being the lowest coefficient of contingency (see Meltzer, 1963).

A REVIEW OF WORKERS' PERCEPTUAL STEREOTYPES

On the basis of two studies on workers' perceptual stereotypes of age differences (Meltzer, 1960, 1964), particularly in a study of age and sex differences in workers' perceptions of happiness for self and others, conclusions were as follows:

1. Perception of happiness in years of life for self and others is different.
2. Perception of years of happiness for others is more consistent, less varied and a more reliable index of stereotype than perception of years for self.
3. Younger years generally are the more favored years; older years are the least favored in happiness for others.
4. In perception of years of life that are happy for self, personal experience plays a differential role.
5. In perception of years for self, women tend to be more varied and less stereotyped than men.
6. Reasons for selecting happy years of life given by women are different from those given by men and are likely to be in accord with society's notion of male and female roles.

AGE DIFFERENCES IN POSITIVE MENTAL HEALTH OF WORKERS

In *Current Concepts of Positive Mental Health*, Dr. Jahoda (1958) paid little attention to the age factor in mental health, but does express an awareness of the significance of the problem in the following words: "The study of mental health in different age groups is a research problem in its own right" (Jahoda, 1958). She suggested criteria relevant for considering all age groups in these words,

> Perception of reality, meeting the requirements of the situation, and problem-solving are the criteria *par excellence* having meaning for all age groups, even though their empirical study will, of course, have to take age into consideration (Jahoda, 1958).

The purpose of the present investigation, with the use of the suggestions given by Jahoda, is to study the relation of age to mental health in an industrial setting. This is in accord with McLean's (1967) outlook that in the future there will be more concern and greater demonstration of employer responsibility for encouraging mentally healthy behavior in employees and less worry about those with mental illness.

The most comprehensive study of mental health in workers has been made by Kornhauser (1964). Age differences are considered but not related to the actual mental health indices used. The implication of studies on personality factors and work output of Peck and Parsons (1956) is that little success has been found in relating mental health, as measured by inventories or other paper and pencil tests, to the way in which a worker does his job or makes his adjustments. In the article they concluded that a picture of his own work story would yield more positive results and that a more adequate analysis of life and work stories interpreted in mental health terms will provide a more adequate basis for study of mental health workers than personality tests.

In this investigation an attempt is made to study, by way of the content analysis of life and work stories, the relation of mental health and age of workers with the emphasis not on mental illness, but on positive mental health. The main purpose of the first study is to explore the age differences in mental health of workers divided into five age groups; the following study is concerned with the study of the relationship of positive mental health of workers to memory optimism or pessimism and work competency.

Method

Subjects and Setting

The subjects in this study were 143 workers in a paper-converting industry located in a stable college community in upstate New York. This paper mill is the only plant of any size in the community, and obtaining a job there at that time was considered the beginning of an establishment to a good many of the people living in the community. For the most part they were semiskilled and skilled workers with large families and strong feelings about their jobs in the industry. The workers in the study ranged from nineteen to seventy-eight and represented about one third of all the workers in the plant. For the purpose of this study they were divided into five age groups used in previous studies (e.g., Meltzer, 1958, 1963, 1964)—twenty to twenty-nine, thirty to thirty-nine, forty to forty-nine, fifty to fifty-nine, and sixty-up. Percentages in each group arranged in sequences were as follows: 21.68 percent, 25.17 percent, 25.80 percent, 18.18 percent and 9.09 percent.

Source Material

The source material used was based on initial interviews with workers who were taken over by a new company. The interviewers* were representatives of the new company, and the attitudes of most of the workers toward them were extremely favorable because of dissatisfaction with the old company. In the interview as structured, the directed questioning about work, family, personal story, present conditions and problems preceded the more projective phase of the interview, which, in this study, was the recall of outstandingly pleasant and unpleasant experiences of life and personified values (see Meltzer, 1950).

Procedure

The interview was structured in the following sequence (Meltzer, 1950): (1) Direct questioning about work, family, personal story and the present conditions or problems; (2) recall of the most outstanding pleasant experience with the question, "And now tell me what comes to your mind when you think of the most outstanding pleasant experience in your life";† (3) recall of other outstanding pleasant experiences; (4) recall of the most outstanding unpleasant experience; (5) recall of other outstanding unpleasant experiences; (6) questions concerning personified values, (a) Who is the greatest person that ever lived? Why?; (b) Who is the greatest person living? Why?; (7) questions

---

* The interviewers were different from the investigator who worked with the data thus acquired.

† Request for pleasant and unpleasant recall did not invite or suggest concern over attitude toward management. The questions were relatively unstructured and invited memories of a lifetime.

concerning personified ideals or aspirations, "Of all the people you've ever seen, heard about, or read about, whom would you rather be like? Why?"

As a single measure of memory optimism or pessimism, the P-U Potency Index* was used. A plus score was interpreted as indicating memory optimism, a minus score as indicative of memory pessimism, and a zero score as indicative of indifference. The work competency index (Meltzer and Ludwig, 1968) was based on the rating of the interviewers at the end of the interview. The interviewers had available the ratings by the respective foremen of the subjects studied to consider as an aid in making their judgments. Scores for various ratings went from 1 (very poor) to 8 (very good). The assessment of dominant value was based on direct reference to such a value in the recall of memories (Meltzer and Ludwig, 1968).

For the purpose of assessing mental health the interview material was broken down into individual sentences and those sentences, approximately fifteen per record, which were felt to be indicative of the worker's mental health were underlined. Each of the sentences was then taken individually, was given a (+) or (−) value, then placed in one of four categories that was chosen to be indicative of the worker's positive mental health. These categories were adapted from Jahoda (1958) and constitute a condensation of her six major categories of criteria for total positive mental health. The categories are self-regard, maturity, personality organization and relation to environment. The judgments involved in this assessment were made by a person who did not do any of the interviewing and were made without knowledge of the optimism or competency scores of the subjects.

SELF-REGARD. The attitudes an individual has toward himself make up the self-regard category. A sentence would be scored positively and placed in this category if it indicated some measure of self-acceptance, self-confidence, self-reliance and sense of identity. A sentence would be scored negatively and placed in

---

* This scale refers to the predominance of pleasant over unpleasant memories derived by subtraction of the number of unpleasant from the number of pleasant memories (first used by Meltzer, 1930).

this category if it indicated a lack of the above qualities (such as lack of self-acceptance).

MATURITY. The maturity category designates the worker's degree of growth, development and self-actualization as reflected in his sense of responsibility and his trustworthiness as a worker.

PERSONALITY ORGANIZATION. Personality organization is an assessment of the personality structure of the worker and designates such traits as resistance to stress, a unifying outlook on life (integration and balance of personality) and good reality orientation. Special consideration is given to the firmness of the personality as opposed to either looseness (lack of firm organization) or rigidity (intolerance).

RELATIONS TO ENVIRONMENT. Relations to environment designates the worker's adequacy in interpersonal relations and efficiency in meeting situation requirements, his sensitivity to others and his adjustment to the situation. Also, consideration is given in this category to the reaction of other people to the worker being interviewed.

After each of the underlined sentences and interviews was scored either positive or negative and placed into one of the four categories, the indices of positive mental health of the worker could be given. The score for each individual category was determined by subtracting the number of negative statements from the positive ones in that category. The overall total mental health index was determined by adding the four category scores.

A second judge (who was a graduate student in psychology) scored twenty-five of the same protocols according to the criteria and categories defined above. The same underlined sentences were used for both scorings. The interjudge reliability for the total index was found to be .85, and the reliabilities for the four categories were found to be .81 for self-regard, .86 for maturity, .71 for personality organization, and .77 for relations to environment.

Results

The findings in the study of age differences in positive mental health as reported in terms of means, standard deviations and f-ratios may be summarized as follows:

1. The thirty to thirty-nine age group scored significantly higher on all mental health indices than all the other age groups. The differences between this age group and the younger (20 to 29) age group and older groups were all significant at the .01 level.

2. The largest difference between the younger and older workers is found in their self-regard. It appears that the younger workers are more idealistic about themselves and are more confident about their abilities than are the older workers who can look back and see failure in meeting their ideals. The next greatest difference between the two groups is found in their relations to the environment. Here again the younger workers seem to be able to adapt to the situational demands and be more adaptable to their environment than the older workers who have apparently become more "set in their ways." There is also some difference in personality organization. The younger workers seem to exhibit a greater resistance to stress and somewhat more reality orientation than do the older workers who begin to wonder about their future and are contemplating the agonies of retirement and old age. There seemed to be little difference in the maturity scale of the two age groups, and it would seem likely that the older workers would score fairly well on this scale because of their dependency on the job.

3. The general picture of the total mental health index reveals a steep rise in the Positive Mental Health from ages twenty to twenty-nine, to ages thirty to thirty-nine with the peak being reached at this latter age. From there a marked decline occurs to the forty to forty-nine age group with a gradual leveling off from there until the sixty-up age group. It would seem that the twenty to twenty-nine age group is going through the initial rough period of adjustment to marriage and vocation, and thus score lower than the thirty to thirty-nine age group which has passed through this period and arrived at established lives. This is in accord with the findings in the age differences in workers' perceptions of happiness of self and others (Meltzer,

1963). Workers perceive their own peak age of happiness as arriving later than those of others. The positive outlook on organization decreases drastically from forty on with the realization of the middle-age decline and the lack of fulfillment of the earlier goals and ideals.

Figure 12-1 presents a graphic illustration of the results of the different age groups on the total index. This index shows a significant increase from the twenty to twenty-nine age group to the thirty to thirty-nine age group and then a significant drop to the last three age groups. The latter three age groups did not differ significantly from each other.

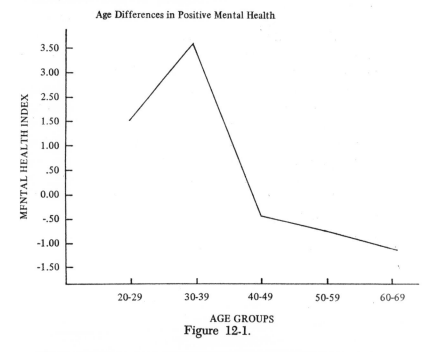

Age Differences in Positive Mental Health

AGE GROUPS
Figure 12-1.

HUMANIZING OR MENTAL HEALTH IMPLICATIONS OF AGING IN INDUSTRY

For the reduction if not elimination of dehumanizing effects and discrimination against the older workers, the studies reveal the following needs for change in programs, policies and attitudes which now prevail:

1. The need for replacing the use of stereotypes with facts to serve as a frame of reference for establishing and developing policies and attitudes. These should include the facts reported concerning age differences and work and life adjustments, age differences in share of happiness of workers, and age differences in positive mental health of workers.

2. The need for special consideration for hiring workers above forty and managers above fifty or fifty-five.

3. The need for restructuring retirement policies and programs based on individual differences in abilities and attitudes to make possible the development of more flexible programs which definitely consider individual differences rather than a rigid standardized rule for all who arrive at a given age, say, sixty-five.

4. The need for many aging workers on the road toward retirement to shift their primary and marginal roles. Otherwise, an abrupt retirement has the possibility of leading many workers from a work role which was all meaningful to no role that has any meaning and makes for a life full of emptiness and often early death.

MENTAL HEALTH PROGRAMS

Based upon a consideration of the foregoing needs, programs that industry would do well to consider are the following:

1. **Counseling older workers on the job for career planning and retirement.** Such counseling should be done by people with industrial experience as well as with psychological knowledge and (in the light of the facts presented in this paper) with knowledge of work attitudes, life-adjustment attitudes, perceptual stereotypes and other knowledge of aging in industry. When a company can afford it and is willing, it would be well for it to start counseling at least ten years before retirement time to prepare people still on the job for not only retirement but for adjustments in later years.

2. **Changing employment policy about hesitancy or resistance against hiring people above forty.** This calls for a complete change

of attitude on the part of many people responsible for hiring. Companies that have pension programs often think they cannot afford to hire older people because such persons would profit from the pension system without spending many years with the company. Some companies resolve this conflict by getting the older person to forego the pension benefits or to agree to an individualized retirement program that does not take money out of the reserves held for those who have worked longer. The problem is more than one of reeducating people in personnel to hire people in terms of capacities, abilities and experience. It involves reeducating top management to the desirability and advantage of hiring older workers. This is not an easy change to bring about, and it calls for national as well as local publicizing of the facts and their significance for hiring. In some instances one might even find it possible and desirable to do what Marrow (1945) did to overcome the resistance to change on the part of the board of trustees of his company.

3. **Planned change for acceptance of change.** This concept implies informing workers as well as management. In this connection, it is well for one to keep in mind the words of Lippitt, Watson, and Westley,

> We need always to remember that when examined closely, all dynamic systems reveal a continuous process of change—adaptation, adjustment, reorganization. This is what we mean by dynamic, by being alive. We call these processes learning, development, maturation, and growth. But it is equally true, as we can learn both from experience and from the results of scientific studies, that all these systems exhibit a high degree of stability, constancy or rigidity, in many aspects of their operation and organization. Often as external observers, we can note that this stability is very uncomfortable or even dangerous, not only for the system in question but for its neighboring systems. In other words, the natural dynamic processes of change do not occur fast enough to keep pace with the very rapidly changing conditions of our world today (Lippitt, Watson, and Westley, 1958).

4. **Organized labor-management mental health programs.** At the 1964 meeting of the American Orthopsychiatric Association held in Chicago, three labor-management mental health programs

were presented. Dr. L. L. Tureen presented one in use for eighteen years by the Labor Health Institute operated by the Teamsters Union in Saint Louis. This service has been expanded since that time and as presented in the Annual Report (Berger, 1973) of the Saint Louis Labor Health Institute, the extent of the nature of the services is indicated by the number of classified cases which include the following: a total of 394 cases for the year composed of eighteen people classified as psychotics, 165 classified as psychosis, 165 classified as neurosis, eight classified as organic brain syndrome, ninety classified as behavior disorders, and others composed of undiagnosed and psychophysiological reactions totaling 113. The predominant form of treatment continues to be individual psychotherapy; however, marital, family and group therapy are being used more frequently than ever before.

The second program presented is one operated by the Amalgamated Clothing Workers of America. The person reporting was Dr. H. J. Weiner, Director of the Sidney Hillman Health Center. Dr. Weiner, a sociologist, is directing the agency to be community-conscious and is definitely making an attempt to pitch services to community rather than union control. Dr. Weiner *et al.* (1973) have continued to work on the program originally described for the Orthopsychiatric Association. The efforts and the results obtained have been recently published in book-form by him and co-authors in a volume entitled *Mental Health Care in the World of Work*. This book describes in detail all phases of the program—how to use the work setting and locate the individual in it; difficulty of functioning on the job, how to help workers stay on the job; and their problem of establishing a mental health care clinic for blue-collar workers; how the clinic organized and emerged from the community; how the clinic can adapt to the life-style of the rhythm of industry; a description of the diagnostic process involved in evaluating the breakdown of the clinic population: rationale and methodology; the multidimensional approach to the solution of problems; harnessing of existing union and management resources; and linking the services with the center's health system. This book also contains a consideration of mental health and work behavior. The central question considered is what is the impact of mental illness on an individual's ability to maintain a work role.

5. **Organizing a flexible retirement program which provides for consideration of individual differences in abilities, skills and contributions to organizational effectiveness.** Solving the retirement problem is not as simple as passing a law against it because it is well-known that unions, leaders in unions and many workers are just as much and even more often advocates of compulsory retirement policies than are the employers and industrialists or the so-called capitalists. So needed is knowledge for people on the labor side as well as people on the management side and also people in government to understand the meaning and implications of the aging process for life renewal as well as for retirement. That calls for something that is also lacking in our society, namely the courage and honesty to deal individually with each person, his competence and ability. The facts of individual differences are disregarded. Instead there is a policy which assumes all people over sixty-five are retired, willingly or unwillingly. Among the many workers that we studied there are many at the age of forty who look upon themselves as too old to get jobs and too young to die.

Even in our universities, compulsory retirement is the general policy regardless of individual differences, competency or vitality. The problem is getting more serious because in 1900 two thirds of the American men who were sixty-five years old were working. In 1971 only one fourth of the people sixty-five or over were working. Between 1940 and 1970 there has been an increase in the number of people aged sixty-five or over from nine million to twenty million; from 6.8 percent of the population to 9.0 percent. With this immense increase and with the young generation emphasizing the present and disregarding the past, the elderly represent the depository of the past. Needed is an awareness of the fact that compulsory retirement keyed to chronological age can be harmful and threatens the health of the individual concerned. This is well-expressed in the beginning of a booklet of the American Medical Association's Committee on Aging called "Retirement—A Medical Philosophy and Approach" (see "Compulsory Retirement . . .," 1974): "The increase in life expectancy and higher health levels will prove of little benefit to man if he is denied the opportunity to continue contributing of his skills at a certain chronological age, whether this be 45, 65, or 85 years."

In the studies presented here, the work took on more rather than less meaning with the aging process. Older people paid more attention and considered work as their primary role, whereas younger workers did have other roles outside of work. In the recent book on *Old Age in a Changing Society*, a sociologist, Dr. Blau (1973), expounds a role exit theory which she described as serving a better frame of reference than the *disengagement theory* for explaining events and conditions known to exist among the aged in our population. The role exit is said to occur

> whenever stable patterns of interaction or shared activities between two or more persons cease. "Divorce," "Separation," "Departure," and "Ending" are terms given to signify exit from social roles which engender feelings of deprivation, sadness, depression, and uncertainty similar in character, if not in intensity and duration, to those precipitated by a loved person's death.

An excellent illustration of the possible significance of aging and retirement is presented on page 78 of *Work in America* (1973). Here a Mr. Winter is described who single-handedly ran an operation that nobody else in his company fully understood. At the age of sixty-five he was forced to retire after he broke in a younger man. In retirement he withdrew, became vegetable-like and was in the hospital emotionally dying. Two years later the apprentice died. The company did all they could to bring Mr. Winter back to life. Four of his best friends finally succeeded in a breakthrough after much effort. They did spark life in Mr. Winter when it finally dawned on him that he was being offered work again, the work that had meant everything to him. Shortly thereafter he was operating at full steam and interacting with people as he had years before. The story of Mr. Winter is one not only of role exit, but of role exit and role renewal. The important consideration for planned programs for the aging process in industry is to provide for renewal and not merely exit.

An excellent perspective on the meaning and possibilities of self-renewal of individuals and organizations can be found in John Gardner's (1963) book entitled *Self-Renewal, The Individual and the Innovative Society*. From this book we can learn some very relevant facts which can serve as a basis for self-renewing processes in the individual in industry or in society. We can, for example, learn that

> . . . Renewal—of societies or of individuals—depends in some measure on motivation, commitment, conviction, the values men live by, the things that give meaning to their lives. . . . Though the only society that can renew itself over a long period of time is a free society, this offers no grounds for complacency. We are not living up to our ideals as a free society, and we are very far from meeting the requirements of an ever-renewing society. But both are within reach. . . It is necessary to discuss not only the vitality of societies but the vitality of institutions and individuals. They are the same subject. A society decays when its institutions and individuals lose their vitality. . . . Men who have lost their adaptiveness naturally resist change. The most stubborn protector for his own vested interest is the man who has lost the capacity for self-renewal. . . . The society can do much to encourage such self-development. The most important thing it can do is to remove the obstacles to individual fulfillment. This means doing away with gross inequalities of opportunity imposed on some of our citizens by race prejudice and economic hardship. And it means a continuous and effective operation of "talent salvage" to assist young people to achieve the promise that is in them. The benefits are not only to the individuals but to the society. The renewing society must be continuously refreshed by a stream of new talent from all segments or strata of society. Nothing is more decisive for social renewal than the mobility of talent.

All of this brings us to the modern emphasis on process, an emphasis suggested in its broadest implication by Arnold Toynbee (1948) when he said, "Civilization is a movement . . . and not a condition, a voyage and not a harbor." This is in accord with Gardner's (1963) impression, "In the ever-renewing society, what matures is a system of framework within which continuous innovation, renewal and rebirth can occur."

REFERENCES

Anderson, J. E. (Ed.): *Psychological Aspects of Aging.* Washington, Am Psychol, 1956.

Anderson, J. E.: *The Psychology of Development and Personal Adjustment.* New York, Holt, 1949.

Argyris, C.: *Interpersonal Competence and Organizational Effectiveness.* Homewood, Dorsey, 1962.

Argyris, C.: *Personality and Organization.* New York, Harper, 1957.

Berger, E. J.: *Annual Report, Saint Louis Labor Health Institute, 1973.* Saint Louis, Saint Louis Labor Health Institute, 1973.

Birren, J. E. (Ed.): *Handbook of Aging and the Individual.* Chicago, U of Chicago Pr, 1960.

Blau, Z. S.: *Old Age in a Changing Society.* New York, New Viewpoints, 1973.

Brozek, J.: Age and functional efficiency: A comment. In Anderson, J. E. (Ed.): *Psychological Aspects of Aging.* Washington, Am Psychol, 1956, pp. 245-248.

Burgess, E. W. (Ed.): *Aging in Western Societies.* Chicago, Univ of Chicago Pr, 1960.

Clark, F. L., and Dunn, A. C.: *Ageing in Industry.* New York, Philos Lib, 1956.

Clay, H. M.: A study of performance in relation to age at two printing works. *J Gerontol, 11*:417-424, 1956.

Clay, H. M.: Compulsory retirement can be harmful. *Newsletter, Am Orthopsychiatr Assoc, XVIII*:9, July, 1974.

Gardner, J. W.: *Self-Renewal.* New York, Har-Row, 1963.

Harris, S. E.: What to do with 18 million aged? *New York Times Magazine,* July 10:8, 1949.

Jahoda, M.: *Current Concepts of Positive Mental Health.* New York, Basic, 1958.

Karsten, A.: Adjustment to old age in industry. *Vita Hum, 2*:87-101, 1959.

Kleemeier, R. W.: Behavior and the organization of the bodily and external environment. In Birren, J. E. (Ed.): *Handbook of Aging and the Individual.* Chicago, U of Chicago Pr, 1960, pp. 400-451.

Kornhauser, A.: *Mental Health of the Industrial Worker.* New York, Wiley, 1964.

Lawrence, D. H.: We need one another. *Scribner's,* May:479-484, 1930.

Lippitt, R.; Watson, J., and Westley, B.: *Dynamics of Planned Change.* New York, Harcourt, 1958.

Marrow, A. J., and French, J. R. P.: Changing stereotypes in industry. *J Soc Iss, 1*:33-37, 1945.

McFarland, R., and O'Doherty, B. M.: Work and occupational skills. In Birren, J. E. (Ed.): *Handbook of Aging and the Individual.* Chicago, U of Chicago Pr, 1960, pp. 452-502.

McLean, A.: *To Work Is Human and Mental Health and the Business Community.* New York, MacMillan, 1967, pp. 273-280.

Meltzer, H.: Mental health implications of aging in industry. *J Genet Psychol, 107:*193-203, 1965.

Meltzer, H.: Age and sex differences in workers' perceptions of happiness for self and others. *J Genet Psychol, 105:*1-11, 1964.

Meltzer, H.: Age differences in happiness and life adjustments of workers. *J Gerontol, 18:*66-70, 1963.

Meltzer, H.: Age differences in status and happiness of workers. *Geriatrics, 17:*831-838, 1962.

Meltzer, H.: Workers' perceptual stereotypes of age differences. *Perceptual and Motor Skills, 11:*89, 1960.

Meltzer, H.: Age differences in work attitudes. *J Gerontol, 13:*74-81, 1958.

Meltzer, H.: Memory dynamics, projective tests, and projective interviewing. *J Pers, 19:*48-63, 1950.

Meltzer, H.: Individual differences in forgetting pleasant and unpleasant experiences. *J Educ Psychol, 21*(6):399-409, 1930.

Meltzer, H., and Ludwig, D.: Memory dynamics and work motivation. *J Appl Psychol, 52:*423-428, 1968.

Peck, R. F., and Parsons, J. W.: Personality factors in work output: four studies of factory workers. *Personnel Psychol, 9:*49-79, 1956.

Tibbits, C. (Ed.): *Handbook of Social Gerontology.* Chicago, U of Chicago Pr, 1960.

Toynbee, A.: *Civilization on Trial.* New York, Oxford U Pr, 1948.

Weiner, H. J.; Akabas, S. H., and Sommer, J. J.: *Mental Health Care in the World of Work.* New York, Assn Pr, 1973.

Welford, A. R.: *Ageing and Human Skill.* London, Oxford U Pr, 1958.

Welford, A. R.: *Work in America.* Report of a Special Task Force to the Secretary of Health, Education, and Welfare. Cambridge, M.I.T. Pr, 1973.

———————————— Chapter 13 ————————————

THE HUMANISTIC ORGANIZATION:
FROM SOFT-SOAP TO REALITY

FRED MASSARIK*

RARELY ARE THE concepts *humanism* and *organization* blended in harmony. Conventional imagery is replete with notions that semantically polarize these basic constructs. Influential treatments of organization rarely consider humanism explicitly, although, of course, ideas—and controversies—surrounding human relations are widely current. The latter label itself has been subject to a checkered history; for some it has become a virtual epithet to be hurled at any style of organization or management that is alleged to be soft, muddle-headed or in some way committed to individual welfare to the presumed detriment of organizational goal attainment.

This paper holds that a clarification and substantive introduction of the concept *humanistic organization* is overdue. Let us note at the outset that this concept by no means proposes that any one set of individual needs, *ipso facto*, normatively must outrank organizational goal attainment, nor indeed is humanistic organization inherently synonymous with any views attributed (largely erroneously) to the human relations movement, viz. views allegedly promulgating unrealistic oversell of happiness/personal satisfaction while ignoring the significance of task objectives.

The notion that *the humanistic* is the necessary antithesis to *the directive* is prevalent in much contemporary management

* Based on an address presented at the Convention of the American Psychological Asosciation in Montreal, 1973.

thought. By way of example, we note an article in *Administrative Management,* a widely-read business systems, equipment and personnel journal, that views the humanist style of organizational leadership as follows:

> This style results from over-reaction to the preachings of human relationists and makes individual happiness the ultimate goal. The seeking of total self-satisfaction for the individual is so important that the objectives of the organization itself are subordinated. This style is sometimes called country club leadership, or "have another martini" management (*XXXV*(10), October, 1974).

This position epitomizes a level of oversimplification that, unfortunately, has characterized much of the accumulated literature.* The search for neat descriptive categories has tended to obscure the complexity characterizing managerial/organizational reality, though contingency theory has been a welcome counterbalance.† While individual managers may find particular modes of functioning more compatible than others, and while some generic commonalities may be observed in these modes, variability in style and environment are the pervasive dynamics. It is this turbulence rather than typological fixedness that provides a basis for the introduction of the humanistic organization concept.

WHAT THE HUMAN ORGANIZATION IS
NOT AND WHAT IT IS

The humanistic organization is neither Weberian bureaucracy nor Maslowian eupsychia.‡ The proposed construct may, how-

---

* But even influential scholarly literature is not immune to oversimplification; a visible example: the Theory X/Theory Y dichotomy of Douglas McGregor's *The Human Side of Enterprise,* New York, McGraw-Hill, 1960, pp. 33-58, which may in fact owe its impact to its apparent simplicity, no less than to its plausibility.

† See for instance, Paul R. Lawrence and Jay W. Lorsch, *Organization and Environment,* Homewood, Richard D. Irwin, 1969, pp. 185 ff. and Jay W. Lorsch and Stephen A. Allen III, *Managing Diversity and Interdependence,* Boston, Harvard, 1973, p. 191 ff.

‡ For views of Weber's concepts, see Stanley H. Udy, Jr. " 'Bureaucracy' and 'Rationality' in Weber's Organization Theory," *American Sociological Review,* 24, 1959, pp. 791-795 and basic sources such as Max Weber In Talcott Parson

ever, partake of the characteristics of both these exemplary types, which, at first glance, appear antithetical.

As a starting point, but with no claim for completeness, we may venture a definition of the *humanistic* organization as follows: An organization* is humanistic if an organizational unit and individuals composing it meet the following criteria:

Key Criterion I   *Valuing*: It recognizes and acts on the
Functional Criteria: affirmation of values by organizations and by persons and assesses its own "goodness."

Criterion II   *Wholistic - Systematic Perspective*: It recognizes and acts on the wholistic-systematic character of organization and persons.†

Criterion III   *Intentionality-Intuitiveness*: It recognizes and acts on the intentional-intuitive character of organizations and persons, including recognition of the "organizational unconscious."

Criterion IV   *Openness-Privacy*: It recognizes and acts on balanced considerations of openness and privacy.

Criterion V   *Identity*: It recognizes and acts on its present identity and its correlative processes of being-becoming and nonbeing.

---

* An extensive treatment of the concept *organization* as such is beyond this paper's bounds. Relevant typologies serve as useful references; see, for instance, Peter M. Blau and W. Richard Scott, *Formal Organizations*, San Francisco, Chandler Publishing Company, 1962, and a plethora of other works.

† This analysis conceptually distinguishes between organizations and persons. Without opening the Pandora's box of argumentation concerning reductionism, we note the obvious—organizations are *sui generis* the creations of persons and ubiquity of structural, technological and economic variables notwithstanding. Organizations represent particular social configurations with emerging synergistic dynamics determined most crucially by the person-variable.

(Ed.), *The Theory of Social and Economic Organization*, Glencoe, Free Press, 1947. Abraham H. Maslow's thoughts on "Utopian Psychological" management are explored in *Eupsychian Management*, Homewood, Richard D. Irwin, Inc. and the Dorsey Press, 1965.

Criterion VI   *Paradox and Variability*: It recognizes and
                        acts on paradoxes, ambiguities and uncer-
                        tainties, including the limitations of formal
                        structure and co-existence of positive and
                        negative processes extant in organization
                        and persons.

Criterion VII   *Creativity and Meaning*: It recognizes and
                        acts on aspirations for organizational and
                        personal creativity and meaning, with
                        awareness of individual variation and
                        realistic external constraint.

Contextually, the concept of humanistic organization takes
account of continuing interplay between organization, person
and technological/socioeconomic forces operating within and
outside the organization's boundary. As initial criterion the
crucial issues of values must be considered to serve as a bench-
mark by which to assess the humanistic organization's effects
and influence.

CRITERION I: VALUING

Some Valuing and Normative Observations

The proposed concept of humanistic organization seeks to
be *realistic* in its thrust and character. *Realism* in this vein is a
value affirmed by the author. Its basic test, underlined by the
valuing process and thus the criterion of *goodness* of organization,
follows lines somewhat along those implicit in the theories of
the nineteenth century utilitarians,

> The organization is "good" if it provides optimum value attain-
> ment—in terms of satisfaction of conceptually-specifiable if not
> always specified values—translated into goals and unconscious as
> well as conscious desires—for the greatest number of persons (as
> variously affected, internal and external to the organization), by
> the organization's nature and actions,* while minimizing corre-
> sponding nonattainment and dissatisfaction (including direct harm).

---

* For relevant philosophic background, see, for instance, the work of
John Stuart Mill.

This proposition is importantly at variance with the notion that the humanistic organization simply is concerned with the needs of the employees, viz. by assuring high morale, participation, etc. To focus predominantly or exclusively on *the worker* or on any one intraorganizational subset is to ignore the fact that, in terms of a genuine humanistic perspective, other publics also are relevant. These include the organization's top executives, other managers, stockholders, affected consumers and members of the public at large. All these too are human, of course, and must be considered in the utilitarian (quantitative or qualitative) equations of *goodness* as well as *employee* or *worker*.

In turn, this formulation puts in different perspective the traditional confrontation of individual and organization; prevailing intraorganizational conflict (which is real enough) must be examined in terms of near-term and long-range goal attainment of *many* publics including persons (and organized entities) external to, at the top of or elsewhere within the organization whose goodness is assessed.

The Multiplicity of Relevant Publics

The above view urges us to look beyond "worker satisfaction" and indeed beyond any exclusively intraorganizational concept as principal criterion of organizational humanism. Rather, we must examine explicitly the impact of the organization's nature and action on a broad set of relevant overlapping publics affected by it, internally and externally. A number of major rubrics may be distinguished,

1. Organization members, at *all* levels of the hierarchy (however structured), e.g., rank-and-file, first line supervision, middle management, upper-level management, staff (at all levels, in all departmental/divisional relationships), the managing officer and members of the management team (top management)
2. Organization policy-setting units, i.e., board of directors, boards of regents, trustees, etc.
3. Proprietary or quasi-proprietary units, e.g., partners in the firm, stockholders, etc.

4. Familial support and reference groups, e.g., family members of employees, of top management, etc.
5. Informal support and reference groups, e.g., personal friends and associates of employees, of top management, etc.
6. Current consumers of the organization's product(s) or clients of the organization's service(s)
7. Potential consumers of the organization's product(s) or clients of the organization's service(s)
8. Professional support and reference groups, e.g., members of the American Management Association, of the American Marketing Association, professional groups in sales, production, etc.
9. Professional evaluative units, e.g., stockmarket analysts assessing the organization's current condition and prospects
10. Governmental and regulatory units relating to the organization as apply in specific instances, e.g., state corporate commissioner, state utilities commission, etc., legislative and judicial bodies
11. Organized influence units, actually or potentially affecting the organization, e.g., consumer and institutional lobbies, environmental protection groups, etc.
12. Other organizations and organization members interfacing with the subject organization, e.g., suppliers, corporate customers, etc.
13. An undifferentiated residual category—the public at large

It is clear that, by the above listing of relevant publics, the humanistic organization, to be meritorious in *humanistic* terms as well as, one may hypothesize, by other criteria of organizational effectiveness, must consider extensively its impact on a wide range of human groupings.

In turn, value judgments must be made by someone, within and/or outside the humanistic organization as to the relative importance or weight that is to be assigned to each of the publics defined as relevant, viz. "Who matters?" It is theoretically possible, of course, to attribute an extremely high and, thus, virtually exclusive weight to one or a limited number of publics.

Such delimitation inherently deviates from the concept of *humanistic* organizational goodness as proposed, viz. the argument is made that the humanistic organization is concerned with optimal welfare and satisfaction across a maximal gamut of publics.

Undue limitation, though one may dispute just what is undue, by its very nature is nonhumanistic as it fails to consider the welfare of significant numbers of persons who are, or may be, affected by the organization's nature and activity. An extreme example of humanistically inappropriate delimitation might be a divine right/absolute ruler-choice of publics (the public identified exclusively, *reductio ad absurdam*, as a single individual). Less extreme, but equally questionable, is the delimitation of consideration to either top management (augmented perhaps by a diffuse attention to stockholders' objectives), or primary (and possibly exclusive) focus on the organization's grass-root, line employees. Operationally, the task remains. How is one to identify the relevant publics and their relative degrees of importance? And who is to do the identifying? The answers to these questions are complex.

Ideally, to be consistent with the concept of optimal welfare and satisfaction, one may construct a hypothetical model in which every person actually or potentially affected by the organization's nature and action assesses the relative weight or importance of each public. It is evident that a construct of this nature, whatever its academic elegance, cannot be readily operationalized; limited levels of awareness in many of the publics, their relative inaccessibility to cast their votes (probably in terms of feeling and opinion rather than by conventional election) and other constraints make this kind of process quite infeasible.

From a research standpoint, a more workable procedure involves the selection of a broad number of publics judged to be relevant on theoretic grounds, e.g., in terms of their structural and functional interrelationships within and outside the organization. Samples of members of the specified publics may then rate or qualitatively assess the relative degrees of significance of the specified publics. Alternatively, knowledgeable observers or formally or informally chosen reference persons may suggest who and what matters in the assessment of organization impact. A possible elitist bias in this procedure, however, must be consciously controlled.

Finally, one may observe that, research and systematic inquiry aside, the judgment of an organization's merit by various publics is a *de facto* process; evaluation of an organization's goodness vis-a-vis particular publics occurs all the time. Typically, such evaluations proceed through implicit and explicit assertions of how things are going and of what's good for people by persons within the organization and by external publics.

Pragmatically, one may conceive of the humanistic goodness of an organization at a particular time in terms of the utilitarian motto by determining the net affirmation (expressed and unexpressed, including unconsciously-rooted) accorded the organization by this ongoing informal process . . . by sundry grapevines, in cocktail-hour conversations, in day-by-day reactions on shop floor and in board room, and by inner feelings of those who are directly and indirectly affected by the organization's nature and actions.

The Multiplicity of Values and Goals

Even for a particular person, of course, there exist many co-acting values and their derivative goals. However, the multiplicity of relevant publics further affirms the corollary concept of *multiplicity of values and goals*. For the sake of convenience we have referred to values or goals. These terms, however, are but shorthand notations for the extremely complex patterns of values, goals and associated processes that prevail in the real world. The following paradigm shown in Figure 13-1 identifies, in simplified form, two major dimensions bearing on the issue of value/goal multiplicity.

The complexity of the value and goal patterns emerges in terms of the number of cells and their interrelations in the resulting matrix. The underlying concept restates the perennial problem of welfare and political theory, particularly as relates to the functions of democracy; the significant variety of publics (viz. in political theory—constituencies, interest groups, etc.)

VALUES/GOALS

	"Top Priority"................................ "Lowest Priority"		
(e.g.) organization members			
organization policy setting units			
proprietary units			
support and reference groups... etc.			

PUBLICS

Figure 13-1.

predicates a requirement to attend simultaneously to constellations of varied goals, some overlapping, some distinct, many irreconcilable. The solution of the *utilitarian equation* postulated earlier by simple majority represents a pragmatic, widely-accepted approach. In humanistic organization research it may be a "satisfying"* solution and *good enough* for various relevant publics under varied and difficult circumstances that offer promise. Still awaiting resolution are issues such as the differential degrees of relevance of the several publics in relation to a given choice situation, the trade-offs involved in meeting the needs of one public to a greater extent at costs to others, and the shifting and decay of particular values and goals in each of the publics over time. Particularly in the latter connection one must note the significance of the time dimension by adding the latter as a third axis to the paradigmatic matrix.

Change in values and goals undoubtedly applies to organizations as such as well as to individuals. With growth and decline in their internal structures, including accession of new incumbents, impact of interest groups, organizational maturing and aging, etc., and in response to changing external demands viz. crises and cyclical trends in economic conditions, changes

---

* See James G. March and Herbert A. Simon, *Organizations*, New York, Wiley, 1958, p. 140 ff.

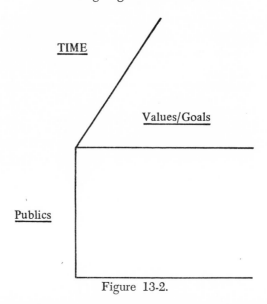

Figure 13-2.

in technology, altered consumer demand, etc., such change is inevitable.

It is evident that a change in one cell in the paradigmatic matrix may cause changes in one or more of the other cells. Thus, external demands may lead to internal value reordering and reorganization, and modifications in goals by one public may affect the prospective goals of others at any one time and over time. Accordingly, *the relationships sketched in the paradigm in fact do not constitute neat, distinct boxes, but rather denote a fluid and dynamic interplay of forces temporally generated by specified publics.*

Many theories of value and goal-setting have observed that *not all values or goals are created equal.* The well-known concept of the hierarchical nature of values, goals (or needs), perhaps identified most lucidly by Abraham Maslow,[*] operates complexly for organizations as well as for individuals. As a goal par excellence, the predominant *bottom line* of net profit cited by profit-seeking organizations may be redefined appropriately in

---

[*] See A. H. Maslow's "A Theory of Human Motivation: The Basic Needs," *Psychological Review, 50,* 1943, p. 395 ff., and *Motivation and Personality,* New York, Harper, 1970.

nonprofit settings as, for instance, in terms of maximum service to clients, viz. in social agency or psychotherapeutic institutions. The problem of operationalizing the latter is methodologically difficult, and efforts in this direction have not been fully successful. This circumstance, however, does not reduce the concept's fundamental importance as capstone in organizational goal hierarchies.

The existence of a bottom line or other *sine qua non* goal notion as a prepotent demand on the organization carries with it the existence of congeries of other goals, variously subordinate at a given time as ends in themselves and/or as means required as preconditions to the attainment of the specified bottom line goal. The process of management in its usual corporate sense and in the sense of personal-life management significantly revolves around resources allocation decisions designed to attain specified means-goals (which, in turn, may become end-goals) and which may serve in striving toward the bottom line goal. *To survive, humanistic organization, too, must meet such sine qua non or bottom line goals.* Failure to do so, which may reflect morally purposeful choice, nonetheless carries with it eventual organizational demise or basic recasting of the organization's nature and activity.

In summary, per the expanded paradigm, the concept of *value/goal constellations* will be identified. These constellations are constituted by the total patterns of values/goals (a) held, consciously and unconsciously, by the relevant publics, (b) at a given time and (c) through time. Value/goal constellations become the appropriate yardstick, in their complexity and possible intractability for empirical study, by which an organization's goodness may be judged.

The Functional Criteria of Humanistic Organization
Criteria II-VII

We turn now to a consideration of the functional criteria of humanistic organization. In doing so, we must recall (a) that the term *humanistic* is not necessarily a synonym for organizationally good, and (b) that how the organization *views* its members and people generally, as those contained by the relevant publics, individually and in relationship, *and* how the organization *acts* (behaves, operates, functions) are basic considerations in assessment of its humanistic character.

The question as to whether a given humanistic organization is in fact *good* is empirical—Does the organization that fits the specified functional humanistic criteria also attain specified levels of goodness, as by optimally satisfying corresponding values and specified goal constellations? Our present emphasis rests with the conceptual rather than with the empirical aspects of this issue, as we briefly review the functional criteria of humanistic organization.

CRITERION II

Wholistic-Systematic Perspective

In accordance with Criterion II, the prevailing mode of thought and basis for action in the humanistic organization is wholistic-systematic. The hyphenated neologism is needed to designate a conceptual union between two modes of approach often thought to be antithetical. On one hand, the humanistic perspective is, and one may roll out a string of related terms, wholistic (holistic), configurational, organismic, responsive to totality and Gestalt of the organization's structure and function.* On the other hand, this perspective takes cognizance of the systemic character of the organization as unit and of person (in relevant publics). It appreciates the complex interrelationships among constituent parts within the organization's boundary and across the boundary, and among and within the relevant publics to which the organization relates. It is not necessary to recite the processes frequently treated under the heading "General Systems Theory"; a substantial literature is available in this

---

* For characteristic Gestalt-theoretic views, see various editions of the works of Wolfang Kohler and Kurt Koffka, especially K. Koffka, *Principles of Gestalt Psychology*, New York, Harcourt, Brace and Company, 1935, Chapter 5, p. 177 ff. and Wolfgang Kohler, *Dynamics in Psychology*, New York, Grove Press, 1960, p. 43 ff. as well as the work of Kurt Lewin, viz. *Field Theory in Social Science*, New York, Harper, 1951, especially pp. 30-59, and 130-154.

field, including numerous applications to organizational issues.*

The criterion of wholistic-systematic thinking asserts that wholistic modes of thought and systemic modes of thought are fully compatible and complementary. In the sense of Gestalt-theoretic viewpoints, organization (and person) may be so regarded that at one point it is the wholistic, complexly-patterned indivisible image that is the *figure,* viz. company character, organizational ethos, etc., while systemic analytic attention to specific interactions among the parts, and systems dynamics remain *ground.* Conversely, for other purposes one must focus on part interactions, viz. transactions among individuals or departments, relationships between marketing and production processes, doctor/patient communication, etc., as figure while the wholistic totality of the organization recedes to ground.

In line with this view, wholistic and systems thinking are not only reconcilable but indeed require one another. The wholistic context provides meaning to the analysis of systems relationships; in turn, the organization's wholistic totality is understood more fully by means of concrete analyses stemming from systems-theoretic thinking.

The wholistic-systematic approach as a criterion constitutes both a mode for looking *at* the organization *by* the organization (and by the organization members themselves, particularly by its key decision-makers), and as a viewpoint focused by organization members on relevant publics.

CRITERION III

Intentionality-Intuitiveness

Criterion III focuses on the humanistic organization's recognition of intentionality and intuitiveness in relation to itself and

---

* For characteristic systems-theoretic views, see various editions of *General Systems: Yearbook of the Society for General Systems Research.* Washington, Society for General Systems Research and Russell L. Ackoff and Fred E. Emery, *On Purposeful Systems,* New York, Aldine-Atherton, 1972; Fremont E. Kast and James E. Rosenzweig, *Contingency Views of Organization and Management,* Chicago, Science Research Associates, 1973, especially pp. 37-56; and David I. Cleland and William R. King, *Management, A Systems Approach,* New York, McGraw-Hill, 1972, especially pp. 29-114 and pp. 142-169.

to person-relevant publics. Organizations, even in a conventional sense, stress their choiceful character. Emphasis on functions such as rational goal-setting and planning are examples of intentional organizational behavior. However, many organizations emphasize their intentionalities while ignoring or denying their less rational aspects.

At the other side of intentionality lies the *non*conscious, including intuitive and inarticulate aspects of the organization's functioning. Accordingly, it is organizational intuition as well as exploration of the *organization's unconscious* that are factors in determining whether the organization is humanistic. Thus, an organization that attends exclusively to its intentionalities or that expects solely intentional responses among its members and/or persons in relevant publics while paying little or no attention to its intuitive and unconscious dynamics falls short in this criterion.

The operation of unconscious goal-striving, as stressed notably in psychoanalytic theory and its derivatives, needs to be considered, for the organization as a unit as well as for individual persons. The *organizational unconscious* is manifest in the organization's collective memory, whether explicitly stated or communicated implicitly in norms and values.* It is internalized in the thought-ways of the organization's key decision-makers and is broadly, but often diffusedly, disseminated throughout the organization structure. Of course, the organizational unconscious, no less than consciously-articulated processes, changes through time, affecting the organization's style and purpose.

---

* The literature of the unconscious, primarily focused on individual dynamics, though on occasion on larger social units, is vast. Some generic approaches, in part applicable to the organizational unconscious, may be stimulated by examination of works such as the following (leaving aside for present purposes Freud's fundamental formulations as such): Henri F. Ellenberger, *The Discovery of the Unconscious,* New York, Basic Books, 1970; A. Bronson Feldman, *The Unconscious in History,* New York, Philosophical Library, 1959; and J. P. Chaplin's paperback, *The Unconscious,* New York, Ballantine Books, 1960. The German-speaking reader will find helpful insights in Donald Brickman's *Probleme des Unbewussten,* Zurich: Rascher, 1943, particularly in his reflections on the works of other germinal figures in the field such as Eduard von Hartmann and C. G. Jung, and on the contributions of lesser known but significant authors such as Christian Wolff and J. G. Hamann.

The humanistic organization functions in balance, intentionally expressing purpose and thrust, but responding as well at appropriately intuitive levels to the deeply internal, implicit and nonconscious aspects of its functioning.

CRITERION IV

Openness-Privacy

A fourth criterion of humanistic organization is a balanced mode of openness by the organization, internally and externally, in dealing with others, concurrent with the recognition of the limitations of such openness and respect for organizational and personal privacy. It is evident that this position does not argue that everything about the organization or everything about persons within the organization should be known to all. The realities of competition, the simple irrelevance of certain kinds of information and the positive personal desire for privacy—all these act as restraining influences to any hypothetical desire for complete openness.

The humanistic organization may seek openness on the grounds that such openness will provide sound and significant relationships within the organization, among organizations and among individuals. It encourages conditions for such openness, particularly when these conditions make possible meaningful transactions among participants, including those who have important differences of opinion and for whom conflict is a fact of life.

The sheer realization that openness may lead to some measure of discomfort is not sufficient basis to avoid it. Often the opportunity to face unpleasantness directly, in the appropriate confrontational setting, compensates, particularly in the long run, for possible conditions of discomfort. On the other hand, some levels of threat and the realistic possibility of destruction of carefully-nurtured relationships, particularly if there is insufficient time to work through complex interpersonal issues, and the limits of privacy establish appropriate boundaries within which truly humanistic openness is defined.

CRITERION V

Identity

A fifth criterion of humanistic organization is the organization's sense of identity, for the organization as a whole and for the persons composing it. While organizations tend to describe themselves, for purposes of public relations and internal convenience (as in employee manuals) in frequently glowing or detailed descriptive terms, such self-description is not necessarily tantamount to the existence of sound identity. The latter notes the organization's *core values* and maintains a thorough awareness of its values, capabilities and potential, and of its modes of response to internal and external demands. One may wonder whether economic and managerial difficulties encountered by many conglomerates following their initial heyday in the sixties were not symptoms of identity loss, if indeed a coherent identity had developed in the first place.

The concept of organizational identity is attuned to the inevitable reality of the organization's life-cycle. While theoretically the corporate entity survives any given set of incumbents, the organization as such is characterized by a course of life of its own; it is founded, it grows and develops its particular uniqueness, and eventually it declines and dies. Some organizations, particularly institutions such as religious movements or political ideologies, may have life spans encompassing hundreds or even thousands of years. This continuity over time-given historical analysis does not support the view, however, that organizations are, *ipso facto*, immortal any more than that individual human beings are immortal.

One pervasive issue concerns the mode in which organizations die; some organizations attempt to perpetuate their existences in the face of substantial evidence that they are obsolescent. Others change their objectives and, in that sense, are reincarnated as different entities, perhaps carrying with them vestiges of a prior life. Some organizations disintegrate as in bankruptcy, and still others purposefully terminate their existence (commit suicide?) when it appears that their goals have been met or that their resources are no longer responsive to changed requirements. Finally, some simply fade away by disuse and lack of interest on the part of those who, at an earlier time, were instrumental in maintaining organizational viability.

This criterion holds that awareness and significant grasp of the organization's current identity in the context of its total, from birth to death, life-cycle is a yardstick of its humanism.

CRITERION VI

Paradox and Variability

In accordance with Criterion VI, Humanistic Organization affirms paradox, and thus ambiguity, and variability in organizational and individual life. The organization does not focus on formal structure as end-all just because the latter is deemed rational and clear—an antidote for uncertainty and a shield against the potentially paradoxical. Rather the Humanistic Organization sees structure as human approximation for relationships that are regarded as significant to attain particular goals, noting that goal-attainment itself relates to multiple goals—some clear, some fuzzy —held by multiple publics and changing through time.

In light of Gestalt-theoretic thinking (see Criterion II), at a given time a particular aspect of the organization's functioning may be salient as *figure* while the others appear as *ground*. Particular functions specified by formal organizational structure may require principal attention on one occasion while others continue normal functioning but at a level of relatively lesser emphasis. For instance, at a given time in an organization's life, the marketing function may be viewed as prepotent while production, finance and other basic activities proceed at standard levels. In turn, persons at different rungs of the organization hierarchy respond more emphatically to particular subunits, normally the ones in which they are imbedded or the ones with reference to which major power relationships exist rather than to others. All these processes act to reduce theoretic neatness and abstract simplicity in organization life. Rather, the *shifting* of emphasis among organization functions and their correlative organization structures often imply paradox and unpredicted variation. *Positive and negative aspects in the organization and in individuals associated with it co-exist,* often in apparent violation of *a priori* logic.

Further, management functions, viz. staffing, organizing, planning, controlling, directing, etc., rarely proceed in clearly separable fashion. The Humanistic Organization recognizes the interplay of these functions in real-world organization process and the variable prominence of these functions at different times and at different levels of the organization. Whatever the circumstances, the Humanistic Organization attends both to stable elements, to turbulence and change, and to the inevitably resulting paradoxes and ambiguities.

CRITERION VII

Creativity and Meaning

Per the seventh criterion, the humanistic organization provides maximum creativity and personal meaning for itself and for persons related to it within the constraint of time, resources and trade-off with goals held by relevant publics. The very admonition that meaning and creativity are to be aspired is, of course, well-known among humanistic psychologists and other theorists concerned with the human condition. However, the concept of Humanistic Organization as advanced here does not propose that absolute maximum attainment of meaning and creativity *at all costs* is a criterion. Rather, these affirmed values stand in the context of other values also related to the organization's functioning. While, for instance, *job enrichment* may prove useful for some workers under certain conditions, job simplification (perhaps with some trade-off with meaning and creativity—for shorter hours, higher wages and other opportunities for compensatory value realization) may be in order, even humanistically! And we must be reminded that meaning and creativity are highly subjective concepts; a working opportunity that appears meaningful to one person may be drudgery to another though the designer of the job may have projected his/her own concept of meaning to the job design without taking account of significant individual variation.

While meaning and creativity may be generic humanistic values, the Humanistic Organization, recognizing the complexities of its existence and those of persons associated with it, considers these values in the broader context of opportunity and constraint, including individual differences, demands generated by competing values and the limitations of resources and time.

REPRISE: ORGANIZATIONAL REALISM

The Humanistic Organization regards its own functioning and that of the participant members as *total* organizational and *total* individual human being(s) respectively in such a manner that positive and negative elements of feeling, cognition and behavior are understood and acted on in balance. The Humanistic Organization avoids both single-minded Pollyanna approaches and persistent gloom or fixed cynicism. It is capable of responding to the genuine complexity of organizations and people, seeing in perspective the plusses and the minuses that present themselves in ongoing organization life. It avoids being locked into any perception of course of action while ignoring concurrent, potentially equally-significant perceptions and courses of action. Rather than stereotyping its own modes of functioning or those of individuals related to it, it seeks its unique identity and deals with the varied realities as these unfold in the matrix of the changing values and goals of a broad set of relevant human groupings.

Chapter 14

BEHAVIOR MODIFICATION PERSPECTIVE FOR HUMANIZING ORGANIZATIONS

Walter R. Nord

If properly understood and implemented, behavior modification can be one of the most humanistic approaches in contemporary behavioral science. In making this assertion the writer is well aware of the numerous writers who have vigorously attacked behavior modification (especially operant conditioning) as antihumanistic.

The purpose of this paper is to examine the validity of some of these polemics as they apply to the use of operant conditioning in organizations. This study will require several steps. It will begin by discussing some criteria of humanism and speculating about why behavior modification is perceived to be antihumanistic. Secondly, it will outline a framework for classifying the assets and liabilities of the application of this approach for humanizing organizations. Using this framework it will then be shown that behavior modification per se is neither humanistic nor antihumanistic. Rather, the evaluation of this approach as a humanizing force is contingent on the nature of reality and the processes used to modify behavior.

HUMANISM AND BEHAVIOR MODIFICATION IN ORGANIZATIONS

No simple criteria are known which unambiguously differentiate humanism from nonhumanism. However, there are two general features which most humanists see as central to their position. To be considered humanistic an approach must (1) treat human beings as ends as opposed to means and (2) advance, or at least seek to advance, the degree to which human beings exercise control over their own outcomes.

Most contemporary models for organizational development are, at least on paper, humanistic in the first sense. Certainly approaches stemming from the work of McGregor, Maslow, Herzberg, Argyris, Likert and others are directed to achieve the full development of people in the organization. The writer has suggested elsewhere (Nord, 1969) that Skinnerian operant conditioning parallels these models in most respects. Skinner and most of his followers have consistently sought to advance human development at (1) the microlevel (e.g., individual therapy), (2) middle-range levels (e.g., classrooms, organizations), and (3) the macrolevel (e.g., the design of social systems, *Walden Two*). While operant "technology" can be used to "manipulate" people, so can almost any advance in knowledge including "participative management" (Gomberg, 1966). In short, on the first criterion, behavior modification is neither more nor less humanistic than other approaches to organization change; whether people are treated as ends or means depends more on how knowledge is used rather than the character of the knowledge itself.

On the second criterion, the degree to which an approach actually has the ability to enhance human potential to achieve favorable exchanges with the environment, behavior modification may turn out to be superior. To help people control their own outcomes a technique or model must work; it must lead to actions which reliably result in the achievement of desired outcomes. Whether or not the approaches of McGregor *et al.* have the ability to make any difference in the lives of people is not clear. While considerable evidence (see, for example, Argyris, 1973) does demonstrate the value of these approaches there is a growing number of skeptics (e.g., Hulin and Blood, 1968; Winpisinger, 1973; Quinn *et al.*, 1973; Levinson, 1970; Tausky, 1973; and Nord, 1974). By contrast, the efficacy of behavior modification has been demonstrated by literally millions of observations at a variety of levels of the phylogenetic scale, including man. Much of this evidence comes from studies conducted in psychological laboratories and hospitals, prisons, schools and related total institutions (see Bandura, 1969; Hamblin *et al.*, 1971).

Less evidence is available on the value of the operant approach for work organizations, but already there has been a clear progression from speculation about the possibilities to evidence of success. Aldis (1961), Nord (1969) and Jablonsky and DeVries (1972) summarized a number of ways in which behavior modification could be useful in managing organizations. Wheeler (1973) suggested that the applications of positive reinforcement to organizations may produce less punitive, less bureaucratized, less authoritarian, more self-managing organizations.

A growing body of empirical research in both laboratory and field settings has supported the value of the operant perspective for managing work organizations. Schneier (1974) provided a comprehensive review of this research. For purposes of this paper, the field work of Goldstein and Sorcher (1974), Luthans (1974) and Standing and Lazer (1973) were selected as examples of the use of behavior modification in organizations.

Goldstein and Sorcher (1974) outlined a strategy for teaching ". . . interpersonal skills relevant to effective supervision." These procedures, which they termed *applied learning,* include modeling, role-playing, social reinforcement and mechanisms for the transfer of training. They discussed a number of cases where the application of applied learning resulted in improvements in performance and satisfaction in work situations.

Luthans has introduced "organizational behavior modification" (O.B. Mod) as a comprehensive strategy for organizational development. O.B. Mod begins with the identification of performance-related behavioral events. Baseline frequencies of the relevant (targeted) behaviors are recorded and the antecedents and consequences of the targeted behavior are analyzed; interventions in the form of manipulation of reinforcers are introduced. Finally, effectiveness is evaluated in terms of bottom line performance. Luthans cited soon-to-be-published research as support for the efficacy of this approach. Both Goldstein and Sorcher and Luthans have shown that behavior modification is effective. However, for the most part, their views of efficacy centered on the achievement of organizational goals rather than human development. Thus, while they showed the ability of behavior modification to score well on criterion two, they neglected criterion one.

Contributors to the Standing and Lazer (1973) symposium, however, gave greater attention to the relationship between human development and the application of behavior modification to achieve organizational goals. In particular Warren discussed several cases where this approach resulted in the transfer of large amounts of power and control to lower level participants, the growth of individual workers and the availability of a greater choice and participation to employees at nearly all corporate levels. Among the examples Warren provided was the following:

> We have a plant in Arkansas that manufactures golf clubs. There is a high standard of productivity, quality, and costs at the plant. By the way, the plant is 90% women.
>
> The organization's objective or desired outcome was to make a better and cheaper club than anybody else. What would be desirable for the people in the plant? We found that freedom and power to control the environment were the two best ways to reach our objective.
>
> Since supervisors take control away, we did away with supervisors. In other words, natural work groups (approximately 50/group) were built, without supervisors. The plant has approximately 200 employees, with only seven management people. Each group was responsible for and controlled its own production, raw materials, and quality.
>
> Work groups that meet or exceed production standards have the authority to select their own breaks, lunch hours, and working hours. They also have the power to hire and fire group members. Those groups who meet efficiency standards also are allowed to participate in additional tasks, on their own time or work time after standard is met. These tasks include working with the plant or industrial engineer in solving plant efficiency problems.
>
> The work groups are presented with the overall annual objectives for the plant. They then break down into their groups, and, with the product manager, set the group's production goals in relation

to the overall goal. Feedback, in terms of individual and group efficiency, is posted weekly on a bulletin board.

Both management and work group members go through orientation before getting into full participation. Employees have a one week orientation to the group and the concepts of plant operations. The seven managers went through one year of team training and were trained in running problem solving groups, contingency management concepts, and how to surrender power.

Similarly, Barnicki (1973) summarized how the performance of work groups and the growth of subordinates had increased through the use of concepts taken from behavior modification.

While much of the data from the business organizations were collected under less than fully adequate research conditions taken together with the carefully controlled studies conducted in other settings, they give some support to the proposition that behavior modification can be effective in achieving a variety of outcomes which would normally be termed humanistic according to the second criterion—the control exercised by individuals and groups over exchanges with their environments. However, most of these reports did not comment on the first criterion— the treatment of people as ends as opposed to means. The writer suspects that this type of omission contributes to the view that behavior modification is antihumanistic.

Why Is Behavior Modification Perceived as Antihumanistic?

In a general way the perceived antihumanism of behavior modification parallels the attacks to which many advances in knowledge have been subjected throughout the last several centuries. In general, the magnitude of these attacks has been positively related to the perceived probabilities that the knowledge will (1) produce real effects, (2) challenge the standing of man as a unique central figure in the universe, and (3) conflict with existing ways of thinking. Behavior modification, especially operant conditioning, is threatening on all three counts.

Efficacy

Behavior techniques have been shown to be effective; there is a long history of scientific evidence and conventional wisdom supporting the view that much human behavior is a function of its consequences. However, despite the fact that so many aspects of our evolving social system appear to be consistent with the assumption that consequences of behavior play a major role in social control, explicit statements of this assumption are seen as threatening to human rationality and free choice.

Moreover, fears about the application of operant conditioning to the management of society in general, and to business organizations in particular, are heightened by the belief that behavioral scientists are prone to become, in Baritz's (1960) words, "servants of power." In fact, concerns about power are among the most frequently-voiced fears by critics of operant conditioning. These charges are expressed through images of Orwell's *1984*, predictions of dictatorial states and polemics against the manipulation of people. In essence these concerns focus on the questions: Who will exercise control, for what purposes, using what methods and by what authority?

Challenge to Man's Position

Secondly, behavior modification challenges the role of man as a rational, self-directing animal. Many people perceive operant conditioning as violating some of the central cultural values and assumptions about human nature; admonitions against treating people as animals are common. Perhaps the best discussion of these issues is still to be found in the classic article by Rogers and Skinner (1956).

Challenge to Current Thought Patterns

Thirdly, behavior modification challenges some basic ways we think about human behavior. Perhaps this attack is most acutely experienced by academic psychologists who find operant conditioners tend to ignore such processes as cognition, personality and motivation. In particular, many dynamically-oriented psychologists charge that behavioral therapies, like earlier hypnotic approaches, are apt to leave the basic causes of maladaptive behavior untouched. Consequently, they charge that behavioral therapies will not produce sustained improvements.

All of these concerns deserve the serious consideration they have been given. Unfortunately, however, most discussions of these issues have reflected rather absolutistic positions. Often, the protagonists, on the basis of a few findings or assumptions, argue that behavior modification is either good or bad. There has been little assessment of the conditions which influence the value of behavior modification. The framework outlined in the next section is offered as a means to less absolutistic assessments.

To Modify or No?—A Cost-Benefit Perspective

Presently, we have a choice about how much we use behavior modification techniques. Simply stated, we can employ little behavior modification or make widespread use of it. What are the costs and benefits of following either course?

Clearly the costs and benefits will be different depending on the nature of the real or true laws of human behavior. For example, if, as the operant conditioners contend, a great deal of human behavior is controlled by its consequences, the results of applying operant techniques will be very different than if little human behavior is subject to such control. Combining these two possible *true* laws of behavior with the two alternatives of applying behavior modification to few situations or to many situations, four sets of outcomes can be envisioned.

These possible states are summarized by the two-dimensional array portrayed in Figure 14-1. Although both dimensions are shown as dichotomies, each is assumed to be continuous. The horizontal axis represents the *actual* state of affairs or *the perfect knowledge* case as to how much behavior is a function of its consequences. At one extreme, perfect knowledge would convince us that little behavior is controlled by its consequences; at the other extreme we would conclude that much behavior is so controlled. The vertical dimension represents the degree to which behavior modification is applied. It can be applied in few or many situations.*

Each of the four quadrants in Figure 14-1 contains a brief summary of the types of humanistic costs and benefits associated

---

* While for simplicity these two dimensions are represented as being independent, in fact they are not; what we do is apt to be a function of what is.

Summary of Relevant Humanistic Concerns from Application

and

Nonapplication of Behavior Modification

Degree to which behavior is controlled by its consequences

		Little behavior controlled by its consequences	Much behavior controlled by its consequences
Degree of Application of Behavior Modification	Little application of behavior modification	Quandrant I Little application, low costs	Quadrant II - Little application, high opportunity costs and costs from social traps (due to failure to use behavior modification)
	Widespread application of behavior modification	Quadrant III - Widespread application, high opportunity costs (due to failure to use more appropriate model)	Quadrant IV - Widespread application, high benefits from effective control, combined with potential costs in terms of freedom, dignity, etc.

Figure 14-1.

with the combination of each degree of application under each state of reality. These outcomes are discussed in more detail below.

Quadrant I

What are the humanistic consequences when behavior modification is not applied and little behavior is controlled by its consequences? There are few costs or benefits which are relevant to this paper. Since behavior modification is not being used, it has few effects. Moreover, since even if it were used it would not be effective, there are few costs due to lost opportunities. Clearly, the choice not to use operant conditioning when it would not work is a wise one; resources are not wasted on an ineffective set of procedures.

Quadrant II

What are the humanistic consequences when behavior modification is not applied and much behavior is controlled by its consequences? The probable costs are high because the failure to apply operant techniques when they would work will mean that people may not achieve what they are capable of achieving.

Many of these costs are well-described by what Platt (1973) referred to as "social traps" and "counter traps." Social traps are

> . . . situations in society that contain traps formally like a fish trap, where men or organizations or whole societies get themselves started in some direction or some set of relationships that later prove to be unpleasant or lethal and that they see no easy way to back out of or to avoid.

Countertraps are really the converse of traps; according to Platt they occur where

> The consideration of individual advantage prevents us from doing something that might nevertheless be of great benefit to the group as a whole. It is, so to speak, a *social fence* rather than a social trap.

These situations are produced by inadequate awareness and design of the reinforcement contingencies which control behavior.

It is important to emphasize that the failure to apply operant techniques under these conditions does *not* mean people are free. The behavior of individuals will still be controlled, but the control will be random or perhaps exercised by a few people who, for a variety of reasons, are using techniques or models similar to those of behavior modification. The results are apt to be antihumanistic in two ways. First, to the degree that behavior remains under the control of random contingencies, people will exercise less control over their outcomes than they could. The design of reinforcement systems which are most beneficial to individuals and groups will not be achieved. Secondly, in the case where a few people control the behavior of many, obviously the many do not exercise control over their own outcomes. In other words, the danger of control by an elite may result from the *failure* of society as a whole to use behavior modification. In general, humans will continue to be more susceptible to chance contingencies and less in control of their own destiny than they are capable of being. However, they will be no more or no less *free* in the *free-will* sense; they will still be controlled by their contingencies.

There are also some direct costs associated with Quadrant II.

The nature and magnitude of these costs depend on the alternative models which are used and the amount of resources devoted to them. If the alternative models assume that little behavior is controlled by its consequences, they are apt to be ineffective; resources devoted to them would be largely wasted. Moreover, the strategies they spawn may involve substantial psychological costs. For example, some strategies might seek to change human behavior by inducing guilt for behavior which is beyond an individual's control.

In sum, the humanistic costs of Quandrant II could be considerable. Importantly they result from the *failure to apply* behavior modification. These costs are overlooked in many discussions of operant conditioning which consider mainly the costs of applying it.

Quadrant III

What are the humanistic consequences of widespread application of behavior modification when little behavior is controlled by its consequences? The indirect costs are parallel to those of Quadrant II in that the most appropriate model is not being used; we are attempting to use operant conditioning when little behavior is controlled by its consequences. Of course, while the magnitude of these costs depends on whether or not a more appropriate model is available, our knowledge of such alternatives is apt to be underdeveloped because of our reliance on behavior modification.

While these indirect costs could be substantial, the direct costs associated with Quandrant III are apt to be even greater. First, the development and implementation of behavioral modification systems could be very expensive. It is probable that the implementation of systems in most industrial settings, especially unionized ones, would involve some form of additional compensation. Moreover, the costs of redesigning jobs and installing the necessary administrative apparatus could be high. Since these programs are apt to have little benefit to the organization, these expenses would be wasted.

Secondly, there are a number of considerations relevant to the general well-being of the participants in the system. These concerns are not the typical ones about freedom, dignity, etc., because the behavior of people cannot in fact be effectively controlled through behavior modification in Quadrant III. Instead, these costs would be a function of the influence the resulting programs have on the lives of the participants. For example, the introduction of behavioral modification will influence the distribution of both material and social rewards. Each individual is apt to receive greater rewards under some systems than under others.* Changes in the distribution of resources will inevitably involve a number of value judgments.

However, in at least one way everyone may be better off under strategies of behavior modification even if they do not influence behavior. At present many of our organizations are punishment-centered; they rely heavily on aversive control. Behavior modification, by contrast, emphasizes the administration of those positive reinforcers which are highly valued by each person. Consequently, everyone might get more of what they want and hence feel better off.

However, on balance, the outcomes of using behavior modification techniques when little behavior is controlled by its consequences are apt to be antihumanistic. Even if people were treated as ends, huge outlays of resources would be allocated in ways which would not improve the exchanges of humans with their environments. In fact, since the search for alternative models might be discouraged, behavior modification could well lead us away from exercising such control. Note again, however, these costs do *not* include threats to human freedom, dignity, etc. These charges against behavior modification are only really relevant when it is applied *and* it works.

Quadrant IV

What are the possible outcomes of the widespread use of behavior modification when a great deal of behavior is controlled by its consequences? Some of them are similar to the results discussed for Quadrant III. The distribution of rewards would be revised, although total welfare might increase since, by com-

---

* On average, people may be equally well off since the losses of some people under one system would be offset by the gains of others.

parison to current practices, the use of positive reinforcement would be increased and the use of punishment would be decreased. Also, there would be considerable direct costs of designing and implementing the new operant systems.

The major difference between Quadrant III and Quadrant IV is the efficacy of behavior modification strategies. Since they are apt to work under the conditions of Quadrant IV, a whole new set of concerns arises. The rest of this paper will focus on Quadrant IV because it describes the conditions where the challenge to humanistic values and traditional approaches is apparently most direct. However, it also describes the conditions under which behavioral techniques may contribute significantly to human welfare. What are the factors which will influence the extent to which successful behavior modification is more or less humanistic?

TOWARDS THE HUMANISTIC USE OF BEHAVIOR MODIFICATION

There are at least three sets of criteria on which the humanism of effective behavior modification can be judged. The first involves individuality and is concerned with pressures which reduce differences in behavior among people. A second criterion is related to power and freedom and is focused on the process used to choose which outcomes will be sought. The third criterion is more academic; it concerns the adequacy of behavior modification as an approach to understanding human behavior.

Individuality

Behavior modification might both promote and retard the development of individuality. For example, operant techniques could reduce the heterogeneity of behavior in a social system which has previously distributed reinforcers in an unplanned way. Since random reinforcement would be replaced by deliberately patterned reinforcement, it is possible that people would behave more like each other. However, planned diversity would also be possible; by deliberately conditioning people to be very different from each other we would actually increase the variance among individuals. Thus, under the conditions of Quandrant IV, the degree of individuality becomes a matter of choice. The techniques themselves are neutral; they aid us in achieving whatever end state we desire.

Conditioning techniques, especially respondent conditioning, could support or violate individuality in another way; they could be used to shape people's preferences. For example, it might be possible to respondently condition large numbers of people to prefer the same reinforcers; consequently, we would reduce the extent to which individuals differ. However, we could also condition people to prefer a greater variety of reinforcers and thus increase individuality. Again, the techniques are neutral with respect to individuality.

Moreover, forgetting the possibility of changing preferences, to be effective operant conditioning must be individuality-centered; only reinforcers which are in some way of value to the individual will work. Operant techniques force us to think about what the individual wants and then to design a system that makes that outcome contingent on performance. In short, if behavior modification is not individually-centered, behavior will not be modified.

Thinking more specifically of the work situation, Hamner (1974) suggested that the application of behavior modification techniques could increase the conditions for the growth of individuality. Hamner argued that as long as there are alternative organizations where an individual can work, each person can work where his or her individuality would be appreciated. Of course it could be argued that often such a choice is not available. However, assuming that we want to encourage the development of individuality by calling attention to the importance of such alternatives for the development of individuality, the operant model would encourage us to design a system which produces the outcomes we desire. In other words, here is an area where the operant approach can enhance what we commonly call freedom by stimulating the design of contingencies which promote job mobility in place of many current policies which restrict movement between jobs.

Choice and Freedom

Many critics of behavior modification have charged that the application of operant conditioning restricts freedom of choice. Undoubtedly this outcome is possible; however, it is neither inherent in behavioral techniques nor an inevitable result of their application. In fact, successful behavior modification may be shown to enhance human freedom. For example, consider the work of Chein (1972).

Chein's book has been heralded in some quarters as a definitive humanistic reply to Skinner despite the fact that Chein explicitly acknowledged his deterministic position. However, Chein argued persuasively that deterministic assumptions are not incompatible with the existence of at least some measure of human freedom.

Chein suggested that motivation (defined as behavior*), constitutional and environmental factors are the three sufficient conditions for behavior. However, he added that

> Behavior is free to the extent that the environment and the constitution . . . do not dictate or preclude a particular action. . . . Within the limits of these constraints, the behavior that actually occurs is determined by the motivation of the actor. No behavior is ever completely free, some degree of freedom being lost as a consequence of the constraints of constitution and environment; but degrees of freedom are also gained from the dependabilities of constitution and environment.

Such a statement is a severe challenge only to extreme statements of operant conditioning. In fact, this position provides a basis for showing that, by increasing ". . . the dependabilities of . . . environment," operant techniques can enhance freedom. If reinforcement contingencies are clear and consistent, individuals will face a dependable, predictable environment. Consequently, contingency management can enhance individual freedom.

The outcomes of behavior modification can also enhance the freedom of groups of people by improving the quality of the exchanges social units can exact from their environments. A

---

* Chein discussed this point fully.

good case in point is Platt's (1973) discussion of Hardin's Tragedy of the Commons as a "social trap." Platt noted that such traps can be avoided by the design of systems in which reinforcements are contingent on behavior which satisfied the interests of the group as well as the individual. If such costly social traps can be avoided, man's control over nature, upon which human freedom depends, could be strengthened. In short, by producing dependable environments for individuals and permitting groups of people to exert greater control over their environments, many direct outcomes of successful behavior modification may contribute to human freedom.

Of course, dependable, controllable environments do not necessarily ensure increases in human freedom and choice. Whether behavior modification restricts or enhances human freedom and development depends on a number of indirect effects which are a function of the process used to modify behavior.

The way that contingencies are designed, i.e., the way we go about deciding who, what, when, where, why and how, has major consequences for human development. For example, consider *Walden Two* (Skinner, 1948). Assuming a large amount of behavior is a function of its consequences the design of Walden Two is consistent with many humanistic principles. While the designer of this community had considerable power, neither the founder nor any other person exerted current control (Rogers and Skinner, 1956). The decision-making process encouraged participation of all members of the community in areas of their competence. Moreover, the major criteria used for decisions were empirical; the courses shown by experimental evidence to have the best chance to achieve the goals of the community were chosen. While full support for the writer's assertion of the humanism of Walden Two would require a paper in itself, by and large, the goals and decision processes of the community treated people as ends and sought to increase the effectiveness of the control its members exercised over their outcomes.

Contrary to the opinions of many writers (most recently Fry, 1974), the use of operant conditioning does not necessarily require an authoritarian system run by an elite. As Hamner (1974) suggested, the design of systems based on operant principles can provide for some form of democratic processes through which many people participate in the decisions about what behavior will be reinforced with what reinforcers. In other words, individuals could have power to determine their outcomes in ways which are not available to them in today's organizations. Support for Hamner's point can be found in Holland's (1974) description of several cases where the principles of reinforcement were used in the design of social systems. Significantly, in these cases, the participants in the system, not an elite, were responsible for the process. These systems allowed lower level participants to exert far more control over their own outcomes than do many current management styles which we call humanistic.

The institution of such processes provides some protection against the manipulation of some people by others. If in reality much behavior is controlled by its consequences, our only choices are whether or not to acknowledge the fact and whether or not to act on it; in other words we are limited to a choice between Quadrants II and IV. This choice is *not* one of control versus no control. Rather, as Bandura (1969) noted, "The basic moral question is not whether man's behavior will be controlled, but rather by whom, by what means, and for what ends." The free will of any one individual will not be changed by our assumptions; the person will still not be any more or less free. However, if we acknowledge this control and are careful about the process of design, behavior modification may help us overcome existing restrictions on human freedom. As Holland (1974) noted,

> It is a shame that those persons most involved in the struggle for justice view Skinner and operant conditioning as the enemy, thereby forfeiting a powerful tool to analyze the control exerted within the system they oppose.

Behavior Modification and Psychological Knowledge

A number of psychologists have argued that behavior modification provides a very limited understanding of important psychological processes such as motivation, cognition and the individual's awareness of himself as a causal agent. Consequently, they suggest that behavior modification may misdirect psychological research.

The writer believes these charges have considerable validity. There are a number of psychological processes which operant conditioning does not help us to understand. To the degree that these processes are significant ones and operant conditioners continue to overlook them, our models of human behavior will be incomplete. However, such an outcome is not a necessary correlate of Quadrant IV; operant conditioning is *not necessarily* incompatible with other psychological models. In fact, it is complementary to many of them.

Contrary to the assumptions of both advocates and opponents of operant conditioning, even if a great deal of behavior is a function of its consequences, the search for understanding the processes through which individual experience is stored and perhaps acquires functionally autonomous, *causative* power is a meaningful area for inquiry. Even if operant conditioning is effective and the operant conditioners do not choose to study motivation, cognition and related processes, these more traditional topics are not thereby rendered superfluous.

Psychologists, including many operant conditioners, often seem to think in surprisingly absolutistic ways. Consequently, various approaches to their subject matter become unnecessarily polarized. Less absolutistic perspectives might reveal a basic complementarity between behavior modification and current advances in academic psychology.

A good example of such complementarity, which has direct implications for the motivation of people in organizations, is the relationship between intrinsic and extrinsic motivation. Hamner (1974) noted that since operant conditioners commonly focus on external rewards, they are often criticized for ignoring the possibility that intrinsic motivation comes from the job itself. Recently this position was supported by evidence reported by Deci (1971, 1972) who found that extrinsic rewards interfered with the development of intrinsic motivation. However, more recently Foster and Hamner (1974) found that the effects of intrinsic and extrinsic reinforcement may well be additive. Based on Foster and Hamner's work, intrinsic and extrinsic rewards appear to complement each other.

While full knowledge of the relationship between extrinsic reinforcement and intrinsic motivation requires additional research even if extrinsic rewards are found to reduce intrinsic motivation, knowledge about the use of extrinsic rewards developed by the operant conditioners may be useful in understanding the nature and effective use of intrinsic reinforcement.

Examination of what we often call intrinsic reinforcers, e.g., achievement, recognition and the work itself, reveals that many of them are not only intrinsic, but are also contingent upon performance in ways which can be expected to produce high rates of performance. For example, such rewards as feelings of achievement are apt to occur immediately after a task is performed successfully. Also, these rewards may occur on some type of a ratio schedule in that they do not occur after every performance, but only after some especially fine accomplishment. Thus, one of the reasons intrinsic reinforcers are effective is that they occur on an optimal schedule. Based on this understanding, the design of tasks which provide optimal intrinsic reinforcement may be facilitated.

Summary

So far the writer has suggested that behavior modification is not inherently antihumanistic; in fact he has described a number of ways, including several actual cases from industry, in which behavior modification may increase the control humans exercise over their environment and enhance individuality. He has also suggested that the failure to use these techniques may be antihumanistic because humans do not achieve what they are capable of, particularly due to the existence of social traps and countertraps. However, it has been stressed that the humanizing potential of behavior modification is a function of two fundamental things—(1) the nature of the *true* laws of human behavior and (2) the process by which the techniques are applied. Finally, an attempt has been made to show that behavior modification and more traditional concerns of psychologists may be complementary rather than antithetical. The writer concludes by commenting on the implications of some of these points for applied behavioral scientists.

BEHAVIOR MODIFICATION AND THE APPLIED BEHAVIORAL SCIENTIST

Assuming that a great deal of behavior is actually a function of its consequences, applied behavioral scientists are faced with several dilemmas. They will have a technique which can have major consequences for society; they can work to apply it (Quadrant IV) or to not apply it (Quadrant II). Once we have a technique that works, it will become increasingly difficult to convince ourselves that our work is value-free. The choice between Quadrants II and IV involves a number of value judgments; many of those judgments involve fundamental aspects of social control.

The decision of applied scientists to work in Quadrant II involves a number of humanistic costs. First, this decision makes it more difficult to actualize human potential. Second, it leaves current mechanisms of control intact. To the degree that these are in conflict with the individual and social development, the choice of Quadrant II is antihumanistic. Finally, there is the possibility that in the future, if not the present, individuals or small groups may be able to use behavioral techniques to achieve their own parochial ends. The choice not to apply behavior modification is neither value-free nor humanistic. The choice of Quadrant IV is not value-free, but it may be more humanistic.

Attempts to modify behavior of people involve a number of concerns about social control. These issues become particularly important when it appears likely that a certain group, e.g., the managers of organizations, will exercise increased power.

Apparently in America the legitimacy of efforts by managers to use scientific knowledge to influence and coordinate the behavior of people is widely accepted. Moreover, many behavioral scientists have been eager to help in these efforts. Presumably, good management is, in part, a function of the amount of influence and control. When a set of techniques appears to have the potential to make the influence and control process manifest and potent, society and behavioral scientists may well ask, "Just how good do we want management to get?"

To the degree that the behavioral scientists have an effective set of techniques and are themselves subject to contingencies which increase the behavior they devote to the service of management, serious value issues arise. If the scientific community fails to actively initiate strategies for influencing the behavior of our members, we run the risk of social traps, etc. If we have a technique that works and fail to control how we use it, we may legitimately be called servants of power.

However, the availability of an effective technique need not be a curse. As the writer has argued, the humanizing potential of behavior modification is a function of the process by which it is implemented and the ends for which it is used. To achieve humanistic goals behavioral scientists will need to do more than provide the techniques. They must become active in influencing the processes by which organizational goals are decided upon and through which they are implemented.

This type of role is new to most applied behavioral scientists; however, behavioral scientists may need to accept these demands if the humanistic goals of having people treated as ends and controlling their own outcomes are to be realized. By pointing out manipulative contingencies and aiding in the design of countercontingencies, operant conditioners can provide a major force against the tendency of the powerful to treat the less powerful as means rather than as ends. By working for decision-making processes which permit full participation of all elements of a social unit in the setting of goals and designing of contingencies for that system, behavioral scientists can help to develop environments which are humanistic at both micro and macro levels. On the microlevel individuals will be encouraged to participate in important decisions; consequently many organizational members will be able to have a greater role in determining their own outcomes than they do now. Moreover, through this participation, they may develop themselves more fully. On a macro level, systems can be designed which increase the effectiveness of groups of people in their exchanges with nature.

In conclusion, contrary to many humanists, the writer believes behavior modification has great potential for humanizing social systems. In fact, to the degree that human behavior is a function of its consequences, behavior modification may be the most effective approach for humanization presently known to man.

Dewey's (1922) discussion of social change provides an excellent summary of the central thesis of this paper. Dewey wrote,

> . . . there are two schools of social reform. One bases itself upon the notion of a morality which springs from an inner freedom, something mysteriously cooped up within personality. It asserts that the only way to change situations is for men to purify their own hearts, and that when this has been accomplished, change of institutions will follow of itself. The other school denies the existence of any such inner power, and in so doing conceives that it has denied all moral freedom. It says that men are made what they are by the forces of the environment, that human nature is purely malleable, and that till institutions are changed, nothing can be done. Clearly this leaves the outcome as hopeless as does an appeal to an inner rectitude and benevolence. For it provides no leverage for change of environment. It throws us back upon accident, usually disguised as a necessary law of history or evolution, and trusts to some violent change, symbolized by civil war, to usher in an abrupt millennium. There is an alternative to being penned in between these two theories. We can recognize that all conduct is *interaction* between elements of human nature and the environment, natural and social. Then we shall see that progress proceeds in two ways, and that freedom is found in that kind of interaction which maintains an environment in which human desire and choice count for something. There are in truth forces in man as well as without him. While they are infinitely frail in comparison with exterior forces, yet they may have the support of a foreseeing and contriving intelligence. When we look at the problem as one of an adjustment to be intelligently attained, the issue shifts from within personality to an engineering issue. . . .

REFERENCES

Aldis, O.: Of pigeons and men. *Harvard Business Review, 39*:56-63, 1961.

Argyris, C.: Personality and organization theory revisited. *Administrative Science Quarterly, 18*:141-167, 1973.

Bandura, A.: *Principles of Behavior Modification.* New York, HR&W, 1969.

Baritz, L.: *The Servants of Power.* Middletown, Wesleyan U Pr, 1960.

Barnicki, D.: A line manager's view of behavior modification. In Standing, T. E., and Lazer, R. I. (Eds.): *Executive Study Conference Summary.* Meetings held in Atlanta, Georgia, Executive Study Conference, December 4-5, 1973, pp. 44-48.

Chein, I.: *The Science of Behavior and the Image of Man.* New York, Basic, 1972.

Deci, E. L.: Effects of externally mediated rewards on intrinsic motivation. *J Pers Soc Psychol, 18*:105-115, 1971.

Deci, E. L.: The effects on contingent and non-contingent rewards and controls on intrinsic motivation. *Organizational Behavior and Human Performance, 8*:217-229, 1972.

Dewey, J.: *Human Nature and Conduct.* New York, Henry Holt and Company, 1922.

Foster, L. W., and Hamner, W. C.: Are intrinsic and extrinsic rewards additive: A test of Deci's cognitive evaluation theory of task motivation. Paper presented at National Academy of Management, 1974.

Fry, F. L.: Operant conditioning in organization settings: of mice or men? *Personnel, 51*:17-24, 1974.

Goldstein, A. P., and Sorcher, M.: *Changing Supervisor Behavior.* New York, Pergamon, 1974.

Gomberg, W.: Democratic management—Gomberg replies. *Transaction, 3*:48, 1966.

Hamblin, R. L.; Buckholdt, D.; Ferritor, D.; Kozloff, M., and Blackwell, L.: *The Humanization Processes: A Social, Behavioral Analysis of Children's Problems.* New York, Wiley, 1971.

Hamner, W. C.: Reinforcement theory and contingency management in organizational settings. In Tosi, H., and Hamner, W. C. (Eds.): *Organizational Behavior and Management.* Chicago, St. Clair Pr, 1974.

Holland, J. G.: Are behavioral principles for revolutionaries? In Keller, F. S., and Ribes, I. E.: *Behavior Modification: Applications to Education.* New York, Acad Pr, 1974, pp. 195-208.

Hulin, C. L., and Blood, M. R.: Job enlargement, individual differences, and worker responses. *Psychol Bull, 69*:41-55, 1968.

Jablonsky, S. F., and DeVries, D. L.: Operant conditioning principles extrapolated to the theory of management. *Organizational Behavior and Human Performance, 7*:340-358, 1972.

Levinson, H.: Management by whose objectives? *Harvard Business Review* 48:125-134, 1970.

Luthans, F.: An organizational behavior modification (O. B. Mod.) approach to O.D. Paper given at Meetings of the Academy of Management, Seattle, Washington, 1974.

Nord, W. R.: Beyond the teaching machine: The neglected area of operant conditioning in the theory and practice of management. *Organizational Behavior and Human Performance,* 4:375-401, 1969.

Nord, W. R.: The failure of current applied behavioral science—A Marxian perspective. *J Appl Beh Sci,* 10:557-578, 1974.

Platt, J.: Social traps. *Am Psychol,* 28:641-651, 1973.

Quinn, R. P.; Mangione, T. W., and Baldi de Mandilovitch, M.: Evaluating working conditions in America. *Monthly Labor Review,* 96:32-41, 1973.

Rogers, C. R., and Skinner, B. F.: Some issues concerning the control of human behavior: A symposium. *Science, 124*:1057-1066, 1956.

Schneier, C. E.: Behavior modification in management: A review and critique. *Academy of Management Journal,* 17:528-548, 1974.

Skinner, B. F.: *Walden Two.* New York, MacMillan, 1948.

Standing, T. E., and Lazer, R. F. (Eds.): Behavior modification in industry. *Executive Study Conference Summary.* Meetings held in Atlanta, Georgia, Executive Study Conference, December 4-5, 1973.

Tausky, C.: Meanings of work: Marx, Maslow, and steamirons. Paper presented at meetings of the American Sociological Association, August, 1973.

Warren, M.: Contingency management. In Standing, T. E., and Lazer, R. I. (Eds.): *Executive Study Conference Summary.* Meetings held in Atlanta, Georgia, Executive Study Conference, December 4-5, 1973, pp. 26-33.

Wheeler, H. (Ed.): Introduction: A nonpunitive world? *Beyond the Punitive Society.* San Francisco, W. H. Freeman and Company, 1973.

Winpisinger, W. W.: Job satisfaction: A union response. *AFL-CIO Federationist,* February, 1973.

FACILITATING THE DEVELOPMENT OF
THE HUMANIZING ORGANIZATION

INTRODUCING PART IV . . .
HOW TO DO IT

How to do it, how to humanize organizational behavior is the main theme of the contributions in Part IV. In Part IV, "Facilitating the Development of the Humanizing Organization," are featured three case studies describing experiences and results obtained in efforts to humanize organizational behavior. Also presented in a comprehensive manner is a very important possible contribution to humanizing the frequently-neglected physical setting. Also included is a survey featuring "The Search for the Effective and Humanizing Work Organization" and a chapter, "On Organizations of the Future."

The road ahead on how to humanize an organization by development programs starts with a contribution by Michael Beer who works for Corning Glass Company and Edgar Huse who is a consultant to the organization. In their description of improving organizational effectiveness through planned change and development, a number of quotes indicate the positive feeling of the people involved. The causes of many manifestations of dehumanizing are ascribed to bureaucratic organization. Because contemporary organizations are still largely bureaucratic they are increasingly experiencing problems in commitment, motivation and adaptability because of changes in markets, technology, information, society and men themselves. The project represents one effort to design at least a part of an organization to cope with these new realities.

The investigators saw in the occasion a unique opportunity for bringing the process of decision-making to a conscious level and consistency by getting the management team to develop managerial philosophy and plan. A McGregor Theory Y assumption was made that employees desire responsibility, challenging work and an opportunity for achievement and growth. Over a period of three years a work environment was created based on this assumption. The details of the processing which led to the whole program as well as the findings and results are presented in the paper. The means of changes are considered in detail. Emphasized were both structural and job changes. Job enrichment and autonomous work teams were the two dominant principles applied for bringing about the change of departments described. The result has been increased involvement in work, commitment to the organization, motivation and satisfaction of needs. Considered also is the style of relationship of the plant with the parent company. The paper ends with a very promising note, namely "as the pace of change increases and the lifespan of technology decreases, a planned strategy of organization development will become an important competitive edge."

The next paper presented, "Humanizing Relations of Key People in Industry," is described as an exploration in experiencing, studying and working with an organization in human relations in one industry for a period of one year from the vantage point of management in action. Specifically, the very first problem confronting the investigator was: can six people who were trained to look toward a general manager for leadership and direction in an industry employing 250 men, be developed into functionally autonomous leaders who could cooperate effectively for common purposes and run the organization? In other words, can persons educated to be subleaders in an authoritarian form of organization be educated to develop enough human insight and maturity to become co-leaders in an interdependent and democratic organization of their making? Attempts made at organizing the creative administration with a description of the earlier situation, which was a reign of authoritarianism, and a description of the organization in transition and then a detailed account of what was, at that time, the earliest attempt to use a clinical approach in organizing are given. Clinical reports are included in the study of all the people involved, their attitudes toward the company, what they did and how they did it. The clinical approach was used only after group approaches did not yield the results desired in a promising way.

The key people were given an opportunity to learn how to solve problems in collaborative fashion as an integral part of the way management was set up. Provisions for the maintenance of improved relations were continuously introduced. This particular program continued for more than twenty years. The article ends with a very simple statement which emerged out of the experience, namely that the need for the development of matured leadership and effective interdependent management is urgent and represents an inviting challenge to organizational psychologists as well as to industrialists and workers.

In the next chapter, "A Planned Humanizing Organization in Action," is a report of what took place in the world of reality in a manner that is very unusual. This small company was planned and designed at the very outset to be humanizing in action. The events which led up to that possibility are interesting. In 1966 a small group of managers, as described by Kenneth Ball, were invited to start a new manufacturing company from a piece of the older company. The older company had developed in an increasingly humanizing manner from 1938 until 1961. Then it was fused with authoritarianism described in the paper. The parent plant was sold and Ball was one of the two vice-presidents who was selected for creating a new organization after five years of sufferance and regression from a previously well-managed humanized plant. The installation of a new company and the design for instituting it included the selection of products as well as equipment needed for making the products. The product structure was consciously selected so it would be too complex for most small competitors, would compete for too small a market for most giant corporations, and require too much technical catch up time for either.

The nature of the organizing efforts and the story of what happened to the company are described in some detail by Ball, who not only is the organizational psychologist involved but who also basically directs the company with freedom of movement on everything that is human. The company has multiplied five times over since its start and Ball is in charge of operations, sales and marketing as well as personnel. The task that is skillfully carried out in this particular organization which is unusual is the integration of informal and formal organization. Thus, the paper does report how a company took advantage of events in its history to provide a program which institutes a humanizing approach at the outset and makes provisions for its continuance and growth.

What Fritz Steele considers in his contribution, "Humanizing the Physical Setting at Work," is often referred to by sociologists as the environmental crisis in human dignity. Steele expresses it in a more practical, realistic way when he says that the physical setting has generally been treated as a "hygiene" issue with attention given only when people are dissatisfied. Attempts to influence it have been thought of as improving the amenities of creature comforts that go with membership in an organization. Steele points out the very important fact that the more complex impacts of the process by which physical decisions are made have tended to remain a hidden dimension of our lives. These influences are always there but we seldom become aware of them and thus able to change them effectively. What he sets out to do in his contribution is to examine these impacts—what will be required in order to humanize the physical settings in work organizations, or as he prefers to express it, to humanize the person-environment interaction system.

In considering this problem, Steele discusses in a relevant fashion what human qualities are, what ways work organizations are presently inhuman, the mode of humanization, main factors in promoting change, and how likely change is. Included also is a review and consideration of the physical facilities and environmental competence of the users. Though he is skeptical about change he gives positive suggestions for ways of humanizing and does include a list of definite positive forces which would aid the process of change toward a more humanizing work setting. The statement he ends with is,

> I suspect that real change is likely to occur more quickly if people become more aware of their own needs for self-control than it is if they sit and wait for higher-level executives to become keen on sharing their power.

In the next paper, Frederic Wickert surveys the developmental history of "The Search for the Effective and Humanizing Work Organization." What this paper attempts to do is consider relevant human inventions with respect to building effective and humanizing work organizations and blend these inventions together to provide a comprehensive eclectic statement of where we are now on the road toward humanizing. In two sections he presents (1) a matrix in organized form which includes the rich array of human inventions that have been designed to date to build an effective and humanized work organization and (2) a review of the several categories of contributions to this book and how they relate to the matrix. In his search, there is an exploration of the "one best ways" over the years which have swung back and forth between effectivism and humanism, with always some of both contained in the one best way of the moment. The level of organization dimension considered as a part of his matrix starts from the simplest level of the individual and goes on toward the large organization, including the pyramid organization. Wickert's hope is that the theory would help give a manager an outlook for seeing things more clearly and therefore acting more intelligently. Some of the suggestions made in this paper would hold regardless of the matrix reference point. Resistance to change is characteristic of small, informal groups in industry and would disappear if the boundaries between formal and informal groups themselves broke down. An open and trusting climate within the group can be a reality.

Chris Arygris, in his chapter, "On Organizations of the Future," starts with knowledge which should be perceptible to all people involved and interested in effective organizations in a human manner, namely that organization deterioration which has taken place is a major force for change. Private and public organizations are increasingly disappointing their consumers with the quality of their services as well as products.

In considering characteristics of the managerial world, Argyris is always aware of the fact that the higher persons go in the organizational hierarchy the more individuals are able if they wish to alter the system. Presented are approaches for inviting people on top to become perceptive enough to see the need for altering the system for their own welfare as well as the welfare of the organization and everybody in it. Argyris' impression is that a good deal of research of organizational behavior is excellent for describing the status quo; but it should not be used by practitioners as guides for future action or else this knowledge becomes a force in maintaining this status quo. Information, science and technology are not enough to depend on for humanizing for the future. Dr. Argyris presents a model to be used to plot the degree of difficulty of any organizational change in the process of changing. Stressed is the need for and advisability of beginning at the top because if the people in power have not accepted the new values and needed behavior, organizational development would not tend to be effective. "New," says he, "is the notion of reeducating people to develop interpersonal and problem-solving competences that will help them become masters of their own fates, architects of their own lives, and managers of their own progress."

Chapter 15

IMPROVING ORGANIZATIONAL EFFECTIVENESS THROUGH PLANNED CHANGE AND DEVELOPMENT*

MICHAEL BEER AND EDGAR HUSE

I love it. I can't get over how tremendous it is and after all the time I've been here I still go home to my husband at night and do nothing but rave about it because it's mostly the nature and freedom of the relationships between the people throughout the plant from the plant manager down. Everyone is so tremendous. They seem friendly, interested and concerned about us. I also feel that I know everything that's going on in the plant and feel that this is very important. It makes things a lot more interesting to understand what is happening and I like going to the meetings and finding out what's happening to the plant sales.

You get involved in your job here and won't stay home because you have a goal to meet.

No matter who you ask to listen, they're interested and they follow through—it's the response of the supervisor; they never shove you aside as unimportant. I'm not afraid to speak my mind because they're always there to listen and they will try it. We know what's going on in our jobs and we can tell them. It makes you feel very important.

T HESE QUOTES WERE taken from interviews with production workers in a small electronics assembly plant. Here are some quotes from supervisory and exempt personnel as well as a visitor to the plant.

---

* The authors would like to acknowledge the innovation and farsighted approaches to management implemented by the managers and supervisors of the organization described. Particular thanks are due to J. G. Sabin, C. F. Wheatley and J. Johnson. Many others were and are involved; we thank them also.

A supervisor: "I have to say it, and I'm not going to try it, but I think that I could be off the floor for three or four weeks and my people would still make schedule."

An engineer: "I wondered about this organizational development (O.D.) approach when I got here and kinda thought that it was for the birds. The thing that convinced me was the way we got those new products into the line. Because of the problems involved in any other plant that I've ever worked it would have been a complete fiasco."

A graduate student to one of the authors: "I'm glad we went on a plant tour instead of the plant manager coming to lecture us. If I hadn't seen it myself, I would never have believed it. I tried to tell my father about it (an executive in a large company), and he wouldn't believe me. He asked me what I had been smoking."

These comments were gathered through interviews in a small electronics assembly plant which was the focus of an experiment in management. The purpose of the experiment was to see if management patterns and work in this organization could be changed so that they more closely reflected the real needs and expectations of employees while at the same time increasing productivity and effectiveness.

Work organizations (industry, government, universities, hospitals, schools, etc.) are facing a crisis in employee commitment and motivation. This trend is being felt most by managers daily engaged in the task of managing the human side of the enterprise. Their experience tells them that traditional patterns of influence, namely the authority vested in them as managers, are no longer as effective as they once were. Their search for new means of motivation is evidenced by their rising interest in behavioral science. They hope to find through this emerging discipline new insights into how they might both humanize work and achieve results.

The crisis in commitment and motivation is apparent in a number of national trends. Fifty percent of all new college recruits leave their first job and company within the first five years. Turnover and absenteeism among production employees have steadily risen since World War II (Foulkes, 1969). Costly strikes have shut down such large employers as General Electric, the United States Post Office and school systems. While these strikes have ostensibly been for wages and fringe benefits, evidence exists that alienation of workers from their organizations is in progress and that money is not the major factor. Other examples of increasing alienation include declining quality of products, resistance to change and unionization among professional employees such as teachers, college professors and engineers.

The cause of many of these problems is the bureaucratic organization. To understand the deficiencies of this form of organization it might be well to examine briefly its historical development. Contemporary organizations were born of the industrial revolution. The early entrepreneur was faced with the task of organizing to make and sell one product consistently and reliably for his lifetime and perhaps that of his children., Organizational stability rather than flexibility was called for. The model for organizing and managing came from the only previously existing organizations—the church and the military. Industrial organizations are characterized by hierarchical, centralized decision-making based on assumptions about people which may have been justified for that era but are increasingly invalid. The assumptions are that employees' most pressing needs are survival and economic security and that loyalty and motivation could be obtained by simply paying people. The *economic contract* was submission to organizational authority in return for security and pay.

Contemporary organizations, which are still largely bureaucratic, are increasingly experiencing problems in commitment, motivation and adaptability because of changes in markets, technology, information, society and man himself. An organization designed for stability will have difficulty with adaptability. The very economic affluence brought about by the bureaucratic organization has freed man from needs for security and has resulted in wants for esteem, independence and self-actualization (Maslow, 1943). The challenge for the future lies, as Warren Bennis has said (1966), in designing organizations that can cope with these new realities. It requires experimentation not only with the structures and administrative systems of organizations, but with the social system itself.

Between 1965 and 1969 we were involved in a program of organization development (O.D.) aimed at putting into practice management patterns that could reverse the crises in organizations. New management patterns have resulted in high commitment and motivation. Evidences of this are (1) low absenteeism and turnover, (2) a reduced need for supervision, and (3) increases in productivity and quality. The ability of employees to respond to change has been demonstrated through rapid product introduction. The interview excerpts above show that the work force is committed to the attainment of plant goals, and, through this, the attainment of their personal goals. The plant is approaching, although it has not reached, the true integration of individual needs and organizational objectives needed to alleviate the crises in contemporary organizations (Argyris, 1964).

THE ORGANIZATION

The organizational development program took place in a plant manufacturing a variety of instruments for medical and laboratory use. Product complexity ranges from relatively simple to highly complex. At the end of the three-year period described in this paper the plant employed approximately seventy hourly employees (mostly women with high school educations), thirty-five weekly salaried technical and clerical personnel, and eleven monthly salaried professional and managerial personnel. Its assembly technology, its small size and the fact that most of the production employees are women constitute uniqueness that must be understood in assessing the meaning and generality of this experiment in management. It should be noted, however, that the plant has tripled in size since 1969 with many of the innovations to be described below still intact. It is our view that the new patterns of management discussed in this paper are not only applicable to larger plants and different technologies, but are more mandatory for these organizations.

In 1965, when the plant was small, Dr. Beer, a behavioral scientist employed by the firm at its headquarters, was asked to visit the plant by the personnel supervisor because of the latter's interest in trying out some new managerial concepts. After a day in the plant it seemed apparent that here was an organization that was still in its formative stages. Crucial decisions were in the making concerning the plant's methods of production, means of setting production standards and controls, personnel policies and practices, managerial practices and philosophy. These decisions were certain to be influenced largely by the traditions and practices of the parent corporation and stood the chance of being inconsistent in their basic thrust.

It became clear that a unique opportunity existed for bringing this process of decision-making to a conscious level and consistency by getting the management team to develop a managerial philosophy and plan. There was enough interest by the management team to start a series of discussions on current concepts in management. The purpose of these discussions was to contrast traditional approaches with approaches suggested by current behavioral research and theory. The discussions never succeeded in getting an explicit decision on the pattern of management that would prevail in the plant, but they did succeed in gaining a commitment to try some new things on a trial and error basis. This constituted much less than commitment to a new pattern of management, but it did constitute commitment to experimentation and examination.

At this point Dr. Huse was introduced as an outside change agent who was geographically closer to the scene and thus able to work regularly with the plant.* This step seemed essential to supplement Dr. Beer's necessarily less frequent visits.

AN IDEAL ORGANIZATIONAL MODEL

If the managers in the plant did not start with a firm commitment to a philosophy of management, how did the change pro-

---

* The terms change agent and OD consultant will be used interchangeably.

gram take shape? It was the change agents in this case who started with some ideas about new management patterns which might increase commitment, motivation, personal growth, satisfaction, innovation and adaptability. These ideas came out of our synthesis of current organizational research and theory. In order for this synthesis to be a practical statement of organization development objectives it had to go beyond the existing data, particularly where conclusive research findings did not exist (in the behavioral sciences this includes almost all situations). For example, one of the key underlying thrusts of the whole effort was to move the organization to a participative or Theory Y management style (McGregor, 1960). As professionals in the field will readily admit, all the evidence about effective leadership is not in. Nevertheless, the overwhelming evidence indicated that participative management stood a better chance than any other to increase commitment, motivation and adaptability. Participative management seemed particularly appropriate because the plant was expecting continuous change in products and because of highly labor-intensive production operations.

The questions, it seemed to us, were not really whether to implement participative management, but how much, how fast? In this regard a dynamic and growth-oriented view of organizations (Argyris, 1958; Korman, 1970) was taken—that is, managerial approaches should not only reflect employees' needs and expectations, but should lead them. At any given time employees are more or less ready or able to work effectively under participative management. The managerial approaches chosen should not only reflect the current state of readiness, but should anticipate a direction of change, i.e., more participation, and lead the employees. In this way the managerial approach chosen can increase the employee's ability and desire to function under such a pattern which in turn will encourage management to take further steps. Thus, the goal was a *positive snowball of change* started by some initial changes, followed by heightened expectations and readiness for more change, followed by further change and so on. In this regard the job of management seemed to the authors to be very similar to childrearing.

THE MEANS OF CHANGE

What were the means employed? The approach has been eclectic and based upon three basic beliefs,

1. That the operating manager will try out and continue to use that which helps him to get his job done better. He will drop or cease doing that which, for him, is not helpful, at least as he perceives it.
2. That the change agents should work primarily toward helping the operating manager do his job better by acting as resources but not telling him how to do his job.
3. That a variety of approaches to change have a place in an organizational development program, and that the change agents should not become wedded to any single tool or technique.

Change was catalyzed by a team of four individuals who raised questions, provided feedback based on observations and other data, and provided counseling and consulting support. This team included the personnel man, Dr. Beer, who was employed by the corporation as a behavioral scientist but was not part of the plant organization, and Dr. Huse, who was hired as an external consultant. The fourth member of the team was a researcher whose main responsibility was to gather data in the organization for evaluation and feedback purposes.

Having gained entrance to the organization, the basic approach was for the two outside change agents to establish working relationships with individuals at all of the management levels of the organization. Stemming from the basic beliefs listed above, the change agents presented themselves to individuals as resource persons who could be used to help solve specific ongoing problems or initiate small experiments in management. The idea was to get someone or some organizational component to start implementing new managerial concepts consistent with the direction of change program. Access to these concepts came through consulting on a specific problem managers were facing or may have come briefly, but without full understanding, through the initial few seminars that were held. (This reference to lack of full understanding will become clear below.) The result was that there were a few individuals in the plant who began, with our aid, to apply some new managerial approaches. As it turned out, most of these early experiments were successful, resulting in reinforcement for the individual and the organization, thereby enhancing interest and motivation to experiment and change. (Encouraging a spirit of experimentation is probably more important than the solution to a specific problem.)

This change and learning process is a reversal of the traditional educational and management development model which stresses formal learning of concepts prior to the time of expected application. One of our most important findings is that the most effective and permanent learning comes after the individual has experimented with new approaches. Through working with a change agent, a manager may try to apply a new means of communication, job enrichment or a new organizational structure. If the new approach is successful, it frequently leads to another try. At the same time, the successful experience begins in a subtle way to change the individual's attitude toward the new management concepts being applied and organizational development as an ongoing process. These changed attitudes lead to a desire for more information and experimentation. As continued experimentation succeeds, new managerial behaviors and attitudes are reinforced and the desire for more learning and change is increased further.

CHANGES IN THE ORGANIZATION

What were some of the management patterns and organizational arrangements tried? These are far too many to be fully covered here and often too subtle to be able to convey on paper. Nevertheless, the new management patterns can be put into two categories—those changes that related to the behavior of individuals and groups, and those changes that related to the technology, task and organizational structure.

Although these two areas will be discussed as though they are separate, work on both proceeded simultaneously, and they are interdependent in many ways. Changes in both structure and behavior are absolutely essential, and change in one facilitates change in the other. For example, improvement in interpersonal trust and cooperation facilitates structural changes, and structural changes, in turn, facilitate the development of interpersonal trust and cooperation.

Changes in Organizational Behavior

In this part of the program work was done directly on organizational processes having to do with interpersonal and social variables; attempts were made to improve leadership and supervision in the plant as well as to improve communications; and new methods were used to establish and develop effective work groups and improve intergroup relationships.

Communications

One of the first concerns was to increase the amount and openness of communication so that high trust levels could be developed. Trust would be needed to create the major changes which were to follow. Although the plant already had developed some communication patterns, these were far less than were thought possible and necessary. What were some of the communications changes?

DEPARTMENTAL MEETINGS. Individual supervisors began, with relatively little training, a series of monthly meetings with their subordinates. This occurred at all levels of the organization, but the most radical change came at the first-line supervisory level. In these meetings the supervisors told their subordinates what was going on in the plant and in the department. They communicated about (a) the monthly objectives of the plant and how the plant was doing in regard to these objectives and (b) how the department objectives fitted in with the plant objectives. At the same time the supervisor tried to get his people to give their comments, ideas and suggestions regarding the objectives that had been discussed, and solicited their feelings about the plant and what was going on.

How did the meetings go? They grew and developed over the next several years into meetings with real two-way communication. One of the interesting things that happened in the meetings, particularly at the production worker level, is that communications changed from *minigripes* to *megagripes*—that is, discussions, questions and comments changed from very peripheral topics such as vacation and sick leave policies to topics of more central task relevance such as quality of products, parts shortages and needed tools.

This shift, particularly among production people, seemed to be part of an evolutionary learning process. All of the people had come from more traditional companies where they had very narrow and limited perceptions of their roles. As one worker put it, "In the last company I worked for, things were different. You were told what to do and you did it. Beyond that, no one told you anything about the company and what you were working on. No one asked you anything about nothing."

COFFEE WITH THE BOSS. A weekly communication meeting was set up between the plant manager and a sample group of hourly and weekly salaried employees (on a rotating basis) to close the communications loop at the top. Again, the discussion showed the same kind of shift over time that has already been described in the departmental meetings.

OTHER APPROACHES. As the meetings changed in content and openness, it became evident that employees at all levels wanted more information about their jobs, how they fitted into the organization, and how the business was doing. As a result plant tours were initiated to show employees from one department what was happening in other departments. After a time, hourly employees gave the tour in their own departments. The effect of these interdepartmental tours is best illustrated by the following quote from someone in the purchasing department.

> I like to know what's going on on the floor and I feel that one of the most interesting things I have had was a tour of the Meter Department. To know what is being made and how what we purchase for people contributes to the product makes my work much more interesting.

In addition, charts were placed at the major traffic point in the plant. These charts, brought up to date monthly, showed actual versus budgeted progress in areas such as sales, inventory, plant effectiveness, and the like. For proprietary reasons it was, however, necessary to leave actual dollar figures off the charts.

Three quotes below further illustrate the feelings of employees about communications,

> In spite of the fact that this is such a big company, you know what's happening. You never knew anything at the company I was at before. They kept you in the dark. One day you were there, who knew about the next day? This company wants you to know things.
>
> It's hard to understand how they can justify taking people off the production floor to listen to a meeting rather than produce. The plant must lose money this way. I think the information they give is important, however, and I'm interested in hearing it.
>
> It's very good to know about what goes into makng a product and the system that it's involved in so you can tell people about the work you do. It's very embarrassing to have someone ask you what an electrode is after you have made one and to have to tell them that you have no idea. The department tours put things into perspective and make you understand the relationship with other people and their jobs. Consequently, you pay more attention to what you do.

The process of increased and improved communication described above may seem deceptively easy to achieve and maintain. Actually the time period over which these communication patterns became institutionalized was well over a year. This was a difficult and precarious stage in the organization development process. It often seemed as if the process of change was agonizingly slow. The change agents would often meet in utter disappointment when they realized that few obvious changes had taken place. In retrospect the period during which communication was developing was a critical period. It was during this period that trust was building and a culture conducive to further change was developing. More on the implications of this to an understanding of the change process later.

Leadership and Supervision

There is no doubt that leadership and supervision of managers has an important impact on the motivation, commitment, adaptability and satisfaction of employees. As described earlier, it was the change agents' aim to move the plant toward a style of management which emphasized delegation, participation, consideration and support of employees. What has already been described about changes in communication patterns clearly indicates that the style of supervision moved in the intended direction. Subsequent descriptions of changes in group process, intergroup relationships, job structure and organizational structure will further substantiate that supervision in this plant increasingly became participative, supportive and delegating in nature. These changes were carried out by the supervisors and managers of this plant and are, therefore, reflections of their changing values and leadership style.

Perhaps the most interesting aspect in the development of participative management was the early difficulty encountered by the managers in understanding the concept and applying it. After participative and supportive management had been discussed in seminars and counseling sessions, several supervisors were found to be interpreting this to mean a hands-off, be-warm-and-friendly-to-everyone-regardless-of-the-situation-type of approach. That is, they were swinging from a directive to a laissez-faire style of management in an attempt to find and establish a new style of management. This was most often reflected in increasing uncertainty about how to handle problems and problem employees. For example, should a supervisor discuss lagging performance with an employee, or should he mention something about increasing absenteeism or tardiness? Concern for people was being emphasized to the exclusion of concern for the task and production. Occasionally the early confusion resulted in wild swings in style from laissez-faire to directiveness. When, not surprisingly, laissez-faire and friendliness did not work, increased frustration on the part of the supervisor would erupt in a new, tough and quite unexpected (from the employee's point of view) approach to a problem. These swings were not surprising and reflected a trial-and-error learning process on the part of the managers much like an attempt to groove a new golf swing. However, these were difficult times for those undergoing the learning process. In the case of one individual, they resulted in a temporary loss of confidence as an old and familiar style was being discarded and a new one was being developed.

The search for an appropriate style of management on the continuum between hard and soft reflects a common confusion among managers about participative or Theory Y management. Participative management does not lie on this continuum at all, and an attempt was made to counsel with supervisors on this matter. It was pointed out that participative management is an integration of concern for people and concern for production through mutual involvement by boss and subordinate in goal-setting and decision-making—that is, concern for people is not best expressed in a lack of attention to the task and the development of a country-club atmosphere. Instead, concern for people is expressed through involvement in the decision, task and objective-setting process. As such, participative management is *not* on a tough-soft continuum. It is a third management alternative of this continuum. It is tougher than directive leadership because the direction and control come from within the individual through commitment (Blake and Mouton, 1964).

Working through these issues led to the utilization of a management-by-objectives or work-planning approach at several levels of the organization. For example, production and other goals were mutually planned and set by the production superintendent and the production supervisors. Mutual goal-setting was also adopted with production workers. Instead of production standards being set by industrial engineers (a direction the plant was heading in when the program started), goals for each department were derived from the plant goal. Individual goals for the week or month were derived from department goals through discussions between the supervisor and subordinates. Interviews showed that workers clearly understood how the goals fitted into the department and plant goal structure, and that this made it possible for them to work on their own without close supervision. In a presentation to higher level management, the plant manager stated that every worker in the plant had a clear idea of what his or her goals were for the next accounting period.

Other examples of supportiveness, participation and delegation by supervisors also existed. Performance reviews were held with all employees, including hourly employees. These reviews were two-way discussions. The supervisor gave his impression of the subordinate's performance, and the subordinate gave his impression of his own performance, and in some cases that of his supervisor. A rate-your-boss form was developed, and several supervisors asked subordinates to fill them out and discuss them. Thus, participation and greater equalization of power were carried over to the performance appraisal process.

A further example of participative management was the practice of communicating to employees the reasons why another employee was terminated. (Performance was the criterion for firing and, together with seniority, was the criterion for promotion.) This surely reflects concern for people, their need to understand what is happening, and their need for security, but it also carried with it the assumption that people are interested in doing a good job and are mature enough to understand such actions.

An indication that managers in the plant learned that participative management is not soft or laissez-faire was reflected in the relatively high rate of involuntary turnover. People were evaluated consistently, and action was taken to terminate them when appropriate. The more open and participative culture of the plant seems to have enhanced the ability of managers and employees to look at themselves realistically and to take individual responsibility for difficult decisions that are often postponed in more traditional cultures. This continuous process of upgrading the quality of employees in the plant not only resulted from the developing plant culture, but was in turn an important factor in the plant's ability to make the many changes in job structure and organization structure described below.

The following interview excerpts may help the reader to understand the degree and kind of change in leadership and supervision which occurred in the plant.

> They should have it this way in all of the different departments throughout the plant. The supervisors praise you here and you work more because you are praised. Praise brings more work. The atmosphere is also different here. It's very clean and all the people are very friendly. You enjoy working.

Since I've been working here, my husband is a much better super-visor in his plant. I tell him what he should do to make his people more interested in what they are doing based upon what our supervisors do here.

No matter who you ask to listen, they're interested and they follow through—it's the response of the supervisors; they never shove you aside as unimportant. I'm not afraid to speak my mind because they're always there to listen and they will try it. We know what's going on in our jobs and we can tell them. It makes you feel very important.

Intergroup Process and Relationship

Work on intergroup relations was important because of the interdependence of departments in accomplishing plant objectives and the fact that differences between department goals and time horizons often created intergroup conflict.

Early in the O.D. program plant professionals and supervisory personnel felt that the relationships between different departments needed to be improved. As a result, a meeting was held with the department managers and the change agents to discuss perceptions of their own and other departments. During that meeting frank discussions were carried on regarding the good and bad points of each department. The change agents were also discussed. For example, it was felt that the change agents were not providing adequately definitive answers, and that they were not performing as much in the role of experts as the plant supervisory personnel felt they should.

Following the meeting it was decided that follow-up meetings of the same type should be held and that the format and style of these meetings should be expanded. As an example, cross-department meetings were established on a periodic basis. In these meetings the personnel of a particular department would meet with another department to discuss expectations, percep-tions, strong points and weak points. Although it is difficult to state precisely what the results of these meetings were, the general consensus was that they had been extremely helpful. As one employee put it,

Before we had those meetings, I really wasn't concerned about the people in 'X' department, except to feel that they weren't doing

their job. After we held the departmental meetings, I began to
understand some of their problems. I began to listen to them and to
work with them. I think that they were helpful.

Group and Team Development

There is substantial evidence to indicate that the development of cohesive work groups can have strong effects on the
performance of individuals if the group supports the objectives
of the organization (Seashore, 1954). A conscious objective of
the change program was to utilize and develop teams wherever
possible for this reason and for the purpose of improving trust
and communications.

The plant manager and his staff formed themselves into a
board of directors for the plant. As a group they would meet
once a month to discuss a plant problem and try to develop a
team solution to the problem. These and other similar meetings
were occasionally attended by one of the change agents as
participants, observers and, occasionally, team facilitators and
developers. In the latter role we sat in on meetings that
managers had with their own staffs, and during and after each
meeting led a discussion of how the meeting might have been
more effective.

Openness developed in the plant because these discussions
stimulated a few individuals to take risks in giving and receiving
feedback while they were dealing with task matters. Some of
this occurred as a result of individual initiative and some of it
with help from the consultants. Openness between peers as well
as boss and subordinates became more and more a reality in the
plant as a result of such initiatives.

The use of groups in accomplishing production work was also
an important part of the O.D. program, but because it was closely
tied to the task and technology it will be discussed in the next
section.

Changes in Technology, Jobs and Organizational Structure

Many of the past efforts to change the culture of organizations have started and ended with improving interpersonal
relationships through laboratory training techniques such as
sensitivity training. While improving a manager's understanding

of his own behavior and his relations with others is clearly an important part of organizational development, it is not enough. First, the high rate of transfer and promotion of managerial personnel in most organizations (not a single salaried monthly employee in the plant today was in the plant during the three-year period when major changes occurred) makes organizational change based only on changes in individuals and relationships highly temporary. Secondly, the fact that behaviors of an individual or group are heavily dependent on situational factors (controls, organization structure, goals, technology, information flow, etc.) is likely to make behavior change, unsupported by changes in these situational factors, temporary. That is, individuals or groups will tend to regress to former behavioral patterns unless jobs, organization structure and technology also change.

Low organizational effectiveness is often caused by the situation rather than the personalities involved. For example, the traditional conflict in manufacturing plants between production and quality control is brought about by differences in tasks, goals and measures. These differences are then often the cause of severe personality clashes that continue independent of the situation which created them.

All this suggests that in order for change to last beyond the individual job incumbents, attention must be given to situational factors such as goals, measures and controls, organization structure and the flow of information, materials and ideas. Changes in these factors can reinforce changes in the social system and the behavior of people, and can in turn stimulate further social and behavioral change. For these reasons the development program has also emphasized structural and job changes. In bringing about these changes the change agents tried to follow two principles—

1. Job Enrichment—They wanted to change the structure of jobs to give individuals more opportunity to handle the whole job with responsibility for *planning, doing* and *controlling* their own work. The objective was to create more interesting and challenging work. These changes, it was felt, would reinforce the evolution toward participa-

tive management and would further enhance employee involvement and motivation.

2. Autonomous Work Teams—They wanted to create cohesive work groups around interrelated or interdependent jobs. The creation of work teams is, of course, both a structural and a job change since relationships and responsibilities change. The purpose was to create further meaning in work through identification with a group. Group cohesiveness in turn could serve as an important position influence on motivation and commitment. These two basic principles were discussed with plant personnel.

The changes came after discussion with the change agents. Several of the structural and job enrichment changes are discussed below.

The Hot Plate Department

After discussing the concepts of job enrichment, an engineer became very excited about this notion. It made a lot of sense to him, and he became interested in trying it out. With the first-line supervisor he began planning for a change in the layout of the Hot Plate Department. This is a department assembling a number of different models of hot plates for laboratory and hospital usage.

At the time this department had already been pretty well streamlined into the normal assembly line operation. There were six women in the department. Each performed a small part of the total assembly. The line had been balanced, and management was generally satisfied with productivity. After considering several alternatives and discussing them with other people, the first-line supervisor and the engineer came up with a design that was radically different from the assembly line. Rather than have an assembly line operation, it was decided to give each of the women the responsibility for assembling the entire hot plate. The idea was presented to the plant manager, and permission was granted to try out the idea.

When the changeover was made, each person was expected to do the whole job. No other changes were made in the department, and no change was made in personnel.

What were the results? First, the people responded positively to the change. As one woman remarked, "Now it is *my* hot plate." Second, there was a drop in controllable rejects (those within the control of the workers) from 23 percent to approximately 1 percent during a six-month period following change. Absenteeism dropped from about 8 percent to about 1 percent in the same period of time.

What happened to productivity? Figure 15-1 shows the results. The changeover occurred in midyear. If one takes the average productivity for the first half of the year and compares it directly with the average productivity for the second half of the year, there is an 84 percent gain in productivity. If one takes the last three accounting periods (an accounting period in the plant is four weeks) in the first half of the year and compares these with the last three accounting periods of the

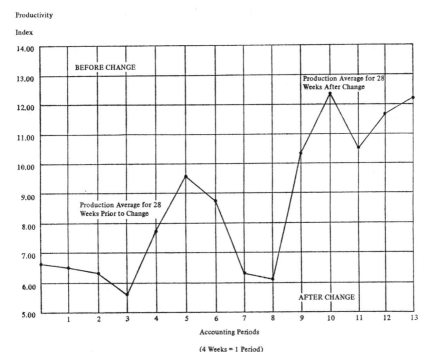

Productivity in the Hot Plate Department

Figure 15-1.

year, there is a 47 percent increase in productivity. By the way, the temporary increase in productivity in Periods Five and Six was a result of considerably increased emergency pressure to get production out to meet a sudden and unexpected increase in sales.

Whether one uses the 84 percent or the 47 percent increase in productivity as an index, the results seem clear. Changing the job structure from an assembly line process to giving each employee the responsibility for the total product had marked and dramatic effects.

The Glass Shop

The next step was in the Glass Shop where women worked on lathes to form glass for electrodes. The supervisor there decided that he was going to try something that had been called the team approach to productivity. At the beginning of the program team formation had been discussed along with the effects of cohesive work units, and it was mentioned that it might be worth trying. At a later stage there had been some discussion about merging two functionally-organized departments and forming work teams around interrelated and interdependent jobs. Without prior discussion with the consultants the supervisor divided his people into teams. He had, however, discussed the change with his boss and the plant manager, and they had given their approval.

The supervisor's approach to his people was very simple. He told his people,

> Look, I think we ought to organize around teams, and you four are responsible for the 'X' electrode. You are going to be responsible for the total task. I want you to know that we're going to need five hundred of these the next accounting period. You as a team decide who's going to do what, how you're going to do it, and you schedule it.

Not all the employees in the Glass Shop reacted favorably to the proposed change. Some saw it as a tribute to their ability and were very enthusiastic. Others were not used to dealing with this type of climate or supervisory style and were suspicious. For example, some individuals wondered if the supervisor was abdicating his responsibility by asking them to do their own scheduling. (This suspicion, which the change agents picked up in their interviews, existed in the initial stages of many other changes.) As it turned out, this particular change resulted in an immediate increase in productivity. There were lasting changes in the involvement and commitment of the employees and their interest in the work. For example, on occasion the workers would stay in the cafeteria after punching out at the end of the day to discuss schedules and manufacturing problems over a cup of coffee. This was the source of the following quote: "Isn't it silly for a bunch of us housewives to stay here after work worrying about how we are going to make schedule? We really should be home cooking dinner." So that the schedules would look neat and presentable, one person took them home at night to type even though she knew that she should not work overtime without pay.

As time went on the composition of the groups changed. At one time the concept was almost abandoned as a new supervisor came in who was, understandably, somewhat dubious about the value of the team approach. However, almost a year later, toward the end of 1969, the new supervisor reported regarding the effectiveness of the work teams, "I wouldn't want to do it, but I honestly believe that I could give the people the schedule at the beginning of the accounting period and come back three or four weeks later and find out that they had met schedule." At this point in time he had just taken over a new department in addition to the Glass Shop and was contrasting the difference between the two. In the Glass Shop the teams knew the schedule, pooled their efforts and swapped jobs as necessary to meet the team's objectives. In the other department it was still necessary for the supervisor to assign work in the early morning to each specific employee as is traditionally done in most manufacturing establishments. Since then, more team and job enrichment concepts have been brought into the other departments.

Materials Control Department

The Materials Control Department has the responsibility for the functions of purchasing, inventory control, scheduling and expediting. The department was functionally organized, and the people were assigned to each of the four specialty areas. However, the plant was being plagued with parts shortages, causing delays in the production of units needed for delivery. This was affecting profit margins as well as service to customers. The department supervisor started by enriching the job of his secretary and finding to his surprise that she was more involved in her work and liked it better, and he had less to do. He then decided that his organizational structure was wrong and that job enrichment could be applied to his whole department. As he put it,

> Look, I think this is all wrong. I don't think these people who are expediting really like expediting. It's not a very challenging kind of job. In addition to that, I think my people are having tremendous problems communicating across functional lines. For example, when the scheduling people schedule a parts flow into the plant and there's a change in the schedule, something gets hung up and the guys in Purchasing don't hear about it until sometimes it is too late.

Rather than having each work group specialize in a particular functional area, the Materials Control supervisor decided to organize his department around product line teams. Each team would have total project responsibility for a particular product line and would perform all four material control functions (expediting, scheduling, purchasing and inventory control). The supervisor felt that this would reduce his parts shortage problem, solve his communications problems and make the work more interesting for his people.

Since this was a radical change, the supervisor moved slowly. He discussed with the plant management, the change agents and his people alternative ways of going about the structural change and its impact upon the department. He felt the need to go slowly and to keep the door open in case a retreat from the project team approach became necessary.

When he made the change, people were ready. What were the results? In a three-month period of time, the parts shortage list was reduced from fourteen IBM pages to less than a page. This was with the same volume of business. It must be pointed out that later, as the volume of business increased and as more complex instruments were introduced, the absolute number of parts shortages increased, although the relative number still showed a considerable net decrease. Also obtained were very positive interview data on the involvement, commitment and motivation of the employees in the department,

> You no longer operate in a vacuum. I used to schedule with only one point of view—that of getting everything produced for delivery to a customer. I never thought about or was concerned about inventory problems or lead time involved in buying. I would never concern myself with other people's points of view. We just didn't communicate and therefore there was very little cooperation.
>
> Ralph and I work so closely together on the problems that we're aware of a parts shortage before it happens. Since I know what lead time is necessary, what the inventory is, and what the orders are, I can schedule their work with all of these things in mind rather than operate independently from these other critical considerations.
>
> We can relate our success to theirs where this was completely impossible before the teams. It gives you a great sense of satisfaction to know that you have coordinated the back-up work for an entire department.
>
> My job is also a lot more interesting since the reorganization. I no longer have to do the same things day after day, and things have real meaning for me.

The Instrument Department

In 1967 the Instrument Department made complex devices ranging in worth up to approximately 3,000 dollars. Here there were both successes and failures in job enrichment and organization development. Early in the development effort, one of the supervisors was faced with the problem of which women to assign to two different production areas. The sociogram techniques for identifying patterns of interpersonal relationships had been described by the change agents in a previous meeting. The supervisor decided to ask his people to fill out a sociometric questionnaire that asked, "Who would you like to work with most? Next most?" and so on. However, he did not prepare his people very well and had not yet established sufficient trust to carry it out. His people rebelled and said, "I'm sorry, Boss, that's your job to tell us who's going to work with whom; that's not our job." At a deeper level they were saying "We're not ready for this kind of change yet. What are you talking about? This is not our proper role."

Some months later when a new supervisor was transferred into the department, he began by being extremely frank and open with his people about things they wanted and needed to know. At the same time he began to have discussions with his people as to how schedules could be met and began working toward involving his people in the planning process. He also began working toward what he called the "total job concept." This is only a different term for what was earlier called job enrichment. He was able to implement this concept so that each person in his department was completely assembling a complex instrument system with up to five hundred parts and twelve printed circuit boards.

While this change occurred, four new instruments were introduced on the manufacturing floor in three months. Rather than having a marked drop in productivity as would be the case in most traditional electronic firms, productivity was reduced by only a slight amount. An engineer associated with the new product introduction raised the question with one of the consultants as to how the change agents knew that the total job approach (job enrichment) was equal to or better than the more traditional approaches. He indicated that he thought that it was good but he wasn't certain as to proof. He was asked simply, "How would the Model 'X' introduction have gone in any other plant where you have worked?" (The Model X was one that, because of delays in design, was introduced to the floor only as a prototype without manufacturing drawings.) After a moment's reflection, he replied,

> It would have been utter chaos. Under the circumstances, we just couldn't have gotten a normal assembly line process going. At least with girls making the entire product, they learned about the problem quickly, you had fewer people to talk to and train, and they were so involved that if they had questions, they came looking for someone or, in most cases, solved the problem themselves by discussing it between them.

He thought a bit longer, then concluded, "I guess you're right—that's the kind of proof that I needed."

At a later date the plant accountant generated figures regarding the effect of the job enrichment program on productivity. For comparison purposes he used a standard model which had been in production for more than two years prior to the change. The average productivity for the previous eight months was used as a base. Although the increase in productivity was not as dramatic as in the Hot Plate Department previously discussed, gains were significant. Productivity increased by $1.75 per hour, or an increase of 17 percent. Quality had improved in similar fashion. The number of rejects had decreased from an average of 25 percent to an average of 13 percent, an increase in the quality of about 50 percent. Absenteeism was reduced from 8.5 percent per month to 3.4 percent, a reduction of over 50 percent.

The following interview quotes illustrate employee feelings about the job and structural changes described above,

> I am now interested in the team and what we can do as a team in terms of our production goal. Sometimes I sit at home and think of how we can better the goal, whether we'll make the goal, and how we can improve the goal.
>
> We started teams and you really know what you have to do. No one has to tell you what to do next, and it helps us to use our time better. They should have it this way in all of the different departments throughout the plant.

Changes in behavioral dimensions such as supervision and communication, together with structural changes in jobs, were to reinforce each other. The organization was to become a more internally consistent system where the individual received few conflicting cues about the kind of organization he was working in and his role in it. One measure of the extent to which this was achieved can be found in the ability of managers to see the managerial philosophy of their organization clearly and to themselves integrate task and production concerns with concerns for people, their motivation and satisfaction.

The following vignette is given as an example of this emerging integration:

During the introduction of a highly complex new product, it appeared that the plant might not meet the manufacturing schedule. As a result, three monthly employees came to the plant manager to tell him that they wanted to come in on Saturday and Sunday to assemble final units. In the discussion the plant manager raised the question as to how the hourly assembly workers, who were also committed to meeting the schedule, would feel about having somebody else complete "their" units. After further discussion the three decided to come in on the weekend and work, but that they would make subassemblies, thus allowing the production workers to have the enjoyment of making the final assemblies.

Changes in Quality Control

One other fundamental change in job and organizational structure was underway and needs mention. The role of the Quality Control Department was changing from that of an inspecting to a consulting department. More and more quality control was being performed by production workers. In the Hot Plate Department all routine inspection was being done by the production workers themselves. A full-time quality control job was eliminated. In the Instrument Department many calibrations and checks previously performed by quality control inspectors were being performed by the production workers themselves, thus their work was enriched through further self-control; indirect labor costs associated with quality control were reduced, and the quality control job was upgraded in its challenge and level of responsibility. This change from external control to self-control by workers themselves resulted from many interlocking structural and social changes. These changes created a new plant culture where individuals were growing in skills, knowledge and need for achievement and involvement.

Implications of Changes for Pay

One of the most frequently discussed issues associated with changes of the kind we have been describing concerns pay. Do people want more pay as they become more involved in their work? Our experience indicates that people do expect to be rewarded equitably for greater personal investment in work and the organization. However, rising expectations for more pay were never disruptive or unmanageable. As jobs were redesigned, jobs were reevaluated and higher pay grades assigned to them. Furthermore, because this was a growing plant, promotions to higher level jobs were given to the higher performing employees; equity came to those who invested more. Finally, a change in the pay system was made to allow a merit increase of 5 percent at the top of each pay grade. This pay increase was another means of rewarding people who were investing more of themselves as a result of the changes in job structure and management.

It has long been recognized that additional changes in the reward system would be necessary to maintain consistency between new levels of worker involvement and their rewards. A profit improvement sharing plan like the Scanlon Plan was one alternative considered. Further development of merit systems was another. Of the two, the Scanlon Plan was the most attractive. The barrier to its introduction has been the difficulties that such a major departure would create in other parts of the corporation. To date, little progress has been made on this front and no major change in reward systems has occurred. Despite this, no major problems have arisen in sustaining the changes described above and pay has not become a major issue. Of course, it is difficult to tell if more progress and change might have been possible had a major change in the reward system been possible.

The crucial point is that pay has not been the driving or leading force in the change effort. Changes in pay are felt by employees to be necessary to maintain equity, but inability to create major changes in the pay structure has not caused regression. (It should be noted, however, that on the average the plant pays well when compared with other alternative employers.) In the change toward greater involvement and commitment by workers, it is assumed that the psychological rewards of greater involvement have been the major driving force.

FINDINGS AND RECOMMENDATIONS FOR CHANGE AGENTS AND MANAGERS

Some of the results of the organization development program have already been discussed, but other conclusions can be drawn which may be pertinent and useful to organizations seeking to humanize work and improve their effectiveness. Of course, it is also necessary to point out that an approach that works in one organization at one point in time may not necessarily be effective in another organization at another point in time. For this reason the recommendations are being presented in a relatively broad and generalized form to make them more applicable to a broad variety of organizations.

The first set of recommendations has to do with the kind of management theory that will contribute to organizational effectiveness and who and what kind of commitment to such a theory is necessary. The second set of recommendations has to do with the change process itself. The last set of recommendations has to do with the relationship of the plant to the parent organization.

A. What managerial theory or innovation is appropriate and who should know about it and be committed to it?

1. A clearcut commitment on the part of the manager to any particular theory or set of values is not necessary for a successful development program to take place. In fact, an attempt to obtain such a commitment from a group of managers in the early stages of organizational development can be threatening enough to cause the withdrawal of commitment to any change. For example, during an early visit to the plant by one of the OD consultants, the plant manager said, "Ed, I feel crucified. I can't make a decision because I keep worrying about whether it is a 'Theory Y' or 'Theory X' decision." At the same time his people were concerned that he wasn't making decisions. The response of the consultant was, "Go ahead and make any decisions that you feel most comfortable with and think are right for the business. We'll worry about theory later."

   If managers are not concerned with theory, what are they concerned about? Simply, they are concerned about getting the job done better. They will welcome help from someone if they perceive it as contributing to the solution of problems. If the help provided assists the manager in getting the job done better, the manager is more responsive and accessible to help the next time. Therefore, rather than asking for commitment to theory or values, the change agent should first demonstrate his ability to help on operating problems. This creates openness to experimentation and has often been called the unfreezing stage of the change process.

2. It is necessary, however, that at least the change agent have in mind a model of how organizations function and a flexible set of concepts about what might be the right managerial approach for a particular situation. The organizational model should be general and should reflect the complexity of organizations and the interdependence of their various components and dimensions. The assumptions about man's needs and values and the consultant's theories of management must reflect current research findings and basic social and historical trends. They can and must be updated and changed as new research findings become available, more is learned about the functioning of the client organization, more is learned about the environment in which the client organization operates, and more is learned about the effects of changes already made in the client organization. Thus, the consultant should be oriented toward integrating knowledge and research with the practical problems the organization is facing. Humanization of the organization will follow from this approach.

3. There is a need for making structural as well as social and behavioral changes. It is frequently easier to change the situation and thereby change the behavior of people than to change such behavior directly. Examples were given earlier of work done in the Hot Plate Department and Materials Control Department that point directly to this finding. On the other hand, structural changes have to be accompanied by the development of new relationships, better understanding of roles, and new personal skills and competences. Both types of changes are important targets for an organization development program.

B. The next set of findings and recommendations have to do with the process of change itself which unfolds over the extended period of an organization change effort.

1. Some individuals are oriented and ready to change as soon as the opportunity presents itself in the form of a change agent, or a general commitment by the plant to try some new things. These individuals go ahead with changes even though they know very little about what they are getting into. A first-line supervisor walked into the Glass Shop Department one morning and announced to his workers that they would be organized into groups with complete responsibility for producing their own product line. An engineer and the supervisor went ahead and redesigned the production operation in hot plates by eliminating an assembly operation and giving each worker total responsibility for the assembly of a product. These change leaders are natural targets for the change agent. In the plant, opinion leaders helped shape a culture that later influenced others in the organization to try some things on their own.

2. Changes set off a circular process in which change in organizational functioning increased not only the effectiveness of the organization, but also changed abilities of people and their capacity for motivation and involvement in work. Rising expectations, increasing need for involvement and achievement, and increasing levels of competence in turn create further opportunities for adjustments in how the organization functions. The real potential in organizational development lies in setting in motion a positive snowball of change, growth and development. This is like increasing the size of the pie rather than cutting it up differently—everyone gains. The changing organization will continually strive to reestablish internal consistency by adjusting how it functions to new levels of abilities and expectations reached by its members. The development and management of such a cycle of change has been one of the key objectives of this organizational development program.

3. The most effective and permanent learning comes after the individual has experimented with new approaches. Here the basic model for learning is a reversal of the traditional educational model. Figure 15-2 summarizes this basic concept. Through working with a change agent a manager may experiment with a new means of communication, with job enrichment or with other approaches. The plans for the experiment are discussed with the change agents and are carried out by the manager. In

Model for Learning About Organizational Change

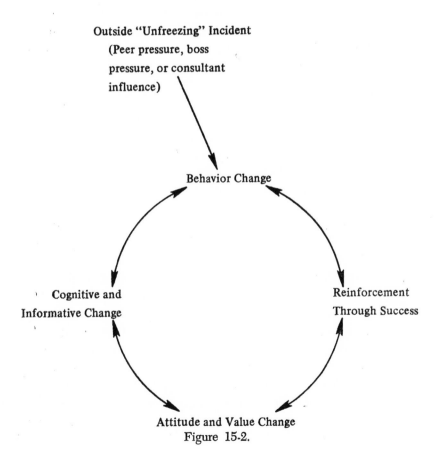

Figure 15-2.

the beginning this is done without complete understanding of the theory and knowledge base underlying the change. The change agent is the resource and translates his knowledge of behavioral theory into questions or alternative solutions relating to the specific situation at hand. In the writer's experience, the first change was typically behavioral, not one of knowledge or even attitude. If the manager was successful in the attempt as judged by his own subjective criteria, this success experience would often lead to some change in attitude toward change and almost always to another try. Several successful experiments lead to a change in attitudes and values with respect to the management of human resources and the organizational development process. With these subsequent attitude and value changes there is less chance that the development program will come to a halt when failure occurs.

After attitude and value changes have occurred, managers request more and more knowledge through reading, seminars and training programs. This is the time when seminars and laboratory training would seem to be of most value. There is a readiness to learn and utilize the learning. The most direct example of this change in the plant came in the change of attitude toward seminars. When seminars were initially suggested, the attitude was so negative that the only way the salaried group could be brought together for learning was through an agreement that only work-related problems would be discussed. The plant insisted that these seminars be called workshops as opposed to seminars. Later, as more and more success was seen by individuals, they sought more theory from the change agents. That learning starts with behavior and experience has been one of the most important things we have learned. The operating, ongoing organization may be the best laboratory for learning, with no problems in transfer of learning to the real-life situation. Obviously, some learning may still be needed in the more traditional training program format. Nevertheless, significant and marked changes in behavior have occurred without training.

4. In order for the individual employee to shift his perceptions of his role and the organization, multiple changes are needed—that is, changes in the social system need to be accompanied by changes in formal structure and technological systems. For example, pushing decisions down needs to be accompanied by redesign of jobs to allow more responsibility, by a pay system that recognizes performance, and by a communication system that is open. All of these complementary changes are needed if the individual is to receive a clear message about *his* organization and *his* role in it. Past attempts to change organizations through human relations and supervisory training have had limited success because other key leverage points have not been changed. Similarly, job enrichment without associated changes in supervision and communications will not change long-held role perceptions and attitudes. In fact, the writers found that unless certain groundwork was laid to develop trust, job enrichment concepts were looked on with suspicion. As one worker asked, "Is the boss trying to give me something he doesn't want?" Thus, changes in trust may have to precede or at least accompany changes in structure, technology or administrative systems.

5. Changes in structure and in systems reinforce and legitimize interpersonal or social changes. Figure 15-3 presents this concept. Certain trust levels have to be achieved before change can occur, but beyond this the change can be in either direction in the model. It is probably better if social and interpersonal changes occur first, but systems and structures can and do change first in many cases. They fail as instruments of total and permanent organizational development when they are not followed up by changes in individual and group behavior.

6. Organizational change occurs in stages—a stage of unfreezing and trust-building in which people get ready to change, a takeoff stage when major changes and learning

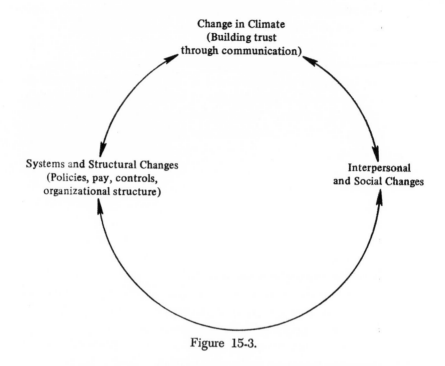

Figure 15-3.

occur, and a stabilization stage. This cycle has been repeated a number of times throughout the organizational development program at the plant. For example, changes in communications took a whole year to get off the ground and become really effective. This seemed like an agonizingly slow process of change. In retrospect this was a critical period during which trust was building and a culture was developing conducive to further change.

Similarly, the change reported in the Hot Plate Department was followed nearly a year later by another upswing in productivity as the employees developed more confidence in themselves and in their supervisor. These changes in trust and confidence allowed elimination of the final inspector, a further major change.

7. The plant became a sophisticated consumer of new ideas and approaches to management. It became an open and

experimenting organization much readier for new and sophisticated approaches to management than it would have been without organization development. New approaches to business management could easily be brought into this organization because the organization and its members have learned to cope with and manage change. They valued it. The greatest potential of OD lies in its development of an organization that is capable of continual self-renewal on all fronts.

C. The last set of findings has to do with the relationship of the plant with the parent company. The plant is geographically separated from the parent company and designs and builds products which are quite different from those of the larger organization. As a result of this and some of the organizational development work going on, differences existed between the plant and the larger corporate system.

1. Initial understanding by top management of a larger organization of where OD will lead an organizational sub-unit is not necessary for change to occur in the smaller unit. Although top management of the organization knew what was happening in general terms, it was never really committed to the organization development program nor, indeed, was it ever really asked to become so committed. It is possible to change a relatively *autonomous unit* of a larger, multidivisional and geographically-scattered organization without the total commitment and involvement of top management. This has been shown by a number of studies and experiences including one by Huse (1965). This is not to say that such commitment and involvement is undesirable, nor that it will not be eventually necessary if organization development is to encompass the total organization.

2. Influence has been exerted upward with great acceptance of new management concepts by individuals at higher levels in the corporation. In this regard this change program has been an experiment in a systems approach to organization development at two levels. In the plant

it has been an attempt to work with multiple facets of the organization to help the plant become more effective. At a corporate level it can serve as a model for the rest of the organization and as an example of how organizational change must be planned and conceptualized. It was hoped that the change program would create such a clearly different culture in the plant that it would become visible to the corporation. Small changes, it has been found, often get lost. With visibility it was expected that people from other parts of the company would visit and become interested in trying new things. This has, in fact, happened, and the plant is now widely-known to be applying new patterns of management. Furthermore, several individuals have been transferred to other locations and have begun to apply similar concepts. It is the writers' feeling that changes in subunits of an organization can have strong influences on the larger culture if the change is carefully planned—seed personnel are transferred to various parts of the organization; a network of change agents (line and staff people) are clearly identified and trained; and change agent resources are used in appropriate places at appropriate times and in appropriate ways. Once again, top management commitment is not a necessary condition for the process of change to begin. Once begun, the process may influence top management to get behind it and ensure its eventual success for the total organization. There are many companies in which a bottoms-up pattern of change is beginning with the hope of this eventual outcome.

3. The interface between the parent corporation and the plant has not always been easy. An organizational development program may at times cause stresses and strains with established corporate practices and procedures. For example, how does one reward workers who have doubled their production under an established pay rate system which is not directly geared to productivity? How does the traditional job evaluation program reflect the fact that hourly assembly workers are now doing the inspection previously required of a quality assurance technician?

SUMMARY AND CONCLUSIONS

The management experiment described has been based on the assumption that employees desire responsibility, challenging work and an opportunity for achievement and growth. Over a period of three years a work environment was created based on these assumptions. Jobs, communications, organizational structure and leadership, to name just a few organizational dimensions, were changed by the managers with the help of consultants. The result has been increased involvement in work, commitment to the organization, motivation and satisfaction of needs frustrated in many traditional organizations. These positive changes verified the writers' assumptions that employees need and want involvement in work, responsibility and challenge. It is, of course, equally probable that the changes in work environment described earlier encouraged employees to develop the kind of needs and interests they were assumed to have in the first place. In either case, employee needs and organization purpose were less in conflict at the end of a three-year period than they might have been without the organization development program. Thus, this organization is clearly a more humane place to work.

The increased integration between employee needs and the organization has not only increased individual satisfaction and involvement in work, but has also enhanced organizational purpose. The effectiveness of the plant organization is high. Voluntary turnover among hourly employees is considerably below that for the area; productivity and quality have improved as changes have been made in department after department; the plant handles more volume with less supervision and indirect labor; the plant has been able to introduce new products quickly and without drops in productivity; and its overall efficiency and financial performance have continued to meet the corporation's objectives. Thus, the plant is not only a more humane place to work, but also a more productive organization than it might otherwise have been.

Not all employees have equal needs for achievement and responsibility, and not all organization development programs can be approached in the way this program was approached.

Nevertheless, working man in the Western World is quickly evolving toward a greater desire for meaningful involvement in work and the organization. Furthermore, accelerating change in the corporation's environment is placing a greater premium on its ability to adapt to and cope with new markets and technology. These forces are presenting a clear challenge to the traditional bureaucratic organization, a challenge from which the corporation will not be exempt.

In order to meet this challenge, corporations will have to initiate organization development programs of the kind described above. Unless the initiative is taken by management, which has most of the leverage on the work environment, the risk of more chaotic, disruptive and less profitable change will be increased. We have pointed out the importance of trust as a basic building block in organization development. Trust was built and maintained in the plant described because management took the initiative and took some risks. To these risks the employees responded with increased involvement and commitment, thereby setting in motion a positive cycle of trust and change that has not been reversed and is not likely to be reversed unless a complete change in management philosophy occurs. Thus, management has avoided getting into the unhappy circumstance of being pressured for change by dissatisfied and alienated workers. It is more difficult to build a positive cycle of trust in such a situation and, therefore, integration of organization purpose and employee needs is less likely to occur. What can management do to initiate change in anticipation of the challenge?

The experiment in management reported here and others like it across the country have demonstrated on a small scale that planned and continuing organization change and development is both possible and practical, and will achieve desired outcomes for the individual and the organization. It is now time for the top management of large-scale corporations to adopt organization development as a major strategy equal in importance to strategies in marketing and technology. In organization development there is a process and a set of tools that will achieve an objective that most managers agree is key in their responsibilities—that of building and developing a human organization capable of achieving organizational objectives.

Organization development on a corporate basis will require the involvement of top management and larger sums of money and personnel than are now commonly apportioned to this effort, but substantially less investment than is being now applied to the development and maintenance of markets, technology and machines. For example, each major organizational component of a large company may require one or more people with responsibility for organization development. As the pace of change increases and the life span of technology decreases, a planned strategy of organization development will become an important competitve edge.

REFERENCES

Argyris, C.: *Personality and Organization.* New York, Harper and Brothers, 1958.

Argyris, C.: *Integrating the Individual and the Organization.* New York, Wiley, 1964.

Bennis, W.: *Changing Organizations: Essays on the Development and Evolution of Human Organization.* New York, McGraw, 1966.

Blake, R. R., and Mouton, J. S.: *The Managerial Grid.* Houston, Gulf Pub, 1964.

Foulkes, F. K.: *Creating More Meaningful Work.* New York, American Management Association, Inc., 1969.

Huse, E. F.: The behavioral scientist in the shop. *Personnel,* 42(3):50-57, 1965.

Korman, A. K.: Toward an hypothesis of work behavior. *J Appl Psychol,* 54:31-41, 1970.

Maslow, A. H.: A theory of human motivation. *Psychol Rev,* 50:370-396, 1943.

McGregor, D.: *The Human Side of Enterprise.* New York, McGraw, 1960.

Seashore, S. E.: *Group Cohesiveness in the Industrial Work Group.* Ann Arbor, Survey Research Center, Institute for Social Research, University of Michigan, 1954.

Chapter 16

HUMANIZING RELATIONS OF
KEY PEOPLE IN INDUSTRY*

H. Meltzer

$\mathbf{M}$ANAGERS IN INDUSTRY are important people. The life course
of many workers is directly or indirectly dependent on them.
The effectiveness and happiness of foremen to a large extent are
determined by them. Because the success of management is in
their hands, the stockholders also have a type of dependence on
them. It is not altogether surprising, therefore, to find Burnham
(1941), in his book, *The Managerial Revolution,* predicting that
to management belongs the future.

Neither was it surprising to find Galbraith (1967) in his
book, *The New Industrial State,* saying that professional management in big corporations had become invincible and incapable
of being displaced even by stockholders or government. It is
understandable that Jean-Jacques Servan-Schreiber (1968), in
his book called *The American Challenge* in English translation,
predicted that American management was taking over the world.
What is surprising is that, according to Drucker (1973) in his
last book, *Management,* in regard to the *management boom,* the
Galbraiths and Servan-Schreibers had begun to sound naive by
1970; and that this prediction of Burnham, Galbraith and Servan-

* From H. Meltzer, "Explorations in Humanizing Relations of Key People
in Industry," *The American Journal of Orthopsychiatry, XII*(3):517-528, 1942.
Reprinted by permission of the author. Copyright, 1942, the American Orthopsychiatric Association, Inc. Reproduced by permission.

Schreiber "appeared at the moment when professional management began to be unseated right and left by the take-over-raiders promising 'asset management,' with the full and enthusiastic support of the supposedly docile and impotent stockholders." The emphasis moved away from the management boom to the realization that it was organizations that needed managing.

THE NATURE OF THE PRESENT STUDY

The explorations described here represent a sort of adventure in experiencing, studying and working with the organization of human relations in one industry for a period of one year from the vantage point of management in action. Its aim is to contribute on a small scale toward what Mayo (in Roethlisberger and Dickson, 1939) referred to as the most important researches of our time, namely the substitution of human responsibility for futile strife and hatred, and the restoration of humanity's capacity for spontaneous cooperation. This objective certainly is not new to organizational psychologists or industrialists since in the main that is precisely their purpose. What is new is the exploratory selection and application of knowledge and techniques relevant as aids for solving some problems in industrial management.

Unusual also is the freedom of movement permitted the investigator. Though an attempt was made to deal with more urgent problems first, no restrictions or compulsory sequences of work which would interfere with planned action in the solving of real problems being explored were placed on the investigator. The chief task with which the investigator was confronted was: can six key people who were trained to look toward a general manager for leadership and direction in an industry employing 250 people be developed into functionally autonomous leaders who can cooperate effectively for common purposes? In other words, can persons educated to be subleaders in an authoritarian form of organization be further educated to develop enough human insight and maturity to become co-leaders in an interdependent and democratic organization of their making? In this instance the problem was not one of restoring spontaneous cooperation, but rather of helping individuals to develop so as to create and maintain such relations.

At the time that this study was undertaken, key people or managers of industry were considered too high to be investigated. More recently, executives and key people have been investigated since industrial psychology has become organized enough to become organizational psychology. By and large, the contributions of psychology in industry as reported in literature have been segmented or fragmentary in nature. They have limited themselves to the discussion of a relatively simple problem, quite often with a disregard of social context, or they have made too much ado about dissatisfied workers as if management had only to get rid of dissatisfied workers and all would be well.

What are the realities of the problems of management in industry? Can they be realistically and comprehensively understood without provisions for a fairly thorough study of personality organization in life situations as they emerge in industry? Can they be understood without an appreciation and study of factors of social organization, informal organization as well as formal organization?

ORGANIZING FOR CREATIVE ADMINISTRATION

The Earlier Situation: A Reign of Authoritarianism

The particular plant* in which these explorations were made is one which had grown relatively rapidly from what twenty-one years ago was a jobbing business to a fair-sized conversion business on a national scale. Expansion and growth often took place without reconstruction in its organization to readjust for changes. When the investigator was first introduced to the plant, the management of it was in the hands of one man, the general manager. This one man was in charge of everything—an office employing thirty people and 250 people in the plant. As the

---

* For their valuable contributions to this work project, the author would express his gratitude to the key people, foremen and participant employees of the Orchard Paper Company where this study was conducted. Particularly, gratitude is due the executives of the company, especially the president, Mr. H. C. Orchard, whose enlightened attitudes made this study possible.

company expanded, the general manager merely took on more duties so that all divisions of work in the plant, as well as all the work in the office, led to his office. He was also responsible for correlating all this for the executives. All workers' complaints led to his office; often they were not attended to, but at least they landed on his desk. If the worker made demands on him, he would promise to take it up with the executives, and he relieved the officers from responsibilities to the workers. By this technique, partly consciously and partly unwittingly developed, the chief executive of the company, an individual whose ingenuity was responsible for its development, became increasingly more and more out of touch with the workers in any meaningful manner. All in all, so far as the workers could perceive, in both the formal and the relatively informal forms of organization in the industry they worked for, the plant they worked in was authoritarian in nature in the sense that all roads led to one man who did the directing, judging and giving of orders. The form of authoritarianism was not very rigid, but insofar as one could perceive a form of organization, it was certainly more authoritarian than democratic in pattern.

The work of the plant naturally divided itself into six divisional departments, each one headed by an experienced, if not adequate, man. During the reign of what we will call authoritarianism, these heads looked to the general manager for direction. One day the general manager, because he was refused part ownership without investment, resigned, and the organization has carried on more democratically as well as more systematically and effectively ever since.

Plant Organization in Transition

The general manager had trained the six key people, heads of the various departments, to be followers, not leaders. With his resignation emerged an interesting learning problem. Could followers educate themselves to become leaders? Developments in the plant brought with them not only the occasion to observe this type of problem, but to test the nature of it because, with the resignation of the general manager, the president invited the key people to organize themselves in a cooperative manner, gave increasing rewards in the form of increased wages, and invited them to take leadership roles.

For a time seemingly all went well. The president of the company met with the key people, and production continued without loss; for a time it even increased. After three months, habit residuals of the people as well as undercurrents which motivated and gave them life interfered with effective cooperative efforts. At the end of one year the executives decided that more needed to be done. Aside from the original spurt it seemed possible for the executives occasionally to arrange short-scale emergencies and motivate the key people to work together again, but when a particular emergency was over, a return to previous patterns would again take place. At the end of the year the executives decided that this emergency technique was not enough and therefore did two things—(1) they called in an efficiency expert to help systematize scheduling and production; (2) they invited the investigator who had been a consultant on previous occasions to explore the human side of their enterprise from the top level down.

Efficiency Versus Effectiveness in Management

In the hope that system would make certain techniques and knowledge more transmissible and therefore acceptable for cooperative efforts, the management hired an efficiency engineer from an industrial engineering firm to do this kind of a job in the scheduling department, and, if it worked out, to do likewise with the departments of the other key people. Possible relations and also conflicts between the phases of the organization, which have been sensibly enough labeled by Roethlisberger and Dickson (1939) as "technical organization" and "human organization," were not considered.

Without a knowledge of or concern with these forms of organization, the efficiency engineer was advised to do his work. The man selected seemed to know something about scheduling and production forms, sheets and processes, but knew nothing about how to work with people. The first key person he was scheduled to work with and train to use the system he was introducing was one who had been with the company for many years. He did have the fault, from the point of view of system, of keeping too much in his head, and it was difficult to teach him to systematize his work so that more of it could be in a transmissible form. The efficiency specialist had this particular person overenthusiastic the first few weeks and completely deflated for the rest of the time. In two months' time he not only succeeded in antagonizing this key person, but, because of his reactions on him, antagonized all the other key people who resented this man's way of working. From their point of view his experiences seemed limited to working with companies that had failed, not successful companies. Justifiably enough they felt that what they had done in the past had yielded good results, and they therefore had the right to expect that their experiences would be sought after and profited from by the efficiency engineer. However, this was not his way of working, and at the end of two months it was obvious that confusion was the only yield of his effort.

It was at this stage of the game that the executives confronted the investigator concerning this problem. It was suggested at this time that it would be inadvisable to work with the key people until the efficiency engineer had completed his job, that in the meantime perhaps a series of talks and informal discussions concerning forms of organization might be helpful. An attempt at this type of group teaching for developing openness and communication was then instituted, but the talks on factors in a communicative system in both formal and informal organization in industry did not help. The engineer could not be educated to consider the human factor, did not desire to try to understand the key people, and the end was, as could have been predicted, that the efficiency methods introduced from the point of view of technical consideration yielded only ineffectual consequences, which is to say that, in this particular instance at least, an attempt to introduce technical efficiency with an utter disregard of the human factor proved to be a complete failure. At the end of less than three months this attempt was called to a halt. During the last month the group teaching approach for influencing behavior of the key people was attempted.

It might be interesting at this point to record that one year later, after the key people had been working together cooperatively for about nine months, an outside specialist was called in for help in improving the cost system. This time the advisability was considered at a meeting of key people for their approval, and this time the work was done without resistance and with wholehearted cooperation. Industrial engineering certainly has a place in industry, but not efficiency engineering which limits itself to technical considerations and disregards factors in human organization.

Exploring Possibilities for Developing Leadership

After these experiences management asked the consultant to educate the six people so they would have some understanding of what it is to participate in organizing creative administration. It was logical for the executive to think that the six well-trained people who knew their fields could learn by classroom procedures how to change themselves from followers to leaders. In these meetings the most relevant contributions from the most reliable sources concerning creative administration in industry were presented in a relatively formal fashion and discussed more informally. Included in such considerations were the principles of organizing communication systems. Also considered was how a new organization comes into being, for example, when there are persons (1) who are able to communicate with each other, (2) who are willing to contribute action, and (3) who aim to accomplish a common purpose.

Another topic well-considered was the open road toward enlightened supervision. This included such facts as the need for placing definite responsibility for results in definite individuals, the need for establishing definite lines of authority, and the need for improvement to set up such coordinating and control plans and units of organization as are necessary to keep activities in line with management's aims and desires.

The foregoing generalization and others similar in nature

were acquired from a selection of such works as Follett's (1924) *Creative Experience,* Whitehead's (1941) *Leadership in a Free Society* and Barnard's (1938) *The Functions of the Executive.* Also considered were the thinking processes in general and barriers to effective group thinking in particular.

Most of the key people seemed to understand the meaning of these relatively simple principles and facts of thinking, but whatever they learned made no difference in their everyday behavior in industry—nothing moved, nothing stirred, nothing was done. Whatever they were when the general manager was there, they still were but did not take up new responsibilities with anything like a new attitude. Such knowledge as was acquired was stored in the heads of these key people, and reactions to that knowledge were also stored. During the period when the group education approach was being tried out, no felt needs or requests for additional psychological service were made.

As a result of all this, it became apparent that the key people could not be moved by any kind of group approach in developing leadership. Too many of the individuals involved needed self-understanding, understanding with each other and to develop attitudes that would make learning possible—attitudes that would develop more effective relationships with co-workers—before results could be expected. Hence, the next logical step was to attempt a more individualized approach—the clinical approach.

The Clinical Approach

With this experience as a background, the group approach was dropped, and plans were arranged for individual interviewing of all key people, all foremen and a sample of the workers to get the feel of the undercurrents. With these preliminary interviews out of the way, a system of interviewing for resolving conflicts and breaking through the barriers was then planned. The scheme consisted of (1) intensive interviewing of every key person to a point where the investigator felt he understood the man's adequacy and that the man had obtained a sense of adequacy concerning himself as a person as well as a sense of

reality about his possibilities for being a more natural cooperative leader; (2) sessions between the president of the company
and each key person; and (3) joint session conferences where
every key person met every other key person.*

In dealing with industrial management it was found definitely
advisable to familiarize each individual at the outset with the
general purpose of the sessions and to describe the interview in
such a manner that the individual would get a clear picture of
the chances for development of his own attitudes in relationship
to his attitudes to others, not only for the sake of release but
also to build him up to be gladly willing to deal with the others
without reserve and conflict.

In practically every instance this meant that the interview
was continued up to a point where the investigator had a feeling
of ease and confidence that the individual was permitting himself
to perceive clearly the role he could play with the information
and experiences he would have so that he could with a feeling
of security and self-assurance cooperate with others. Also, of
course, the nature of the therapeutic relationship between the
interviewer and key people in an individual management problem
does not remain on the same behavior level. There are certain
shifting levels that are necessarily implied. There is need, too,
for considering arrangement and sequence of interviews.

Such therapy as is involved in dealing with industrial management problems of the kind described here takes on more of the
characteristics of direct rather than indirect therapy, though some
indirect therapy is involved. The interviewer or clinician in an
industrial management problem also plays different roles, at times
being most concerned with internal pressures of a single individual, at other times more concerned with the sources of external
pressures as they exist in the organization. The solution of
different problems also calls for different techniques and approaches. In some instances it means clearing of an individual;

---

* In planning and organizing these interviews, the investigator profited
from the writings of Mayo (1933), Piaget (1929), Follett (1924), Moreno
(1934, 1937) and Lewis (1936) concerning techniques, and Korzybski (1933)
and Ogden and Richards (1923) concerning thinking.

in other instances it means actual manipulation of the industrial situation. Also, the clinician is in the position of so setting the stage that the people capable of doing the most effective jobs are invited to participate in such a manner that effective co-ordinated work results, and this is a major contribution to the development of industrial morale in dealing with management problems.

The Expressions of Individual Attitudes

The six key people could be described roughly as having the following attitudes at the beginning of the interviews. Person A was the most educated and one of the best organized with an engineering degree in his specialty, and teaching and working experiences. Emotionally well-balanced, he managed the staff in his own office well, go along well with the foremen, and is respected for his knowledge and ability. To the executives, however, he seemed at times too complacent and lacking in initiative. As it turned out, he had both initiative and insight, but the nature of the social structure of the plant when he came into it did not call forth the release of either, except in spurts. The spurts did not characterize his temperament as it did his response to emergency demands from the executive group.

This man had a sensory defect. Instead of so arranging his work so this defect would not handicap his efforts, he read into it implied inferiority and tried to compensate by knowledge and intelligence, which he almost succeeded in doing. The mistakes made because of the defect were costly, and he was held responsible. Because of this he lost prestige with some of the other key people. At the same time he was struggling with a frustrating ambition—namely, with the resignation of the general manager there was a feeling on his part, as well as key person B, that one of the six would be made plant superintendent or else a plant superintendent would be hired from outside. His characteristic response to frustration was a new surge of aspiring behavior typically well-considered and intelligently carried out. With the significance of this type of compensatory adjustment explained to him to a point of emotional acceptance and discussed with him again with his approval in the presence of the president, arrangements were made for a phase of the work in which this defect was a handicap to be taken over by someone else in his department. It took two hours to get him to the point where he was eager to take up all relevant matters with the president. After this arrangement a more natural and spontaneous cooperative release of energies was developed, and it has continued.

Person B was the most ambitious of the key people, had been with the company for many years, had his hand in every new development, and had knowledge of machines and men that was very useful to the plant. Despite his value to the company at the time of the first session, it was obvious that this man had a feeling he had lost prestige with the company and that things were done over his head, which clearly indicated that his judgment was no longer respected. He admitted pulling two boners, partially because of lack of communication on his part with other key people, but he also cited instances where, from his point of view (and there was some factual basis for it), things were done over his head even in his own department. He was particularly irritated by two instances where a man in his own department had been advanced without his being consulted. His characteristic response to frustration was extropunitive (see Rosenzweig, 1935), usually expressed with lengthy, logically-constructed content of which the undercurrent was a drive for omnipotence. A rationalizing logician, ready to uphold his end and then some, describes his frequently manifested pattern of behavior. He had been accumulating this emotional overload in a relatively unconscious manner over the past four months. The attitude of the efficiency man reinforced this impression. The knowledge of the fact that one of the key people considered him arrogant did not help his feelings. Because of these many undercurrents practically all day was spent clearing with him. Early in the interview, before he began opening up, he expressed the opinion that if a man works for a company he has been loyal to and has gained much from, and a point is reached where confidence in him is lost, severance is the only solution. After the all-day session, including the lunch hour, his attitude changed and he was at least ready to discuss problems with the president. The interview with the president the following day went easily, smoothly and clearly, and took not much more than half an hour. Each successive interview from that point on was easier; the purpose seemed clearer.

Person C was a man who had formerly worked under person B when the two offices were together. This man, who had been with the company for more than fifteen years, was a man of action; he was anxious and restless. Many in the sales office as well as some of the key people found him difficult to deal with. From their point of view, he was moody, temperamental and had to be treated like a child. Though his work was important, it was not nearly as important as he made it seem, when, at times, his actions gave the impression that unless he did just so right now the whole plant would cave in. He did much running around, kept many things in his head, and was against changing procedures in his office to make them more transmissible in spite of his desire to cooperate with the firm, for which he had a deep loyalty. He readily criticized everyone but himself. It was difficult for him to take criticism, and his frustration tolerance ratio was very low. His style of response to frustration was extropunitive, usually manifested in an explosive outburst. His attitude to the general manager, however, was one of appeasement. Blaming was for the small fry. His characteristic emotional pattern was ambivalent. At home he was fairly submissive to his wife.

Person D was the most withdrawn of all. Because of his distrust for person B, whom he described as being arrogant and undermining, particularly to him, he began organizing his department as if it were a small business within a larger one. He refused to have central functions taken over by central departments. In a sense, person D was not only an isolationist, but ran his department with a defensive Maginot Line built up as a defense for fear of being undermined by person B. Reassurances concerning his value, concerning the purpose of the interview, and goals aimed at made it possible, however, for him to agree not only to a joint session with the *arrogant under-miner*, but to permit the functional interrelationship of his department to the general central processes of the plant as a whole. His typical style of reaction to frustration was further recoil and the building of reinforcements in his department, his Maginot Line. Repressed hostility toward offenders he merely deposited in his body system. Some of his responses to frustration were intropunitive in nature, but most of them merely appeared so on the surface.

Person E was a relatively new man; he had been with the plant for less than two years. At the time he was interviewed he seemed sunk and lost in routine. He had a ten-year history behind him of fear of failure and defeat from the depression years, and it was impossible for him to completely relieve himself of the anxieties experienced during that time. Though his job called for numerous tasks all over the plant, one of his chief positions was to stay close to the men in his own department because this was the focal point for all other activities for which he was responsible, but demands for insignificant things came so often that in a relatively short time he was almost out of touch with the staff of his main department and internal departmental troubles developed. This person had enough problems in building up his prestige with the other key people so that he was hardly aware of the difficulties of other key people. His characteristic style of reaction to frustration was restless movement referred to by some of the key people as the *jitterbug technique*.

Key person F was the smoothest personality of all in some ways, and he was proud of the fact that he had made for himself a full-time job out of what person B had merely touched on and left behind while he was running into other things. His characteristic response to conflicts and frustration was conciliation almost to a fault. Some of the men in the plant referred to him as a "smoothy."

These six key people had value judgments; they even had insight, but they also had emotional prejudices, blind spots, anxieties, feelings of insecurity and were victims of habits of a previous social structure which were difficult to get away from. This and much more came out in the interviews. No attempt was made to do a full-time therapeutic job with each person. It was considered enough to clear each sufficiently so that he would gladly, and with an understanding purpose, meet with the others. All sessions of each key person with the president went smoothly, and in these the investigator merely assisted as a sort of catalytic agent to make communication easier and to bring out possible sources of misunderstanding and conflicts which needed to be cleared. In the sessions between each key person with every other key person, the procedure was more like joint sessions between husbands and wives after each one has been cleared separately, but carried with them the additional need of not only clearing each with each, but preparing them to contribute their all for the mutual purposes outlined.

A closer analysis of the learning difficulties of the six key people reveals many facts and principles of learning and, even more so, the significance of emotional attitudes which make learning possible or difficult. It also reveals the importance of the conditions of learning in a learning process. As long as the social conditions, i.e., the social structure did not invite spontaneity, none emerged. When the change was invited, plans for the change in social organization of the business were provided, and the nature of the leadership changed, learning began to take place on the part of practically all the key people relatively rapidly.

Provisions for Maintenance of Improved Relations

When the interviews were finished, the plans were to arrange for maintenance of the attitudes that had been cleared by the organization of key people meetings. The purpose of these was to serve as a sort of clearing depository not only for release of emotional tensions but for the solving of mutual problems. It was assumed that unless such provisions were made, the attitudes developed as a result of the interviews would not persist. That this assumption is warranted was revealed early in the efforts to organize the joint sessions. The sessions were successful in spite of the relapse of person C. The first time an arrangement was made during working hours to discuss the purpose and arrange for monthly key meetings, this person snapped, "I will give you five minutes." Facial expressions of the other key people were the only answers this evoked, and to save face, person C said of course he was in favor of the meetings, he did not mind five minutes, but he thought it advisable to have evening sessions. Evening sessions were therefore arranged. All went well until, as a part of this program, each key person was invited to present the workings of his own department, to indicate particularly all functions that were at the time in a transmissible form and those that were not, and consider with the others how in the most effective manner the remaining features could be made transmissible.

When it came to person C's turn for presenting his department, having relatively little confidence in his ability to present organized material, he had a temper tantrum throughout the session. He was questioned by the chairman and key people and, by and large, presented most of the facts concerning his department which he did know. Some months later he admitted that it was fear of inability to run that kind of meeting in an organized manner rather than a desire not to cooperate that was responsible for his behavior. He has since been as communicative and contributory as the others. These key meetings were planned to provide for continuity in organization and function in terms of relevance and significance for changing times. Everything was discussed in an informal but organized manner.

For the next many years following this organization of key people to be a leader group, the consultant introduced a variety of psychological procedures for helping increase the firmness of organization in the plant. The procedures and situational changes included the following: (1) a job evaluation plan that was extremely well-accepted by the workers and the foreman, all of whom were used in developing the plan; (2) a merit-rating system (this was exceedingly well-received because it counteracted in some departments the unpopular, unfavored incentive plans provided for human communication with both the supervisors and select personnel staff); (3) a key people meeting was institutionalized to meet monthly for the purpose of reviewing and planning, a foremen's training course was instituted, followed by the organization of foremen's meetings (the foreman met with all members in his department for an hour once a month); what the workers received from that was a feeling of having a time and place for making a contribution or reacting to what was being considered for the department and its planned change; (4) the universal use of tests in the light of clinical kinds of interviewing was implemented for evaluation and promotion, both selection and upgrading; (5) a suggestion system was set up where workers were participant judges; (6) counseling provisions for special personnel problems were established.

The whole story makes an interesting drama, and from it can be obtained many illustrations of facts, conditions and principles of learning in industry, some of which are listed in the conclusions which follow.

CONCLUSIONS

1. Interdependent leadership for democratic living in industry can only be developed by the application of knowledge and techniques which carry with them insight concerning the significance of social organization as well as personality organization. It cannot be developed by legislation from the top, which permits coordinated effort for only a small span of time for emergency purposes.

2. The style of efficiency which disregards the human factor introduces more nuisance value and barriers toward effective human relations and in the long run reduces production. Only effective approaches where the human factor is accepted as relevant material to be considered in relationship to the jobs that must be done, as well as the systematizing of the jobs, promise well.

3. Increasing transmissibility in industry is advisable and necessary, but unless people are assured of security and relieved of anxiety, secrets which permit bargaining for power will remain the style of behavior of those who will see to it that the transmissible systems which might be given to them will not function. Transmission systems are good only if human communication systems of the people who work the systems are good.

4. Resistances in the form of habit residuals as well as cultural residuals from previous organization often manifest themselves in individuals who work their way up to the top, and only clinical understanding of their nature and ways of dealing with them can eliminate such resistances.

5. The sources of frustration of key people as well as workers are extremely individual in nature and should be considered individually.

6. In dealing with managerial problems it is advisable to pay more attention to the general meaningfulness of the interviewing procedure in each session, and more advisable logically to present the meaning and purpose of the interview at the outset, and summarize or sound out in summary fashion at the end.

7. It was interesting though not surprising to discover in industry, as in international and national relations, that terms bandied about for a number of years are often used to describe the pattern of behavior—isolationism, exploitation, appeasement policies, Maginot Lines are all easy to discover in industrial relations. Even the type of noncommunicativeness, probably best-labeled excommunication, which existed between the Army and Navy before Pearl Harbor is observed between leaders of what should be two coordinating departments in industry.

8. Follow-up is fundamental in industrial relations, though easier than in psychiatric social work or in child guidance. Spontaneous recovery of past habits can inhibit release of new ones. Relapse or regression to previous patterns may be expected unless provisions are made for maintenance of newly-acquired patterns and attitudes.

9. An interdependent arrangement for division of labor among the managerial group definitely tends to lessen anxiety tensions of all members of the group. Each individual, when this job is done well, has an easier possibility for loading and unloading his own emotional burdens in a more balanced, effective manner.

10. After a relatively small amount of clearing, arranging for individuals antagonistic toward each other to work together

is often simpler in reducing antagonism and developing more integrative ways of working together than more analytical techniques.

11. Throughout, it is revealed over and over again that key people are human, and that they, too, need a feeling of belongingness before they are willing to give up their personal ideas as the only way of playing for power in a search for fictitious security which they will not give up until they can more clearly perceive realistic security and ways and means of attaining more realistic goals.

12. Also revealed was the fact that, as in a nation too full of the privilege of democracy without the responsibilities of democracy, disunity all too often prevails. Despite its prevalence, an oncoming emergency can at least temporarily produce unity enough for an emergency purpose. An emergency request from the executives did result in a temporary lull of undercurrents and other barriers to coordinated efforts. A regression to the more inherent patterns of the individual, however, occurred after each emergency. In industry as well as in international relations it is apparently possible to win a war and lose a peace. In this instance further effort made the continuance of a more understanding and promising peace possible.

13. Child guidance experts and mental hygienists know the effects of consistencies and inconsistencies in child training; these are equally applicable in industry. In the child guidance field it is known that techniques and attitudes in line with mental hygiene are definitely preferable to traditional ones, but even traditional ones are often better than inconsistent or confused mental hygiene techniques. This is certainly applicable in industrial relations because, if the top structure in a business organization does not make possible the application of anything but authoritarian approaches, the availability of democratic techniques lower down in the hierarchy of authority is likely to result in confusion and inconsistency.

14. History all too often repeats itself in industrial relations as well as in other relations merely because no provisions are made for learning and profiting from our experiences. A repetition

of the same stupidities which formerly yielded bad results will again yield them. This law of human nature holds in all areas of human relations, and one of the areas in which it is easily perceived is industry. Observe the *business as usual* policy against the claim of *united effort* persisting after many months when it is obvious to everybody that only united efforts will give the results wanted. Observe also the farm bloc and at times the labor bloc. Certainly a reorientation toward a consideration of man's adventure in life from the vantage point of humanity in general is needed.

In industry as well as elsewhere, H. G. Wells' race between education and catastrophe has been going on. Years ago Wells emphasized the fact that "a sense of history as the common adventure of all mankind is necessary for peace within as it is for peace between nations." In the words expressed by James Harvey Robinson (1921),

> There can be no secure peace now but a common peace of the whole world; no prosperity but a general prosperity, and this for the simple reason that we are all now brought so near together and are so pathetically and intricately interdependent, that the old notions of noble isolation and national sovereignty are magnificently criminal.

In industry as elsewhere, the need for the development of matured leadership and effective interdependent relations is urgent and represents an inviting challenge to organizational psychologists as well as to industrialists and workers.

REFERENCES

Barnard, C. I.: *The Functions of the Executive*. Cambridge, Harvard U Pr, 1938.
Burnham, J. T.: *The Managerial Revolution*. New York, John Day, 1941.
Drucker, P. F.: *Management: Tasks, Responsibilities, Practices*. New York, Har Row, 1973.
Follett, M. P.: *Creative Experience*. London, Longmans, Green, 1924.
Galbraith, J. K.: *The New Industrial State*. Boston, HM, 1967.
Korzybski, A.: *Science and Sanity*. Lancaster, Science Pr, 1933.
Lewin, K.: *Principles of Topological Psychology*. New York, McGraw, 1936.
Mayo, E.: *The Human Problems of an Industrial Civilization*. New York, MacMillan, 1933.

Moreno, J. L.: Interpersonal therapy and the psychopathology of interpersonal relations. *Sociometry*, I:9-76, 1937.

Moreno, J. L.: Who shall survive? A new approach to the problems of
human interrelations. *Nervous and Mental Disease Monograph Series,
Number 58.* Washington, Nervous and Mental Disease Publishers
Company, 1934.

Ogden, C. K., and Richards, I. A.: *The Meaning of Meaning.* New York,
Harcourt Brace, 1923.

Piaget, J.: *Child's Conception of the World.* New York, Harcourt, Brace
and Company, 1929.

Robinson, J. H.: *The Mind in the Making.* New York, Harper and Brothers,
1921.

Roethlisberger, F. J., and Dickson, W. K.: *Management and the Worker.*
Cambridge, Harvard U Pr, 1939.

Rosenzweig, S.: A test for types of reaction to frustration. *Am J Orthopsychiatry*, V:4, 1935.

Servan-Schreiber, J.: *Le Defi Americain* (English translation, *The American
Challenge*). New York, Atheneum, 1968.

Whitehead, T.: *Leadership in a Free Society.* Cambridge, Harvard U Pr,
1941.

```
┌─────────────────────── Chapter 17 ───────────────────────┐
│                                                            │
│              A PLANNED HUMANIZING                          │
│              ORGANIZATION IN ACTION                        │
│                                                            │
│                     KEN BALL                               │
│                                                            │
└────────────────────────────────────────────────────────────┘
```

IN RECENT YEARS articles relating to humanizing industrial organizations have appeared with increasing frequency in the psychological literature. Many of them have discussed humanizing in the context of potential program applications. Some have explored theoretical underpinnings from the psychology of the individual to the sociology of the group. Some have integrated both. If organizations are to move toward humanizing, there is a need for the reporting of applied programs in the ongoing industrial setting.

The purpose of this paper is to help satisfy that need by reporting one company's planned approach to humanizing in action. Conscious attention will be paid to programs employed, theoretical assumptions and observed results. It is the reporting of real events over a period of many years. The full scope of the company's industrial life as it relates to this study encompasses more than three decades. Most of the reporting is from the author's perceptions and participation as a professional psychologist and an executive of the company.

A HUMANIZING OPPORTUNITY

In 1966 a small group of managers had the unique opportunity to start a new manufacturing company from a piece of an older company. The events emerged from the company's history and provided new patterns for future growth.

The parent company was forty-six years old. The printing of packaging materials for retail application represented more than two-thirds of its sales volume. This major part of the business was sold along with almost all of the equipment and the entire plant facility in which it was housed.

The president selected two vice-presidents and met with them to map product and organizational strategy for a new beginning. The author was one of the vice-presidents and was afforded the unusual opportunity to participate as both psychologist and executive in a real humanizing adventure.

First, a new product-base had to be selected. A small segment of the old company known as the Technical Products Division was chosen. These were printed or coated products used in the building and furniture industries or other industrial applications. The product selection was determined on the one hand by excluding the larger product divisions which were sold and had become significantly less profitable and, on the other hand, by selecting products requiring a high degree of technical and proprietary know-how, long-term R & D backup, relatively heavy capital investment and relationship to growth markets and industries. Chances for a profitable future would be optimized if the product structure was too complex for most small competitors, would compete for too small a market for most giant corporations, and require too much technical catch-up time for either.

A new plant was found, and managers were selected. Again, there was a unique opportunity to pick leaders from the old company with prior firsthand knowledge of the individuals. The executives had a number of meetings where they analyzed the company's history including its earlier successes and some of its more recent failures. These were related to the more successful styles of management. The recent six years had been characterized by autocratic executive management at the top as compared to an earlier period which was group-centered and human relations-oriented.

The president expressed his unhappiness with some recent mismanagement and directed the search toward those who had demonstrated not only job effectiveness, but the ability to function well in the more open, sharing atmosphere. Similar considerations were given to the selection of the sales group. It was felt that the future sales successes required a small marketing group where each member could function in a self-directed manner as a small entrepreneur. Each would be given responsibility for a product group's marketing and sales.

A meeting was held in the president's office with the new management and marketing people. The plans for the new company were presented, and the group was told why it had been selected. There was an open discussion where feelings were vented, particularly as they related to the frustrations which had built over the past few years. Establishing a commitment to an open style of management emerged from the meeting. Area responsibilities were outlined, and one could sense everyone's desire, agreement and understanding that there was this one chance to develop some kind of real, honest and effective participative management.

The president and vice-presidents indicated that they would function as a team. On a daily basis each would split executive responsibilities, the president taking sales and marketing; one vice-president (the author) taking operations, personnel and human relations; and the other vice-president taking finance and technical areas. The supervisors and department heads were challenged to work out their departmental definitions and the manner in which they would interrelate.

The president reviewed some areas of mismanagement where leadership created factions, defensiveness and broken communications. He indicated that the new management must function openly and would be redirected if new signs of departmental and individual "wall-building" recurred. The feeling generated was that the company could be successful financially and people could have fun while working toward that goal. This was the kind of spirit with which the new company began.

Only a few problems remained before the two companies

split. Factory and office personnel were selected. There was not 100 percent freedom of choice since personnel in certain departments were in the part of the business which had been sold. There was open selection from the other areas, and those not selected remained with the purchasing company. Choice was relatively easy since there had been prior experiences with all of the people. The selection criteria were a combination of skills needed and people who could function well in an open company. Although some of those selected expressed fears about the unknown in a new venture and a few even elected to remain with the purchasing company (ostensibly due to travel distance to the new location), in a few months a new spirit was evident throughout the new organization.

An executive vice-president who was not needed in the management of the old company and would not fit the style of the new left soon after the plant move. Until then, his management activities were curtailed. To put this into proper perspective, the organization must be viewed in its historical frame of reference.

THE COMPANY—VIEW FROM THE TOP

The historical beginnings of what is now called a humanizing effort were in the forties. The founder-president of the company sought professional psychological guidance for organizing an effective and more democratic organization. As the company had grown from its inception in the twenties, the common small entrepeneurial growth-pattern occurred. One-man leadership grew to a need for shared leadership. As often occurs, human conflict inhibited planned direction and growth. In the forties, management opened all parts of the company to psychological consultation for the patterning of a humanizing organization (Meltzer, 1942, 1956).

The key to the program subsequently developed, and their effectiveness was the positive attitude of the president toward humanizing programs and goals. Moving from the old style organization toward shared leadership was not without conflict, but with what might have been called a people orientation, the company grew.

What were then relatively new organizational and individual growth techniques for industry were employed—group problem discussion, in-plant individual counseling, assessment and evaluation techniques. In all, the company was characterized by employee openness not usually associated with the more typical autocratic leadership. Beginning with the president, throughout, to the first line of supervision, the company's leaders learned new ways of dealing with people and new bases for motivation. They found that more democratic principles could be effectively applied in an industrial setting. The plant worker was finding that when so invited, he could, in fact, respond to a more open setting and find from participation new avenues for satisfaction.

In the fifties, after the death of the founder-president, his son became president. The same types of programs continued. In many respects they were intensified, particularly as they were put into effect at companies purchased during an expansion phase. At these companies, decisive human organization action was usually required to implement broad changes. This was made possible by the president giving a psychologist and vice-president of human relations freedom to act.

In the late fifties, significant changes in the company began to occur. The business had grown larger with more plants, people and product complexity. The president's attention shifted away from internal functions. His leadership role of giving freedom to develop humanizing programs diminished. He took the alternative of moving the management organization toward more rigid structure with classical lines of authority relationships.

A line of vice-presidents came through the company as the president sought to reinforce this new management style. The vice-president of human relations left. The author was brought into the personnel area from a manager's position at a subsidiary plant. Having been with the company as a graduate student prior to this transition period, he was available to help reestablish a new humanizing management when called upon in 1966. This was made possible because the author kept up a relationship with workers and to a less extent with the supervisory group throughout the dehumanizing or confusing authoritarian period.

In attempting to attract loyalties and become a focal leader, each of the new vice-presidents applied his own version of authoritarian behavior. One emphasized "the carrot and stick" philosophy of motivation, tried to look angry and create action through fear. Another preferred to have supervisors reporting alone and frequently to his office rather than work together as functional groups. Another actively sought loyalties by going between departments issuing on-the-spot directives. All succeeded in fragmenting informal communications. Rigid lines of communications created blind spots and barriers. Any form of participative management was limited or eliminated as in the case of supervisory meetings, employee departmental meetings and safety meetings. The executive vice-president in particular was fluent with humanizing phrases, but in reality seemed to consciously set the stage for more of a dehumanizing period.

Turnover at all levels grew drastically, including key people; group labor unrest developed; product management problems grew; and the total company growth and profitability were severely impeded. A negative kind of spiral developed—problems grew, management felt pressured to use more inhibiting techniques, creating more unrest, communication breakdowns and greater problems.

At the plant level, vestiges of employee-centered programs from the personnel department shielded some of the effect. Individual considerations continued from the department and through its influence over first-line supervisors. This was important in retaining a core for a rebuilding, the beginnings of which have been described.

PROVISIONS FOR HUMANIZING PROCEDURES

Characteristic of the company referenced here is that in size by number of employees, dollar volume and number of plant operations it would be categorized as a small medium-sized company. The company's headquarters are located in the suburbs of a large midwestern city. Basic human relationship patterns established in the forties have persisted to the present day. The company at that time was among the first to seek consultation from a clinically-oriented industrial psychologist. From the late forties through to the present the company has employed industrial psychologists functioning out of the personnel-industrial relations area and as an integral part of top management.

While the company does not have a great number of unskilled employees, it has many factory employees who would be classified as skilled or semiskilled. The primary operation is technical, utilizing heavy equipment, where skills are necessary to be developed and training is important for the success of the company.

At the time of the company's move and rebuilding there was conscious effort on the part of the author to define with top management those programs which would be reinforcing in the desired, humanizing direction. These were then converted into action programs with the supervisors.

The development of trust has been viewed as multidimensional or a necessary component in relationships between individuals at each level, within levels and between levels. Meltzer (1963) called for "a cultivation of an emotional atmosphere that invites self-development and the actualization of these skills, abilities, and experiences that are productive as well as satisfying to the individual." He reported programs and opportunities structured to serve for "initiating and developing a relationship" between the organization and employees. The programs he reported, and which are among the many employed by the company described here, range from the more common appraisal interview to counseling, and include the more unique "daily rounds." Here, key management people, particularly an industrial psychologist out of the personnel or human relations department, make daily contact with employees in all and any work areas. In an informal manner, people's tensions, whether or not job-related, can be considered on the spot and frequently reduced or provisions made for follow-up.

Selection and Early Development

Consideration is sought for individuals as striving human beings from the moment they are hired and throughout their personal and job growth. The total assessment situation relates specifically to the individual, not only for job fit, but also for a broad review of skills, development and growth needs. The most important humanizing orientation takes place in the personnel department—usually the first point of contact. The objective is to relate individual and company in an atmosphere of mutual need and, hopefully, trust. With this kind of selection procedure it is easier to initiate circumstances conducive to both job and personal counseling during subsequent career and personal growth.

When an applicant reaches a point for final consideration, the supervisor, a personnel man (usually a psychologist) and the applicant get together for an unstructured but goal-oriented talk. The objective is to set the stage for each to open up to each other as a first step in assessing and establishing an ongoing life-style between the two individuals who must work together in an open atmosphere. This provides an opportunity to initiate conditions conducive to individual growth while satisfying organizational needs.

The induction procedure is highly individualized. The employee is given an unharried advantage to understand the organization, the opportunities within it and various programs as they relate to him. Subsequent follow-up is aimed at similar objectives. In the factory, where most of the hiring takes place, there are maximum review time periods such as thirty days following the starting day.

At these reviews the employee, his supervisor and a personnel man sit down for an open-ended session which might last from fifteen minutes to one hour. The employee is given the opportunity to evaluate his own progress and opportunities. He is encouraged to test whether, in fact, his first expectations were realistic and, if not, whether a mutually satisfying and realistic picture can be developed. From this point the supervisor can carry on the discussion with the individual, solidifying the relationship in the context of job review, reinforcing progress and thereby developing some sense of mutual sharing and trust. It is important that this review take place with the personnel representative who can act as a relatively uninvolved guide to a fruitful discussion.

Following the thirty-day review there are more and frequent reviews until the employee becomes established on the job. There are also formalized merit-reviewing procedures twice a year for all nonmangement employees. One of the merit ratings each year is a self merit-rating as well as supervisory rating. Using the same form, the employee rates his progress on the job over specified factors and his supervisor rates him. The two ratings reviewed together function as a vehicle toward shared understanding for both personal development and job goal-attainment. This procedure stimulates discussion, stimulates more conscientious ratings and self-ratings, and provides a kind of measure of mutual understanding and self-awareness.

Growth and Opportunity

Giving substantive backing to individual considerations, and perhaps most important for a genuine humanizing atmosphere, counseling is made available. It is not uncommon for employees to request tests to help determine what direction they may want to take in their own lives, even without consideration for specific jobs within the company. From this kind of vocational and personal counseling, a *good* employee may leave the company to seek satisfaction elsewhere. That this does occur, at least infrequently, might be taken as an indicator of a successful actualizing program. It is also a test of the company's ability to provide opportunities if in fact one accepts the tenet that company success is tied to employee growth and success. If realistic growth cannot be achieved within reasonable (as mutually defined) time limits, then, in any event, either the employee will be lost or a disruptive force may persist.

More recently the company embarked on a program to identify career development needs as they relate to company needs. In this endeavor all employees were asked to outline career objectives and relevant factors, including assistance needed such as educational opportunities for vocational growth. They can request testing, personal interviewing or guidance counseling.

It is most important for credibility of the developmental program to permit employee movement, even if it might not seem to fit with the short-range objectives of the company. For example, often an employee will want to move laterally in order to gain a broad range of experiences, but the move might seem to create an unnecessary training need. Sometimes where there is a different point of view it may be important for the employee to test himself on a job with all due counseling and guidance, and without putting him in an environment where he is doomed to fail—"letting him hang himself."

THE MANAGING ORGANIZATION

Most characteristic of the structure of the company is its minimum number of layers and short-circuited informal communications system. Basically there are three supervisory levels—executive management, middle management and first-level supervisory management.

The executive group is small and, on goal-setting problems, works almost as one with the middle group. These managers supervise broad functional areas such as manufacturing, technical, engineering and sales, working together defining operational needs, analyzing performance and carrying on the business of the company in its broadest scope. They also work closely with first-line supervisors in goal-setting and problem-solving.

The functional aspects of the company are centered around a problem-solving orientation. Bennis (1970) predicted that the industrial organization of the future would be run by ad hoc committees existing in time primarily to meet demands of rapidly changing challenges and problems. Problem-solving committees cut across all lines of formal structure and may include non-supervisory personnel.

Approximately once each year key managers for large segments of the company, i.e., manufacturing, meet with the psychologist as conference leader to define or redefine problems in their segment. Discussion is related to optimizing goal attainment relative to supervisory strengths, developmental needs and preferences for contribution. These discussions may progress over some weeks with consideration given to feedback sessions held with each of the individuals involved. This approach is designed to accomplish two important organizational objectives— (1) patterning the organization around problem areas rather than ego-power interest, departments or other rigid structures and (2) minimizing resistances to change through participation in developing the pattern and inviting involved persons to have some control over their own destiny, growth, et cetera.

Strengths are emphasized. Weaknesses are only recognized as training needs as long as strength areas can still find avenues of expression in problem-solving. This approach tends to strengthen open and honest communications since the need to protect areas for prestige or recognition is minimized. A man's contributory strength is defined through his personal strengths and is not forced into the mold of a structured department. This tends to emphasize security, opens communications and enhances the opportunities for satisfaction through self-actualization. This does not mean that there are no departments. It is rather that the departments emerge from problem-solving needs and/or continue to carry on daily business as part of a structure within which daily organizational habit patterns can occur.

After all of the preliminary discussions and feedback sessions have been completed, a chart representing organized communications flow is prepared for presentation to the total group affected. The chart is a functional one where each key enclosure is descriptive of a problem.

The name of the individual assigned to a particular problem area is indicated near a statement defining the problem along with lines to associated problem areas and people. The intent is to plan the organization as fluid and problem-solving-oriented. Where a problem's solution requires a coordination of approaches from different disciplines or people, they are both shown with communications lines to the problem with a statement indicating the coordinated responsibility. This is not problem-solving by unresponsible (through vague sharing) committees. It is rather perceiving the interface as a place where problems should be solved. This is intended to overcome tensions and conflicts which are counterproductive for defining what is to occur. It is designed to invite openness and trusting rather than create fear, suspicion and defensiveness.

With this functional concept, a supervisor's contribution is not necessarily related to any factors other than problem-solving. Thus, one supervisor may have the assignment, as in one case, of putting together a large department and develop a training program. On the other hand, a supervisor who had managed problems in a large department the previous year was assigned to coordinate multiple efforts to solve a particular problem with no one reporting to him.

How do employees in a department feel in terms of security, for example, if there are changes in supervision? In discussing guidelines for successful change, Seashore and Bowers (1970) indicated acceptance of change requires that the employees have confidence in managers' "humane" values which can be earned only if it is reciprocated by placing confidence in the employees.

The supervisory overtone which this company tries to set is that the supervisor is not a policeman or watchdog, but rather a planner, coordinator, counselor and problem-solver. Departmental meetings are used not only as a form of relating between the supervisor and the group, but to foster a problem-solving spirit between employees with the objective of giving them freedom to perform to the extent that they are capable.

It is important not to lose sight of each employee's need level. For example, the company was at one time not experiencing the degree of success it thought it could expect with hard-core unemployed ghetto people. This failure was measured primarily by attrition and absenteeism. Investigative interviews soon revealed that these employees felt lost. They had different needs and required security from more constant feedback. Their learning needs were more basic. Many actually verbalized a desire for closer supervision.

THEORETICAL FOUNDATIONS—NEW REALITIES
AND REFERENCE POINTS

Humanizing efforts were considered in the context of the individual, the total organization and subgroups. If such an industrial organization undertakes a broad humanizing effort, there must be implicit assumptions about the organization's needs, objectives and individual and social relatedness.

The many facets of humanizing considered by the company are expressed in the following summary from the symposium at the 1973 American Psychological Association Convention on "Humanizing Organizational Psychology" chaired by H. Meltzer and as reported by Wickert (1974),

> For Levinson a humanizing organizational psychology would make a point of recognizing . . . three phases each manager goes through during the course of his working career. A humanizing organizational psychology would work toward designing organizations to utilize their members in ways appropriate to these career stages and not inappropriately as they now all too often do.

Lawler's concern was less for managers and more for a humanizing program benefiting the blue-collar worker. To achieve this he would assess individual differences not only in competencies, but in motivations, as well as relate these to critical differences in tasks, jobs and organizational design. Hall focused on young managers and their frustrations with the slowness of the established organization to accept humanizing values—the need for organizational psychology to teach them social change methods. Massarik defines the humanistic organization as "balanced," not dominated by structure or extreme ambiguity, thereby over-emphasizing the individual and becoming "humanistically dysfunctional."

Maslow (1954) provides the theoretical framework within which consideration can be given to the individual and his growth potential—man and his creative potential. When considering the individual in the total organizational context, McGregor (1960) and Bennis (1969, 1970) provide the theoretical framework.

Industry has become increasingly aware of changes in man's expressed attitudes toward his work, and now we find representations of this from Studs Terkel in his recent book, *Working* (1974). He provides us with popularized insights into understanding the need to create work in a humanized climate rather than what it has come to be. In his opening paragraph he states,

> This book, being about work, is, by its very nature, about violence—to the spirit as well as to the body. It is about ulcers as well as accidents, about shouting matches as well as fist fights, about nervous breakdowns as well as kicking the dog around. It is, above all (or beneath all), about daily humiliations. To survive the day is triumph enough for the walking wounded among the great many of us.

Subsequent interviews with people from a multiplicity of occupations do not fully validate the original tenet that all work is, in fact, drudgery. We see emerging from Terkel's little vignettes essences of the work atmosphere which seem to make the difference between a humanized and nonhumanized situation. This differentiation seems to relate to each individual's interpretation of his total work environment.

Awareness of changing mores, values and attitudes increased as student behavior was manifested in the sixties. As curricula change and adapt, those entering industrial life will come with new expectations and needs to be met.

Mosher and Sprinthall (1970) suggested that a curriculum for psychology education in secondary schools would include effective objectives which are "crucial"—to enable the individual (among many other things) . . . to understand himself, express his feelings, be spontaneous and creative, to act in behalf of personal value, to perceive what he wants to become, to change direction, etc. Educational systems, in fact, seem to be turning more organized attention toward these kinds of human development goals. Into what kind of an industrial organization can we then expect the high school graduate to fit?

Considering broader socioeconomic factors, as described in a January, 1974, article in the *New York Review* by Robert Heilbroner, industrial leaders are becoming aware of limitations imposed upon what might be called the industrial frontier in the United States. Endless boundaries no longer exist. Man is beginning to be confronted in most dramatic ways with the effects and results of his dehumanizing of society. We see this around us exemplified by problems of pollution, overpopulation, the aged, the poor, et cetera—human needs expressed in the form of social, political and economic objectives and goals.

Even from the most pragmatic viewpoint of the industrial leader, there are reasons why it makes sense to consider a more humanizing approach to industrial organizations. Behavioral science studies in the last few decades have at least given strong indications that people perform better and use their abilities to a greater degree and their intellects to greater capacity in a trusting, open environment where abilities and intellect are more likely to flourish.

Simply stated, industry risks losing the very people it must develop and loses its attractiveness to the very people needed for successful growth without some modicum of a humanistic approach to organization.

It is even becoming prudent in today's society for the industrial organization to couch its profit motive in broader and more publicly acceptable goals. These are becoming increasingly identified with individual, group and general welfare—from ecological considerations to minority groups to concern for the problems of the worker.

SUMMING UP

The descriptions of one company set forth in this paper only highlight one approach taken in organizing facilities and people in a company guided by certain humanistic objectives. The paper reports how a company took advantage of events in its history to provide programs which would reinforce management's humanizing efforts.

Since reorganization eight years ago, the company has grown in both sales volume and profits at an overall rate in excess of 30 percent per year. Both are considerably larger than what had been achieved in the prior forty-seven years. The company consistently has lower turnover rates than its industry or area, usually by as much as 50 percent. Comparable absentee and accident rates are difficult to obtain, but it appears that the company is well below the national average in absenteeism. Historically, its safety record has been better than the average in its industry, although recent statistics have placed it closer to the average. Finally, grievances causing work interruptions for a single employee for even an hour are extremely rare.

Giving consideration to individuals in the organization begins with group training and personal counseling, particularly for those with supervisory responsibility. Employee programs include those which are relevant to individual needs. Similarly, supervisors are exposed to relevant training to learn to deal with human problems in ways which promote self-understanding for personal growth. The typical authority relationship of supervisor to subordinate is replaced by a relationship which fosters maturity and growth.

Underlying the company's orientation toward people is a realization that effective humanizing cannot be proselytized into manipulation. Conscious effort has been given for reflecting genuine concern through patient, persistent humanization programming from the top throughout the organization. Having experienced a brief dehumanizing period, management has become sensitive to manipulators. There is full recognition that results can be disastrous for individuals and the organization if people are led to a false level of expectation, and, similarly, paternalism is viewed as the anathema to the humanizing experience. The managing environment accepts conflict openly and deals with it as a motivator. Answers to management problems tend to emerge from relationships, not from preconceived organizational formulas.

The planned humanizing efforts related here are continued in the company today. In its effort to strengthen the approach the management has found that the alternative to rigidity can be organizational firmness rather than uncontrolled looseness. While planning for continued future successes, the company's managers have learned from experience that trust and openness foment human growth and contributions toward planful, creative management. Planned procedures for changing communication channels in human relations with technological and growth changes are provided.

REFERENCES

Bennis, W. G.: *Organization Development: Its Nature, Origins and Prospects.* Reading, A-W, 1969.

Bennis, W. G.: A funny thing happened on the way to the future. *Am Psychol,* 25:595-608, 1970.

Maslow, A. H.: *Motivation and Personality.* New York, Harper, 1954.

McGregor, D.: *The Human Side of Enterprise.* New York, McGraw, 1960.

Meltzer, H.: Explorations in humanizing relations of key people in industry. *Am J Orthopsychiatry, XII* (3):517-528, July, 1942.

Meltzer, H.: Mental health realities in work situations. *Am J Orthopsychiatry,* 33:562-565, 1963.

Meltzer, H.: Roads to misunderstanding in industry. *Am J Orthopsychiatry,* 26:394-399, 1956.

Mosher, R. L., and Sprinthall, H. A.: Psychology education in secondary schools: A program to promote individual and human development. *Am Psychol,* 25:911-924, 1970.

Seashore, S. E., and Bowers, D. G.: Durability of organizational change. *Am Psychol,* 25:227-233, 1970.

Terkel, S.: *Working: People Talk About What They Do All Day and How They Feel About What They Do.* New York, Pantheon, 1974.

Wickert, F. R.: Comments on humanizing organizational psychology. *The Industrial-Organizational Psychologist, 11*:32-35, 1974.

Chapter 18.

HUMANIZING THE PHYSICAL SETTING AT WORK

FRED I. STEELE

INTRODUCTION

MANY DIFFERENT VARIABLES have been used in recent attempts to improve the quality of work life for members of organizations. Jobs have been redesigned; methods of doing basic tasks have been examined and altered; communication patterns have been increased or redesigned; treatment of minority groups has been challenged; new processes for planning for possible futures have been instituted; autonomous work groups have been created; work teams have engaged in developmental activities to improve their functioning as a unit and so on.

There is, however, still an area of organizational life that tends to be treated in very simplistic ways (if at all) when attempts are made to humanize organizations. This is the area of peoples' interactions with their physical settings. The physical setting has generally been treated as a hygiene issue, worth attention only when people are dissatisfied. Attempts to influence it have been thought of as improving the amenities of creature comforts that go with membership in an organization. The more complex impact of the person's influences on and by the setting as well as the impact of the process by which physical decisions are made have tended to remain what Hall calls a "hidden dimension" of our lives; these influences are always there, but we seldom become aware of them and thus able to change them effectively.*

This chapter will examine some of these impacts, and what would be required in order to humanize the physical setting in work organizations, or, more precisely, to humanize the person-environment interaction system. The topics which will be discussed are :What are human qualities, In what ways are work organizations presently inhuman? Modes of thinking that promote dehumanization. Main factors in promoting change. How likely is change?

The writer's comments are based on three main sources—(1) some general propositions about human beings, derived from the work of humanistic psychologists such as Goldstein, Maslow, Rogers and Argyris; (2) the writer's experiences as a general organization development consultant; and (3) the writer's observations and personal research while serving as a consultant on physical settings in organizations.

WHAT ARE HUMAN QUALITIES?

The following are some of the basic qualities of humanness to try to keep in mind when working on physical setting changes.

Similar Basic Needs

Every living organism has certain basic needs which must be met to ensure survival. For human beings it will be assumed that there are the following basic needs: physiological inputs (food, etc.), physiological and psychological safety, social contact, symbolic communication, esteem from others and from one's self, and some degree of self-actualization or growth. Humans are similar to one another in that they have basic needs and require environments that facilitate the satisfaction of those needs over the long-run. To date, more attention has been paid to the environmental needs of other organisms such as plants than it has to the needs of humans at work.

---

* See Edward T. Hall, *The Hidden Dimension*, Garden City, Doubleday, 1966.

Individual Differences

Although their categories of needs are similar, people also vary as to the pattern of needs that are important to them at particular times and in particular situations. People vary as a result of different adaptation levels, comfort zones, styles, histories, moods, rates of change and other factors.

Survival Orientation

One of the most basic human needs is the force toward survival as an organism—to not have experiences which deteriorate or destroy one's self.

Fallibility

One of our most prominent human qualities is the limitation on our judgments and information-processing. We are not always right the first time we make a choice, and we often have the need to correct or alter earlier decisions, choices or attitudes.

WHAT MAKES WORK ENVIRONMENTS INHUMAN?

On the whole, work settings in the United States today tend to do a relatively poor job of allowing or encouraging their users to experience their human qualities to the fullest extent. Sometimes basic physiological needs are poorly served—the setting provides too little control over temperature, moisture, noise, dust and the like. Sometimes the setting threatens psychological survival by providing no alternatives in the social contact area—either people must interact even when they do not wish to do so, or they are isolated from one another when they would prefer some stimulating interaction.

In the areas of growth and self-actualization it is often the system's characteristic mode of decision-making about settings which serves as a block to full humanness. A person in an organization grows in his sense of personal effectiveness through the process of identifying problems or goals, making choices, taking action and obtaining feedback about the results of his actions.

In most organizations, however, decisions about facilities tend to be heavily controlled from the top of the system. This control tends to block or reverse the growth cycle. Low-power members of the organization spend most of their waking hours in a setting where they have little or no opportunity to take any action or engage in any learning. People are being trained implicitly not to take responsibility for the quality of their surroundings. They do not own their own surroundings either economically or psychologically—the company owns it all.

A related dehumanizing force is top management's desire for integrated design or regimentation in the style of facilities and their use. This regimentation is often rationalized in terms of (and in fact may sometimes even result in) cost savings from buying in volume, but it tends to cover up the individual differences between persons and within one person over different time periods. These differences are a part of what it means to be human, and there is a human cost to denying them.

Perhaps the most dehumanizing force of all is the tendency in organizations to develop policies which communicate a high concern for the maintenance of things and a low concern for the maintenance or enhancement of the people who use them. For example, when a company has a new building constructed many new policies are usually created to ensure that the users do not deteriorate the new, slick facilities. The premises are hygienic and may be aesthetic improvements, but they are also sterile and very expensive in terms of the human spirit. Peoples' excitement and enthusiasm for exploration is often sacrificed to the preservation of pristine plaster walls. No surprises are allowed and no tinkering with a fixed solution which was judged to be the right configuration. All of this tends to communicate that the users are there to serve the setting rather than to be served by it. It also denies the basic human traits of fallibility and changing needs.

MODES OF THINKING THAT LEAD TO DEHUMANIZING SETTINGS

The patterns described in the previous section do not occur by chance. They are the resultant (and cause, as they feed themselves) of assumptions and modes of thinking which are, ironically enough, also very human tendencies. The following are a few of the key modes of thinking which the writer believes contribute to dehumanizing settings.

Proprietary Thinking

As a part of the pattern of power differences and power balances in an organization, top management tends to think of it as their duty (and their right) to be proprietary about the physical facilities of the system. They dole out goodies as if they were door prizes, usually basing their decisions on policies about who should be rewarded for fitting the company's norms well enough to have risen to a certain formal level. The writer's observations indicate that the doling out function is most strongly protected by top management in those organizations where employees do not find their work tasks intrinsically rewarding.

Fantasies of Perfection

As in many other areas of organizational problem-solving, managers who make facilities decisions tend to believe that there is one elegant, right solution to every physical settings problem. They therefore see their task as discovering that right solution and implementing it. The implementation may be through imposing it unilaterally or through selling it to the users ("once they understand it, they'll see that it's the way we have to go," said one manager). But in either case, the underlying theme is that there is one right answer, and the good executive is able to divine it.

The need to have something finished and perfect before it can be given to people to use is a force toward *deadening* our settings and our experiences while using them.* The more finished something is, the less the users can bring to it, and the less they can make it feel alive, experience it as their own and

---

* For a lovely description of how slick, complete design leads to deadness, see "Plans and Plants, or, The Administration Block," in C. Northcote Parkinson, *Parkinson's Law and Other Studies in Administration.* Harmondsworth, Penguin, 1959.

identify with it. This alienation from their own setting is definitely not a perfect relationship between users and their setting.

Focus on Conspicuous Costs

When decisions about physical facilities are being considered there is a strong tendency to focus on certain criteria to the exclusion of others. Traditionally, organizations have paid most attention to selected economic costs that are specifiable in advance such as initial installation and maintenance costs of the new space.* They have paid much less attention to the less quantifiable costs to the organization's human resources (energy, growth, vitality, mutual stimulation, etc.) of physically shaping the system in one manner versus another. The capital outlays are conspicuous costs while the human system costs (and gains) are fuzzy, inconspicuous and may depend in part on how the change process itself is handled (which is also the case with the money costs, although this is seldom acknowledged).

Over time, savings on physical facilities become an end in themselves as if investments in work spaces were the company's business rather than a means to fulfilling its primary tasks. This mode of thinking is particularly evident in periods of economic pinch. For example, a company may save on meeting spaces and thereby reduce the frequency or quality of problem-solving interactions. This, in turn, can reduce the probability that new ideas will be generated which would get them out of their slump.

The focus on conspicuous costs is probably one example of a more basic mode of thinking, which is a *low tolerance for ambiguity.* As noted, this lower tolerance shows itself in the emphasis on quantifiable numbers even when those numbers have no particular factual basis. Avoidance of ambiguity is also evident in sets of impersonal rules about how facilities are to be used. Many executives seem to fear that if spatial decisions are not controlled by policies from the top, then vague irresolvable conflicts would occur which would drain the system of its energy and be an embarrassment to all concerned. Precise rules which

---

* Although in practice these "specifiable" costs often turn out to have been badly underestimated. The initial figures were not facts, they were just *numbers.*

tie facilities' rights to positional level in the hierarchy are usually an attempt to avoid this sort of ambiguity. The inconspicuous costs of this pattern are usually ignored—the loss of the energizing force that ambiguity can contribute toward dealing with unrecognized, underlying problems; and the extent to which avoidance of open dealing with conflicts tends to stunt employees' growth in their ability to handle such conflict efficiently.

Model-Board Mentality

This is a rather poor term for a very interesting phenomenon. As executives get involved in physical system decisions, they talk about it one way but feel another. They describe it as a chore that is distasteful, but that has to be done by someone so they have stepped in to fill the breach. At the feeling level, however, they may be quite excited by and caught up in the process. It is very exciting to see drawings and models of possible future settings; it is quite intriguing to be a part of the process of creating something that will be used by many and may still be an influence when you yourself have left the system. This *model-board mentality* is another force which tempts executives to hoard their influences over facilities and to make decisions for others which reduce the others' opportunities to experience a similar excitement in the creative process.*

MAIN FACTORS IN PROMOTING CHANGE

If we assume that the patterns described above do have some impact on the humanness of work settings, what can be done about it? If we wish to create more humanizing settings, where should our energies be applied? Although space limitations preclude a long discussion of change strategies, it is possible to suggest some major points of attack.† These include (1) the

---

* For the classic documentation of this hoarding process in action, see Speer's descriptions of Hitler and his programs for new buildings in Germany. (Albert Speer, *Inside the Third Reich*, New York, MacMillan, 1970.)

† If you wish a more complete discussion of the process of changing physical work setting, see F. I. Steele, *Physical Settings and Organization Development*, Reading, A-W, 1973).

physical facilities themselves, (2) the organization's decision processes about facilities, (3) system rules about use of facilities, and (4) the environmental competence of the users.

The Physical Facilities Themselves

An obvious target for change is the shape of the physical setting itself. In a given situation, any number of improvements might be made—spaces opened up so that people are more visible to each other, materials used which allow influence and tinkering by the users, controls built in so that people can alter the amount of physical or social stimulation they receive, locations of people altered so that contact is easier for those who want it, brighter and more varied colors used to communicate more visual excitement and so on.

The key to these types of changes is an expanded view of human needs and how the environment impacts on them. If one uses traditional, narrow views of the setting as either a morale problem or a cost-minimization exercise, then design changes are not likely to make much real difference to the humanization process. (They are more like attempts to design a better zoo for the animal inmates.) What is required is a diagnostic stance toward the needs and styles of the employees with an expanded diagnostic model that includes human as well as economic factors. The writer uses such a model in his own work based on six functions of the setting,

1. Shelter and security
2. Symbolic identification (information communication)
3. Social contact
4. Task instrumentality
5. Pleasure
6. Growth

The writer's book in the Addison-Wesley Organization Development Series (Steele, 1973) contains a detailed description of these dimensions and their use in diagnosing the impact of an organization's physical settings.

One crucial feature worth special mention is the capacity of a setting for easy change as needs and users change. The more fixed a facility is, the more likely it is to represent a historical monument to past ways of working rather than a flexible tool for the present. To combat this rigidity, Robert Propst has designed an office furniture system specifically to encourage change and adaptation of the office as the user's needs or preferences change.* "Office Landscaping" (Buroland-schaft) is another example of an office system designed with components that can be rearranged at a lower cost (in time, energy, and money) than the usual office layout. If the organization encourages the use of this flexibility, these systems can be a useful contribution to more human, nonstatic environments.

Spatial Decision Processes

In the second and third sections of this paper, the writer described some modes of thinking which tend to promote top-down control of facilities decisions in organizations. If true humanization is to occur, these decision processes must be openly examined and new alternatives explored. No matter how beautiful employees' work spaces are, if they feel powerless to influence them, they will be dehumanized just by being there (the "animals in a comfortable zoo" image comes to mind again). By and large, the writer believes that those who use a setting are likely to have the best information about what functions that setting should provide.

The writer tries to help executives loosen their control over facilities as a part of their more general experimentation with the expansion of responsibility at lower levels in the organization. In addition, the writer encourages them to reduce their use of facilities decisions as symbolic statements about power distribution. The facilities have enough of a role to play in terms of work of the system, and there is a real cost in having them serve the double duty of ritual power demonstrations as well.

Rules About Use of Facilities

Another change target is the combination of formal policies and informal group norms which control how existing facilities

---

* Robert Propst, *The Office—A Facility Based on Change*, Zeeland, Herman Miller, Inc., 1968.

can be used or altered. A part of the person's alienation from his work setting results from the constraints placed on what he can do with it. Two main issues around this use are *personalization* and *utilization.*

Many rules and norms limit the extent to which individuals can personally influence their immediate work space through visual displays, rearranging furniture, adding new objects, changing colors or whatever. Constraints are no doubt necessary in some cases to maintain some sort of coordination, but the constraints often go far beyond this requirement and result in alienation of the person from his own place. One of the writer's indicators of the degree of humanization in a work setting is the extent to which there are visible personal droppings which provide clues as to who uses the setting and what they are like as people.*

The utilization issue is created by both norms and policies that limit how a setting can be used. An organization may have more facilities than it needs, yet people feel cramped because they are underutilizing these facilities. For example, a policy that limits the use of a board room to four quarterly meetings of the board of directors each year is very costly in a company that has few other meeting spaces, yet the writer has encountered numerous examples of just such policies. Similarly, a group often develops norms which prescribe appropriate settings for talking, reading, relaxing, holding impromptu meetings and so on. These norms usually block more varied uses for a given space and can be very costly in the long run.

For both personalization and utilization, the first step is an honest assessment of what exists in terms of current constraints on facilities use. This assessment is often resisted since it raises issues about taboo subjects such as differences in competence, but it is generally necessary to acknowledge current rules about use before they can be altered to provide richer opportunities for the members of the system.

---

* In contrast, many systems have anonymous droppings provided by the organization such as prescribed lines of furniture, art, plants, etc. These provide information about the *roles* people are fulfilling, but very little about the people themselves.

Environmental Competence of the Users

The writer's final change target is not concerned with the facilities themselves nor with characteristics of the social system, but with the competencies of the members themselves. One way to help people experience greater humanness in their settings is to help them become better able to use their own skills and abilities in those settings.

The writer sees environmental competence as having two components—(1) the person's ability to be aware of the surrounding environment and its impact on him, and (2) the person's ability to use or change his settings to help him achieve his goals without inappropriately destroying the setting or reducing his sense of effectiveness or that of the people around them.

This competence is not something that can be taken for granted, nor is it equally present in all people. Yet, most companies have spent next to nothing in developing this type of competence in their employees. Facilities changes are instituted with no attention to new skills or awareness that may be required to use the new facilities well. If the changes do not appear productive, the blame is usually placed on the design or on the intransigent employees rather than on the company's lack of provision of the developmental activities which should have been a natural part of a systematic change process.

If we really want settings to be more humane for employees, then we will also be willing to pay for some training, reflective experience and trial periods that will enhance users' environmental competence. These will be built into design projects as a natural parallel activity. If they are not, then there is some real question about the seriousness of the change intentions.

HOW LIKELY IS CHANGE?

Although the writer is convinced that changing physical settings and physical decision processes can help create more human work organizations, he must end on a somewhat pessimistic note. Most of the discussion here has been about what should or could be done to improve settings for human use, but how likely is it that these changes will be attempted in the average United States organization?

Some definite positive forces which should aid the process of change toward more human work settings include

1. An expanding interest on the part of behavioral scientists, economists, managers and public officials in the problems of dehumanization at work
2. A lower tolerance for regimentation on the part of younger employees in the United States work force
3. Cross-cultural experiences between countries, between companies and between different types of organizations fostered by the growth of multinational corporations which demonstrate that there is generally no single right way to do almost anything
4. The increasing frequency of organization development programs and other system-wide interventions which generate both an awareness of process and concrete activities which have a humanizing influence
5. An expanding interest in the field of environmental psychology, including the interaction between person and environment in the work setting*

On the whole, however, the writer would estimate that the average probability of real change in facilities management is low. Control of the physical setting is a very visible symbol of entrenched executive power; controlling things and how they are used is still considered to be a central indicator of power and status in the United States culture. Those who hold this power are unlikely to share it unless the balance of perceived incentive is changed. If it were seen to be in their own vested interests to allow greater subordinate impact on settings, then it might happen. It is probably more likely that subordinates may find some means of rearranging the balance of forces so

---

* For a sampling of sources in this developing specialty, see the following: Roger Barker, *Ecological Psychology*, Stanford, Stanford University Press, 1968; *Environment and Behavior* (a quarterly journal); E. T. Hall, *The Hidden Dimension*, Garden City, Doubleday, 1966.

that they can demand a certain minimum of control of their own life-space as a condition for being willing to participate in the system at all. Of the two routes, the writer suspects that real change is likely to occur more quickly if people become more aware of their own needs for self-control than it is if they sit and wait for higher-level executives to become keen on sharing their power.

ADDITIONAL READINGS OF INTEREST

Newman, O.: *Defensible Space.* New York, Collier Books, 1973.

Perrin, C.: *With Man in Mind.* Cambridge, MIT Pr, 1970.

Propst, R.: *The Office—A Facility Based on Change.* Zeeland, Herman Miller, Inc., 1968.

Proshansky, H.; Ittelson, W., and Rivlin, J.: *Environmental Psychology.* New York, HR&W, 1970.

Sommer, R.: *Personal Space: The Behavioral Basis of Design.* Englewood Cliffs, P-H (Spectrum), 1969.

Steele, F. I.: *Physical Settings and Organization Development.* Reading, Addison-Wesley, 1973.

Chapter 19

THE SEARCH FOR THE EFFECTIVE AND HUMANIZING WORK ORGANIZATION

FREDERIC R. WICKERT*

IMAGINE AN ORGANIZATION that would go to the trouble of first finding out each supervisor's leadership style and the climate in each of the many work teams in the organization, then matching supervisors and work teams on the basis of their mutual compatibility. Further imagine that each supervisor is encouraged to develop the leadership style which is most actualizing for him, and each work team doing a similar set of tasks is encouraged to operate differently from every other work team doing that similar set of tasks. What all this amounts to is that each work team is encouraged to develop a work team style most actualizing for the particular mix of persons in the team. The teams are not in any way forced to follow standardized practices. Now go one step beyond this and imagine that each work-level member of the organization is encouraged to join the work team that he feels is most actualizing for him or her. What a great place to work in! Here is humanizing to the nth degree.

Of course this extreme humanizing has a price tag. A great deal of time and other resources like money have to be spent finding out about varied preferences and styles and then doing all the matching that is needed, e.g., matching supervisors and work-level organization members and work teams. Nevertheless,

* Based on contribution to the Symposium on Humanizing Organizational Psychology, at the Convention of the American Psychological Association, Honolulu, Hawaii, 1972.

according to Lawler, in a freewheeling, informal talk he gave several years ago, the above represents real humanizing and could possibly be justified from an effectiveness as well as a humanizing point of view.

The search for both an effective and a humanizing work organization is hardly a recent phenomenon but obviously has been going on for a long time. There is every reason to think that this search will go on in the future for as long as work organizations exist.

Human progress toward the effective and humanizing work organization has taken place in a way very much like progress in other areas of human thought and corresponding action. The best way of handling a commonly-encountered, complex, persistent problem is discovered and exploited. As the bloom fades from a particular *one best way,* human inventiveness develops another *one best way.* The best of the most recently faded one best way is retained, but it is no longer the center of attention. Eventually the next one best way also fades to be replaced by still another. Nonetheless, something of each one best way, as it fades, usually remains and becomes absorbed into eclectic practice. Eclectic practice over the years is gradually enriched, and there is progress.

It is the purpose of this chapter to take into account relevant human inventions with respect to building effective and humanizing work organizations and then blend these inventions together to provide a comprehensive, eclectic statement of where we are now. It will be found that much of the essence of the preceding chapters reappears and joins together in this integrating chapter.

This chapter consists of two main sections. The first and far longer section develops the eclectic statement referred to above that portrays the rich array of human inventions that have been designed to date to build effective and humanizing work organizations. The second and shorter of these two sections reviews the four distinctive categories of contributions to this book—that is, its four parts—and relates them back to the eclectic statement.

THE MATRIX: INTRODUCTION

The comprehensive, eclectic statement is presented here in the form of what may loosely be referred to as a matrix. The two dimensions of the matrix are (1) the succession of one best ways, gradually developed by management theorists over a long period of time to make work organizations more effective and humanizing; and (2) the level of organization. The level-of-organization dimension is the familiar one that runs from the individual at one end of the scale through the work group or team somewhere in the middle, to the whole organization at the other end. The underlying idea is that one can make the organization more effective and/or humanizing by doing things or carrying out programs at each of the several levels. The cells formed by the intersections of the categories of each of the two dimensions of the matrix provide space to record how each one best way is expressed at each level. See Figure 19-1 for a rough sketch of such a matrix.

Rough Sketch of the Matrix

LEVELS

	Individual.................Small Group.......Whole Organization		
One Best Way$_1$	cell	cell	cell
One Best Way$_2$	cell	cell	cell
One Best Way$_n$	cell	cell	cell

Figure 19-1.

THE MATRIX:
THE SUCCESSION-OF-ONE-BEST-WAYS DIMENSION

Of the two dimensions of the matrix, the most basic one, and for this reason the logical one to begin with, is the chronological succession of one best ways.

Probably the earliest one best way, and one that persists in many subtle ways, yet is almost never mentioned in organization behavior texts, is the following. The best way to put together a work organization is to assemble a group of relatives and/or friends among whom there is a modicum of trust and inter-dependence. Paternalism, favoritism and buddy-ism will no doubt abound. Persons who join the organization later as it grows and who are not friends or buddies of the original inner group may feel left out, uninvolved and generally frustrated.

An example would be the form of business so common in East Asian cities that is built around the Chinese extended family. Far Eastern governments are reported to have been irritated for a long time by the limitations on their economic potential imposed by this form of business structure so dear to commercially dominant but minority-group businessmen. These businessmen allow only family members into the inner circle while members of the majority culture remain inconsequential, frustrated, low-level employees. Further, folklore has it that the size of business under this structure can include only up to about fifty or sixty persons and remain effective, with the consequence that business units remain too small to get into operations that technologically require a larger organization. It is true that in other cultures at other times this form of favoritism-governed organization has been used in much large-sized units, e.g., whole government in Europe up to about the time of the French Revolution.

Despite all the difficulties, this way more or less works, and worldwide it could still be the most commonly-found one best way to organize. The already-mentioned dehumanizing feeling of being left out can lead to disloyalty, subtle sabotage and other symptoms of organizational ineffectiveness. Moreover, this one best way, though the organization is humanizing for some of the inner group, represents a form of humanizing that is not well-distributed throughout the organization. Even many family members may feel put-upon, exploited and second-class citizens.

The one best way that came along next and was designed to overcome the family-buddy way to organize was Max Weber's ideal bureaucracy. Favoritism was displaced by impersonal, impartial, even mechanical organizational procedures. On the surface and by reputation, ideal bureaucracy would appear to be the very antithesis of effectiveness and humanizing. However, to the extent that it replaced politics and favoritism and introduced impartial interrelations among organization members and mechanical efficiencies to organizational functioning, it did something to dignify life by assuring more equal if not always satisfactory treatment to both bureaucracy members and the people to whom it provided services. All this is a kind of humanizing over what existed previously, at least for some people.

Closely related to Weber's conception of the ideal bureaucracy, the next one best way and sometimes merged with it, is looked on nowadays as rational, closed-system theory, the Theory X of McGregor. This theory in turn can be subdivided into two subtypes—(1) at the broad, total organization level the classical theory of Fayol, Urwick, Gulick and Koontz and (2) at lower organization levels, most commonly within the various manufacturing departments of an industrial company, the scientific management of Taylor, Gilbreth and the other early industrial engineers. Rational, closed-system theory at both total organization and manufacturing department levels systematized and rationalized work and thereby, especially when first installed, greatly enhanced organizational effectiveness if not degree of humanizing. Since managers and engineers earned respect for looking as though they knew exactly what they were doing, the organization could at least be humanizing for these classes of organization members. More important, the more effective work organizations poured out cheaper and better goods for the masses which, at that time, was considered as enhancing appreciably the quality of life.

Although it is easy to point out the dehumanizing effects of this one best way on employees (incidentally, the term *one best way* was possibly Taylorism's main device to dehumanize employee-level work), there were a variety of humanizing aspects for employees, surprisingly enough. In addition to the benefits of more and cheaper goods already mentioned, as has often been pointed out, Taylor himself saw that his precise study of motions and times and then getting employees to follow the methods the studies developed would work well only if individuals were selected who had the physiological and psychological capacities to perform the work. To the extent that this selection worked, scientific management could be considered humanizing. At the very least, the resulting industrial climate made selection testing and traditional industrial psychology wanted and acceptable. Later this industrial psychology made some contribution toward humanizing as it began making employee morale and motivation explicit goals for managements to try to achieve.

Then, too, at the time classical theory and Taylorism were riding high, there were actually also a number of other forms of humanizing around. However, it was the sort of humanizing that fitted the Zeitgeist and not what nowadays one would consider too satisfactory. For example, the personnel function, one of the essential classical management functions, was widely seen as a way to get employees' interests and welfare represented in top management deliberations. Personnel management during this era was often highly paternalistic yet it also was a form of expression of management's wanting to treat work-level employees as fellow human beings.

Despite what humanizing there was in classical-scientific management theory, its dehumanizing aspects were so much more apparent that the next one best way that came on the scene overreacted by being too humanizing if that is possible. This next one best way has become known as the human relations movement. Some well-known concepts of this movement are the informal group developed from the Hawthorne experience, McGregor's Theory Y and Likert's System 4. It also has been called *power equalization* and *influence without authority*. Its effectiveness for organizations has been seriously questioned but hardly its humanizing.

The following one best way, neoclassicism, was an attempt to merge the advantages of the old classical theory with its often clearly evident surface effectiveness on the one hand and human relations theory with its humanizing on the other. Such mergers sometimes even more or less worked.

From this point on in the search for effective and humanizing one best ways began to emerge in such profusion that instead of replacing the one best way that had gone on before, various advocacy groups and even cults developed their own one best ways, a number of which then came to coexist and even compete.

One such advocacy group was made up of organizational sociologists. They saw successful organizational adjusting to ever-changing technology as the key to organization effectiveness. For them, the effective organization was one that organized itself to handle and adjust to the changing technology it had to use to survive and grow against the competition of other similar organizations. Humanizing manifested itself, the little that it could, in organization members' satisfactions from their technical specialties. This whole theory has come to be called technological determinism. Technology was seen as determining organization structure and thereby the relations among organization members.

Another coexisting one best way was derived from the human relationists like McGregor. Its focus, in contrast to that of the technological determinists, was on process rather than structure. It is best known for its faith in the efficacy of group dynamics and sensitivity training. The most accurate name for this one best way is probably *typical group interpersonal interactionism* (Bowers, 1969) because of its assumption that the dynamics within any given small face-to-face group was about the same as that of any other such group. Further, typical group interpersonal interactionism achieved its applicability to the whole organization by assuming that the whole organization was nothing but a hierarchically-arranged collection of overlapping small groups. For example, assume that work groups A, B and C are independent and side-by-side, each with its own first-level supervisor. Now assume a second-level supervisor to whom the supervisors of work groups A, B and C report. Then it can be said that the second-level supervisor plus the first-level supervisors of work groups A, B and C make up a four-person small group separate from any of the three work groups. In turn, the second-level supervisor and his peers and their immediate superior go to make up a hierarchically higher typical group, separate from any of the hierarchically lower groups. One may analyze the organization into overlapping typical groups up to the group made up of the president and his vice-presidents or the chairman of the board and his board members. The key to the effective and humanizing organization then, according to the typical group interpersonal interactionists, lies in the processes taking place in each typical group, processes essentially analyzable in terms of those that take place inside T-groups. Interpersonal interactions in each such typical group would then lead to understanding and solving almost all organization problems at both a personal and an organizational level.

The proponents of this particular one best way certainly thought of themselves as being as humanizing as possible, but others saw this cult as dehumanizing. The others especially objected to the invasion of privacy, the discomforts of encountering, and other similar disagreeable and dehumanizing features of this one best way. Nevertheless its contributions have been legion, and with its variations it possibly still remains among the more popular if controversial sets of answers to problems of organizational effectiveness and humanizing.

Other recent one best ways, perhaps not yet fully developed but moving toward becoming so, are the two variations of open-system theory—planned open system theory and natural open system theory as well as two others, behavior modification theory and humanistic theory. The two variations of system theory mainly supplement and add to other theories. These two theories call attention to analyzing complex events into systems and subsystems so that each hierarchy of system is in turn considered, including humanizing aspects of the organization, its component subsystems and the organization itself as a subsystem in its environment, which in turn is simply looked on as a still larger system.

Planned on the one hand and natural open system theory on the other simply refer to the degree of planning involved. There is no doubt a degree of planning and a degree of naturalness in any human system that exists. Nevertheless, the planned open system school operates on the assumption that, within limits, the organization can do much to control relevant events inside and outside itself. The natural open system school, on the other hand, is far less sanguine (or more realistic) with respect to how much the organization, through planning, can control much if anything. One is reminded here of the long-standing controversy between the two extremes of leadership theory—the theory that a great leader like Napoleon can shape huge segments of human behavior versus the Tolstoian-type theory that the leader is but a small pawn in a field of forces so powerful as to be irresistible.

Behavior modification or Skinnerian theory is concerned with favoring positive rewards over aversive or negative ones when possible. These positive rewards or reinforcements are administered on an empirically discoverable schedule efficiently to induce desired behavior change. In social settings a series of reinforcement exchanges takes place between the changer and changee so that both are involved in a mutually-controlling exchange system so systems concepts enter in here. The mechanical, planned character of behavior modification made it at first blush appear to be dehumanizing even though it might be effective. Writers like Nord (1969) have shown that behavior modification need not be dehumanizing but could be as humanizing as McGregor's organizing scheme.

Humanistic theory is just beginning to be developed for practical work organization settings. Lawler's ideas about going to all the trouble of matching supervisors' styles of leading with the character of the available work groups, as presented in the opening paragraphs of this chapter, give some notion of what may be involved in this one best way.

It should also be recognized that most of the time in practical work organization settings today, one sees the application of a mix of one best ways. One should, then, expect mixes rather than pure types, despite the stress here on pure types.

By way of summary one might reflect back on the title of this chapter, "The Search for the Effective and Humanizing Organization." That search has been marked by a succession of one best ways. The emphasis of these one best ways has swung back and forth between effectiveness and humanizing, with always some of both in any for-the-moment-popular one best way. If any trend is discernible, it is probably toward more humanizing as American and Western European society generally matures, yet, with many not-very-humanizing rough spots remaining. Nevertheless, the search still goes on.

THE MATRIX:
THE LEVEL-OF-ORGANIZATION DIMENSION

The second dimension of the matrix, it will be recalled, is made up of a succession of levels which range from the individual to the work team to the whole organization. Each one best way takes on a somewhat different look at each level as will soon be shown in greater detail.

What the various levels along this second dimension should be has turned out to be more complex than the usual categorization of levels into individual-group-organization commonly found in organization behavior texts. Working with the matrix of one best ways and levels indicates that the following levels are needed to bring out the richness of several if not all of the one best ways.

The simplest level should be that of the individual. One makes the organization more effective and more humanizing by working with or on each individual one at a time. The idea at this level is that one can effect change by changing each individual one at a time through training, therapy, job enrichment or some other individualizing treatment.

There is a second way, however, a way often neglected in organization behavior texts, to operate at the individual level. Experimental and social psychology, in contrast to the clinical psychology focus on each whole individual, have abstracted out from individuals such processes common to many individuals, including, of course, organizational members, as attitudes, beliefs, emotions, stereotypes, motivations, perceptions, etc. Organizations may be made more effective and/or humanizing through working at this abstracted psychological processes level. An example would be doing surveys of attitudes including attitude feedback. Conducting an attitude survey feedback program and possibly adding to the program a propaganda campaign directed at influencing attitudes would be clear cases of attempting to work toward organizational effectiveness and humanizing through an abstracted process, attitudes.

The next level could be the dyad, the interactions that take place between two persons. There is a rich literature on the wide variety that exists of that dyadic interaction familiarly called the interview. The counseling interview has from time to time been seen as the answer to all organizational effectiveness and humanizing problems (Dickson and Roethlisberger, 1966). Also, whole organizations may be visualized as nothing but collections of overlapping superior-subordinate pairs with each superior being involved in quite a few pairs as a member of a dyad with each one of his subordinates. As with counseling, a focus on superior-subordinate dyads has been seen as the key to solving managerial organizational human problems. An example would be the M.B.O. or management by objectives periodic session between each superior and each of his subordinates in the organization.

One step up from the dyad is the small face-to-face group— the work crew or team or even the committee. At this level, movement toward the effective and humanizing organization takes place through concentrating on the development of intra-small group functioning, e.g., the functioning of a committee.

Following the small group is a level which, in recent years, is finally beginning to get the attention it deserves, namely that of intergroup relations. The view at this level is that the key to organization improvement lies in getting those groups, which are obviously parts of the same organization and should always have the best interests of that organization in mind, to collaborate instead of counterproductively fight each other. Examples would be relations between work groups engaged in a sequential production process, the day shift and the night shift, organization functions like production and sales where production wants long, uniform runs while sales wants outputs tailor-made for each customer.

Beyond intergroup relations comes the level of the whole organization. The approach at this level is to change the whole organization or some important facet of it. For example, one facet, the changing of which could lead to a greater degree of organizational effectiveness and/or humanizing, is the reward structure; a change in reward structure could change the whole organization over time as the effects of the change permeate the organization.

Last, and at the most complex level, is the attempt at change by changing the organization's environment or some significant aspect of it so that the organization will have to react in a new and hopefully improved way. An example would be a new law that would require the organization to behave differently.

So much, then, for the points along the levels dimension. As is true of the one-best-way dimension, any particular program for making an organization more effective and/or humanizing could well involve a mix of points along the levels dimension. For example, Blake and Mouton's (1969) organization development format involves first working with the "behavior dynamics" of work teams in an organization (the small face-to-face group level), then doing things with "the interworkings between organized units of the company where cooperation and coordination is vital to success" (the intergroup relations levels), and finally a series of planning and implementing operations at corporate level (the whole organization level). Elsewhere they report that it is useful for organization members of manager status to have gone through sensitivity training (the individual level) before beginning the other organization development procedures.

THE MATRIX:
INTRODUCTION TO CELL CONTENT

The two dimensions or axes of the matrix have now been laid out. To construct the matrix itself (refer again to Fig. 19-1) let us draw the one-best-way dimension as the vertical axis and the organization level dimension as the horizontal axis. The cells formed by the intersections of the categories of the two dimensions become available space in which to write out how each one best way would manifest itself at each organization level (matrix rows) as well as how each organization level is handled by each one best way (matrix columns).

No definitive generally agreed on matrix based on the intersections of these two dimensions has been prepared, although at least one attempt has been made (Wickert, 1972). Of what value would such a filled-in matrix be? To what uses might it be put? Experience to date suggests two sets of uses—(1) general and theoretical and (2) specific and practical. With respect to general uses, students report that for the first time they understand the whole parade of organization theories and their relevance for mastering the folklore every management student is expected to master. The filled-in matrix could organize the complex field of organizational behavior for the teacher and researcher as well. The researcher, for example, could examine carefully the content of cells at each row and column intersection to see how adequate or inadequate they were. Cells with inaccurate or little or inadequate or even no content could be ripe for research development.

At the more specific, practical level the matrix may be useful for both the manager considering or using an organization development program and the organization development consultant. The manager, for his part, could identify each of the cells within which the organization development program proposed as taking place in his organization, and determine how it was to operate or was actually operating. He could raise searching questions with his consultant that would get his consultant to defend his concentration on some cells and his neglect of others. The consultant whose approach was narrowly limited by his cult orientation might soon find himself with fewer consulting jobs. The organization consultant, for his part, would be alerted by the matrix to take the whole range of known possibilities into account before deciding on some specific point on which to concentrate his attack.

A paragraph from a recent article by Zand (1974) illustrates clearly the problem faced by the manager who is exposed to too narrow a personal or organizational development focus or set of organization theories (in matrix language, to too limited a number of cells) by his particular training or organization development program. The paragraph reads,

> The manager's confusion is sometimes compounded by laboratory-method, organizational development programs. Sensitivity training, grid laboratories, and variations of group methods focus on improving the manager's skill in individual and group behavior, but rarely introduce relevant organization theory. When a manager applies his new knowledge to his formal organization, he usually encourages open questioning of goals and methods, which blurs formal boundaries between jobs. Other managers interpret his action as undermining authority and disrupting the formal organization, so they resist and discard his changes. The manager is in theoretical limbo; without concepts he cannot explain to other managers what he is doing in terms they can understand.

The writer does not think that the confused manager in Zand's paragraph is going to get himself out of his difficult situation by pulling a copy of this matrix out of his pocket and showing it to his fellow managers. He does think, however, that his comparing the rows and columns within which he is operating and those within which his fellow managers are operating will give him some ways of seeing for himself what he is doing in an understandable, theoretical frame of reference; then he will be in a position to explain to his colleagues what he is doing in their terms. Theories (or one best ways) all in relation to each other are made explicit by the matrix for all to see.

THE MATRIX:
SPECIFIC EXAMPLES OF CELL CONTENT

To communicate something of matrix content, below are developed the matrix rows for two rather different one best ways. Each row shows what each of the two one best ways might do to make effective and humanizing organizations at each of the several organization levels. These row statements might not be too polished, but they will give the flavor of the possibilities.

The first one best way worked out here is the scientific

management at manufacturing department or shop level combined with classical organization theory at the higher organization level.

With respect to the entry in the first cell in the scientific management row and the whole individual column of the matrix, the entry might be thin because scientific management on the surface was supposed to have little to say about the whole individual. Nevertheless, describers of scientific management delight to point out how Taylor himself carefully considered the overall temperament of each worker, the worker as a whole person. Then, with respect to the next column—that is, abstract psychological processes—it needs to be pointed out that scientific management also considered appropriate physical characteristics of employees—height, weight and energy level. The best known example is that of the Pennsylvania Dutchman whose behavior Taylor was supposed to have so carefully regulated as he so efficiently moved the pigs of iron from one spot to another. This Dutchman was picked by Taylor for his phlegmatic temperament, his huge physical size and his energy (recall how, after working long hours for Taylor, he could run up a mountain and work on building his house there by moonlight). The incentive plans of scientific management assumed that workers had highly rational, self-interested, economic man motivations, yet were technically not too bright so that they could be permitted little or no technical discretion. On the other hand, managers as human beings, with their special set of abstracted processes, were not only rational but omniscient, omnipotent, not to be questioned and preferably engineers by education and training. All this should be squeezed into the *Individual* cell for this row.

When it came to the dyad and the small group level, neither scientific management nor classical management paid much attention. At the small group level occasional and reluctant use was made of group incentive plans, but preference was to work with each individual worker. Taylor, of all the scientific management industrial engineers, made a special point of suggesting the idea of functional foremen to handle the complexities of the leadership of the work group, but this idea never commanded much of a following, probably because of its conflict with the classical theory dictum of one man, one boss.

At the intergroup level, the classical one best way, if it were asked about the matter, probably would say that one should draw clear lines of responsibility and authority to minimize conflict. Staff and line should keep to their places. When appropriate, as among sales groups or even parallel production units, intergroup competitions could be held with prizes awarded to the winners. The writer once knew a forge foreman who clearly used this form of classical theory. He divided his total crew into the two principal ethnic groups, blacks and Poles, and week after week these two groups fiercely competed to outproduce the other group for more piece-rate paid out money as well as for greater honor.

At the whole organization level there could be a number of ways of making the organization more effective (and humanizing, if humanizing occurred to top management at all). One way would be to redraw the organization chart and watch organization members change their behavior to fit the job titles on the new chart and thereby hopefully make the organization more effective. Related would be a new division of labor plus new and more searching control and coordination procedures. Rational propaganda could help the cause. Drives could be put on to cut costs, temporarily forbid adding new people, etc. What humanizing there was often took a rationalist-paternalist approach —if I, the top management give you, the workers, some benefit such as a year-end bonus, then you, the workers, out of gratitude, will be more loyal and work harder.

At the environmental level the free enterprise system, under which outside interferences with company operations were as few and far between as possible, was espoused. If government did have to intervene through regulations, laws and taxes, these would be rationally and automatically obeyed.

One can begin to see by this time that the interpretation of what a given one best way advocates at a particular level is based to some extent on guessing and conjecture. At the same time, however, one begins to see a pattern of behaviors emerging that quite thoroughly and fairly characterize each particular one best way.

Now, by way of great contrast, let us turn to the typical group interpersonal interactionist row to see what that group of theorists would advocate at each level (or matrix column). At the individual level, preferably every organization member, but at least all managers, would be required to undergo sensitivity training or one of its more recent variants such as encountering. In this way each individual would be sensitized to all other individuals, and everyone would behave admirably toward everyone else. Sensitivity training of each individual, if nothing else were done, would go a long way toward both making effective and humanizing the organization. Many problems, including those in dyads, would simply disappear in the resulting delightful, open and trusting organizational climate.

With respect to small groups, the small group situation becomes the *sine qua non* for carrying out the program of sensitivity training. Beyond its central training use, the open and trusting work team, trained as a team to be open and trusting to every other team member, would work far more effectively and humanizingly than the mistrustful work team in the mine run of nonsensitivity-training-exposed organizations. The resistances to change so characteristic of informal small groups in industry would disappear as the boundaries between formal and informal groups themselves broke down in the open and trusting climate within all groups.

As concerns intergroup problems, Blake and Mouton (1969) type intergroup sensitivity training would be so conducted that each working team or organization function would be sensitized to each other, then work more effectively and humanizingly with all these other working teams or organization functions. As Blake and Mouton describe this process, it is a long, perhaps neverending one (1969). There is also the danger that needed structural changes might be neglected because of the strong process rather than structural emphasis characteristic of the sensitivity training orientation.

At the whole organization level, to achieve effectiveness and humanizing ends, not unexpectedly there would be a series of process rather than structural interventions by a change agent team. That change agent team would attempt to get the people in the organization not to concentrate on rearranging organization structure to improve the organization although some structural modifications could develop as a consequence. Rather, the change agent team would concentrate on making the organization more effective and humanizing by getting organization members to study, then improve interpersonal and intergroup processes. Beer, in his typical group interpersonal interactionist approach to organization development in this book (Chap. 15), stresses that the path to success is to change behavior, presumably through process, and then the other desired events hopefully will follow. Structural changes can then be made to support behavioral changes. In his experience he says that to change structure alone is likely to accomplish little (Chap. 15).

At the level of initiating change in the environment of the focal organization in order to move it toward becoming more effective and humanizing, the typical group interpersonal interactionists have been creating a climate through their writing and talking that indicates that their program is receiving widespread acceptance and works well in a wide variety of real-life organizations. In so doing they have created a cultural climate that extends beyond the boundaries of any one company and is supportive of using their set of techniques. In addition, they have also organized a set of formal consulting organizations that further legitimizes their activities.

We have now seen two of the rows of the matrix developed for two rather different one best ways. It is obvious that there is nothing very sacred about the particular way these two one best ways were described here. Almost anyone could come along and polish these two sets of descriptions. The point is that once the vertical and horizontal dimensions have been adequately delineated, filling in cell content becomes to a large extent an exercise in expressing individual preferences. Nevertheless, some suggested cell content, such as that contained in the descriptions of the two rows given here, is clearly helpful for communicating the specific nature of the matrix.

THE MATRIX AND THIS BOOK

The matrix developed in this chapter, first with its thoroughgoing historic perspective and its optimistic utilization of the best of the past, and second with its built-in cross references to each of the various sizes of people units or levels, serves as a convenient frame of reference to pull together the book as a whole. In addition, concepts found in each of the book's four parts will frequently be observed to stretch and enrich the matrix in its role as an inclusive frame of reference and even to suggest significant additions or refinements to it.

Part I of the book, with its emphasis on the contemporary scene and the problems industrial society is currently facing with respect to the members of work organizations, represents a collection of statements that present a compelling case for continuing and extending humanizing efforts. It also touches on some matters that stretch the matrix. Its mention of factors in the general culture that create the need for humanizing suggests that the organization environment extreme of the succession of levels dimension might also well include the general culture within which organizations necessarily must exist. Its mention of minorities and women and unions and their members also suggests possibilities for the matrix; unions as a rational economic response at a rather inclusive people level indicates that a cell entry where the relevant row and column intersect should say how unions play a collective bargaining role for a significant part of organization members. Unions, as an emotional response, need to be worked into cell content in several rows and columns.

Part II of the book, with its concern for diagnosis, represents one of the many uses to which the matrix may be put. The matrix, with its display of cells arising from the intersections of the two dimensions, becomes an important diagnostic tool. The matrix also suggests areas already receiving enough or more than enough attention as well as areas needing more attention. In this way the matrix could serve as an additional tool in the organizational diagnostician's kit.

Part III, the individual and the organization, has two rather separate connections with the matrix. First, Part III invites attention to the individual in the organizational setting, a concern of the first column of the matrix. One can let his eye follow down the *Individual* column in the matrix to ascertain the extent to which and the way in which each one best way, with its distinctive and enduring contributions, treats the individual and develops expectations about the individual's role in the organization. Similarly, one can look down the row of cells in the *Organization* column to see how each one best way perceives the organization as a setting within which the individual organization member necessarily lives. The individual organization member, as such a look will demonstrate, has a strange conglomeration of organizational nuances to put up with in his life as an organization member.

Part III has a second impact. Its making explicit the relation between the individual and the organization suggests that each scale point on the various sizes of people unit dimension could be related to every other scale point, e.g., the relation between the individual and the small group or work team, the individual and significant organizational intergroups as well as the individual and the whole organization. The development of all these interrelationships is beyond the scope of this paper, but it remains a further job to be done eventually.

Part IV, of all the four parts of the book, is most congruent with the matrix. Each chapter in Part IV discusses one or more organization development (O.D.) issues or methods. These O.D. issues or methods concern ways of making the organization more effective and humanizing. Each one of these issues or methods can be located in one to several cells in the matrix with little or no modification.

The matrix, in summary, has in large part although perhaps not completely, stood up to the complex and difficult task of serving as a unifying frame of reference for the book as a whole. It may come to represent a useful and used way, at least until some better arrangement is invented, of reminding us of how the apparently hopelessly countless and disparate facets of the search for the effective and humanizing organization can nevertheless be brought together and handled with a substantial degree of conceptual unity.

THE BOOK AND THE MATRIX

It is the book, obviously, and not the matrix that makes up the flesh and blood of organizational humanizing. The matrix is merely one possible kind of skeleton that tries to hold together the many aspects of this area of vital human concern.

These nearly the last pages of both this chapter on the matrix and the book might well exploit a key concept from the matrix— the environment of both the work organization and this book. The environment of work organizations today is obviously pervaded by humanizing. Moreover, humanizing is clearly the dominant force in the environment that has prompted this book. The point has been reached in this chapter and book where one should ask what is happening out there in that environment that provides thoughts appropriate to bring all this to a memorable conclusion.

Basil J. Whiting (1974), from his strategic position in the Ford Foundation, comments on the forces surrounding one humanizing device—job enrichment. His remarks could readily be extended to apply more generally to all humanizing of work life.

Whiting points to four "fundamental pressures" that he sees will make the nature of work, particularly its humanizing, more salient during the last quarter of this century. Two of the pressures are for greater human productivity and growing world-wide competition and the energy and materials crisis. Both of these call for the intelligent and loyal participation of organization members in collectively making millions of decisions in support of the specific organizations they work for and the society of which they are members. It will be useful for work organizations and the societies in which they are embedded to humanize work situations to the fullest degree possible in order to create a collaborative climate between them and their members. For their part the members themselves will be under great pressure to cooperate, but they will be more enthusiastic and ingenious about cooperating on the largely unobserved and uncontrolled decisions they are to make if the work climate is more rather than less humanizing.

The remaining two pressures particularly characterize the situation within Western and American culture and may not be quite so world-wide as the first two. These pressures are the enormous increase in the educational levels of organization members and the concomitant and nagging problem of the perceived, if not always actual, underutilization at work of organization members' knowledge and skills. These last two pressures not only suggest the promise of humanizing—that humanizing has a real chance of taking place since available will be high levels of understanding generated by high levels of education well-distributed throughout work organizations—but also the challenge to humanizing—that the work of organizations is perceived as mostly flat and uninteresting and deficient in good jobs that utilize the high level of education in the work force.

Whiting goes on to point out that the above pressures will reinforce other on-going trends—(1) "competition for the society's relatively few 'good' jobs will intensify; (2) pressures for improvements in pay, working conditions, and benefits will increase; (3) programs in adult and continuing education will develop more rapidly." Further developments may include (1) "an increase in social problems deriving from status inconsistency; (2) the gradual moderation of the American success ethic by a 'suffice' ethic; and (3) a possible increase in the political constituency supporting egalitarian social and economic policies."

It is clear that in the environment sketched above humanizing of work life has a series of intricate involvements. The hope is that the eclectic approach of this book and that of the matrix in its own small way will have made a contribution by calling attention to the most significant facets of humanization in the world of work of today and the next several decades and the ways in which these facets interlock and interact.

REFERENCES

Beer, M.: Improving organizational effectiveness through planned change and development. In Meltzer, H., and Wickert, F.: *Humanizing Organizational Behavior.* Springfield, Thomas, 1976.

Blake, R. R., and Mouton, J. S.: *Building a Dynamic Corporation Through Grid Organization Development.* Reading, A-W, 1969.

Bowers, D. G.: *Work Organizations as Dynamic Systems.* Technical Report. Ann Arbor, University of Michigan, Institute for Social Research, September 30, 1969.

Dickson, W. J., and Roethlisberger, F. J.: *Counseling in an Organization: A Sequel to the Hawthorne Researches.* Boston, Harvard University, Graduate School of Business Administration, 1966.

Nord, W. R.: Beyond the teaching machine: Operant conditioning in management. *Organizational Behavior and Human Performance, 4:*375-401, 1969.

Whiting, B. J.: Job enrichment: Some future trends? *Public Opinion Quarterly, 38:*432-433, 1974.

Wickert, F. R.: Recent writing in organizational psychology and theory. In Piret, R. (Ed.): *Proceedings, XVIIth International Congress of Applied Psychology, Liege, Belgium, August, 1971.* Brussels, Editest, 1972.

Zand, D. E.: Collateral organization: A new change strategy. *J Appl Beh Sci, 10:*65, 1974.

─────── Chapter 20 ───────

ON ORGANIZATIONS OF
THE FUTURE*

CHRIS ARGYRIS

INTRODUCTION

THE MOST CRITICAL fact about present complex organizations is that they are infected with dry rot, a cancerous illness that threatens to disable and cripple seriously their effectiveness and efficiency. Consequently, the citizenry has become increasingly disenchanted with organizations. The youth who someday will be asked to manage these systems may become (or have become) so disillusioned that they may seek ways to alter them, destroy them or bypass them (and none of these strategies is presently viable).

One way to begin to overcome these problems is to base the new organizational designs upon a richer and more complex view of man. Organizations should be designed to achieve their objectives in such a way that their employees are encouraged to be less pawns and more origins, less concerned with conformity and more with growth, less passive and more activist, less compliant and more self-responsible. Under such conditions, technical competence and substantive excellence will be even more highly

─────────
* These excerpts from "On Organizations of the Future," by Chris Argyris are reprinted from Sage Professional Paper in Administrative and Policy Studies series Volume I, Number 03-006. © 1973 by permission of the Publisher, Sage Publications, Inc.

valued, more easily identified and rigorously protected and rewarded.

In examining the organizational literature, two trends seem relevant. First, with one exception, few groups of organizational theorists have taken the problems identified above seriously. Second, those scholars who have taken these issues seriously have tended to underestimate or ignore the importance of first changing the *behavior* of the participants, especially those at the top, to mirror and make credible the new organizational ethic that takes human beings seriously. They have conducted research on how to design new organizational structure, new management information systems and new control systems that could encourage human realization and organizational effectiveness. Yet, experience to date suggests that employees are justifiably reticent about believing in management's commitment to these new ideas because, whenever administrators behave, their behavior does not mirror the rhetoric of humane organizations.

Finally, when one focuses seriously on helping people learn the new behavior so well that it does not wash out under stress, one discovers quickly that this will be a very difficult task to accomplish. The new organizations will require competences that may require basic value and behavioral changes that may more than match the changes that individuals are typically required to make during their lifetime.

ORGANIZATIONAL DETERIORATION: A MAJOR FORCE FOR CHANGE

There are several reasons why organizations are going to have to change if they are to survive in the future. Public and private organizations are increasingly disappointing their consumers with the quality of their services and products. Ralph Nader and the appointment of consumer representatives at various levels of government are but two indications of consumer unrest. Public organizations are coming under careful scrutiny, especially in the large cities where they seem to show remarkable capacity to consume increasing amounts of taxpayers' money, yet provide a constant or decreasing quality of service. The result is that the consumers feel that they are being shortchanged and simultaneously have decreasing influence on altering their organizations (Kaufman, 1969; Long, 1971; and Smith, 1971). The structure and functioning of universities are also under serious challenge by students and faculty (Newman, 1971).

Public and private organizations seem to be full of internal conflict that cannot be surfaced or discussed; they are surrounded by an increasingly disappointed if not hostile environment designed with, and managed through, the use of concepts that tend to reinforce the forces toward ineffectiveness, leading to a self-sealing cluster of trends slowly but surely leading to a social explosion. The most optimistic prediction made recently has been by Schon (1971) who suggests that organizations will gravitate toward a steady state of "dynamic conservatism" where survival will be their central focus while learning and innovation will be difficult, unrewarded and, in some cases, not sought. Argyris has predicted that public and private organizations are presently designed and managed in such a way that they will exhibit "organizational entropy"—that is, slow deterioration (Argyris, 1964 and 1968). Under the more or less optimistic diagnosis there is agreement that organizations are able to produce valid information for unimportant problems and invalid information for the important and threatening problems.

One can conceive of a future for our society where thousands of organizations will exist, each chugging along, producing marginal services and products at increasing costs. At the same time the organizations will tend to increase the strength, vitality and rootedness of their self-sealing, antilearning, resistance-to-change forces. In the public sector the regulatory agencies designed to keep organizations in the service of society will also manifest the same problem of dry rot.

To the extent that the consumers feel frustrated and helpless they may strive to coerce change through legislation. However, it is doubtful that one can legislate effectively against apathy, noninvolvement and organizational entropy. Ironically, such legislation could also be supported by the employees who, also feeling helpless, may view its passage as reinforcement for the wisdom of their withdrawal and the accuracy of their view that organizations are deteriorating. These may be some of the reasons that have led John Gardner (1968) to conclude that it is not unrealistic to think that in the foreseeable future our society could come crumbling down because the organizations upon which it was built were full of dry rot and unresponsive to their environment.

If this perspective is valid, then there are millions of youths who are growing up in the milieu where public and private organizations are seen as deteriorating and the consumer is ignored. It is not likely that youth will accept this legacy without reacting. One very clear trend is the genuine questioning of the present modes of designing and managing organizations. Organizational authority that was revered, cherished and aspired to as symbolic of status and competence is slowly becoming mistrusted and condemned; and the major aspirations evolving around it seem to concern how to destroy it (Bennis and Slater, 1968; Katz and Georgeopoulos, 1971; and McGregor, 1960). Miner (1971) has shown that the cause of student activism was less due to a minority of extremists and due more to the low student levels of competitive motivation and negative attitudes toward authority figures and toward assuming managerial roles in bureaucracies. This is even true for the more conservative samples of our population. Ewing (1971) has reported a survey of a large sample of *Harvard Business Review* readers. He notes that they are clearly questioning the traditional view of organizational authority, and he predicts that organizations of the future will spend much more energy in developing genuine member involvement.

One can predict that one of management's primary concerns in the future will be how to prevent their organizations from being torn apart by younger members who push for internal changes and older members who, knowing of no viable alternatives, fight hard to maintain the posture of dynamic conservatism.

Management will therefore strive hard to tighten up their ship. New controls will be developed. However, given the underlying logic of present control systems, they will tend to be the wrong response to the right problem. The problem is the members' increasing lack of responsibility and commitment, but the cause may be the very control systems (and organizational structures) that are used in the first place.

Consumers will escalate their demands for increasing effectiveness. Since these demands will probably not be fulfilled, the consumer will request further involvement and control. This, in turn, will probably make managers even more uptight, and they will design even tighter controls.

The youth may feel doubly angered and frustrated. They may view organizations as products of their elders and see little need to show the reverence paid to them by their creators. They may demand that organizations be redesigned to fit a new, more complex model of man. They will not be satisfied with blue ribbon commissions that move organizational boxes around, or information from science-based experts who basically do the same thing underneath the apparent complexity of computer models or information systems.

There is no evidence, to the writer's knowledge, that the youth have any workable organizational models to substitute for the present ones. If one examines the attempts of some to create new organizations, one must conclude that their systems are designed in a way that almost denies any necessity for specialization of work, for differential power and for information. The results are primitive communes which one scholar suggests may be doomed to failure (Kanter, 1970). The majority of the youth, however, tend to enter into traditional organizations, but are increasingly restive about living under such conditions for very long.

What Are the Causes of Organizational Deterioration?

There is a growing body of literature that is exploring the causes of organizational deterioration. Basically, these scholars tend to see some of the causes (but not the only causes) as stemming from the oversimplified view of man assumed by traditional organizational designs and the lack of attention paid to the way people actually deal with one another as individuals (interpersonal relations) or in groups (group dynamics) while making decisions, plus the realities of intergroup rivalries and organizational norms that support these activities (Argyris, 1964; Bennis, 1966; Golembiewski, 1967, 1969; Herzberg, 1966; Katz and Kahn, 1966; Likert, 1967; McGregor, 1960; Marrow, Bowers, and Seashore, 1967; Maslow, 1970; Tannenbaum, 1968; and Whyte, 1969).

Recently the writer has attempted to summarize some of the findings of this group regarding human and organizational problems at the lower and upper levels (Argyris, 1971).

Characteristics of the Lower-Level World

1. Work is highly specialized and fractionalized; it is broken down to the simplest possible motions. It is assumed that the easier the work, (a) the greater the productivity, (b) the shorter the training time needed, (c) the greater the flexibility for interchangeability of the workers, and (d) the greater the satisfaction of the employee because the less the frustration and/or responsibility that he will need to shoulder.

2. Responsibility for planning the work, defining production rates and maintaining control over speed is placed in the hands of management and not in the hands of those actually producing.

3. Responsibility for hiring employees, issuing orders, changing work, shifting employees, evaluating performance, defining and disbursing rewards and penalties is vested in top management.

The exact degree to which these assumptions or premises are followed varies with the organization.

Characteristics of the Managerial World

1. The higher up they go in the organizational hierarchy, the more individuals are able, if they wish, to alter the system. They are not as bound by the structure, technology and control systems as are the members at the lower level. Assuming as we have from the outset that the members have the necessary technical competence, we see that the biggest barriers to change at the upper levels are the interpersonal relationships, the group and intergroup relationships, and the system's norms. These

barriers to effectiveness are rarely potent when the system is dealing with routine, programmed and nonthreatening information. The barriers become especially difficult to identify and overcome when the system is dealing with innovative, nonprogrammed and threatening information.

2. Why do administrators tend to create interpersonal, group and intergroup relations that inhibit system competence precisely when it is most needed? Part of the answer to that question is that they are programmed from an early age with interpersonal incompetence (Argyris, 1968). The cause of the incompetence lies in the fact that most people who aspire toward positions of power and are educated in our schools are taught to internalize the values of the engineering-economic-technological world which dominate our lives.

The writer's research indicates that there are three such identifiable values. They are

(a) The significant human relations are the ones which have to do with achieving the organization's objective. In studies of over 265 different types and sizes of meetings, the indications are that executives almost always tend to focus their behavior on getting the job done. In literally thousands of units of behavior almost none shows that men spend some time in analyzing and maintaining their group's effectiveness. This is true even though in many meetings the group's effectiveness was bogged down and the objectives were not being reached because of interpersonal factors. When the executives are interviewed and asked why they did not spend some time in examining the group operations or processes, they reply that they are there to get a job done. They add, "If the group isn't effective, it is up to the leader to get it back on the track by directing it."

(b) Cognitive rationality is to be emphasized; feelings and emotions are to be played down. This value influences executives to see cognitive, intellectual discussions as relevant, good, workable and so on. Emotional and interpersonal discussions tend to be viewed as irrelevant, immature and not workable.

As a result, when emotions and interpersonal variables become blocks to group effectiveness, all the executives report feeling they should *not* deal with them. For example, in the event of an emotional disagreement they would tell the members to get back to facts or to keep personalities out of it.

(c) Human relationships are most effectively influenced through unilateral direction, coercion and control as well as by rewards and penalties that sanction all three characteristics. This third value of direction and control is implicit in the chain of command and in the elaborate managerial controls that have been developed within organizations.

3. The impact of these values upon the interpersonal relationships within an organization is to create a pattern of behavior which may be identified as Pattern A. The ideology of Pattern A may be summarized briefly as follows.

To the extent that individuals dedicate themselves to the value of rationality and getting the job done, they will tend to be aware of and emphasize the rational, intellective aspects of the interactions that exist in an organization and to suppress the interpersonal and emotional aspects, especially those that do not seem to be relevant to achieving the task. For example, one frequently hears in organizations, "Let's keep feelings out of the discussion," or "Look here, our task today is to achieve objective X and not to get emotional."

As the interpersonal and emotional aspects of behavior become suppressed, we may hypothesize that an organizational norm will tend to arise that coerces individuals to hide their feelings. Their interpersonal difficulties will either be suppressed or disguised and brought up as rational, technical or intellectual problems. In short, receiving or giving feedback about interpersonal relationships will tend to be suppressed.

Under these conditions, we may hypothesize that individuals will find it difficult to develop competence in dealing with feelings and interpersonal relationships. In a world in which the expression of feelings is not permitted one may hypothesize that the individuals will build personal and organizational defenses to help them suppress their own feelings or inhibit others in their attempts to express their feelings. If feelings are suppressed, the tendency will be for the individual not to permit himself or others to own their feelings. For example, the individual may say about himself, "No, I didn't mean that," or "Let me start over again. I'm confusing the facts." Equally possible, one individual may say to another, "No, you shouldn't feel that way;" or "That's not effective executive behavior;" or "Let's act like mature people and keep feelings out of this."

4. Another way to prevent individuals from violating the organizational values of rationality and from embarrassing one another is to block out or refuse to consider (consciously or unconsciously) ideas and values which, if explored, could expose suppressed feelings. Such a defensive reaction in the organization may eventually lead to a barrenness of intellectual ideas as well as values. The participants will tend to limit themselves to those ideas and values that are not threatening so they will not violate organizational norms. The individuals in the organization will tend to decrease their capacity to be open to new ideas and values. As the degree of openness decreases, the capacity to experiment will tend to decrease, and the fear of taking risks will tend to increase. As the fear of taking risks increases, the probability of experimentation is decreased and the range or scope of openness is decreased, which in turn decreases risks. We have a closed circuit that could be an important cause of the loss of vitality in an organization.

To summarize, to the extent that participants are dedicated to the values implicit in the formal organization, they will tend to create a social system in which the following will tend to *decrease*:

Receiving and giving nonevaluative feedback.
Owning and permitting others to have their own ideas, feelings and values.
Openness to new ideas, feelings and values.
Experimentation, risk-taking and new ideas and values.

If these characteristics do decrease, hypothesize that the

members of the system will tend not to be aware of the interpersonal impact upon others. If individuals are in social systems in which they are unable to predict accurately their personal impact upon others and the impact of others upon them, they may begin to feel confused. "Why are people behaving that way toward me?" "Why do they interpret me incorrectly?" Since such questions are not sanctioned in a rationally-dominated system, much less answered, the confusion tends to turn to frustration and feelings of failure regarding interpersonal relations. In an attempt to maintain their sense of esteem the members may react by questioning the honesty and genuineness of the interpersonal behavior of their fellow workers. Simultaneously, they may place an even greater emphasis upon the rational and technical interactions in which they are probably experiencing a greater degree of success. The increased emphasis upon rationality will act to suppress the feelings even more; this, in turn, will decrease the probability that the questions of confusion and the mistrust of self and others will be explored.

As interpersonal mistrust increases, and as the capacity (individual and organizational) to cope with this mistrust decreases, the member may tend to adapt by playing it safe. The predisposition will be to say those things that cannot be misunderstood and to discuss those issues for which there exist clear organizational values and sanctions. The desire to say the right thing should be especially strong toward one's superiors, toward one's peers with whom one is competing, and toward one's subordinates who may bypass their superiors. As a result, conformity begins to develop within an organization. Along with conformity, the interpersonal relationships will tend to be characterized by *conditional acceptance* (to use a Rogerian concept), and the members will tend to feel accepted if they behave in accordance with certain organizational specifications. Because of the existence of mistrust, conformity and dependence, it may be hypothesized that the members' commitment to the organization will tend to be external as far as interpersonal activities are concerned. By external commitment, the writer means that the source of commitment to work for any given individual lies in the power, rewards and penalties that individual may use as influence. Internal commitment exists when the motive for a particular behavior resides within, for example, self-realization. A certain amount of internal commitment restricted to rational activities may be possible in this system if the rational, intellective aspects of the job are consonant with the individual's abilities and expressed needs.

External commitment will tend to reinforce the conformity with conditional acceptance of, and especially dependence upon, the leader. The subordinates will tend to look for cues from the leader and will be willing to be influenced and guided by him. In fact, they may develop great skill in inducing the leader to define the problems, the range of alternatives and so on. The subordinates will tend to operate within limits that they know to be safe. As the dependence increases, the need for the subordinates to know where they stand will also tend to increase.

Thus, interpersonal mistrust, conformity, conditional acceptance, external commitment and dependence tend to be outputs of decreasing interpersonal competence. Each of these attitudes feeds back to reinforce itself. All, in turn, feed back upon interpersonal competence to decrease it further or to reinforce it at its existing level.

All these factors tend to act to lower the effectiveness of the decision-making process. For example, in situations where executives with mathematical and engineering background were observed dealing with highly technical issues, they developed strong emotional attachments to these issues. During discussions held to resolve technical, rational issues, the emotional involvements tended to block understanding. Since the men did not tend to deal with emotions, the inhibiting effects were never explored. Since the arguments were attempts by people to defend themselves or attach blame to others, there was a tendency for the rationality of the arguments to be weak. This, in turn, troubled the receiver of the argument who tended to attack obvious rational flaws immediately. The attack tended to increase the degree of threat experienced by the first person, and he became even more defensive. Similar impacts upon rational decision-making were also discovered in areas such as investment decisions, purchasing policies, quality control standards, product design and marketing planning.

Summary and Implications

1. Some of the most important causes for organizational deterioration and entropy are related to the fact that organizations have been designed and managed on a too-restricted view of man. Engineering-man, rational-man and happiness-man need to be expanded to include such deeper human qualities as self-acceptance, originality, an increasing sense of responsibility, psychological success and essentiality.

Note that these qualities are in addition to the necessity for rationality and technical competence. A total and contributing human being encompasses rational and technical competencies. Indeed, without these competencies it is doubtful that he could be a productive member of any organization.

Interpersonal competence does not supplant the rational and technical. The view presented here is that the lack of interpersonal competence (and its consequences in group and intergroup behavior) has helped to create such an internal environment that the rational and technical competencies of individuals are continuously being blunted and inhibited. Moreover, high interpersonal competence is not a substitute for low technical competence. Indeed it is the existence of the components of high interpersonal competence (trust, risk-taking, openness) that makes it possible for individuals to confront their areas of intellectual and technical incompetence.

2. Respect for our present organizations will decrease, especially among the youth who are to be the future agents of such organizations. Their commitment toward maintaining and enhancing organizational health will tend to decrease. At best they may see their organizations as places to get economic rewards through minimal involvement in order to purchase elsewhere the services and experiences that they value.

If the causes of organizational deterioration identified above are not checked, not only will the dry rot increase at an accelerating rate, but the organizations will be populated with people who do not care or who may even relish seeing their organization deteriorate.

3. The participants in future organizations may not object to working hard or to the idea that organizations have a right to health (efficiency and effectivness). They will simply raise the ante for responsible participation and genuine concern for organizations.

4. If the validity of the concept of the organization (public or private) is to survive, the new designs will have to raise the level of the quality of life within the system and genuinely value high-quality living as much as efficiency. As Harris (1972:40) has noted, "The revolution of rising expectations (has) broken beyond its materialistic limits. It's as if some idiot had raised the ante on what it takes to be a person." This genuineness will be indicated by the degree that the requirements of complex men are integrated into the everyday working policies and relationships, in the design of organizational structures, in the control systems and in the leadership behavior of those with power.

What types of changes will be required if organizations are to be redesigned to take a more complex view of man into account? Broadly speaking, the answer is that organizations will have to make changes in their structure, technology, leadership and managerial controls that reverse the three basic properties in modern pyramidal systems. These are

1. specialization of work		a. dependence b. low fate control c. impoverished work d. psychological failure
2. centralization of power	and their concomitants of:	e. psychological withdrawal f. "market orientation" g. low openness, trust, individuality
3. centralization of information		h. low risk-taking, learning and motivation

ORGANIZATIONAL RESEARCH AND
INTERPERSONAL COMPETENCE

Organizational Change Begins at the Top

There is another requirement about the strategy for organizational change implicit in the moral ethic being suggested. If the new structure cannot be designed for or imposed upon the members, then the involvement for change must begin where the power lies. Those that presently hold responsible positions and control organizations are also responsible for beginning the changes.

But, some may ask, is this not forgetting the people at the lower levels? The answer is that it is out of concern for the people at the lower levels that one begins at the top. There is nothing more hollow or vicious than to begin changes at the lower levels only to find the top intentionally or unintentionally repudiating these changes. For example, job enrichment has become popular these days. Enlarging and enriching jobs of employees almost inevitably leads to taking away tasks from their superiors. They in turn seek to replenish their jobs and seek tasks from their superiors and so on up until the top executives are confronted with letting go some of their activities. If they are not prepared for such a change (and so far most groups have not been prepared) the top balks, politely but firmly. The polite balk is communicated throughout the organizational structure, magnified as it spins down toward the employees who experience it as a deafening rebuff, confirming for them that management did not really mean to alter the organization.

Does this mean that our approach is based on beginning with society as it is? Are we suggesting that government, for example, cannot order such changes? Government, like organizational planners, may serve a useful purpose by bringing designs to the attention of the people. They may also pass laws that become legal charters toward which society aspires. They cannot, however, institute these changes by coercion because that would violate the moral ethic. History is full of examples where governments have ordered changes. As we indicate below, none of them has brought about the changes in the quality of organizational life being recommended herein.

Another reason why the change processes should begin at the top is that, given the existing power structure, if superiors internalize the new ethic, then they can immediately unfreeze rigid and dysfunctional policies, encourage further experimentation and develop the resources necessary for further change.

Is the writer implying, then, that top managers should act in ways that will ultimately lose them their organizational power? There are several interdependent points to be made in trying to give an answer to this very knotty question. First, the top must begin to recognize that as organizations are overcome by dry rot and become rigid, the actual impact of their power will increasingly deteriorate. In other words, given the deterioration of the pyramidal structure, the top has already begun to lose its power to make a significant difference in the organization. In the language of financial analysis, the history of organizational life seems to be that the costs not under the control of the top are increasing while the costs under their control are decreasing, and those costs not under their control are central to the creation of organizational dry rot.

Second, the management of the organization of the future will depend more on technical and interpersonal competence of individuals rather than their formal power. Individual competence will be inferred from the number of effective decisions made and implemented. These, in turn, will be increasingly influenced by a wider scope of information, thus few managers will be able to have expert knowledge in all areas that may be necessary in making and implementing a decision. There will be an increasing need for subordinate involvement and internal commitment. These two factors can be increased if the subordinates' power or control are increased. As Tannenbaum (1968) has shown, when this is done effectively, the power-pie is enlarged and subordinates increase their power without reducing the power of their superiors.

To summarize, the process of changing from the old toward the new must mirror the values of the organizational morality.

This means that organizational designs should be under the control and management of the participants and that the change processes should begin at the top.

ORGANIZATIONAL CHANGE IN THE EXECUTIVE SYSTEM

Processes of Changing

Recently the writer developed a model to be used to plot the degree of difficulty of any given organizational change. This model, presented below, may be a useful way to set the foundations for the logic that leads us to state that the organizational processes are paramount in thinking about and designing the organizations of the future.

Each dimension is hypothesized to be relevant in considering how difficult change will be. Thus, the easiest change is one that requires behavior that can be plotted on the left-hand side of the continua. The most difficult change would be one that falls on the right-hand side of all the continua.

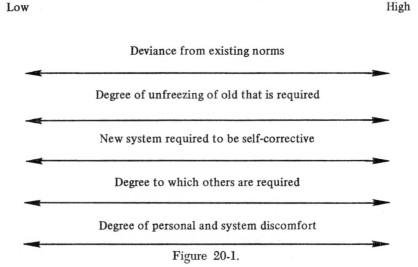

Conditions for Effective Change

Low   High

Deviance from existing norms

Degree of unfreezing of old that is required

New system required to be self-corrective

Degree to which others are required

Degree of personal and system discomfort

Figure 20-1.

Let us hypothesize that one model of the organization of the future seeks to enrich work, minimize unilateral dependence (for important issues), increase openness, trust, risk-taking and the expression of feelings by creating a working world that emphasizes conditions that produce psychological success, confirmation and feelings of essentiality. These conditions are almost 180 degrees out of phase with the requirements of present organizations. Moving toward this new organizational structure and process will tend (1) to mean a high degree of deviance from existing norms, (2) to require a high degree of unfreezing, (3) to require a system that is fully self-monitoring and corrective, (4) to require the participation of others, and (5) to imply a high degree of personal and system discomfort.

This is one important reason why pain, frustration and turmoil are very high among the executives who attempt to redesign their world to enhance self-actualization, interpersonal competence and trust in order to increase the effectiveness of decision-making and problem-solving.

Consequently, the changes will necessarily be slow. People will tend not to have the required competences, but will also have to unfreeze their old values and views about effectiveness. No one can preprogram the speed of unfreezing and the rate of new learning.

However, the very fact that the new behavior required is incongruent with the old means that the clients will be faced with new, puzzling, ambiguous situations. The very newness and ambiguity makes it possible to provide conditions for learning.

The implication is that, for the foreseeable future, since the new directions toward which individuals and organizations will aspire are so different from the present, it is not necessary nor advisable to have complete and detailed maps of the changes that should take place. If such maps were available, then the participants would have significantly less opportunity for experiencing and testing the very conditions that they are being asked to evolve. Detailed maps of the desired organizational forms and of the processes to achieve these forms would tend to lead to change processes that are as pyramidal and mechanistic as the present nature of most organizations.

What is needed is a specification of the kinds of conditions that lead to growth and effective decision-making, e.g., psychological success, trust, openness and essentiality, plus the behavioral skills necessary to achieve these goals. These conditions can be used as guideposts for the participants. It would be up to them to decide how much they wanted to accomplish toward each guidepost at any given time of this development and under different conditions.

SOME POSSIBLE GUIDEPOSTS FOR ORGANIZATIONAL STRUCTURES

What are some of the guideposts that can be identified from research that has focused on man as a complex and actualizing-seeking system?

1. The organizational structure, technology, managerial controls and leadership styles require changing in the direction of increasing people's opportunity for self-control, i.e., decreasing dependence and submissiveness, and for increasing the use of their important abilities.

2. Changes will probably take place in incremental steps so that present organizational forms will be kept but relegated to use under specific conditions. Thus, the traditional pyramidal structure will not be discarded. It will be kept for the decisions for which it is most effective. Similarly, an administration will not be asked to become completely participative and cease behaving authoritarianly. The new organization will permit a whole range of participative and authoritarian leadership styles by defining the conditions under which each may be most effective.

Under what conditions are the pyramidal structure and authoritarian leadership most effective? Four different kinds of organizational structures and leadership styles have been developed to be used in the organization of the future. The structures and leadership styles may each be described along several continua beginning with highly controlled and authoritarian, to a sharing of power and control, to the other end of the continuum where every member, regardless of rank, has equal power for a specified set of decisions. The tight, authoritarian organizational structures and leadership styles are relegated to the programmed, routine decisions where little employee internal commitment and innovation are required. The structures and styles which enlarge everyone's power, but especially those at the lower levels, are for major policy decisions about goals of the organization and the ways by which it should be run (Argyris, 1962; 1964). Thus, the traditional pyramidal structure with its concomitant authoritarian leadership style is not dismissed; it is assigned to be used for the more routine matters of the organization.

Likert (1967) has proposed that organizations aspire toward becoming System IV organizations. Under these conditions, leadership is based on confidence and trust; subordinates feel free to confront upwards; rewards support active involvement; decision-making and goal-setting are widely done throughout the organization (although well-integrated through linking processes); and the control processes are subject to the direct influence and management of the people being controlled so that the systems may be used for self-guidance and coordination.

Golembiewski (1967) has proposed a colleague model for line and staff groups which, in effect, is a model for organizing and managing much of the administrating levels of organization. His model also focuses on structural arrangements that encourage co-equal cooperation, issues defined by the participants, leadership varied according to the function being performed and the abilities of the individual to perform them.

Jay W. Forrester (1965) has been interested in using management information systems in order to decentralize the organization genuinely and to provide the maximum possible autonomy for people at the lower levels. He proposes to eliminate the traditional superior-subordinate relationship and replace it with individual self-control and self-discipline made possible by a sophisticated management information system which will provide adequate intelligence about managerial activities as well as those of others with whom managers are interdependent.

Schon (1971) has developed a model of how an organization can become more open to learning and innovation. His model begins with genuine decentralization and the creation of a network of discrete parts, each working on organizational problems, responsible for their immediate integration with other parts, and continually feeding to the management information which permits it to plan through an inductive approach rather than the traditional one which is defining for the parts through central planning and unilateral communication of the top to the lower-level parts.

Kaufman (1969), in an exploratory paper, argues that increasing representativeness is going to be necessary in public administrative agencies. Beyond the traditional strategy of appointing representatives, Kaufman endorses the concept of organizational ombudsman and notes, especially in the antipoverty programs, the insistence on participation by the poor. Marris and Rein (1967) have documented the difficulties with developing such participation. Indeed, if the experiences in industry are indicative, the public agencies have thoroughly underestimated the competence required to make participation effective (Argyris, 1971).

3. Jobs at the lower levels may be redesigned wherever possible to increase the degree of self-control, autonomy and the use of a larger number of abilities plus the more central ones of the individual.

Reducing dependence and submissiveness and enhancing autonomy and self-control can be begun by designing work that is more automated (Blauner, 1964; Shepard, 1971). Another possibility is job enrichment where jobs are redesigned to provide greater use of more important abilities and to encourage self-control and responsibility. Preliminary experiments with such changes have been gratifying to both individuals and the organization (Ford, 1969; Herzberg, 1966).

As noted above, job enrichment programs can raise basic

questions that may threaten all levels of management. Such questions will, in the present state of management systems, tend to be suppressed, but, if they are suppressed, the employees will soon find themselves in an intolerable position because they will not be permitted to follow the requirements of their new jobs. If this happens, then they will tend to see the job enrichment program as a manipulative trick.

The same kind of confrontation of management tends to occur with other changes that might be possible at the lower levels such as the Scanlon plan, optimal undermanning, the redesign of budgets and so forth (Argyris, 1964). Needless to say, the structural and process changes implied in the suggestions of Golembiewski, Forrester, Kaufman and Likert will require long unfreezing and reeducative processes of the people with power.

We arrive again at the conclusion that organizational change begins best at the top. If the people in power have not accepted the new values, and therefore neither behave according to them nor reward others who do, then organizational change of development will not tend to be effective.

Tinkering With the System

There are at least two ways to evaluate the recommended changes within an organization. The first is to focus on the formal structures, especially upon the centralization of power, information, control and the specialization of tasks. Given this perspective, the true or real changes are those that transfer the power, control and information to all the employees, especially the lower-level employees. The idea, at least as old as Marx, is to give the control of the technology and technocracy to the lower-level employees.

The evidence is clear that such transfer has not, as correctly predicted by Weber, brought about significant changes in the work world as experienced by the employee. For example, British nationalization did not make for a more equal distribution of power; employees did not gain more freedom, and the industrial structure did not become more democratic (van de Vall,

1970: 47). The socialist and capitalist organizational designers, by and large, operate with the same impoverished concept of man (Fleron and Fleron, 1972). The structures that they create do not therefore differ significantly. Indeed, one can make the argument that to give the workers ownership of organizations which cause the psychological difficulties outlined above is to place them in a double bind; if they decide to hate their job, they become politically vulnerable since they may not agress against the very system they own and for which they are politically responsible.

Hough (1969) has recently made it clear that Russian industrial organization and administration are based upon the traditional bureaucratic model. The Russians, he reports, express a degree of mistrust of this model for the same reasons that we have included under organizational entropy. In order to reduce the danger emanating from bureaucratic dry rot, the Russians have created group decision-making at the highest levels (a structure, familiar to Americans, known as the Office of the President and, at lower levels, as matrix organizations). The Russians have also set alongside the industrial bureaucracy a political bureaucracy which is supposed to correct for any excesses and unfairness on the part of the former. Hough suggests that such corrective measures have some degree of success. Unfortunately, he does not explore the issue as to why the political bureaucracy does not develop its own excesses, as theory predicts that it would. (After all, it too is subject to the same forces leading toward entropy.) Indeed, he implies the contrary; the political bureaucracy has its own internal rigidities (Hough, 1969:82-100, 184-186, and 252-255).

In a few socialist countries, experiments have been conducted to alter the traditional pyramidal structure (Zupinov and Tannenbaum, 1968). The results have been modest. Difficulties still revolve primarily around such factors as openness, trust, risk-taking and effective communication within the organization.

Similar experiments have been attempted in American industry. For example, the concepts of project management and matrix organization are based on more equalitarian sharing of power and information. The biggest difficulty with project management is that too often, especially under stress, people behave in accordance with the pyramidal structure and values (Argyris, 1967).

The same may be said for the many experiments attempted recently in creating alternative schools, free universities and community participation. Here again the radical structural changes were unsuccessful primarily because people could not behave effectively in accordance with the requirements of the new structures. Thus, high school students became as authoritarian as their teachers, college students as controlling as their professors, and citizen-participation groups have led to as much cancelling out of the unique contribution by members as did the smoke-filled rooms controlled by political hacks. The result is that organizations may soon become closed to learning about how to improve their effectiveness. One can sense the degree to which people are programmed with behavior that is congruent with the pyramidal structure when one realizes that, after decades of experiences by hundreds of thousands of people in experiential learning, and thousands of pages of articles, individuals uninitiated to T groups still tend to begin them with attempts to create little pyramidal systems within their group.

Why these failures? Because a change is a change for human beings only when they are able to behave in accordance with the new morality upon which the new structure is based. In order to assess whether a change has truly taken place, and not just tinkering with the system, one has to examine what actually goes on in the organization—how people deal with each other as they are making and implementing decisions.

Overthrowing unilateral pyramidal power relationships without reeducating human beings is not anything new, nor does the writer believe it will lead to effective long-lived change. What *is* new is the notion of reeducating people to develop interpersonal and problem-solving competences that will help them become masters of their own fates, architects of their own lives, and managers of their own progress. These competences are at the heart of the change strategy being proposed. Participation based on the three values of generating valid information, free and informed choice, and internal commitment requires skills most people do not have regardless of the political and social structural arrangements in which they live. To illustrate how fundamentally this view differs from those that are presently available, one need only remind the reader that, according to this view, business executives, archbishops, socialist commissars, Black Panther leaders, radical activitists and Naderites are all in the same boat in that they tend to be manifesting the same interpersonal competence skills and, therefore, given the freedom to choose and create, they will choose and create human relationships of the pyramidal variety.

It is the realization that changes are not effective until the people develop ownership of them, and that, given the present culture, ownership of the new organizational morality requires behavioral changes which will take a long time, that leads the writer to focus on a change strategy that begins within the system.

Some writers have implied that such a perspective ignores the environment. The writer does not believe so. As internal organizational deterioration increases, the search process becomes narrower in scope, the openness to new information is diminished, and the amount of learning possible greatly reduced. Under these conditions, organizations that are inherently open systems make themselves closed systems. The environment then has little influence. If organizational learning and the openness to the environment are to be increased, and if increased means people actually behave differently, then one has to begin with the people concerned. Thus, straightening out the internal environment should lead to greater attention to, and effective dialogues with, the external environment. Elsewhere the writer has suggested that the opposite strategy suggested by some theories actually leads to stagnation among the systems already imbued with a policy of status quo maintenance (Argyris, 1962).

Another way to make the point is to say: if one's concern is with human dignity, growth and realization beyond the level of economic subsistence, then altering the political system is a good example of tinkering with the system.

There are some scholars, especially among educators and young left theoreticians, who seem to believe that if one could do away with the pyramidal structure and all that goes with it, one then would really change the system. Aside from the fact that people would still be programmed to create pyramidal structures in free situations, there is another important reason why this strategy is not apt to be effective. This reason is also based on the concept of man as seeking self-acceptance, psychological success and feelings of competence, being an origin and essentiality. These qualities require some degree of structure; growth does not occur in chaos or in an undifferentiated culture. Too much choice can be frightening (Blos, 1970, recently suggested that this is a problem with contemporary adolescents); too much variety in work can be overwhelming; peak experiences are greater, but, as Maslow pointed out, they need to be followed with rest and some routineness. No evaluation of performance of effort can leave individuals bewildered and with a magnified interest in finding out whether or not others would confirm or disconfirm their evaluation of themselves or of their work.

Many years ago Lippitt and White (1947) showed experimentally that laissez-faire groups experienced a lower quality of human relationships, more discontent and less productivity than either authoritarian or democratic groups. The laissez-faire groups actually restricted the space of free movement of their members because of mutual interference and ignorance. The laissez-faire climate is a particularly devilish one with which to punish people because the leaders can objectively say they are doing little to reduce the members' freedom.

But, one could retort, that may be true because human beings do not have the skills to use such large amounts of freedom effectively. This does not seem to be supported in experience. For example, T groups typically begin with a highly unstructured situation. As the members try the traditional structure and become dissatisfied they may swing to no structure. They soon discover that basically each individual is an incomplete human being; that he gains a sense of wholeness from interdependent relationships with others, that the only way so far developed to learn from and to use others, as well as to give and to help others to learn, is to create some degree of order and patterning, which is another way to define structure. Again the key issue is who defines, controls and influences the structure. If the individuals (or their representatives) can control the structure, then there is a greater probability for success.

But designing and monitoring structures is a time and energy-consuming task. It should therefore be preserved for those decisions that are important. As suggested above, the pyramidal structure may be best suited for the routine and programmed decisions. Three other structures have been proposed for the innovative, nonprogrammed decisions that require a high degree of internal commitment on the part of the members implementing the decisions.

But again and again the research is clear—place people in structures that sanction and reward interdependence and growth, and their tendency will be to behave so as to botch things up.

The medium is the message of lasting change; and in organizations the medium is human behavior.

REFERENCES

Allison, G. T.: *The Essence of Decision.* Boston, Little, 1971.

Argyris, C.: Some problems and new directions for industrial psychology. In Dunnette, M. (Ed.): *Industrial and Organizational Psychology.* Chicago, Rand, 1975.

Argyris, C.: *The Applicability of Organizational Sociology.* Cambridge, England, Cambridge U Pr, 1972.

Argyris, C.: *Management and Organizational Development.* New York, McGraw, 1971.

Argyris, C.: On the effectiveness of research and development organizations. *Am Sci, 56*(4):344-355, 1968.

Argyris, C.: Today's problems with tomorrow's organizations. *Journal of Management Studies, 4*:31-55, February, 1967.

Argyris, C.: *Integrating the Individual and the Organization.* New York, Wiley, 1964.

Argyris, C.: *Interpersonal Competence and Organizational Effectiveness.* Homewood, R. D. Irwin, 1962.

Bennis, W. G.: *Changing Organizations.* New York, McGraw, 1966.

Bennis, W. G., and Slater, P. E.: *The Temporary Society.* New York, Harper, 1968.

Blauner, R.: *Alienation and Freedom.* Chicago, U of Chicago Pr, 1964.

Blos, P.: *Young Adolescent.* New York, Free Press, 1970.

Cyert, R. M., and March, J. G.: *A Behavioral Theory of the Firm.* Englewood Cliffs, P-H, 1963.

Ewing, D. W.: Who wants corporate democracy? *Harvard Business Review, 40*(5):12-28, 1971.

Fleron, F. J., and Fleron, L. J.: Administrative theory as repressive political theory: the Communist experience. Delivered at the National Conference on Public Administration, American Society for Public Administration, New York, March, 1972.

Ford, R. N.: Motivation through the work staff. American Management Association, 1969.

Forrester, J. W.: A new corporate design. *Industrial Management Review, 7*(1):5-18, Fall, 1965.

Gardner, J.: America in the twenty-third century. *New York Times,* July 27, 1968.

Golembiewski, R. T.: Organization development in public agencies. *Public Administration Review, 29*:367-377, July, 1969.

Golembiewski, R. T.: The laboratory approach to organization development: The schema of a method. *Public Administration Review, 27*:211-220, September, 1967.

Harris, T. G.: Some idiot raised the ante. *Psychology Today,* February, 1972.

Hertz, D. B.: Has management science reached a dead end? *Innovation, 25*:12-17, October, 1971.

Herzberg, F.: *Work and the Nature of Man.* New York, World, 1966.

Hough, J. F.: *The Soviet Prefects: The Local Party Organs in Industrial Decision-Making.* Cambridge, Harvard U Pr, 1969.

Kanter, R. M.: Communes. *Psychology Today,* July:52-57, 1970.

Katz, D., and Georgeopoulos, B. S.: Organizations in a changing world. *J Appl Beh Sci, 7*(3):342-370, 1971.

Katz, D., and Kahn, R. L.: *The Social Psychology of Organizations.* New York, Wiley, 1966.

Kaufman, H.: Administrative decentralization and political power. *Public Administration Review, 24*(1), 1969.

Leavitt, H. H., and Whisler, T. L.: Management in the 1980's. *Harvard Business Review, 36*(6):41-48, 1958.

Likert, R.: *New Patterns of Management.* New York, McGraw, 1967.

Lippitt, R., and White, R. K.: An experimental study of leadership and group life. In Newcomb, T. M., and Hartley, E. L. (Eds.): *Readings in Social Psychology.* New York, Henry Holt, 1947, pp. 315-330.

Long, N. E.: The city as a reservation. *Public Interest, 25*:22-38, Fall, 1971.

Marris, P., and Rein, M.: *Dilemmas of Social Reform.* New York, Atherton, 1967.

Marrow, A. J.; Bowers, D. G., and Seashore, S. E.: *Management by Participation.* New York, Har-Row, 1967.

Maslow, A. H.: *Motivation and Personality.* New York, Har-Row, 1970.

McGregor, D.: *The Human Side of Enterprise.* New York, McGraw, 1960.

Miner, J. B.: Changes in student attitudes toward bureaucratic role prescriptions during the 1960's. *Administrative Science Quarterly, 16*(3):351-364, 1971.

Newman, F. (Ed.): *Report on Higher Education.* Washington, U.S. Department of Health, Education, and Welfare, Government Printing Office, 1971.

Schon, D. A.: *Beyond the Stable State.* New York, Random, 1971.

Shepard, J. M.: *Automation and Alienation.* Cambridge, M.I.T. Press, 1971.

Simon, H. A.: *The New Science of Management Decision.* New York, Har-Row, 1960.

Simon, H. A.: *Administrative Behavior.* New York, Free Press, 1957.

Smith, D. H.: Voluntary organization activity and poverty. *Urban and Social Change Review, 5*:2-7, Fall, 1971.

Tannenbaum, A. S. (Ed.): *Control in Organizations.* New York, McGraw, 1968.

Van De Vall, M.: *Labor Organizations.* New York, Cambridge U Pr, 1970.

Wagner, H. M.: The ABC's of OR. *Operations Research, 19*:1259-1281, 1971.

Whyte, W. F.: *Organizational Behavior.* Homewood, R. D. Irwin, 1969.

Zupinov, J., and Tannenbaum, A. S.: The distribution of control in some Yugoslav industrial organizations as perceived by members. In Tannenbaum, A. S. (Ed.): *Control in Organizations.* New York, McGraw, 1968, pp. 73-89.

NAME INDEX

G

Gaight, 118
Galbraith, J. K., 320, 338
Gardner, J. W., xii, 228, 229, 396, 419
Geiger, T., 135, 148, 151, 156
Gemmill, G. R., 161, 162, 174
Georgeopoulos, B. S., 396, 419
Gerontological Society, 211
Gilbreth, 374
Ginzberg, E., v, 6, 7, 33
Gleser, G. C., 93, 99, 100
Glickman, A. S., 133
Goldberg, P., 77, 84
Goldstein, A. P., 94, 101, 252, 271, 358
Golembiewski, R. T., 398, 411, 413, 419
Gomberg, W., 251, 271
Gompers, S., 60
Gordon, R. A., 137, 156
Gorz, A., 187, 191, 192
Gouldner, A. W., 176, 186, 188, 190, 192
Grant, D. L., 116, 117, 132
Guion, R. M., 89, 101
Gulick, 169, 374

H

Hackman, J. R., 141, 157
Hall, D. T., ix, vi, 106, 142, 158, 159, 163, 166, 170, 174
Hall, E. T., 352, 357, 358, 368
Hamann, J. G., 244
Hamblin, R. L., 252, 271
Hammerschlag, C., 120, 121, 132
Hamner, W. C., 262, 265-267, 271
Harris, E. F., 66
Harris, S. E., 214, 229
Harris, T .G., 405, 419
Hartley, E. L., 419
Hatchett, S., 128, 133
Hayek, F. A., 136, 156
Heilbroner, R. L., 180, 192, 353
Herbst, P. G., 154, 156
Hertz, D. B., 419
Herzberg, F., 50, 66, 67, 95, 101, 178, 251, 398, 412, 419

Higgin, G. W., 120, 133
Hillman, S., 61
Hively, W., 95, 101
Hoffa, J., 61
Holbrook, J., 130, 132
Holland, J. G., 265, 271
Homans, G. C., 178, 192
Hornstein, H. A., 113, 132, 133
Hornstein, M., 133
Hough, J. F., 414, 419
Hudson, R. A., 61, 67
Hulin, C. L., 251, 271
Hull, C. L., 89, 101
Hunt, J. G., 156
Huse, E. F., vi, 275, 281, 315, 319
Hyman, H. H., 128, 133

I

Ittelson, W., 369

J

Jablonsky, S. F., 252, 271
Jahoda, M., 216, 219, 229
Jeanneret, P. R., 101
Jencks, C., 178, 192
Jerdee, T. H., 77, 80, 84
Johnson, P. D., 94, 101
Jung, C. G., 244

K

Kahn, R. L., 90, 102, 125, 133, 206, 210, 398
Kanter, R. M., 397, 419
Kardiner, A., 168, 174
Karsten, A., 212, 229
Kasindorf, J., 78, 84
Kast, F. E., 243
Katz, D., 396, 398, 419
Kaufman, H., 395, 412, 413, 419
Keller, F. S., 271
Kelman, H. C., 127, 133, 153, 156
Kelso, L., 136, 157

SUBJECT INDEX

A

Absenteeism, 11, 35, 70-72, 74, 121, 140, 144, 282, 284, 292, 299, 305, 351, 355
Accident rate, 355
Accountability, 54
Action research, 97
After school care center, 30
Age discrimination, 211, 222
Agency shop, 49, 65
Age stereotype, 198, 213, 216, 223
Aggression, 77, 79, 121, 122, 173
Alienation, 11, 22, 44, 112, 114, 117, 142, 143, 151, 173, 181, 283, 318, 362, 366
Amalgamated Clothing Workers of America, 225
American Assembly, 22-24
American Management Association, 236
American Marketing Association, 236
American Medical Association's Committee on Aging, 226
American Orthopsychiatric Association, 224
Anxiety, 70
Aptitude test, 88
Arbitration, 19
Assembly line, 6, 7, 20, 33-46, 142-144, 206, 298, 300, 304, 310, 316
Asset management, 321
Attendance contest, 70, 71
Attitude, 107, 121, 122, 224
   employee, 6, 8, 11, 14, 23, 69, 70, 81-83, 153, 188, 197, 198, 206, 218, 219, 223, 276, 290, 291, 294, 295, 300, 301, 305, 311, 313, 322, 327-333, 336, 337, 353, 359, 379, 380
   employee's family, 29, 30, 331
   life adjustment, 212-215, 223

   management, 72, 73, 117, 153, 281, 312, 323, 325, 343, 397
   society, 13, 16, 168, 222, 223, 353
   youth, 396, 397
Attitude index, 118
Attitude survey, 380
Attrition, 52, 351
Authoritarianism, 162, 207-209, 252, 265, 276, 277, 321-323, 337, 345, 410, 411, 415, 417
Authority, 123, 124, 130, 148, 159, 169, 253, 255, 282, 283, 337, 344, 355, 375, 383, 385, 396
Automation, 142, 145, 412
Autonomous work group, 34, 37, 39, 201, 253, 276, 298-301, 321, 357
Aversive conditioning, 260

B

Behavior, 90, 92, 98, 99, 118, 119, 121, 128, 169, 212, 244, 249, 275, 289-296, 373, 378, 379, 381-383
   employee, 15, 35, 36, 55, 57, 91, 94, 96, 99, 144, 155, 167, 178, 181, 187, 189, 202-205, 217, 226, 288, 289, 297, 309, 311-313, 327-330, 334-346, 384-387, 394, 400, 402, 403, 408, 409, 415, 416, 418
   expressive, xi
   management, 79, 148, 155, 161, 207, 288, 296, 297, 312, 313, 326, 345, 394, 399, 401, 405, 413, 416
   society, 20, 186, 256-261, 263-270, 415
   union leader, 61-64, 66
   youth, 161, 169-172, 353
Behavioral measurement, 90, 96, 100
Behavior disorder, 225

429